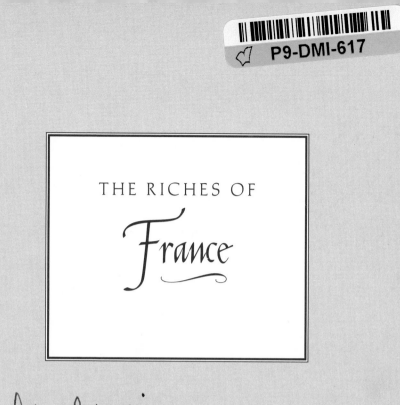

THE RICHES OF

France

For Guy Geslin,
May this book lead you
to many discoveries on your
road trips throughout France.
Happy touring!

With best wishes,
Maribeth

March 2000

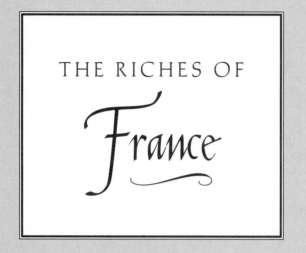

THE RICHES OF

France

*A Shopping and Touring Guide
to the French Provinces*

MARIBETH CLEMENTE

ST. MARTIN'S GRIFFIN
NEW YORK

Design by Nancy Resnick
Maps © 1997, Mark Stein Studios

Library of Congress Cataloging-in-Publication Data

Clemente, Maribeth.
    The riches of France : a shopping and touring guide to the provinces of France / Maribeth Clemente.
        p. cm.
    Includes index.
    ISBN 0-312-15640-5
    1. Shopping–France–Guidebooks. 2. France–Guidebooks.
I. Title.
TX337.F8C44 1997
380.1'45'0002544–dc21   97-7064
                                                             CIP

First St. Martin's Griffin Edition: August 1997

10 9 8 7 6 5 4

To Phil,
whose exuberant spirit accompanied me
throughout my travels.

B.T.S.B.

With love,
B.

CONTENTS

ACKNOWLEDGMENTS

DURING THE RESEARCH and writing of this book I encountered many, many people who helped me in big ways and in small. The welcome I received throughout France was stupendous, and my mind will forever be imprinted with images of the French—open and willing to share their riches with me. Many a craftsperson, shopkeeper, museum guide, *hôtelier*, and *restaurateur* took time out of their busy work schedules to present their prized goods to me, providing explanations and demonstrations that stemmed from a source of pride rather than *commerce*. Thank you to all of you, and please excuse me if at times I appeared gruff, but there was so much to see and do that I could never spend too much time in one place.

None of this would have been possible without the support of numerous French tourist organizations. *Merci mille fois* to all of the people from the various *Offices de Tourisme, Comités Départementaux de Tourisme,* and *Comités Regionaux de Tourisme* who helped me before, during, and after my travels throughout your beautiful country. I was constantly impressed by your wealth of knowledge and my only regret is that I don't have enough room here to list you one by one. Thank you also to Michèle Andrieux at the Maison de la France in Paris for having so efficiently helped me to round up the last-minute verifications of store hours and openings.

The first sorting and organizing of information occurred in 1994, a rather daunting task that was accomplished with the help of a few interns. Thank you for your assistance during this tedious phase of preliminary research, and please contact me to tell me how you're doing since I no longer know of your whereabouts.

The journey I embarked upon while researching and later writing this book at times seemed like a lonely one, and it wasn't until my editor at St. Martin's, Anne Savarese, took the helm that I could comfortably sit back and watch my manuscript take book form. Thank you also to the rest of the team at St. Martin's, particularly to Nancy Resnick for the elegant design of this book, to Judith de Rubini for your most conscientious copyediting, and to Kendall Heitzman for helping to push the work through.

Other key players include my agent, Sam Summerlin, for his undying enthusiasm toward "my cause" and Stéphane Ricour de Bourgies, who wins hands down for cheering me on. Steph, you encouraged me from the very conception of this project to the rather tenuous end; for this, and for so much more, I will always be grateful. Thank you also for the handsome photos and for having spurred my creative spirit and love for French goods way back when.

I would like to acknowledge my many friends on both sides of the Atlantic for their love and support. Special mention goes to my Franco-American buddy, Michèle Brothers, for making me feel very at home in Paris when Paris was no longer my home. Thanks also to Jeanne and Price King, who enabled me to get through the drama of having my luggage stolen during one of my trips, and to Steven Patrick, who introduced me to yoga at a time when I needed it the most.

Some of my most memorable moments were had with my handful of travel companions and I thank all of you for having so willingly turned yourselves over to the trials of unearthing the riches of France with me. Our days were often long and tiresome but I hope you look back on those French-filled times as fondly as I.

The realization of this book, in many respects, became a family affair. Every family member at one time or another said or did something to cheer me on. Cousins, aunts, nieces, and nephew had their say, but certainly my brothers, sister-in-law, and parents were most called upon to demonstrate that one extra vote of confidence needed to get the job done. I thank you all from the bottom of my heart. But I can't close this long list of acknowledgments without giving recognition to my beautiful mother for having imparted to me an appreciation for lovely things many years ago and to my hard-working father for having instilled in me a real sense of perseverance.

Thanks also to God and to Kitty, too.

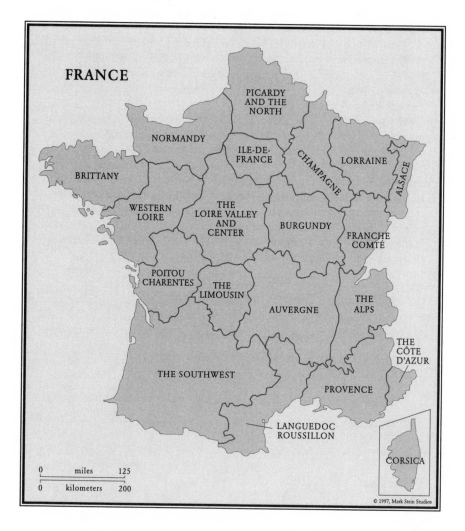

FRANCE

PICARDY
AND THE
NORTH

NORMANDY

ILE-DE-
FRANCE

CHAMPAGNE

LORRAINE

ALSACE

BRITTANY

WESTERN
LOIRE

THE
LOIRE VALLEY
AND
CENTER

BURGUNDY

FRANCHE
COMTÉ

POITOU
CHARENTES

THE
LIMOUSIN

AUVERGNE

THE
ALPS

THE
CÔTE
D'AZUR

THE SOUTHWEST

PROVENCE

LANGUEDOC
ROUSSILLON

miles
0   125

kilometers
0   200

CORSICA

© 1997, Mark Stein Studios

PARIS AND BEYOND

I DISTINCTLY REMEMBER a time when I thought Paris meant everything in France—particularly in terms of shopping. Those sentiments stemmed from my own ignorance that Paris is and always has been backed by centuries-old craftsmanship—nearly all of which grew out of the provinces. It was easy for me to refer to the Right Bank of Paris as France's showcase for the best of everything; the finest hotels, restaurants, and boutiques reign there in regal splendor. But since then, I've come to think of Paris as a *vitrine*, or shop-window, that reflects the traditions and *le savoir faire* from every part of France.

As I became increasingly involved with Paris shopping and tourism, I started to tune in to the many connections that Paris has with the provinces. My ears perked up when I heard about the factory and discount store of Gien, the renowned maker of faience, or refined earthenware, just two hours outside the capital. After a trip there, and then to the little known faience center of Nevers, I yearned to go to Limoges. A visit to the Alsatian Christmas markets followed on the heels of a culturally enriching and shop-filled trip to Brittany; by then I was hooked, and even more important, convinced that there was much more in the provinces than I had ever imagined. As I started to build my files, soon I heard more and more about a sort of rivalry between Paris and the provinces. I began to think that maybe it would take an American to shed a little light on the subject.

Much is said about the gastronomic uniquenesses of the many regions of France, but in comparison, little mention is given to the many other riches of this tremendously endowed country. I became more and more astonished as I did the research for this book; sure, I knew about Limoges china, Gien, Nevers, and Quimper faience, as well as Baccarat, Daum, and Saint-Louis crystal, but I hadn't cultivated a true appreciation for the centuries' worth of artistry that stood behind every house.

Goods that once seemed almost banal to me began to take on an entirely different meaning once I visited their places of origin: simple pleasures like warming a glass of pure amber cognac, in my hand, for example, have since become reverential acts. And even the buttery Breton cookies that I enjoy at teatime have been elevated to near epicurean status. Certain lesser known regional goods, such as Laguiole knives, have skyrocketed in international value since the original conception of this guide. Although it's anyone's guess which product will be the next to shake off a century or two of dormancy and emerge as the trendiest, most desired product of the moment, the value of such classics as *beret basque* or Provençal prints will remain forever. And as far as antiques are concerned, the pickings don't become more poignant than those ferreted out in an old farmhouse surrounded by a dewy mist in the middle of the Norman countryside.

The Riches of France is designed to help you discover each region of France along with its products. If I have done my job well, you will sense the intense flavor of each region as you turn every page. Much like Paris, the provinces of France can become addictive. It became my mission to uncover the most significant riches of France, yet I'm sure that a few treasures escaped me nonetheless. I nearly killed myself in Corsica when, only an hour and a half before I had to catch a plane, I decided that I could not leave the island without seeing the vineyards of Patrimonio. I embarked upon a treacherous drive that led me far up into the mountains, just twenty-five minutes from Bastia. It was the scariest, but also the most divine, ride of my life: it almost seemed as though I had arrived in heaven as I crept along the sinuous route, which was shrouded in a thick blanket of fog. A little goat stepped out in front of my car like some sort of an odd apparition as soulful Corsican songs droned on my cassette player.

These are the sorts of experiences I encourage you to seek out during your trip—albeit in a far less risky fashion. Music heightened the sentiments I felt throughout my travels, so I recommend that you listen to each region's traditional songs to enhance your sensations as well. And as much as I tried to overturn every stone, it truly became impossible. For your sake, I hope that you will enjoy France but not become as obsessed with it as I have been. This book is my personal ode to France, and the opportunity to share my many discoveries with you makes me the happiest of all!

How to Use This Guidebook

THE FRENCH ADMINISTRATION divides the country into 22 regions, but for my purposes of organizing information, I made a few minor adjustments and ended up with a total of 21. Before you delve into the regional sections of the book, you may want to consult "The Essentials," the introductory section that provides information and tips to make your shopping and touring experience easier throughout France. If you are not fluent in French, refer to the glossary in the back of the book, and carry a phrase book with you to further enhance your exchanges with the French people. Also remember that by referring to the chapter "The Provinces in Paris" you can have a grand time shopping the provinces without leaving the capital!

At the beginning of each chapter, the title of the region is written in English, with its French equivalent next to it in italics. The list of goods that follows is meant to give you a gander at the sorts of products associated with the region; this list is by no means comprehensive, but it tells you what you might encounter on your shopping forays. The towns and villages follow alphabetically, and in certain cases I have created subdivisions within each chapter when appropriate. The Alsace chapter, for example, has been broken down into three different headings: "Northern Alsace," "The Wine Route," and "The Cities." Although the region is small, the distinctions make geographical and thematic sense.

Each region of France is made up of an average of four *départements*, counties of sorts which I also often refer to as provinces. The *département* in which each of my chosen cities or villages is located is indicated in parentheses. The vital statistics that follow are self-explanatory; TGV refers to France's high-speed train (*train à grande vitesse*), and unless otherwise stated, the travel time provided is that for a train *originating in Paris*. As far as the markets are concerned, I chose to highlight those that I feel would be of most interest to visitors; so keep in mind that you may always experience a chance encounter with another *marché* that I had ended up nixing from the list. In most instances, I also include an introduction for the town or the village, and often in those preludes, I mention certain places that did not require a full description. For museums, I do not provide the address if they are all clearly marked within the towns and villages.

Shops have been listed alphabetically. Boxed entries indicate places where you are sure to "restore" yourself, such as hotels, restaurants, spas, and museum-type centers; other museums are listed similarly to boutiques. Keep in mind that some of these establishments have shops or small sales spaces, something that I note whenever possible (the price guidelines indicated for these entries do not necessarily apply to the goods in the shops).

Choosing exactly who and what to write about for each city or village was not easy. The one rule I tried to follow was to feature those places that most reflected the spirit of the region. At certain times I couldn't help but be swayed by my personal tastes, but overall I hope you'll find my choices close to democratic. With the wineries, for instance, I included one vineyard from virtually every major wine region, which left me confident that you will discover others along the way. My reasoning was much the same for boutiques and other establishments; if you keep your eyes open as you travel from one place to another, you just might end up visiting a good portion of those addresses that I had to put aside for another day.

THE ESSENTIALS

WHEN TO GO

In Season vs. Off-Season

CHOOSING WHEN TO go to France is key—a choice that depends largely on *where* you intend to go and *what* you plan to do there. As a general rule, the best time for travel throughout all of France—especially if you are looking to play more of a tourist than a beachcomber—is during the spring and fall. The month of May can be a little bit tricky because there are so many holidays, yet if you take them into consideration ahead of time, you shouldn't have any problem.

If you decide to spend most of your time in Paris and plan to make just a couple of side trips outside the capital, then the time of year is less important—unless, of course, gloomy weather leaves you truly glum and non–air-conditioned boutiques make you feel faint. If that is the case, you should probably avoid the winter and summer, and certainly if you want to steer clear of hordes of tourists, you should rule out the busier parts of France during August. The period from mid-July through the end of August brings a funny kind of ghost-town feeling to the more residential sections of the capital that is none too disagreeable. Parisians tend to clear out of town during this time, so don't be surprised to find a certain number of shops and restaurants closed at different intervals throughout these summer weeks as well.

For the rest of France, you'll want to determine whether you will be traveling during "the season" or not. *La saison touristique* generally refers to the period between Easter and November 1, the time when shops and restaurants open up either on a full-time basis or on weekends in order to benefit from the passage of fair-weather visitors. Peak season is July and August, when travelers often find themselves amidst throngs of tourists. In most parts of France, the crowd level is still somewhat tolerable in July, but once August hits, be aware that you risk becoming entangled in the flood of tourists who inundate France, largely from neighboring European countries.

For many North Americans, it's hard to fathom that most Europeans receive four to six weeks of vacation per year and that they take much of this time off *all at once*. Yes, entire factories do indeed shut down for the month of August, creating a mass exodus that leads to all kinds of mayhem along many of France's highways, and even back country roads, and the havoc you have to deal with once you've arrived in the most popular resort destinations is nothing to sneeze at either. Consider this: a good number of Germany's eighty million citizens and other sun-starved Europeans typically spend their vacations basking in the glorious summer sun of the French Riviera. The majority of the French flock to the same tourist centers as well, so if you do opt to visit any of the hot spots, plan it so that you can dodge the crowds as much as possible. A quiet, somewhat secluded hotel, with visits and shopping excursions planned according to the more off hours, can shelter you from the diminishing effects of an overabundance of fun seekers. The safest bets include those regions more toward the north such as Brittany, Normandy, Picardy, and Champagne. The summer can be a marvelously colorful time of year in the land of the Gauls, since this is when folkloric fêtes and cultural festivals abound in a highly animated ambiance of merriment and local tradition.

If you're traveling to France during the off-season, know that although life quiets down in the smaller, less-publicized resort areas like Ile-de-Ré in Poitou Charentes, other seaside destinations such as Biarritz and Cannes remain hopping year-round. Establishments in many of the regions, including Alsace, Burgundy, Champagne, Limousin, Lyon and Romans, and more, are barely affected by the change of seasons, which means that you can count on finding most places open most of the time.

Christmas in the Provinces

All of France trims itself with a modest display of adornment during the end-of-the-year holidays, but if you really want to capture the spirit of Christmas in France, you must head for Alsace, Lorraine, or Provence. The people of Alsace and Lorraine have been greatly influenced by the Germans' enthusiasm for *Noël* and have, of course, adopted certain Germanic traditions such as the celebrating of the *fête de la St-Nicolas* on the sixth of December. Special celebrations take place in both regions to honor this patron saint of Christmas, but in Nancy and in the nearby town of St-Nicolas-de-Fort, the festivities vibrate with a spectacular array of processions, folkloric customs, and fireworks. I have written about the importance of *pain d'épice*, or gingerbread, consumed in Alsace throughout the year, but Christmastime is indeed its crowning season; beginning toward the end of November, virtually every pastry and chocolate shop features an appetizing display of gaily decorated St. Nicks made of freshly baked gingerbread and glossy chocolate. As in Germany, the tradition of *Christkindelsmarkts* or Christmas Markets has become a large part of the holiday scene in Alsace, and the one at Kaysersberg is by far the best. This traditional *Marché de Noël* takes place annually over the three weekends preceding Christmas in a folksy outdoor setting peppered with vendors who sell everything from handmade pottery to hot spiced wine. Christmas in Provence revolves primarily around *santons*, the painted clay figurines used to decorate the mangers. You can buy these endearing expressions of Provençal folklore at town markets or specialized *santon* fairs, which normally take place in Aix-en-Provence the last week in November through the first week of December, and in Marseille from the end of November to the end of December. *Le Salon International des Santonniers*, which occurs annually in Arles toward the first two weeks of December, exhibits a fantastic display of *santons*, although few are actually for sale. The beautiful little village of Séguret in the Vaucluse *département* is widely reputed for its *crêche*, or manger, and if you happen to be there for its midnight mass on Christmas Eve, you will take part in one of the great traditions of *Noël en Provence*.

WHAT AND WHERE TO BUY

The scads of information chronicled in this book focuses largely on what and where to buy—entries which were culled from research that had revealed even more wonderful regional products. My selections, for the most part, were determined by the idea that each purchase should reflect an important dimension or flavor of the region. In highlighting the following categories, I just wanted to bring to your attention some of the primary shopping themes that have been emphasized throughout the chapters.

French Classics

This book takes you to the towns where the world's finest table arts are actually made; Limoges china, Baccarat, Daum, and Saint-Louis crystal, and Gien and Quimper faience figure among the best-known destinations. In certain instances you can buy on the premises, where the selection is often spectacular and the prices run low, particularly at the factory discount stores of these world-famous manufacturers. Shipping seldom poses a problem, and the thrill of purchasing something at the mother house is uncontestable. Lesser-known, yet highly prized, French classics include table linens from Alsace (Beauvillé) and the Vosges mountains (Jacquard Français).

Local Crafts and Artwork

Most of the goods included in this book represent some of the most elevated forms of artisanal work that exist in the world. Handcrafted items such as Provençal *santons*, Alsatian pottery, Savoy bells, Norman and Southwestern copperware, and Basque linens are just a few of the examples of works that have grown out of traditions which have existed for centuries. More artful and exotic products include stained glass panels from Chartres, Basque walking sticks called *makilas*, and string instruments from Corsica and Lorraine. Art in its purest form is best sought out in the reputable galleries along the Côte d'Azur, although I also list a number of dealers in Brittany, Normandy, Western Loire, and a few other regions which showcase works from some of their best local artists.

Museum and Château Shop Souvenir Items

As you tour through France, you will probably visit an incomparable number of museums, historic sites, and *châteaux*. You can bet that each of these attractions has a selling space where you can pick up a memento or two from your visit. Unfortunately many of these shops might leave you a bit disappointed with their often sparse collection of goods, but nonetheless one could easily amass enough souvenir items to fill up an extra suitcase. Many of these products serve as reasonably priced gifts for friends and family back home. Some of the best loved museum gift shops include those of the Mémorial in Caen, Monet's house in Giverny, the Saline Royale d'Arc et Senans in the Jura, and the Musée de Toile de Jouy in Jouy-en-Josas, to name a few.

Antiques

The number of antiquing possibilities in the provinces is staggering, and best of all, prices tend to average about 30 percent less than those of Paris. There is no need to feel daunted, either, about the prospects of buying a huge eighteenth-century armoire in the hinterlands of France and then having to find a way to ship it home. Not only will such a purchase prove more savvy than a similar one in the capital, but you'll end up paying far less (even with the cost of shipping and insurance) than you ever would in your own country. Antique dealers in the U.S., for example, might end up asking at least five times the price of what you paid in France. This is true for everything from high-end antiques to *brocante*, the kind of secondhand items that many non-Europeans would refer to as antiques even though the French do not. I love shopping for *brocante*, and some of the best finds may be unearthed at quaint little bric-à-brac shops and at the many flea markets that I have listed throughout the regions. Country French enameled coffeepots and salt boxes from the first part of this century that typically command exorbitant prices abroad come a dime a dozen in France. Savings can sometimes be extraordinary on everything from old faience to champagne memorabilia, but as a general rule I tell people if you like it, buy it.

In addition to antique shops and flea markets, most towns also hold *salons* or antique shows that take place annually during a two-week period. I chose to list only the really well known shows; to obtain a comprehensive listing of what kind of antiquing is going on when you're in the country, pick up a copy of *Revue Alladin*, a monthly magazine that lists all of the shows, markets, and auctions that you need to know about. You'll find the very best deals at auctions—but you'd better go to them equipped with flawless French or a very trustworthy translator.

Note: If you do purchase a quality antique, be sure to request a certificate of authenticity that states the age of the piece and what the dealer claims it to be; this paper should be stamped, dated, and signed by the vendor. You should also ask for a separate certificate or receipt that states its value.

Food and Wine

You could get fat just reading about all of the food and wine entries included in this book. I don't know whether the French consider chocolate a staple, but they have so much of such tremendously fine quality that it clearly is an important part of their carefully balanced diets. This, in addition to the fact that I am known to seek out my own daily dose of delectable *chocolat*, did not help to bar me from mentioning the majority of top-drawer sweet shops across the land. In many of the towns, I also include the best source for a cross-section of regional specialties, such as wines, cheeses, and countless other gourmet food items. A stop here would provide you with an array of goodies necessary for an impromptu picnic and/or numerous affordable gift ideas of local flavor.

Market Bounty

You haven't lived until you've experienced all of the wonderful aromas, colors, and animation of France's open-air markets. These are also the best places to go to for an immediate slice of local flavor. Although there are similarities among the *marchés* throughout France, you'll also notice a great number of differences as you glance at the day's catch in Brittany or at the pizzas in Provence, fresh from the roaming pizza truck's woodburning oven. Shopping here does not have to be limited to the day's picnic provisions, either, since most markets sell such highly transportable food products as jars of homemade jams and honeys, olive oil, pâtés, and specially preserved goat cheeses. Depending on the region, you also can delight yourself with everything from earthenware kougelhopf molds in Alsace to vibrantly colored and whimsical fabrics, frocks, and tablecloths in Provence!

MONEY

A Few Words About Prices

I have listed all prices in French francs, not to force you to exercize your math skills (or calculators), but instead to avoid confusion resulting from fluctuations in the exchange rate or conversions from currencies other than U.S. dollars.

Noteworthy hotels and restaurants are identified as Inexpensive, Moderate, Expensive, or Very Expensive. These categories are meant to serve as a gauge of comparison with other French establishments; bear in mind that Expensive in France might be considered Very Expensive in another country, or vice versa. To find out the exact prices, call or fax the hotel or restaurant ahead of time.

Note: Prices listed for goods in the various boutiques should simply serve as a guideline; you'd do well to anticipate increases across the board.

Exchange Rates and Cashing In

The exchange rate that you receive at most banks or exchange offices generally is lower than the one posted in your daily newspaper or on CNN. Commissions are usually tacked on as well, fees that can vary as much as the exchange rates. When in the provinces, you have little choice, and it's probably not worth your time to shop around for the best rate; most times you're lucky enough just to find a bank open willing to handle *le change*! Know that you always receive a slightly better exchange with traveler's checks, and if you're looking to exchange US$100 bills, you may have to look long and hard before you find a bank or an exchange office that will agree to take them. It's always best to avoid exchanging currencies in hotels— not to mention in actual boutiques or restaurants—because in virtually all instances, this is where you'll receive the least desirable rate of exchange.

In Paris, the American Express office can be a handy and comforting place for a number of reasons: if you are a cardholder, you may cash personal checks here or draw on your credit card for cash advances. Anyone may change money here, and if you've lost your AmEx traveler's checks or left them at home, you can be issued new ones within about thirty minutes. Cardholders also can receive mail and messages here addressed to them in care of:

> **American Express**
> **11 rue Scribe**
> **Paris**
> **tel.: 01.44.77.77.07**

American Express is located in the 9th Arrondissement (9ᵉ) and the local Métro stop is l'Opéra.

Open Monday-Friday 9 A.M.–6:30 P.M.

Automatic Banking Machines

Travelers have come to rely more and more upon automatic banking machines (ATMs) throughout France. You can even find ATMs in some of the most remote villages of the land, making it increasingly easy to turn up one that is compatible with your banking system at home. As added reassurance, find out before you leave for France which logos identify the ATMs that will be able to handle your transactions. Once you've figured this out, using them is a cinch since the instructions are always listed in several languages.

Note: As much as you could probably count on ATMs to provide you with most of the cash you'll need during your travels in France, don't forget that, depending on your bank or credit card, the interest can pile up significantly with each withdrawal. If you do use ATMs, try to do so just before the end of your billing period so that you won't be socked with an unpleasant heap of service fees and interest when you arrive home.

Payment

For regular shopping and living expenses, paying with credit cards is the best way to go. Not only will this help you to keep better track of your funds (unless you're one of those who runs wild with plastic), but it also prevents you from having to carry around too much cash or keep track of oodles of traveler's checks. Better yet, credit cards offer the best rates of exchange on purchases without tacking on significant additional fees (the rate used is that of the day that the transaction occurs). Most major credit cards are widely accepted; although American Express may be readily used for restaurants and hotels, however, the majority of shops take only VISA. The French peoples' credit cards necessitate PIN numbers when making purchases, whereas yours may not; so if by any chance an absent-minded person in a boutique or any other establishment tries to run your card through a high-tech hand-held gizmo—you may want to indicate that your card does not require you to punch in a PIN number.

Note: In this book I have indicated which shops absolutely do not take credit cards; for the rest, you can safely assume that they accept at least one of the major cards such as American Express, MasterCard, or VISA.

As in many other parts of the world, cash really can come in handy in France. When you visit one of the local markets, be sure to have a few bills tucked safely away on your person. If you are shopping for antiques, know that any purchase—big or small—may become more interesting with the added leverage of cash. This is the one time in France where you can openly bargain (or negotiate in more elegant shops), and depending on the vendor's mood and your persuasive, yet subtle powers, you can drive the original asking price down by an average of 30 percent.

For lost or stolen credit cards call the following numbers in Paris:

American Express, tel.: 01.47.77.72.00
VISA, tel.: 01.42.77.11.90
MasterCard, tel.: 01.45.67.53.53
Diners Club, tel.: 01.49.06.17.17.

Tax Refunds

Savings are much greater in France when you can benefit from the *détaxe*: the tax amount that everyone, except French residents and members of the European Community, are entitled to collect on all purchases made in France amounting to a total of 1,200F spent within one boutique. Currently the TVA (value added tax, VAT) is about 20 percent, a tax that is already incorporated into the prices advertised in shops. Once you reach your minimum, and after doing a bit of paperwork, you should have the right forms in hand that will allow you to recuperate this tax after you have left the country. Once processed, the actual savings does not turn out to be a full 20 percent, yet more like 18 percent—but definitely worth the effort nonetheless.

The problem I have found, however, is that this all works quite well in Paris, but in the provinces you may have to deal with excuses such as "We don't have the forms," or even worse, "I don't know how to fill them out." I've had a number of shoddy and highly exasperating experiences with this myself but unfortunately there's not much you can do unless you want to start protesting about calling the better business bureau in some remote part of France. Every shop is supposed to be able to handle this paperwork for you, and they should all have a supply of détaxe forms for you to fill out. When you're dealing with a quaint little hole-in-the-wall in the middle of the Alps, however, you may very well be one of the first non-French or non-European persons that they have sold to in quite some time. So if these country folk are not prepared, you may very well feel intrusive about causing a ruckus.

If you've made your 1,200F minimum and the store can handle the paperwork, here's how to proceed. Keep in mind that if you fall just a bit short of the 1,200F, it's worth it to add on a knickknack or two to bring you up to this amount; this should be an added incentive for you to make several of your smaller purchases at one boutique so you can cash in on the *détaxe*.

- Pay with a credit card so that you don't have to worry about cashing your tax refund check issued in francs back home (banks charge hefty commissions on foreign checks).

- There are two different ways of handling your refund on a credit card: crediting you for the tax amount or never charging you for it in the first place. The latter is the most common method; instead of charging you for the full tax and then later crediting you for this amount, most boutiques write up two sales slips: one with the purchase amount not including the tax, the other with the tax amount. Once you have processed your papers correctly, the boutique will then tear up the sales slip with the tax amount and you will only be charged the tax-free price.

- At the moment of the purchase, the salesperson will help you fill out the tax forms (it's important to have your passport or just your passport number with you at this time). The salesperson will put the forms in a stamped envelope that bears the address of the boutique.

- Show these papers along with your plane ticket and passport to the customs officer at the airport the day of your departure from France. (The same may be done at the border if you are traveling by train, boat, or car.) This must be done within three months from when you made your purchase. Do this before you check your luggage or have your purchases with you in a carry-on; chances are slim that you will be required to show your goods, but if you are asked where they are, you should at least have your bags with you. The customs officer will stamp your tax forms and show you which one to mail back to the boutique (the mailbox is right at the customs counter); you keep the green slip for yourself.

- Once the boutique receives your tax form, the sales slip with the tax amount will be torn up, or in some instances your account will be credited. If you don't go through the paperwork, you will of course be charged for the tax.

- If you have paid with cash, check, or traveler's checks, either you will receive your VAT check in the mail (this takes two to three months) or you may arrange to pick it up at the boutique if you plan to be in that town again within the upcoming months. If you do go the VAT route, note that two reputable U.S. companies will cash these checks for nominal fees: Thomas Cook Services Inc., with eighty offices, or Ruesch Int'l with five locations nationwide.

Note: You should receive compensation within ninety days after filing; if it goes much beyond that, you may want to contact the store where you made the purchase and/or the French consulate in your country. Claims are valid a year after the date of purchase. Note also that if your purchases totaling 1,200F or more are shipped directly to you from the store, the tax is automatically withdrawn and you do not have to go through this paperwork process.

Facing the Music: Your Country's Customs and Duties

Leaving France with your purchases is a real snap—unless your stash includes goods such as artwork bearing a 1,000,000F price tag or highly prized antiques which might be considered part of France's national patrimony. If this is the case, the dealer from whom you bought these rareties should help you to make the necessary arrangements for extracting these treasures from the French government's clenches (if they shy away from handling this paper trail for you, then you should question the reputation of the vendor). If you choose to explore the matter yourself, contact:

> **French Customs Information**
> **23 rue de l'Université**
> **75007 Paris**
> **tel.: 01.40.24.65.10; fax: 01.40.24.65.30**

Bringing goods back to your home country, either by hand or by mail, requires you to pay considerably more attention to your own government's regulations. In the U.S., for example, each person (including babies) may be exempted from paying duty on purchases amounting to a total of $400 as long as they have not benefited from this exemption within the past 30 days. Anything over this $400 exemption is subject to a flat duty rate of 10 percent up until the next $1,000 worth of goods, and then beyond that, different rates of duty are levied for each particular item. The good news is that antiques at least 100 years old (with certificate of authenticity), books, bona fide artwork, and diamonds are entirely duty-free.

In the U.S., or any other country, it's up to you to decide how you want to proceed, but know that if you are caught trying to "smuggle in" goods, you risk having to pay the duty *and* a stiff penalty. The same is true for food items; remember that bringing in fresh produce, milk products, and meats from Europe is definitely off limits for U.S. customs. (There are so many cute little beagles sniffing luggage these days that even I gave up trying to sneak in my token *camembert au lait cru*.) Canned pâtés and terrines of goose or duck foie gras are acceptable, but pork liver is not. If you really want to know where you stand with your country's regulations, it's worth it to request the U.S. Customs Information pamphlet as you put together your other trip arrangements. Write to:

U.S. Customs Service
P.O. Box 7407
Washington, DC 20044

The rules and regulations for duty on goods that have been shipped tends to be as involved as those for purchases brought into the U.S. by hand—just one more reason to obtain the complete rundown before you go.

Hint: When flying back into your country, you may not want to look terribly chic. There's no sense in advertising to the customs officer that you may be a potential shopping maven. The red flag is bound to go up if you saunter through with matching Louis Vuitton luggage. (Maybe that's why so many people today look as though they're traveling in their pajamas!)

SHOP TALK

Openings and Hours

If you've ever rushed over to a shop in Paris at 6:45 P.M. to sneak in just before its supposed 7 P.M. closing—only to find it *exceptionellement* closed—I can tell you that these kinds of inconsistencies increase tenfold in the provinces. In addition to these unpredictabilities, most store hours often include countless variations according to the seasons. The hours and seasonal changes listed in this book were accurate at the time of writing, but if you're planning a visit to an out-of-the-way place, call ahead to see if it will be open. Unlike Paris, most shops, museums, and banks in the provinces close at lunchtime (generally from noon to 2 P.M.); the closing day for museums is often Tuesday.

Note: Many stores, both in Paris and in the provinces, are closed on Mondays, either all day or just until 2 P.M. Note also that stores open earlier in the provinces than in the capital.

Returns

Returning goods in France unfortunately often sets you up for an encounter with a less than understanding salesperson or shop owner. Although merchandise in the U.S. usually is taken back with a smile *and* a full refund or credit, this is rarely the case in France. It has been my experience that returns policies depend more on the mood of the person you have to deal with than on any hard and fast rules. Sometimes it's easier in the smaller shops where you can often speak with the owner directly, although the owner also can be the most reluctant to accept the return. One thing is definite: you will always get ahead quicker if you play into their sympathies. A good sob story goes a long way in France, and if you lay on a fair amount of *politesse*, everyone could come out smiling in the end. Do not, however, expect a full refund in France; if you can't find an item to instantly replace what you want to return, you will most likely end up with a store credit.

If you run into any truly unjust scrapes and want to file a complaint, contact:

**Direction Départementale de la Concurrence, de la Consommation, et de la Répression des Fraudes
8 rue Froissart
75153 Paris 15003
tel.: 01.40.27.16.00; fax: 01.42.71.09.77**

Discount Shopping and Sales

The best discount shopping in France lies outside of Paris in a multitude of factory stores dispersed throughout the country. Troyes in Champagne, Cholet in Western Loire, and Roubaix just outside of Lille in the north are the three main cities with huge factory outlets and discount complexes. The cities of Limoges, Quimper, and Gien warrant a trip for their factory stores alone, particularly if you have a penchant for table arts *à la française*. These are only a few examples of the discount shopping that you will find as you travel through the regions, so read carefully and highlight the discount boutique entries if bargain hunting is your thing.

Sales, or *soldes*, typically occur in France during the month of January and July, although in recent years they have been creeping up earlier, beginning more toward the third week of December and June. This you can always count on in fashion boutiques in Paris, but if you're looking to pick up *un string* (string bikini) on the cheap in Saint-Tropez, you may have to wait until September. Most of the kinds of shops in this book are not prone to fabulous sales, but keep your eye out for boutiques' *coins d'affaires* (deal corners), where assorted castaways sell at reduced prices.

Shopping from Your Home

You can have almost as much fun shopping from home as actually venturing to the many off-the-beaten-path boutiques described in this book. You will notice that some of the establishments in this book have mail-order catalogues. Although the French seem to be catching on more and more to this idea of *vente par correspondance* or V.P.C., the mail-order business is not nearly as developed in France as it is in the U.S. Be aware, however, that catalogue or not, many shops that sell unique and hard-to-find goods would just love to hear from you. I have included fax numbers whenever possible so that you can carry out all of your special ordering without leaving the comfort of your home. A perfect solution for the armchair traveler/shopper, I hope that this repertoire of boutiques will help you to bring more of "the best of France" into your own home. Don't hesitate to contact the boutiques directly in English by phone or fax, and remember, the only true barrier between the two of you is the expanse of the Atlantic!

Something About Sizes

You'll probably only have to deliberate over sizing a handful of times during your trip, since just a fraction of this book concerns fashion. There are two rules to adhere to: If you're buying for yourself, always try it on, and if you're buying for someone else, always buy big. Size conversions can be misleading since actual sizes vary according to cut, fabric, and brand. Salespeople can be helpful in sizing up customers according to how their merchandise fits.

For women, most shops only carry up to size 44, which supposedly converts into an American size 14, but I have tried on 44s that were cut more like U.S. 10s. Large-sized women will have difficulty shopping in France (big men have an even tougher time); your best bet for picking up more amply cut fashions is to shop at the big-name boutiques in cities such as Lyons, Bordeaux, Deauville, Cannes, and many others. Finding the right shoe size also can be maddening, since the models don't come in varying widths, and half sizes and large sizes (over 40) are difficult to come by. Buying men's and women's shirts and sweaters is less unnerving since sizes are marked S, M, L, and XL for small, medium, large, and extra-large or 1, 2, and 3 for small, medium, and large. Children's clothing sizes are also easy to figure out since they run according to the age of the child; sizes are marked for babies aged 3, 6, 12, and 18 months, and for kids aged 2, 3, 4, 6, 8, 10, 12, 14, and 16 years.

Note: If you buy sheets in France, stay away from the fitted ones, since bed sizes run differently here. Table linens are less of a problem, but to be really safe, carry a measuring tape that has the metric system on one side and inches on the other.

BRINGING AND SENDING HOME THE GOODS

By Hand

There is no surer way to get something home than to bring it under your own steam. This is the obvious solution for smallish items, but don't rule it out for more cumbersome pieces such as a painting or a lamp as well. Remember that the hassle of adding an unwieldy package to your entourage may entail only a temporary inconvenience–particularly if you are on the last leg of your trip. Most of the shops in France are very conscientious about protecting their merchandise, so be sure to specify that you would like a travel-ready package. (If you don't want to deal with too much bulky bubblewrap, you can always pad your purchases with dirty laundry!) Try to arrive in France with only one suitcase for your personal belongings so that you can bring home an extra piece of luggage filled with your stash. Collapsible bags are okay if you plan to put the more fragile items in your suitcase; otherwise, I've been known to pick up a large cardboard box along the way that serves as a sturdier solution (unfortunately, the downside of this is that their cargo-like appearance can spur more questioning at customs).

Tip: As soon as you find a place in France that sells poster tubes, you may want to buy one for the *affiches* and prints you might pick up along the way; such tubes are not always easy to locate.

By Airmail

A good number of stores in Paris will readily mail off packages that you've purchased in their establishment, although this added service is considerably less common in the provinces. If you are staying in a luxury hotel, the concierge should be able to deploy his or her energies for you; otherwise, you may opt to handle the chore yourself. Fed Ex, DHL, and UPS are relatively easy to find in most major French cities, although French versions of Mail Boxes, Etc. are still rather scarce. You can also mail packages from La Poste (France's post offices) by a number of classes. It's one of the most efficient postal systems in the world, but be prepared: a trip to La Poste is almost always a time-consuming and frustrating experience. *Ça, c'est la France!* You can feel confident, though, about sending a large boxful of Basque linens home *par économique* (this class takes about one month to reach the U.S.) or a prized bibelot by Chronopost (the French form of Express Mail). You can buy mailing boxes of varying sizes, and post offices in wine regions such as Sancerre also sell special protective packages for mailing bottles of wine.

Shipping

Wherever you go, whatever you see, know that it can be shipped. This is particularly important to remember for antiques: you will see many beautiful ones throughout France, and any fears about getting them home should not prevent you from buying the piece of your dreams. Upscale dealers are usually qualified to make the shipping arrangements for you directly, but even if you stumble upon a must-have piece in the farthest corner of France, you can contact the following shipper to have them ship it home for you:

Camard
28 rue Cristino-Garcia
93210 La Plaine–St-Denis
tel.: 01.49.46.10.82, or Saturday at 01.40.12.84.45 and Sunday at
01.40.11.49.43; fax: 01.48.09.18.96

Shipping costs can be steep, but depending on the value of the piece, this added expense is more than worth it. Be sure to be particularly vigilant about the paperwork. For antiques, this involves several key components including the certificate of authenticity of your find and usually two different receipts: one that indicates the value for customs purposes, the other that you might want to use for insurance estimates once the piece has arrived at your home. It's also a good idea to take pictures that clearly show the condition of the piece at the time of purchase in case it doesn't look quite the same way upon arrival. You must insure your purchase(s) for this very reason, and if by any chance you are shipping more than one piece, you may want to consider an itemized inventory list instead of a grouped one. (This will facilitate your cashing in on a claim in case only part of the shipment arrives damaged.) Remember that the trip home can be a long one (two to three months, depending on where the shipment is going), a voyage that will probably have your newly acquired piece passed from truck to ship to truck and so on, so you need to take every precaution possible *and* always read the fine print. If you do all of that, everything should work out splendidly.

People interested in shipping precious works to the U.S. with *the* most utmost care may also contact the following U.S.-based shipper that coordinates packing and shipping arrangements worldwide for such clients as Sotheby's:

Thomas Sullivan Transportation
3121 Middletown Road
Bronx, NY 10461
tel.: (718) 892-9388; fax: (718) 829-6957

If you purchase a piece that requires special attention, contact:

> **Sotheby's Restoration**
> **P.O. Box 657**
> **Claverack, NY 12513**
> tel.: (518) 851-2544; fax: (518) 851-2558

PACKING TIPS

I did so much traveling in France that I could not possibly keep up with logging how many kilometers I had traveled by car, plane, and train, but I could come pretty close to remembering everything that I had packed on each trip!

I'm sure all of you have already read numerous times in fashion magazines about the core wardrobes travelers are supposed to pack. I could never restrict myself to such a monastic assemblage of garb, so in addition to the recommended basics, I would always add a few more lively pieces to turn the blah beiges and boring blacks into perkier fashion statements (remember that the French flaunt color much more freely than cosmopolitan types stateside). Lightweight accessories consistently saved the day, so I always traveled with a stack of colorful silk, cotton, and wool challis scarves and just a pouchful of baubles. Whether you're talking about an elegant Hermès *carré* or a vibrant Provençal foulard, you can always add a dash of color and chic to your outfit with this quintessential French *accessoire*. Keep the shoes down to a minimum since they take up a lot of space. There's really no reason, either, to bring more than two handbags: a large shoulder-type tote for day and a small purse for the evening. I travel almost exclusively with knits, silks, and cotton tees or turtlenecks for comfort, ease, and packability, saving more high maintenance items like crisp white blouses for home. Jackets are a bulky luxury, and even on lengthy trips I never travel with more than two. Depending on the season, you will probably want to bring two types of coats that will enable you to pull off a smart look for fair weather and foul.

This may sound like a lot to you, but it allows me to coast through two to three weeks of travel, changing hotels on the average of every other night. Even if you change lodgings every three to four nights, I doubt that you want to pack and unpack each time. My system allows you not to do so, and here's how I suggest you fit it all into a medium-large sized suitcase (anything bigger will create a lot of hassles for you): roll your knits and sleepwear and place them on the bottom of your suitcase; in the remaining space you should have room for a stack of scarves and other small accessories, your lingerie, and even your toiletry case (this will save you from carting in any other bag other than your pocketbook). Slip your shoes in along the sides and on top of all of this, and you should have plenty of room to place your few silks, jackets, travel robe, and extra coat—all of which are best kept on hangers and covered with plastic dry-cleaner bags (a little tip I learned from the *haute couture* department at Chanel). The system works like a charm since the plastic bags prevent any wrinkling. So whenever you arrive in a new place you only have to hang up a handful of clothes, take your toiletry bag out of your suitcase, and *voilà!* Certainly, men can apply this technique, too—but be sure to pack at least one foulard and several pocket squares to ensure a bit of the suave European spirit.

To further enhance your stay away from home, you may want to bring a few washcloths since most French hotels do not carry them; a supply of individually packaged moist towelettes will get you through many long, sticky days as well. Like most Americans, I can be a little nutty about cleanliness, yet although I often washed out my underwear in the hotel sink (if you travel with more than six pairs of bras and panties you're taking up too much room), I never went so far as to buy those ugly inflatable hangers that you're supposed to use for hand laundry. You might also want to put a small supply of scented candles into your luggage before you leave; not only will they freshen every room (the persistent smell of smoke can become unpleasant in France), but their aromatherapeutic effect can make you feel relaxed and as though you're in a familiar place everywhere you go.

DEALING WITH LOST OR STOLEN LUGGAGE

In my quest to experience almost everything in France, someone up above (or below) must have decided that I should have my luggage stolen. The effect was dramatic—I lost all of my personal belongings and many work materials, but fortunately still had my pocketbook with my passport and credit cards. But as long as there is no bodily harm, you just have to regroup and forge on. I knew I had such a heavy schedule planned that it left me barely any time to pick up a change of clothes, a pair of pajamas, and essential toiletries, but I made do little by little and in the end I was surprised at how liberated I felt living without all that extraneous stuff!

This sort of thing happens even in France, a country that has always made me feel incredibly safe; don't ever let anything like this ruin your trip. The best you can do is to take precautions ahead of time: it helps to have a good insurance policy that will cover such losses. If you do, you should become a keeper of receipts—both past, for goods previously purchased, and present, for goods that you will be replacing during your trip.

Remember also that some places invite crime more than others, and no matter how well you conceal your belongings in your vehicle, and even if the doors and the trunk are locked, you are a sitting duck when you leave your car in a parking lot or village known to be frequented mostly by tourists. You don't have to be a pro to recognize a rental car and to know the chances are good that the trunk is filled with loot. Trunks, of course, are not fool-proof, as in my case, you often don't know that you've been ripped off until the criminals are long gone. Certainly the best way to avoid this kind of theft is to travel from one hotel to another without making any stops along the way. If your luggage is lost or delayed during your trip to France, try to view it as a good excuse to outfit yourself *à la française*!

PARLEZ-VOUS ANGLAIS? (A MINI-GUIDE TO INTERACTING WITH THE FRENCH)

I'll admit that it's sometimes difficult for me to be objective when talking about the French. It's true that language does not present a barrier for me, and I've come to know which buttons to push with them in order to obtain my most desired results; yet despite my own personal navigations through the intricacies of the French mentality, I've also come to the conclusion that sometimes the more you know, the more complicated things tend to be. It's nice to preserve a certain freshness, a particular sort of spontaneity—call it even a good dose of naïveté. I came to this conclusion largely by observing how my various travel companions interacted with the French. I truly was charmed to see how much of an exchange people can have with nods and smiles. My translations didn't seem to matter that much because everything passed through the eyes, and when there was laughter it was always sincere and glorious, even though most of the time I was the only one who could explain what was funny.

I began to observe other tourists in France as well, and at the same time thought about an intense trip that I had recently taken to Asia where I felt somewhat distraught about not being able to communicate with the people. It wasn't until I began to relax and started to take my clues from them that I realized that you don't have to understand words to communicate. This same realization kept coming back to me in my subsequent trips through France. The French are lovely, quirky people with complexities as vast as the history of France—but I think you'll have a better time exploring that on your own and then finding your own way of dealing with them rather than having me provide you with a formula.

The most important thing to remember, however, is to treat the shop people and their goods with great respect. This means greeting them with *bonjour, madame,* or *bonjour, monsieur,* and often patiently waiting to be served rather than picking up items yourself.

Interactions tend to be more formal in Paris (and, of course, it helps to dress up more), whereas exchanges flow more easily in the provinces. For a much closer look at the complexities of Franco-American/Anglo-Saxon relationships, I suggest you read *French or Foe?* (Chicago: Distribooks, 1996), a fun and highly informative book available in bookstores throughout the U.S. It was written by a good friend of mine, Polly Platt, a woman who has been coaching people in this subject matter for a number of years.

TOURING IN FRANCE

I can't emphasize enough how much more you will derive from this book if you refer to it as much for touring tips as for shopping information. As I traveled to all of these marvelous places in France, I came to feel as though I would be cheating my readers if I included only my reports on the boutiques. Unlike other well-known guidebooks, my objective is not to provide you with an exhaustive amount of information about how to fare well in France; because my approach is highly personal, anything I decide to share with you is something that helped me when traveling throughout the country. I lived in France for eleven years and my knowledge of the French language and culture is strong, but I had to manage under time and budget constraints like any other traveler.

Key Information

Tourism is the number-one industry in France, and having been blessed with an extraordinary number of riches to promote, the French do a great job providing information about their country's attractions. There is at least one French Government Tourist Office or Maison de la France in virtually every developed nation whose purpose is to promote tourism in France. Their documentations department can help you find such information as how to rent a farmhouse in France, who to contact for a bird-lovers' tour through the country's marshlands, or where to find a shuttle that will take you from Charles de Gaulle Airport to the Champagne region. If you are in the U.S., you can call the following number for answers to your queries: **Maison de la France hotline:** (900) 990-0040 (costs 50 cents a minute).

Once in France, you would do well to make use of the many *offices de tourisme* (tourist—or as I say, tourism—offices) throughout France. Truly, no matter how small the town or village, you will probably be able to walk right up to a tourism office upon your arrival. These offices were formerly called *syndicat d'initiative* and have signs marked by the lower-case letter i in a box ℹ I made extensive use of them, mostly to obtain a map of each city I visited. Since the layout of French urban centers bears absolutely no resemblance to the gridlike pattern of most modern cities, you will drive yourself nuts trying to navigate the maze of centuries-old streets without the proper map. Many of these offices close at lunchtime, so if you arrive during these hours and need directions, go to La Poste (the local post office), where you will find a city map clearly displayed out front.

Whether or not I have thus far dispelled or reinforced certain myths you may have had about dealing with the French, you should nonetheless feel confident about attempting to communicate with them over the phone. The telephone is an essential tool in today's world, and it would be a shame to let any language barriers prevent you from getting the most out of your trip, (Many French people do speak English, so even if you can't utter a word in French, you should at least give it a try.) It definitely comes in handy when you want to reserve a restaurant or a hotel, but also when you want to verify that a shop is open or even to ask the shop owner if he or she carries a certain product. You'd be amazed at the wonders you can work, and it's not at all unusual for someone (particularly an artist's atelier) to remain open at lunch or at the end of the day especially for you. Be aware that you rarely can just step into a phone booth in France, put in a coin, and place a call. Instead, plan ahead and buy a telephone card at the post office or at one of the many *tabacs* (tobacco shops); these can be used for local and long-distance calls.

Note: In 1996 the telephone system changed in France, dividing the country into five different zones or area codes: 01. for Paris and its environs; 02. for the northwest; 03. for the northeast; 04. for the southeast, including Corsica; and 05 for the southwest. For all calls inside France, dial 0 before the 9-digit number: i.e., Paris 01.-- -- --, Marseille 04.-- -- --. (Do not dial 0 when calling from outside of France.) For information and directory assistance, dial 12.

Making telephone calls from hotels is often easier but quite expensive. To call abroad from France, dial 00. If you want to use a calling card to call outside of France, be sure you know the access code ahead of time. To call all numbers in France from outside the country, dial the nine digits (without the 0) after the access code 33.

Travel Options by Train and Plane Within France

I'll leave it up to you to find your way to France. If you plan to travel within the country it's best to make arrangements before you arrive; however, when it comes to picking up a train or a plane ticket for travel within France, it *is* sometimes easier to purchase it in France. This is particularly true, for instance, if once in Paris you decide to take off for Lyons or Bordeaux for a few days. For trips to major French cities from the capital, certainly the best way to travel is by the TGV, France's high-speed train. For more long-distance destinations such as Nice or Corsica, flying is more efficient. Flying within France also can be pricey, although you can sometimes benefit from special deals. Either way, you can make arrangements at one of the many travel agencies that line the avenue de l'Opéra in Paris, or by checking with a travel agency in the provinces. For train tickets it is often easier to go directly to *la gare*, or train station, ahead of time, particularly in the provinces. Don't bother aggravating yourself by attempting to make these kinds of travel plans over the phone. Before you leave for your trip, you can obtain information about train travel in France and the rest of Europe: call 800-4-EURAIL (800-438-7245) in the United States. For specifics about taking the Chunnel train, or Eurostar, call 800-EUROSTAR (800-387-6782).

Note: Taxis can be horribly expensive in the provinces—much more so than in Paris.

Driving Around

As much as Paris is meant for walking, certainly the best way to discover the provinces is by car. Driving gives you the freedom to explore back country roads or to cruise along the highway at your own pace. You'll find this book most useful if you're driving, because there is much to discover between points A and B. If you're driving from Paris to Provence, for example, it could easily take you a month if you decided to take in every highlight that I have listed in the regions along the way; a more typical scenario, however, might involve stopping off to buy some faience in Gien and Nevers, then crossing over to sample some of the nectars of Burgundy before you experience the rustic delights of the Alps. After all this, I think that you'll find this book *and* your car to be just as *indispensable* once you've finally arrived in Provence.

Many people are intimidated about driving in France, and I will openly admit driving was one of my biggest challenges during my research. The most frightening part involved dodging cars on *le péripherique* (the highway that encircles Paris), but aside from that, I really got into the groove. It helps to have a copilot, particularly when it comes to reading signs. You'll find everything, however, to be incredibly well marked in France and if you know what the following three signs mean, you're golden:

> *centre ville*—city center
> *toutes directions*—all directions
> *autres directions*—other directions

Whether you're puttering along on a small road or zooming on *l'autoroute* (highway), simply follow the signs for the town that you want to go to (or the next biggest one)—then believe me when I say that these three signs will lead you wherever you want to go. To simplify this short driving course even more, I found *toutes directions* and *autres directions* to mean basically the same thing!

Parking areas in towns are well indicated by a capital *P* in a box ℗ , and if you park curbside, look for meters that dispense tickets (you're supposed to leave this ticket visible inside your car behind the windshield). Parking in the provinces is free at lunch, after 7 P.M. and on Sundays. In Paris most parking is scot-free the whole month of August.

Renting a Car

Whichever rental company you choose, be sure to reserve your vehicle *before* you arrive in France; otherwise you will end up paying considerably more. Also remember to ask about trunk size when choosing your model, an incredibly important factor for even just two people traveling around France. You'll also want to allot a good-sized budget for gas and tolls, two expenses that cost noticeably more in France than in the U.S. Finally, remember to request an automatic transmission if that's what you're accustomed to driving, since the majority of the French drive standard-shift cars.

Your travel agent is a good source for lining up rentals with the major companies such as Avis, Hertz, and the others. If you plan to rent a car for a minimum of seventeen days for travel throughout Europe, however, Renault offers the most economical and service-oriented plan. Their Eurodrive program allows you to pick up and drop off brand-new vehicles at countless locations throughout France and at a half a dozen or so cities throughout Europe. In most cases, you should reserve a month in advance, although they do allow for a certain amount of last-minute requests. For information about **Renault Eurodrive**, call (800) 221-1052 in the U.S.; (800) 3-Renault in Canada, or contact them in New York by fax at (212) 725-5379.

Tip: The easiest map you can use to accompany the information listed in this book is the basic Michelin map of France (916). I found the more detailed maps to be more confusing than helpful.

Selecting the Right Culinary Experience and Lodging

Certainly there is no right or wrong choice—what matters most is what suits you the best at any given time, and there's no question that during a trip our needs and moods change. Depending on where you are going and at what time of year, you should decide whether or not you want to be "locked into" your accommodations in advance or whether you just want to play it by ear. In any event, dining and lodging options are indeed vast in France and you can't always act spontaneously. For a down-home lunch filled with hearty helpings of local flavor you can make a pit stop at any number of the country's *relais routiers* (truck stops), but you'll most likely have to make plans in advance to reserve a table at one of the country's coveted three-star

Michelin restaurants. Lodging options run the gamut from *gîtes ruraux* (farmhouse cottages) to charming bed-and-breakfast establishments to four-star luxury hotels, and more. I have included many of my favorites throughout the book, places that touched me by their charm and décor in addition to the comfortable room and/or delicious meal. My hope is that they will stir the same feelings of contentment within you.

As you begin to plan your trip, you may want to contact the following lodging providers to obtain catalogues and brochures about distinctive properties—many of which house fine restaurants. These numbers should also come in handy for reserving your accommodations both from the U.S. and in France.

Relais & Châteaux
tel.: 212-856-0115 in the U.S.; 01.45.72.96.50 from France

Concorde Hotels
tel.: 1-800-777-4182 in the U.S.; 0800.05.00.11 from France

Lucien Barrière
tel.: 1-800-221-4542 in the U.S.; 01.60.77.87.65 in France

Sofitel
tel.: 1-800-221-4542 in the U.S.; 01.60.77.87.65 in France

Relais du Silence
tel.: 1-800-653-7262 in the U.S.; 01.45.66.53.53 in France

Châteaux et Hôtels Indépendants
tel.: 1-800-553-5090 in the U.S.; 1-800-673-1286 in Canada; 01.48.78.04.00 in France

Warwick International Hotels
tel.:1-800-203-3232 in the U.S.; 0800.46.34.41 in France

Leading Hotels of the World
tel.: 1-800-223-6800 in the U.S.; 0-800-136-136 in France

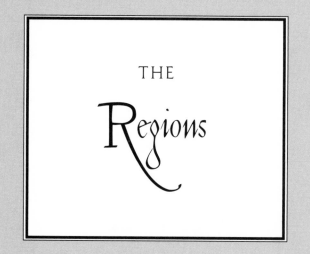

THE

Regions

THE ALPS
Les Alpes

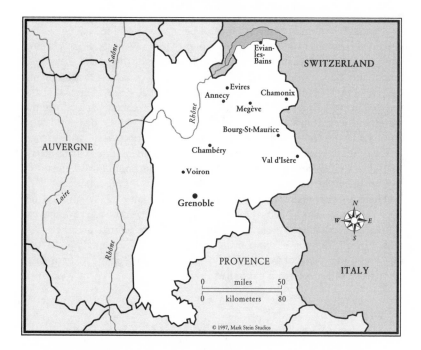

blueberry pies • mountain honey • pottery • painted pine furnishings • cow bells • ski and surf clothing and equipment •
cheeses • walnut, pine, and larch furniture • mountain attire and
gear • hams • water and souvenirs from Evian • sausages • Savoy
crosses • *glaçons de Megève* • ski pants • hard candies • chic *après
ski* clothing and accessories • red and green fabrics • luggage •
mountain collectibles • luxurious bed, bath, and table linens •
handwoven woolens • knickers • chocolate truffles • trompe l'oeil
paintings • Opinel knives • wines • walnut treats • gloves •
Chartreuse

THE MENTION OF "The Alps" triggers myriad images right out of a storybook. Jagged mountains stand tall like stiff peaks of meringue; wood-framed
chalets gently hug hillsides, far from the threat of charging avalanches; and
village churches sit quietly at the center of valleys as if poised for the viewing
pleasure of passing visitors. As you begin to explore this region, you'll dis-

cover that behind all of these picture-perfect scenes is a whole life rich in tradition that goes far beyond the fun and sport that attracts most people here in the first place. You will come to realize that mountain life in its simplest forms was here long before the Alps became associated with recreation.

Although mountain customs may not be as widespread today, many have remained—less out of necessity than as part of alpine culture. Fresh cheeses, sausages, and hams that were once consumed to properly "fuel" the rugged inhabitants now warm vacationers' souls after a long day on the mountain. Convivial meals center on fondue or raclette, whose name comes from the verb *racler*, to scrape; this dish consists mainly of cheese scraped off the wheel and served up sizzling hot along with warm potatoes, ham, and baby onions and pickles. Whether you're talking about food products, antiques, or local crafts such as pottery or glove-making, all of this is part of the ambiance that so distinguishes the Alps from other mountain destinations around the globe.

There are two main *départements* in the Alps: Haute Savoie and Savoie, both of which may be jointly referred to as Savoie. Although distinctively alpine, each possesses certain characteristics unique to that province. The most obvious difference between the two is in the houses: in Haute Savoie, they are mostly made of wood, while in Savoie they are constructed primarily from stone. I'll leave other particularities for you to discover on your own!

HAUTE-SAVOIE

Annecy (Haute-Savoie)

TGV: 3½ hours
Main shopping streets: rue du Pâquier, rue Royale, rue Carnot
Markets: In the Vieille Ville (old town) Tuesday, Friday,
and Sunday 8 A.M.–noon
Flea market: In the Vieille Ville (old town) the last Saturday of
every month 8 A.M.–7 P.M.

It is unlikely that you will encounter busloads of foreign tourists in Annecy, but the town buzzes with tanned and trim outdoorsy types who come to ski, bike, hike, sail, and swim. The main attraction is *le lac*, one of the largest and cleanest lakes in all of France. The lake not only provides a constant source of amusement and wonderfully scenic views, but also extends into the heart of town via a series of centuries-old canals that give Annecy the nickname "Venice of the Alps." These mini-inland waterways, and the old stone bridges that cross them, create a charming and serene setting ideal for strolling. As you weave in and out of the old Renaissance arcades, duck in to **L'Atelier du Sarvan** (rue Perrière), the best address in town for regional crafts such as pottery and painted wood items. This historic center becomes particularly animated on market days when people come down from the hills to sell their homemade cheeses, sausages, and honeys. If you miss market day, stop in at **L'Alpage** (2 rue Filaterie), a rustic little grocery store that is always well-stocked in *spécialités de Savoie*. Across the street, **Le Vieux Necy** (3 rue Filaterie) serves up rich and cheesy regional dishes at irresistible prices in an old savoyard farmhouse.

Around Annecy (Haute-Savoie)

Fabrique de Poteries Savoyardes

As you travel through the Alps, you will see a plethora of pottery, but this out-of-the-way place is worth a visit. Jean-Christophe Hermann is the master behind all of the pottery that is for sale upstairs from his tiny atelier, and although his pieces sell throughout the Alps and in Paris, this is the place to discover the roots of this humble man's passion for *la poterie savoyarde*.

Start with a visit to the adjacent museum, a cavernous old barn that houses Monsieur Hermann's private collection of regional pottery highly respected by experts from such art centers as the Smithsonian Institution. The fruit of more than thirty years of collecting, some 2,000 pieces trace the history of this utilitarian pottery from the twelfth to the early twentieth century. Displays are arranged by type of product; for example, rows of shelves are lined with hundreds of different types of polka-dotted milk pitchers.

Other motifs include flowers, birds, and more abstract geometrical patterns or *jaspage*, a swirly pattern similar to jasper. Green, rust, creamy yellow, and brownish-black make up the traditional palette of colors. (Although widely used today, blue was not introduced until the beginning of the twentieth century.) Monsieur Hermann's own works are based on these traditions. All of his pottery is entirely handmade and fired in a wood-burning kiln. A pitcher or plate costs about 75F here; many of these same pieces sell for as much as five times that price elsewhere.

- 74570 Evires (about 3k from Evires on the RN 203; follow signs for *poterie*); tel.: 04.50.62.01.90
  No credit cards
  Best to call first, especially for the museum

Fonderie de Cloches Paccard

It was here, just outside of Annecy, that I learned about the making of the Liberty Bell. Many people know that the first Liberty Bell was cast in England and broke upon arrival in America. It was then recast in Pennsylvania, but as luck would have it, it cracked with the first gong. Monsieur Paccard exuberantly reeled off this quick history lesson to me because although his family's bell foundry just missed the order for the Liberty Bell (La Fonderie Paccard has been in business *only* since 1796), it was commissioned in 1950 to cast replicas (complete with false cracks) for each of the fifty U.S. states. Paccard also made a 400-pound doorbell for pop singer Michael Jackson!

You will learn all about this and more at the museum that Monsieur Paccard created for his wife in 1985. The process of casting bronze bells has barely changed since 2000 B.C., and the French remain among the most respected in this ancient art. This is one of only three principal bronze foundries in France; the last one in the U.S. disappeared just before World War II. The small museum shop sells miniature bells and concert recordings of some of the most famous carillons in the world. For bigger orders—a ten-ton bell with a 300-kilo clapper, for example—address Monsieur Paccard personally.

- Route des Saintiers, 74320 Sévrier; tel.: 04.50.52.47.11; fax: 04.50.52.66.11
  Open Tuesday–Saturday 10 A.M.–noon and 2:30–5:30 P.M.;
  Sunday and holidays 2:30–5:30 P.M.; open Monday during July and August
  Tours of the Foundry: June–September Friday 2:30–6:30 P.M.; Saturday 10 A.M.–noon and 2:30–6:30 P.M.; Sunday 2:30–6:30 P.M.

Chamonix (Haute-Savoie)

Markets: place du Mont Blanc 8 A.M.–noon Saturday

The most impressive part of Chamonix is the ever-present, snow-topped mass of the Mont Blanc that looms in the distance. Tourists who take the hair-raising ride up the Aiguille du Midi are often caught off guard by the weather, which can include sub-zero temperatures and cutting winds. If you haven't dressed warmly enough for this excursion, **Sanglard** (23 avenue Michel-Croz) stocks the latest in ski and mountain clothing and equipment.

Sanglard attests to the fact that Chamonix is truly a sports resort. People do not come here so much for the ambiance as for the challenge of the mountain. Although you will find just about anything you need for outdoor sports in this snug little town, most of the shops along the main thoroughfares lack charm. **L'Alpage des Aiguilles** (91 rue Joseph-Vallot) is an exception: visitors can savor the rich, earthy smell of cheese and sausage as they browse among the hams that hang from the ceiling and the painted wood cabinets chock full of local wines, liqueurs, and jams. If you're craving sweets, **La Lune** sells many snowy confections in white chocolate, appropriately presented in clear plastic and icy blue wrappings. Its classic tearoom is the perfect place to linger over a hot drink and a blueberry tarte before moving on to more "happening" places.

Le Dogue Bleu

The warm, wooded interior of this charming boutique is filled with regional pottery (including pieces by Jean Christophe Hermann), rustic cow bells, and interesting *objets* such as calf muzzles and gamine-like sleds and rocking horses, both old and new. The sober and often rugged spirit of mountain life also shows in the shop's unique collection of antique furnishings. Mostly constructed out of pine or larch, savoyard furniture tends to be simple and utilitarian. I fell in love with a shepherd's table (7,500F), a tallish piece whose front panel neatly folded down to become a table and exposed narrow, pantry-like shelves.

- 168 avenue Michel-Croz, 74400 Chamonix–Mont-Blanc;
  tel.: 04.50.53.34.01
  Open in season Tuesday–Saturday 10 A.M.–noon and 3–7 P.M.;
  Sunday 3–7 P.M. Off-season Tuesday–Saturday 10 A.M.–noon.

Evian-les-Bains (Haute-Savoie)

TGV: 4 hours

L'Espace Thermal Evian

Known throughout the world, Evian mineral water needs no introduction. Many people may not know, however, that the source of this water, prized for its cleansing and therapeutic properties, springs forth at Evian-les-Bains, a small town located on the French side of Lake Geneva (Lac Léman). Here lake and mountains create an idyllic setting entirely devoted to the *bien-être*, or well-being (a concept far more popular in France than elsewhere). Thermal springs and their resulting spas have long been an essential part of health maintenance throughout Europe, and some people even partake in a *cure* for such medical reasons as urinary or digestive problems. Today Evian's focus is perhaps more on *remise en forme* or "getting into shape," which generally means dropping a few pounds as you tone up and detoxify your body by drinking liter after liter of Evian daily. A regime of *soins*, or treatments, is said to jump-start your circulatory system and allow the healing minerals of the water to penetrate your skin. This is accomplished through a series of baths and showers (a word rather loosely employed, because the consenting *curist* is actually hosed down with near geyser-like force while standing against a wall, with or without a swimsuit). Whether you stay a week (about 6,000F in a three-star hotel with meals included) or a day (310F, towel and bathrobe provided), you'll leave here with your skin glowing.

If you're only passing through town, stop at the gift shop. Here T-shirts, loungewear, bath towels, tote bags, umbrellas, and pens all sport the crisp blue, white, and red Evian logo that symbolizes the crystalline beauty of the French Alps.

- place de la Libération, B.P. 21, 74502 Evian-les-Bains; tel.: 04.50.75.02.30; fax: 04.50.75.65.99
  Spa/Boutique
  Open Monday–Saturday 9 A.M.–12:30 P.M. and 2:45–7:30 P.M.; closed Christmas week

Megève (Haute-Savoie)

Market: Esplanade du Palais des Congres 8 A.M.–noon Friday

If ambiance, character, and charm are high on your list of prerequisites for the ideal alpine getaway, then Megève is for you. In 1916, the Baronne de Rothschild set out to establish a French ski resort that would rival that of the Swiss star, St. Moritz. Although the name is not as recognizable as St. Moritz or even Aspen, over seventy years later, Megève enjoys the same star-billing status as these two other glitzy destinations—without as many of the drawbacks. Fairy-tale chalets owned by such famous people as Hubert de Givenchy and Patrick Poivre d'Arvor (France's own Tom Brokaw) pepper the environs of Megève, yet the word "condo" is still somewhat of a rarity in this discreet Savoy village.

Well-heeled people do, of course, breed high-end boutiques, but nothing seems ostentatious or out of place in this fashionable little town where horse sleighs may just as easily take you out for fondue as drop you off at **Cartier** for a quick fix in gems. **Joly Pottuz** (21 rue Ambrose-Martin) sells hand-crafted Savoy crosses, including the cross of Megève, in 18-karat gold. Each intricately worked piece hangs from green, red, or black silk cords like glistening snowflakes preserved for an alpine queen. Before you become too engrossed in shopping, though, pay a visit to the **Musée du Haut-Val d'Arly** (88 ruelle du Vieux Marché, not far from the tourism office), a living museum where gracious women, clad in traditional costume, keep the spirit of this tiny eighteenth-century farmhouse alive. The costumed staff presents many of the elements essential to life on an alpine farm and also takes great pride in organizing fireside chats called *veillées* around the old woodburning stove.

If this visit inspires you to pick up a piece of Savoyard pottery, go directly to **Pâtisserie La Rivolette** (38 quai du Prieuré), which in addition to sweets sells works by Jean Christophe Hermann. **Pâtisserie du Mont-Joly**, in the village center, is the originator of the *glaçon de Megève*, a chocolaty almond and hazelnut praline hand-dipped in sugary meringue icing. If your hankerings lean more toward salt, **La Cheminée** (rond-point de Rochebrune) is the preferred address for Savoyard hams, sausages, and cheeses.

Teatime is an important part of the day in this socially-oriented *station*, and nestled in at the base of Le Chamois cablecar route is **Chez Maria** (Les Marronniers), an endearing *crêperie* whose blue-and-white-checked tablecloths, doily-draped hanging lamps, and color-coordinated collection of old metal coffeepots will warm you on the most chilly day. The menu features raclette and fondue, but no matter what you order, your check probably will arrive in a little wooden shoe.

Allard

In 1930, a village tailor named Armand Allard responded to the need for a special pant that would allow the skier greater mobility and warmth. The ski pant, or *fuseau*, was born, and Monsieur Allard's focus on elegant practicality gave way to a pair of supremely cut, streamlined trousers destined to become *un grand classique* on the mountain.

Alas, the prices are in keeping with the quality, so unless you can afford to go on a major binge, you may want to content yourself with one precious Allard item such as a plumed Tyrolean-inspired hat at 700F (more fitting for the streets than for the slopes) or a luxurious silk scarf (950F) whose glorious wolfish design pays tribute to the wilds. Mountain themes are omnipresent, largely in the traditional colors of red and green. Most of the clothing (including the ski pants) and accessories for both men and women are made exclusively for Allard and are sold only here. The Allard line of luggage and bath and table linens further mark the company's notion of alpine *art de vivre*. Three-day sales take place annually during the last weekends of April and August.

- 148 place de l'Eglise and 37 quai du Prieuré, 74120 Megève; tel.: 04.50.21.03.85; fax: 04.50.58.73.31
  Open in season Monday–Saturday 9 A.M.–1 P.M. and 2:30–7:30 P.M.; Sunday 10:30 A.M.–12:30 P.M. and 3:30–7:30 P.M. Off-season 9:30 A.M.–12:30 P.M. and 3–7:30 P.M.
  Annual closing early May–June 15. 37 quai du Prieuré open same hours in season. Off-season Monday–Saturday 9:30 A.M.–12:30 P.M. and 3–7:30 P.M. No annual closing.

Henri Duvillard

Ski enthusiasts might recognize this name as the champion of the World
Cup Skiing Competition of 1969. In any event, Monsieur Duvillard has
made excelling on the mountain the main objective in his own brand of
women's and men's ski clothing. Megève may not be known for its steep
summits (in fact, about half of its trails are intermediate), but you will be
ready to meet any challenge with this store's fashion-forward and perfor-
mance-oriented approach to French sporting attire.

- 147 rue Charles Feige, 74120 Megève; tel.: 04.05.21.20.32; fax:
    04.50.21.44.91
  Open in season daily 9 A.M.–8 P.M. off-season Thursday, Friday, and
    Saturday 9:30 A.M.–12:30 P.M. and 3–7 P.M.
  Summer daily 9:30 A.M.–12:30 P.M. and 3–7 P.M.

La Grange aux Moines

The English translation of this shop's name–The Monks' Barn–gives no
inkling of the wonderful antiques and assorted *objets* you'll find inside. The
dimly lit all-wood interior is packed from floorboard to rafters with a plenitude of interesting goods that will leave you with only three problems: where
to put it, how to pay for it, and how to get it home.

The creative force behind this unique emporium of *le rustique* is Jacqueline
Maillet-Contoz, a decidedly discriminating collector who doubles as an interior decorator in her spare time. Her love for the rare and the unusual
from mountains as far away as the Himalayas, is revealed here in unique

Les Fermes de Marie

If you don't yet have a sense of the true art of living in the
French Alps, you owe it to yourself to come here–for a stay of
a few days or at least long enough to coddle a brandy while
sitting in one of the red and green plaid armchairs in the pine-
paneled bar at Les Fermes de Marie. I dare not refer to this as
a hotel, because like the owners' other establishments in town,
Le Mont-Blanc (place de l'Église), **Les Fermes du Grand
Champhameau les choseaux**, and **Au Coin du Feu** (route
Rochebrune), the accent is first and foremost on the authenticity
of mountain style–all in keeping with a comfortable and tasteful
way of living. Attention is paid to every detail, and the small
hamlet of Les Fermes de Marie is in fact a collection of old
alpine farmhouses transplanted here from the nearby hillsides.

Two restaurants, one traditional, one gourmet, also provide good
reason for stopping by.

- Chemin de Riante Colline, 74120 Megève,
  tel.: 04.50.93.03.10; fax: 04.50.93.09.84
  Hotel/Restaurant: Expensive–Very Expensive
  Open May–September and December–April

items such as a century-old lamp fashioned out of one single deer antler.
Quilts and table throws in cozy English fabrics of coordinating red and green
checks, plaids, and stripes have been fashioned exclusively for the shop at
prices that are not for the average passerby. As you leave, you may want to
take a look next door at her daughter's shop, aptly named **Squaw Valley** in
honor of an agreeable sojourn that she spent in that other mountainous part
of the world. The selection of goods is far more mainstream there, although
between both places you can furnish your very own mountain châlet.

- rue des Comtes-de-Capre, 74120 Megève; tel.: 04.50.21.53.70
  Open daily 9:30 A.M.–12:30 P.M. and 2:30–8 P.M.

SAVOIE AND BEYOND

Bourg St-Maurice (Savoie)

Yves Delavest

The more I heard about the Savoy crosses, the more determined I became
to seek out the best address for them. The response to my queries was pretty
much unanimous: Yves Delavest, a jewelry store located almost halfway between Albertville and Val d'Isère. These traditional folkloric pieces recently
regained preeminence with the release of a heavily documented book entitled *Les Croix de Savoie*, by Jean-Pierre Trosset.

Monsieur Delavest began to recognize the importance of the crosses over
thirty years ago when area women brought in their old ones for repair. He
came to know and love the crosses, and then proceeded to start making
replicas of his own. His son continues the business today and has added
earrings, bracelets, and rings to the selection of traditional crosses. Ranging
from pure and simple designs to highly ornamental pieces, most of them
are still fashioned out of gold (Savoy women once wore gold to Sunday mass
and silver during the week). Count on spending at least 2,200F for an interesting piece.

• 63 rue Desserteaux, 73700 Bourg St-Maurice; tel. and fax: 04.79.07.05.90
Open Tuesday–Saturday 8:30 A.M.–noon and 2:30–7 P.M.

Beyond Bourg-St-Maurice (Savoie)

Filature Arpin

Heading east beyond Bourg St-Maurice lies this old woolen mill, in existence
since 1817. An institution of sorts, the Filature Arpin weaves its own wools
into clothing and home furnishings with two primary objectives: to provide
warmth and durability. The look is simple and rustic in an L. L. Bean kind
of way; although here the quality is top drawer, and everything is handmade.
Their elegant woolen knickers practically put contemporary mountain apparel to shame. As Paul-Emile Victor, one of France's famous explorers, once
said of them, "You will wear out your skin before you put a hole in them."
He and his team wore them on at least one major expedition to Greenland.

You can insulate your home with Filature Arpin curtains, cushions, and
blankets in understated solids and plaids. Their throws allow you to wrap
yourself in this handsome alpine tradition for many years to come, and their
prices are honest.

• La Fabrique, 73700 Séez; tel.: 04.79.07.28.79; fax: 04.79.07.02.10
Open Monday–Friday 8:30 A.M.–noon and 1:30–6 P.M.; Saturday 9 A.M.–
noon and 2–6 P.M.
Visit of the atelier: Monday–Thursday 8 A.M.–noon and 1:30–5:30 P.M.;
Friday 8 A.M.–noon

Chambéry (Savoie)

Main shopping streets: place St-Léger, rue Croix d'Or, rue de Boigne
Markets: place de Genève Saturday 8 A.M.–1 P.M.
Flea Market: place St-Léger every second Saturday of the month

The name Chambéry is as melodious as the town's carillon of seventy bells,
which happens to be the biggest and most sonorous in Europe. (The bells
were made by the Fonderie Paccard in Annecy.)

As the capital of Savoy, Chambéry has benefitted from its strategic location throughout history; the town's architecture reflects both the financial
and cultural rewards of the city's former role as toll collector, which enabled
the bourgeoisie to build the elegant *hôtels particuliers* (town houses) that remain today. Pretty pastel façades add a certain Italian note, a reminder that
Chambéry sits at the crossroads of many main axes such as the highways

that lead toward Italy and Switzerland from the north, east, south, and west of France—something worth noting as you plan your trip through this region. With all of this *richesse*, I set out to find an antique shop that would showcase some of the wonderful pieces that people have accumulated here. I fell for **Patrick Bellemin** (9 place de l'Hôtel de Ville; tel.: 04.79.75.09.54), named for its owner, a young, handsome dandy in a corduroy jacket who looked as though he just stepped off the set of *The Age of Innocence*. Patrick proceeded to shyly talk with me about his interest in antiques, the perfect complement to his other passion—that of trompe l'oeil. No wonder the shop glowed with such wonderfully warm colors. A few of his trompe l'oeil paintings provide a bright contrast to his primarily rustic collection of regional furniture. Some items, such as an eighteenth-century–styled lavishly decorated screen (3,000F), are made to order.

If you missed out on the Savoy crosses in Megève and Bourg St-Maurice, the gift shop **Rozier** (90 place St-Léger) also sells a handsome collection of them, and the owners are most helpful in telling you about the provenance of each cross. Opinel knives, rudimentary cutting instruments recognizable by their smooth pine handles, are also typical of the Alps. If you missed the Opinel museum in St-Jean-de-Maurienne, take a look at them here at this fishing supply store called **Au Spécialiste** (2 rue Favre). Opinel knives are fairly inexpensive (about 40F for one of medium size), so you may want to pick one up if you're planning a mountain picnic.

Provision hunting for this outing should start at **Denis Provent** (2 place de Genève), cheese master par excellence. In the cellars (which were used as bomb shelters during the war), he supervises the delicate aging process of his cheeses with utmost care. The cheeses, rich in milk from cows that have grazed in the Savoy pastures, slumber here in the form of tome, reblochon, and beaufort, to name a few. Just down the street at 11 place de l'Hôtel-de-Ville is **La Cave Jeandet**, a wine shop that features Savoy wines such as Gamay, Chignin, and Apremont, a dry white wine most often served with fondue and raclette.

If you are not yet having a *crise de foie* (liver crisis—the French never talk about heartburn), stop by **Mazet** (2 place Porte-Reine), a candy store that has been in business since 1820. Although they sell chocolates, they are best known for their tangy hard candies. All nine of their flavors, which range from licorice to mint, are made on the premises from carefully measured proportions of pure juices and sugar. Hand-wrapped in tiny squares of wax paper marked by the red cross of Savoy, these gourmet treats keep for up to three months.

The confectioner and tea salon **Au Fidèle Berger** (15 rue de Boigne) is also known for its sweets, although of a considerably more decadent order: chocolate truffles. In business since 1832, this traditional establishment claims the powdery chocolate ball that much of the civilized world has come to know as a truffle was first created in Chambéry in 1896. Choose from about a half a dozen flavors, including rose and thyme, of these chocolate-and-cream, melt-in-your-mouth little nuggets and then sit down to sample them with coffee.

Outside Chambéry (Savoie)

Château de Candie

It suddenly occurred to me as I approached this noble château that I had encountered very few edifices of this kind throughout the Alps. It was after 8 P.M. before my traveling companion and I arrived. The room was big and grand enough to hold a small party, and the bathroom alone far surpassed the size of the average person's bedroom, with a huge ball-clawed porcelain tub. I was expected in the dining room, and although I preferred to wile away the evening hours in the privacy of my luxurious quarters, I found myself seduced by more unrivaled elegance as I sat down at the table.

- rue du Bois de Candie, 73000 Chambéry-le-Vieux; tel.: 04.79.96.63.00; fax: 04.79.96.63.10

Hotel/Restaurant: Expensive

Open year-round; the restaurant is closed Sunday evenings

Grenoble (Isère)

TGV: 3 hours
Main shopping streets: Grande Rue, rue de Bonne, avenue Alsace-Lorraine
Markets: place St-André Tuesday–Sunday 6 A.M.–1 P.M.
Flea market: Marché Hoche, place André Malraux
the first Saturday of every month 7 A.M.–1 P.M.

The 1968 Winter Olympics put Grenoble on the map for the rest of the world. Stendahl's description, "There is a mountain at the end of every street," is true: despite the citylike look of Grenoble, the Alps are never far away. And what would life be like in the mountains without skis? There is no better way to fully appreciate the development of skiing over the past few centuries than to spend an hour or so at the Musée du Ski. Housed in the *Musée Dauphinois*, it's just a short, StairMaster climb up the hill from the center of town. The displays trace the history of skiing from its origins, when man dabbled in it as a means of getting around (particularly for hunting), to modern-day racing.

After this trek, you'll feel deserving of at least one of the mouth-watering walnut specialities made fresh daily at the pastry/candy shop/tea salon, **Les Ecrins** (11 rue de Bonne). Walnuts have been grown extensively in the environs of Grenoble since the end of the nineteenth century, and here their rich, nutty flavor is revealed in full glory in a variety of cakes, candies, and liqueurs. Referred to as *les noix de Grenoble*, this shop's best-loved confections consist of two candied walnut halves sandwiched together by homemade almond paste.

To die for!

For a hearty meal, try the historic **Café de la Table Ronde** at 7 place St-André. Opened in 1739, this popular gathering place ranks as the second oldest café in France. Its yellowed walls, and overall tattered edges, preserve its charm.

Gant Notturno

This century-old glove shop, situated a bit of a distance from the center of town, is worth the walk. This is the only remaining glove-maker in Grenoble, known as one of France's glove capitals in the nineteenth century. Millau, a town in the southwest, also claims to have been a leading maker of gloves over the last century, but nearly all Grenoble gloves are made of kidskin, while those in Millau primarily are made with lambskin.

Aside from the differences in leather, the attention to craftsmanship in both places is very much the same. All of the creamy-smooth gloves sold in Notturno's tiny shop are made entirely by hand upstairs in the atelier and also are sold to a handful of select boutiques. The over-the-elbow milky-white kidskin gloves apparently draw a certain amount of attention at Saks Fifth Avenue in New York just before the débutante balls. The rest of the collection is far more practical, and aside from a few bright colors, most of the men's and women's gloves are quite classic. Equally attractive prices, like 300F for a pair of ladies' cashmere-lined kidskin gloves, also make the trip hard to pass up.

- 11 rue Humbert II, 38000 Grenoble; tel.: 04.76.46.56.60
  Open Monday–Saturday 9 A.M.–noon and 2–6:30 P.M.
  Workshop visits by appointment

Beyond Grenoble (Isère)

Chartreuse

Which came first, the color or the liqueur? In fact, neither one. Although the color does take its name from the liqueur, the liqueur was named after the Chartreuse monks, who live in the Chartreuse mountains that border Grenoble. The cellars are so well known that about 200,000 visitors tour them each year. The liqueur recipe, a combination of over 100 different plants and herbs originally concocted as a special elixir, has been closely guarded since 1604. Of the forty monks who live at the monastery today, only three are said to know the mysterious formula. You will not see any of the monks on the tour; they devote their lives to silence, solitude, and prayer.

• 10 boulevard Edgar-Kofler, B.P. 102, 38503 Voiron; tel.: 04.76.05.81.77; fax: 04.76.66.19.35
  Open Easter–November 1 daily 8:30–11:30 A.M. and 2–6:30 P.M.; July and August daily 8:30 A.M.–6:30 P.M.; Off-season Monday–Friday 8:30–11:30 A.M. and 2–5:30 P.M.

Val d'Isère (Savoie)

I had not planned to go to Val d'Isère, but as I approached the end of my research in the Alps, I was left with an undeniable yearning to see great peaks—the kind of giant moonscape, above-the tree-line terrain that holds you in awe from the very base of the mountain. One heading from a travel brochure stuck in my head: "Arriving in Val d'Isère is a dazzling experience." Yes, I had already looked dropped-jawed at le Mont Blanc, but now I was ready to be dazzled.

The breathtaking mountain scenery actually begins on the road to Val d'Isère from Bourg St-Maurice. If you truly want to take in views on this drive, such as a typical Savoyard Baroque church perched high on a hilltop, it's best to be the passenger. The main street of Val d'Isère (avenue Olympique) cuts through the mountains like a great divide. It is here, among the rugged yet stately slate and stone-pillared buildings, that you will find nearly everything you need to remind yourself of your stay in this World Cup resort. **Tee Top** is a shop piled high with attractive tees and sweatshirts for men, women, and children. **Killy Sport,** which specializes in ski essentials, is hard to miss; it's owned by the brother of the town's gold medal-winning native son, Jean-Claude Killy. For more craftlike goods from the region (and other parts of the world as well), stop into **Les Trois Marmottes,** which is almost next door to a splendid little Baroque church.

As with any popular vacation spot, Val d'Isère has an almost infinite selection of eateries, and choosing the right one is rarely easy. My travel companion and I decided to celebrate our last night of a week of tiresome touring and often white-knuckled driving (particularly when the windshield of our car froze over as we inched our way down from the heights of Chamonix: European cars are not always filled with antifreeze)—but where to go? Thanks to Jane, the lovely and most efficient P.R. wiz from the tourism office, we found an authentic little restaurant on the fringes of town, appropriately named **La Vieille Maison,** for a hedonistic repast of fondue and *vin de Savoie.* Call ahead to reserve (04.79.06.11.76)–and for an extra cozy soirée, ask for the table that faces the fireplace.

ALSACE
Alsace

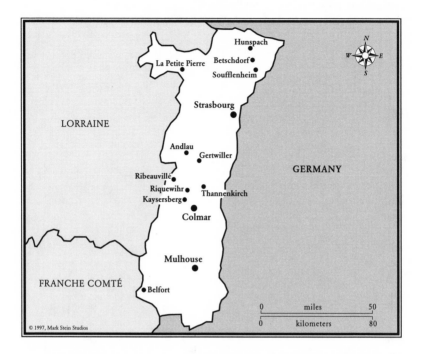

sauerkraut • pottery • wines • rhubarb pies • foie gras • *springerle*
plaques • gingerbread • wood sculptures • reproductions of ancient stamps • traditionally patterned tablecloths • *eaux-de-vie* •
polychrome furnishings • faience • long-stemmed wineglasses •
cheeses • Hansi illustrations • regional folk art and crafts • marquetry • engravings • collectible cards • kougelhopf • old books
• paintings • reproductions of museum pieces • pewter • chocolates • antiques • heart-shaped chairs

I AM EMBARRASSED to say that I lived in Paris for at least eight years before
going to Alsace, a storybook land where storks nest in chimney tops and
festive village celebrations of people dressed in folkloric costumes are com-
monplace. Forever in search of sun, many a Parisian gives a "thumbs down"
response to the idea of vacationing in the far eastern part of France because
the climate and the people are reputed to be dreary.

How wrong those Parisians can be; I could write pages and pages about how unique and enchanting Alsace and the Alsatians tend to be—and the weather is nothing to shrug about either! It must be the German connection that makes the Parisians nervous—but it is the German/French mix that has given Alsace its character. Alsatians are first and foremost Alsatian, an identity that they have forged as numerous factions have fought over their region for centuries. Physically, the people look more Germanic than Latin, and sometimes their robust nature can seem overbearing, yet they possess all of the subtleties of the French—and it is this curious mixture that makes them so interesting.

As for what the Parisians often refer to as coldness, they must be mistaking the Alsatians' often initial reserve for distance (you'd be wary, too, after so many invasions). I met the greatest number of warm, friendly people in this region of France. Coincidentally, an Alsatian assured me that there were more differences between Parisians and Alsatians than between Parisians and Americans. The only difficulty I had was in pronouncing, and particularly understanding, so many of the German names. Alsatians are accustomed to bouncing back and forth between French and German (many primarily speak Alsatian, a dialect of German).

This rich crosscultural heritage is reflected in nearly every aspect of Alsatian life, including food, architecture, crafts, and folklore. Christmastime, a season filled with much merrymaking in Germany, is also greatly celebrated in Alsace. Brightly illuminated decorations and traditional Christmas markets, such as the one in Kaysersberg, the most heart-warming and authentic of them all, enlivens the region during a typically sullen time of year.

This historic little village of Kaysersberg is but one of the highlights along *la route des vins*, uncontestably the most picturesque wine route in all of France. As you drive along this well marked route, you pass through village after village, each with its own distinct flavor, and even more impressive is that each has been beautifully preserved over the centuries. Alsace, particularly the wine route, is a colorful place: even if you travel here in the dead of winter, the rosy pinks of the houses and the rusty reds of their roofs will envelop you with the warmth of this poignant land.

NORTHERN ALSACE

Betschdorf (Bas-Rhin)

The look of the pottery of Betschdorf and Soufflenheim is as different as the villages themselves. Soufflenheim pottery generates great universal appeal, while the more rustic pottery of Betschdorf attracts more of a niche market of folk-art enthusiasts and collectors. The quiet little village of Betschdorf delights visitors with its handsome and generous assemblage of half-timbered houses, many of which date back to the eighteenth century. I suggest you start with a visit to the **Musée de la Poterie**, located in the center of the village: open daily from Easter to November 1, 10 A.M.–noon and 2–6 P.M.

As soon as you step in to this old farmhouse, you might recognize the blue and gray color scheme of the Betschdorf stoneware—probably after having seen it in souvenir shops and other boutiques since your arrival in Alsace. A unique salt-based glaze typifies this hand-turned pottery, a process that has been used in the Rhine region for centuries. A few pieces in this museum date back as far as the Middle Ages, and others transport us to the seventeenth, eighteenth, and nineteenth centuries through supreme examples of pitchers, jugs, and the proverbial beer steins. The last room of the museum exposes samplings from more than a dozen potters who still work in this traditional method. If you wish to visit the studios of the potters whose creations you like best, the museum provides a list of names and addresses.

Hunspach (Bas-Rhin)

It's definitely worth going just a bit farther north to take in this Hansel and Gretel–like setting, one of the most beautiful villages of France, especially if you visit when the window boxes spill forth with cascades of blooming flowers and curling vines. The streets are tranquil, since most of the commercial or farm-related activities take place within the confines of the inner yards of Hunspach's massive, half-timbered dwellings.

As I admired each of these superbly preserved houses along the rue Principale, my eyes blinked twice when I thought I had spotted a tea salon. Sure enough in the middle of the charming, superbly preserved houses along the rue Principale is a tea salon run by Madame Fischer, who gleefully pointed out to me the Alsatian specialties that have been sold in the *boulangerie/pâtisserie* of **Fischer & Fils** for the past five generations. After much indecision, I chose a pinky-green slice of meringue-encrusted rhubarb pie, knowing that it would more than amply tide me over until my next copious meal of *choucroute* (sauerkraut) and beer.

La Petite Pierre (Bas-Rhin)

Although this tiny hilltop village is almost an hour and a quarter from Strasbourg, the journey there is half the fun. The highway part is boring but fast, and once you find yourself on the country roads that lead up to La Petite Pierre, you'll quickly feel transported back in time. As you pass through quaint villages punctuated by pretty pastel-colored houses, you will marvel at how much of this land has remained unspoiled and free of any unsightly modern addendums.

La Petite Pierre teeters on the border of Alsace and Lorraine, a strategic stronghold that has been coveted and captured by many a warlord throughout the ages. Like the rest of Alsace, its history is complex and you'd have to be a true scholar to fully comprehend its intricacies. Monsieur Charles Haudot, curator of the village's **Musée du Sceau** and **Musée des Arts et Traditions Populaires**, is a scholar of an unusual sort. He has designed little plaques, consisting of a color-tainted mixture of stucco and resin, to illustrate ancient seals and cookies for these two small, yet hard to miss, museums in the village center.

In the past, documents in this region were sealed with a dollop of hot wax, then stamped by the official seal of the bearer, whether it was that of a town, a religious order, a trade guild, or any other number of institutions or policy-makers. The rich collection of symbols and images at the crafts and folklore museum is of a different order: the key word here is *springerle*, German for "to spring," which is exactly what happens when you tap the special baking tins used for the classic Alsatian Christmas cookies so that the elaborately patterned treats can pop right out. Developed in the fifteenth century, the *springerle* tradition has practically died out today. It's probably because these dry, faintly anise-flavored cookies weren't made so much for their taste as for their allegorical designs, which expressed a broad range of romantic sentiments and religious beliefs. The plaques on display here show how cookies made from the *springerle* tins would look. Both of the museums sell many of the same plaques from their collection at prices that range from 50F to 100F.

- **Musée du Sceau**: tel.: 03.88.70.48.65
  Open Saturday and Sunday and during school holidays except Monday 10 A.M.–noon and 2–6 P.M.
- **Musée des Arts ets Traditions Populaires**: tel.: 03.88.70.48.65
  Open Tuesday–Sunday July–September 10 A.M.–noon and 2–6 P.M.
  October–June Sundays 10 A.M.–noon and 2–6 P.M.

Soufflenheim (Bas-Rhin)

A village of potters since the twelfth century, the Soufflenheim of today seems to sigh with the weight of the throngs of tourists who come to see the earthenware most frequently associated with Alsace. Not all of the ateliers are open for visits, and of course not all the pottery is of the highest quality. It's not always easy, either, to see the difference because so many of the kougelhopf molds, terrines, and oven dishes begin to look alike after a while. Used both for decorative and culinary purposes, Soufflenheim pieces have simple, countrylike designs of stylized flowers and swirls, richly glazed over classic hues of midnight blue, bottle green, and buttermilk. **Friedmann** and **Wehrling** are two different potters whose work most closely resembles that of the old *art populaire*–particularly important for those who are looking for pieces worth collecting. Look for their wrought-iron sign as you enter the town.

THE WINE ROUTE

Andlau (Bas-Rhin)

Domaine Marc Kreydenweiss

There are so many vineyards that sell wines of varying qualities along the wine route that it's difficult to choose which one to visit. If good wine is part of your criteria, keep your eyes out for a sign that classifies the wine as *grand cru* (great growth, or top-ranking wine), of which there are about fifty in Alsace. I conducted a little bit more research than that–which explains how I found the Domaine Marc Kreydenweiss, a house that has been making wines for more than 300 years. Locating the winery itself took a bit of doing, since this village is not clearly marked. Go first to Barr, then follow signs for Le Hohwald and later Andlau.

I was greeted by a lovely, young and appropriately blond, Alsatian woman I later learned was the wife of Marc Kreydenweiss, the innovative winegrower who has received acclaim on both sides of the Atlantic. He runs a tight operation that produces only about 60,000 bottles a year, so you may want to call ahead–particularly during off-season–to request a visit to the cellars. Although small, the *caves* are worth seeing for their typically Alsatian, eighty-year-old and hugely oval-shaped oak *foudres* (large vats or casks); exquisitely sculpted wood carvings of fish, mermaids, and grapes that adorn the spigots of these tall receptacles; and for the twelfth-century stone column that was found on a summit in the region and planted like a theater prop!

The wines distinguish themselves by their labels (in this regard, Kreydenweiss is the Mouton Rothschild of Alsace) and by their taste. For a true Alsatian experience, be sure to consider one of the wines from their *sélections de grains nobles*, delicately sweet and aromatic vintages born from the nectar of noble rot.

• 12 rue Deharbe, 67140 Andlau; tel.: 03.88.08.95.83; fax: 03.88.08.41.16
Open Monday–Saturday 9 A.M.–noon and 2–6 P.M.
Telephone ahead for visits.

Gertwiller (Bas-Rhin)

Pains d'Epices Lips

In my search for Andlau, I stumbled upon Gertwiller, a little town known as the gingerbread capital of Alsace. Michel Hasbiger, the owner of its foremost gingerbread bakery, closely guards his scores of recipes but eagerly told me the rich history and tradition of *pain d'épice*, or spice bread, which can be traced back at least 2,000 years to China. Marco Polo introduced this rather dense mixture of flour, sugar, honey, and spices, which included ginger, nutmeg, cinnamon, and clove, to Europe during the Crusades, and it became most popular in the lands now known as Alsace, Lorraine, and Germany. The bakery produces many variations on one theme: from apricot-filled to chocolate-covered, *pain d'épice* is consumed year-round, although Christmas remains the biggest and brightest season. Don't miss the *pain d'épice* museum, a newly installed space filled with countless old labels and molds that bear testimony to Monsieur Hasbiger's unchallenged fervor for this traditional Alsatian treat.

- place de la Mairie, 67140 Gertwiller; tel.: 03.88.08.93.52;
  fax: 03.88.08.53.78
  Open Monday–Friday 8 A.M.–noon and 1:30–7 P.M.; Saturday 8 A.M.–
  noon and 1:30–6 P.M.; Sunday 2–6 P.M.
  Museum is open Sunday 2–6 P.M. and during school vacations.

Riquewihr (Haut-Rhin)

The walls of this centuries-old town remain intact today, although you have to park your car outside the city's borders. I arrived here about 10 A.M. one spring morning, not early enough to beat the crowds, nor to avoid the annoying oom-pah-pah of the nearby vendor so desperately trying to sell his cassettes of regional folk music. Despite the touristy atmosphere, if you're a lover of illustrations of tremendous regional flavor and charm, it's worth coming to Riquewihr just to visit the **Musée Hansi**. The ground-floor boutique is filled with rather poor reproductions of Alsace's most revered illustrator's works, but upstairs, chances are you will be generously enchanted by the images of Jean-Jacques Waltz, who was affectionately known as Hansi. Alsatians young and old, dressed in traditional costumes and bearing such typical Alsatian goods as kougelhopfs, Riesling, and pretzels, have been endearingly immortalized here in a prolific array of watercolors, lithographs, advertising posters, greeting cards, and pages from entire albums consecrated to the works of "Oncle Hansi."

- **Musée Hansi**: 16 rue du Général-de-Gaulle; tel.: 03.89.47.97.00
  Open April 1–December 31: Tuesday–Sunday 10:30 A.M.–6 P.M. and
  Mondays during July and August 2–6 P.M.

January: Saturday and Sunday 2–6 P.M.; February–March: Tuesday–Sunday 2–6 P.M.

Thannenkirch (Haut-Rhin)

I couldn't find this little mountain village on my wine route map but was told that it was just a short distance from Illhaeusern. That it was, and I was amazed at the difference in terrain just a few kilometers from the valley. The multiplication of wooden houses, along with the sudden jump in altitude, told me that I had indeed entered the foothills of the Vosges mountains. Even the air smelled fresher and I later learned that Thannenkirch had been named a *station thermale*, a sort of label that ensures the purity of a resort town.

Three little figures, carved entirely out of wood, guided me to my ultimate destination: the atelier of **Pascal Bosshardt** (5 rue Taennchel; tel.: 03.89.73.10.94; fax: 03.89.73.10.66), a master Alsatian woodcarver. Pascal works mostly from special order, although a handful of pieces displayed in his workshop are for sale. Nearly all of the woods come from the region. Hearty woods such as oak or chestnut are best suited for the outdoor sculptures, while *tilleul* or linden, a tender but firm wood, lends itself to the more decorative interior pieces. In keeping with this down-to-earth art form, the primarily folkloric themes revolve around mountain life, animals, and religion. Passionate about his craft, Pascal gladly welcomes visitors, and if you drive by when he's not around, at least stop to take a look at the hand-carved façade of his home and atelier.

It poured rain as I left this quiet village, and since it was lunchtime anyway, I ended up finding a great place to take refuge from this gloomy day. With the exterior painted all in green, I should have realized that the **Waldstebel** (24 rue Ste-Anne; tel.: 03.89.73.11.84) would guarantee me a warm, mountainlike atmosphere. And that it did. A stuffed bobcat, a magnificently-carved cuckoo clock, and an animal horn chandelier provided additional mountainy touches to the stone and wood interior of this homey establishment. The view, a distant silhouette of one of the region's best known landmarks, the Château de Haut Koenigsbourg, only further enhanced my 105F luncheon feast of fresh *crûdités, boeuf au pinot noir*, and the region's own cheesecake–a far lighter and more delicately flavored version of anything that I have ever tasted back home!

Ribeauvillé (Haut-Rhin)

Market: place de l'Hôtel de Ville Saturday 8 A.M.–noon

Another one of the musts along the wine route, visitors appreciate Ribeauvillé for its picturesque Alsatian town qualities as much as for its important vestiges of medieval history. Although Ribeauvillé is not too overrun with tourists, it's best to avoid peak vacation periods, and if you're driving, keep in mind that parking can be a problem.

Beauvillé

To me, the number-one reason for going to Ribeauvillé is to stop at the Beauvillé factory discount store, where prices of this world-renowned textile maker's goods are as much as 30 to 60 percent lower than regular French retail prices. Beauvillé or M.I.E. (the official company name which stands for Manufacture d'Impression sur Etoffes) is a classic Alsatian house known for the color and designs of its prints. Its tablecloths, which started to become de rigueur at Parisian dinner parties nearly ten years ago, are considered mainstays in French linen closets—particularly since many of these prints have been an integral part of the Alsatian tradition for centuries.

Although Beauvillé was founded in 1838, some of its fanciful yet eloquent patterns are based on woodblock prints from the seventeenth and eighteenth centuries, and some from fifteenth-century designs. Color schemes range from a single-colored pattern on a plain white background to a riot of hues of often astonishing nuances. Some of the items are seconds, although most of the merchandise is flawless. It's not a bad idea to do a bit of stockpiling, because Beauvillé tablecloths can cost as much as five times the regular French price in high-end department stores abroad. The factory and store are located just outside of town along the route to Stes-Marie-aux-Mines.

• BP 46-F, 68150 Ribeauvillé; tel.: 03.89.73.74.74; fax: 03.89.73.32.17
Open Monday–Saturday 8–11:45 A.M. and 2–5:45 P.M.

Jean-Paul Mette

Eau-de-vie is always tough to translate into English. It literally means water of life, although the word firewater seems far more appropriate. In any event, Monsieur Metté distills close to 100 different kinds of these power-packed brandies, from the most transparent whites to the glossiest browns—all from fruits, vegetables, herbs, and plants that he tenderly cultivates in his own garden. Taste-testing here proves to be far from a sobering experience, especially if this is your last stop after an entire day along the wine route. The tasting room is indeed charming, and as I sat on a little wooden Alsatian chair with my spine against its traditional heart-shaped back, my only worry was which brandy to sip next! If I remember correctly . . . I stopped after the four most classic flavors of quince, pear, raspberry, and plum, having decided to leave the more exotic asparagus, woodruff, and garlic spirits for the next time!

• 9 rue des Tanneurs, 68150 Ribeauvillé; tel.: 03.89.73.65.88;
    fax: 03.89.73.30.11
Open Monday–Friday 9 A.M.–noon and 2–6 P.M.

Hostellerie des Seigneurs de Ribeaupierre

If you're planning to spend a few nights in the region, this
quaint hotel, run by two very friendly and helpful sisters, might
just transport you back a few centuries in time. I fell in love
with their breakfast room, a huge, stone-walled, fifteen-feet-tall
chamber where only a sliver of light was able to eek in through
the small windows set high up at ground level. Originally used
as a cellar, today this rather dramatic-looking space is enlivened
by tables dressed with pretty green Alsatian prints and crisply
colored faience.

• 11 rue du Château, 68150 Ribeauvillé; tel.: 03.89.73.70.31;
    fax: 03.89.73.71.21
Three-Star Hotel: Moderate
Open early March–mid-December

THE CITIES

Belfort (Haut-Rhin)

On the first Sunday of every month, antique aficionados arrive at Belfort's
renowned flea markets as early as 6 A.M. with flashlight in hand to have first
dibs on the best bargains. The finest showing of antiques and secondhand
goods in the east takes place within the maze of streets in *Vieux Belfort*.
Come early, because the show's over by 1 P.M.

Colmar (Haut-Rhin)

Main shopping streets: rue des Clés, rue des Marchands,
rue des Têtes, rue des Boulangers
Markets: place de l'Ancienne Douane and place de la Cathédrale
Thursday 8 A.M.–noon and place St-Joseph
Saturday 8 A.M.–noon
Flea market: place de l'Ancienne Douane every first and
third Friday of the month 8 A.M.–6 P.M.

Just a stone's throw away from the wine route lies lovely Colmar, a city that once prospered from the nearby wine industry and today is extremely attractive for its historic buildings and manageable size. The real bonus is that the residents far outnumber the tourists! It's hard to talk about the old section of town because so much of the city is old, but any visit to the *vieux quartier* merits a stop at **Pâtisserie Jean** (6 place de l'Ecole, tel.: 03.89.41.24.63), Colmar's best address for chocolates and typically Alsatian treats. If you continue to wander these streets, which are laced with history and art, you will find yourself near the Maison Pfister, a most eye-catching house which is inevitably listed in all of the guidebooks. Almost just across from this historic landmark, be sure to visit the boutique **Au Fond de la Cour** (rue des Marchands), where Dany Geisman displays her *meubles à polychrome,* or painted wood furniture (primarily nineteenth-century pine) whose traditional Alsatian motifs of hearts and flowers resemble classic Pennsylvania Dutch designs. Colmar has a profusion of antiques–and you'll uncover many more great finds as you continue down the rue des Marchands to the place des Anciennes-Douannes. If lunch or dinner is on your mind, though, try **La Maison des Têtes** (19 rue des Têtes; tel.: 03.89.24.43.43), the recently refurbished restaurant of the historic Renaissance house of the same name. It has become one of the most elegant gastronomic addresses in all Colmar!

The textile industry has always been important in Alsace. One store, **La Cotonnerie d'Alsace** (1 rue des Clefs), specializes in fabrics, table and bed linens under the name of Paule Marrot, a designer who left her mark by using elements of traditional Alsatian prints in more modern patterns. To me, the designs, such as a tablecloth color-splashed with highly stylized flowers and leafy motifs, pales in comparison to that of Beauvillé, although if you find yourself on this busy commercial street, you should stop by.

Arcana

See description on page 59.

• 1 rue des Tanneurs, 68000 Colmar; tel.: 03.89.24.09.78
  Open Monday 2–6:30 P.M.; Tuesday–Friday 9:30–noon and 2–6:30 P.M.;
  Saturday 9:30–noon and 2–6 P.M.

Jean-Paul Bidermann

When I first entered this Ali Baba's cavern of antiques and bric-à-brac, I questioned how much of it was actually from the region. After looking more closely at this amusing conglomeration of furniture, faience, and *objets,* I realized that many of the pieces did indeed come from the East. The owner of this interesting little shop, Jean-Paul Bidermann, mused about the sorts of items that attract different buyers: the Germans and the Swiss, for example, are particularly fond of the long-stemmed, mostly engraved, Alsatian wineglasses—probably because so many of these glasses were lost in their own countries during World War II. I discovered another typically Alsatian piece, a sober-looking pine armoire with a "robin's tail," a wooden fixture that would allow the piece to be dismantled within five minutes. A clever invention for people who were unfortunately forced to be occasionally on the run!

• 6 rue du Conseil-Souverain (place du Marché aux Fruits), 68000 Colmar; tel.: 03.89.23.65.20
Open Monday–Saturday 2–6:30 P.M.

Georges Keller

After leaving the Hansi museum in Riquewihr frustrated with the poor reproductions of this beloved illustrator's works, I came to Colmar in search of the real thing. Having stumbled upon Georges Keller's shop by chance, I was thrilled to see that Hansi originals are his forte. Many of the lithographs and watercolors are signed by the artist, and although some are a bit pricey, I noticed that old postcards sold for 350F—and framed, no less! Most striking to me are the large posters that Hansi created toward the first part of this century as advertisements for local banks and the Alsace Lorraine railways—all handsome depictions of Alsatian life and priced between 6,000F and 10,000F.

Georges Keller's handpicked selection of regional engravings and lithographs from the seventeenth to the early part of the twentieth century reveal all of the traditional and folkloric images of Alsace. Marquetry is another typically Alsatian art form, and works by Spindler are among the most treasured. One tableau, priced at 7,000F, represented a classic Alsatian scene of half-timbered houses and storks with such skill and finesse that it seemed to bring the wooden images to life. Other, more current favorites include the ceramic folk art of Jo Heim, an artist who may be best described as having adopted a Botero-esque view of traditionally costumed Alsatian people. His works are priced from 1800F to 5,000F.

• 8 place du Marché aux Fruits, 68000 Colmar; tel.: 03.89.24.22.51.
Open Tuesday–Saturday 9 A.M.–noon and 2–7 P.M.

Around Colmar

Au Pont de la Fecht

Almost halfway between Sigolsheim and Colmar, hidden within the vineyards of the plain, sits this large, family-style restaurant whose every facet embodies the lively spirit of Alsace. Known for decades as a *lieu de rencontre populaire*, or local meeting place, this unique gathering spot has remained one of the best-kept secrets in Alsace. It would look like a Hollywood movie set if it were not so very real and authentic. The huge terrace is meant for parents to sit for hours, laughing and telling stories over pitchers of perfectly chilled Riesling, while their children amuse themselves on swing sets or by driving around in toy cars. Everything seems to have been designed with the idea of fun, and even the farm animals that mill about on this land of milk and honey appear content.

In talking about the tasteful décor of the restaurant's interior, one of the owners, Monique, who was honored with the title of "queen of the wines of Alsace" nearly twenty years ago, says "you find everything inside that is outside." By this she modestly refers to her vast collection of barnyard-inspired *objets* that includes watering cans, milk pails, frogs, ducks, and various other collectibles in every imaginable shape and form. A tribute to Alsatian country life, these accessories further enhance the warmth and charm of the *winstub* (Alsatian for wine bar) and dining room, which have been handsomely decorated with traditional painted furnishings, vibrantly colored Beauvillé tablecloths, and brilliant wall murals. Monique's husband, Hubert, spends most of his time in the kitchen cooking up savory Alsatian dishes for hearty appetites.

- Sigolsheim, 68000 Colmar; tel.: 03.89.41.48.12; fax: 03.89.24.51.44
  Restaurant/Café: Inexpensive–Moderate
  Open daily except Tuesday

Mulhouse (Haut-Rhin)

Main shopping streets: rue du Sauvage, place de la Réunion,
rue des Boulangers, rue Henriette, rue des Marēchauy
Markets: Canal Couvert (rue Aristide Briand
Tuesday, Thursday, and Saturday 8 A.M.–7 P.M.

Undeniably the most modern and industrial city of Alsace, Mulhouse does not exude much character or charm, but people will travel from great distances for its big name shopping. If you're not in the market for an Hermès scarf, focus on the **Musée de l'Impression sur Etoffes**, a textile museum that is in itself worth the trip. The textile industry in Mulhouse began in

1746 with the opening of the first factory entirely devoted to the printing of dyes on fabrics. Prior to that, most of the prints, called *indiennes* (because they originated from India), usually were made by local craftspeople. This began the industrialization of Mulhouse, an expansion that continues today. If you like fabrics, you'll love this museum; it presents an incredibly colorful repertory of prints in a phantasmagoric collection of designs!

The **Musée du Papier Peint**, or wallpaper museum, is equally entrancing, particularly to decorative arts enthusiasts. People often say that this museum is in Mulhouse, although it is actually located just outside the city at Rixheim, a town that began making wallpaper toward the end of the eighteenth century. This industry continues today, and decorators from all over the world place orders here for the special scenic wallpaper that presents near 300-degree views made up of about twenty-four panels. Displayed upstairs, these incredible murals lead you on a decorative journey through exotic lands and historic sights: one beauty, which was made for the White House, encompasses views of New York City, West Point, the port of Boston, and Niagara Falls—all in one giant panoramic landscape.

Unfortunately, the sparsely supplied gift shops in each of the museums are disappointing; their collection of cards, however, based on richly patterned textiles and wallpaper, make for delightful remembrances of your visit.

Strasbourg (Bas-Rhin)

Main shopping streets: rue du Chaudron, rue du Temple-Neuf,
rue Sanglier, rue des Orfèvres
Markets: boulevard de la Marne 7 A.M.–1 P.M.
Tuesday; place Broglie 7 A.M.–6 P.M.
Wednesday; place du Marché-aux-Poissons
Saturday 7 A.M.–1 P.M.
Flea market: rue du Vieil-Hôpital and place de la Grande-Boucherie
Wednesday and Saturday 9 A.M.–6 P.M.

Strasbourg is a big, beautiful city, so you should plan to spend *at least* a day here. Although old and traditional in appearance, the city definitely has a cosmopolitan spirit. Its massive pink-stoned cathedral will humble you, and the weeping willows along the canal-like sections of the river Ill will stir the most romantic sentiments of your heart—but the web of cowpathlike streets will annoy you, particularly if you don't like getting lost! In my attempt to master the lay-of-the-land, I collected at least a half-dozen different maps of the city—each harder to figure out than the next. Be patient as you try to make your way around the city.

The cathedral is hard to miss, and thankfully some of the best shopping takes place in this quarter. The adjacent Carré d'Or refers to a section of stylish streets that includes the rue des Orfèvres and the rue du Chaudron, where you can gorge yourself on everything from high fashion to foie gras. Yes, foie gras is an Alsatian speciality, and some people claim that it originated here before it appeared in the Southwest. The *charcutier* **Fritz-Lutz** (16 rue des Orfèvres) sells both fresh and canned foie gras prepared in a variety of ways. Just across the street is **Naegel** (9 rue des Orfèvres), one of the city's best addresses for kougelhopf, a yeasty bread made in a tall, crownlike shape. Once reserved for Sundays, it has become an Alsatian staple.

The *pâtissier/chocolatier* **Christian** has two addresses in town. One is just a few steps from the cathedral at 10 rue Mercière; the other at 12 rue de l'Outre is recognizable by its gorgeous trompe l'oeil façade. The treats from this reputable house are indeed delicious, and you can savor them in the tea salons, but the service at both shops can be slow and less than friendly.

If you are a collector of antique books, stop at **Ancienne Librairie Gangloff** (20 place de la Cathédrale), a little shop that specializes in old Alsatian books and engravings. They also sell some beautiful books on the region, but not many of them are in English.

The **Musée Alsacien** is the number-one attraction in the region for learning about *les arts et les traditions populaires*. On my way there, I passed through a peaceful little street called **rue du Vieil-Hôpital** where *brocanteurs* often set up stands to sell assorted antiques and bric-à-brac. Although I passed on a Wednesday, most of the vendors come out on Saturday. Be sure not to miss the shop, **La Brocanterie**, which is permanently established at number 18. Two brothers run it, and in addition to their regional offerings of pottery from Soufflenheim and Betschdorf, marquetry, and sometimes even a rare eighteenth-century wrought-iron sign typical of Alsace, they also feature certifiably authentic pieces of artwork from China and other parts of Asia.

Just a short walk over the bridge toward the place Corbeau, you'll arrive in front of the nearly imperceptible entrance of the **Musée Alsacien** at 23 quai St-Nicolas. Housed in a grouping of exquisite Renaissance dwellings, the three floors of this museum pay homage to the rich Alsatian traditions of crafts and folk art. Most of the rooms show how the farmers, winegrowers, and mountain people lived in centuries past; and, of course, you will notice that the utilitarian items of yesterday have become the treasured art forms of today.

Arcana

The *coin boutique* of the Musée Alsacien disappointed me as much as all of the other museum shops that I had encountered throughout the region. Their collections are so rich, yet they sell so few reproductions for visitors to take home. Two very clever women from Colmar decided to fill this void by creating a collection of gift items that are actual reproductions of traditional pieces from the lesser known museums of the region. They opened two shops about five years ago, one in Colmar, and this one in Strasbourg, which is located just down the quay from the Musée Alsacien. All prettily displayed in this small corner shop, products range from hand-painted polychrome boxes, which were used for storing secret love notes, to wool challis shawls in paisley motifs–certainly essential components of the nineteenth-century Alsatian woman's boudoir. Prices vary as much as the goods themselves. Ask about their mail-order catalogues.

- 18 quai des Bateliers, 67000 Strasbourg; tel.: 03.88.14.03.77; fax: 03.89.41.84.65/mail order
  Open Tuesday–Friday 10 A.M.–noon and 2–7 P.M.; Saturday 10 A.M.–noon and 2–6:30 P.M.

Ch. Bastian & Fils

When I asked different sources about the best address in Strasbourg for regional antiques, everyone mentioned Ch. Bastian & Fils. Situated across from the cathedral and in business for more than 120 years, this well-appointed antique emporium is indeed somewhat of an institution. As you enter this *haut lieu* of tradition, you find yourself face to face with an extensive collection of faience, most of which was made in the eastern part of France during the eighteenth century. Jacques Bastian, a specialist in this domain, has been called upon by many museums, including the Metropolitan Museum of Art in New York, for his expertise. Don't stop here, though, because the store snakes around to the back and then next door to a bigger selling space crowded with furniture, paintings, and assorted other decorative items from the artistic and culturally plentiful region of Alsace.

- 22–24 place de la Cathédrale, 67000 Strasbourg; tel.: 03.88.32.45.93; fax: 03.88.75.97.92
  Open Tuesday–Friday 10 A.M.–noon and 2:30–7 P.M.; Saturday 10 A.M.–noon and 2:30–6 P.M.

Bernard Pfirsch

Before you enter this closet-sized temple of *l'art populaire*, take time to admire the window display, which is in itself a true study of Alsatian crafts and folklore. The knowledgeable owner Bernard Pfirsch has filled this space with some of the finest examples of pottery, glassware, pewter, faience, engravings, and a slew of other interesting fragments that have been woven into the very fabric of Alsatian life for the past few hundred years. Monsieur does not speak much English, nor does he talk very much in French, but his pieces speak quite strongly for themselves.

- 20 rue de la Nuée-Bleue, 67000 Strasbourg; tel.: 03.88.32.72.73
  Open Monday–Saturday 9 A.M.–7 P.M.

La Boutique d'Antoine Westermann

Famous for his three-star Michelin restaurant, Le Buerehiesel, Antoine Westermann opened this gourmet shop in 1995. Many of the products sold here are prepared at the restaurant. Even if a meal at Le Buerehiesel does not quite fall within your budget, you can still feast on some of their delicacies such as foie gras or *les orangettes*, the ambrosial sweets that are served with each and every cup of coffee. The vaulted cellar downstairs is almost as impressive as the selection of wines and *eaux-de-vie* contained within these ancient walls. The finest Rieslings, Gewürztraminers, Tokays, Pinot Gris, and more keep excellent company with a wealth of other delicious wines from all over France.

- 1 rue des Orfèvres, 67000 Strasbourg; tel./fax: 03.88.32.72.73
  Open Monday 2–7 P.M.; Tuesday–Saturday 9:30 A.M.–12:30 P.M. and 2–7 P.M.

AUVERGNE
Auvergne

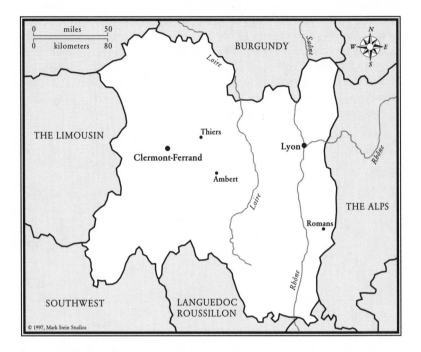

Vichy water • cutlery • cheeses • *pastilles de Vichy* • wines • hand-made paper products • sausages • honeys • *potée auvergnate* • pâté • books on knives • Volvic water • liqueur de verveine • hams

KNOWN MAINLY FOR its agriculture and rusticity, the shopping scene in Auvergne is not too sophisticated. People venture here to experience "the great outdoors," which is accomplished, for the most part, by embarking upon long treks along the volcanic terrain that so typifies this centralmost part of France.

The regional food products are hearty enough to keep a hiker going for days. Cantal is the name of one of the departments and also of a dense, cheddarlike cheese that is indisputably one of the French peoples' favorites. The bleu d'Auvergne and the fourme d'Ambert are two rich and creamy blue cheeses whose calories are worth the extra bit of hiking you'll have to do to work them off! Auvergne's hams, honeys, and pâtés can be equally as wholesome, and the region's two most best-known products, knives and handmade paper, make it easy to sample this wholesome country fare and then to write home about it!

Ambert (Puy-de-Dôme)

Moulin Richard de Bas

Oh, how we take for granted the paper on which we write every day! After a visit to this more than 500-year-old paper mill, you'll never look at paper quite the same way again. The Moulin Richard de Bas is a living museum on a site in the middle of the Auvergnate countryside that is in itself magnificent to behold. Several different rooms represent the business of papermaking from centuries past, but visitors will be most interested to watch the actual crafting of the paper, a labor-intensive process that has served as the very lifeblood of this mill since its origin.

It all begins with rags, whether from scraps of old shirts or shreds of worn out bed linens. The energy harnessed from the nearby river also plays a vital role, enabling the rags to be ground down into cellulose and then eventually pressed into individual sheets. So many of the different aspects of this process are beautiful to see, but one of the most mesmerizing takes place in the room where hundreds of sheets of paper are hung to dry, like cod that has been salted and cured in a Nordic barn.

The boutique displays a large collection of famous texts, sayings, speeches, and books—all of which have been printed on the mill's handmade paper. My favorite pieces are the wonderful cards and papers that have locked the local wildflowers and grasses within their fibers.

- 63600 Ambert; tel.: 04.73.82.03.11; fax: 04.73.83.25.41
  Open daily except for Christmas and New Year's Day 9 A.M.–noon and 2–6 P.M.; July and August 9 A.M.–8 P.M.

Thiers (Puy-de-Dôme)

Market: place du Marché
Thursday and Saturday 8 A.M.–1 P.M.

Thiers (pronounced *tee-yair*) is the knife capital of France, and you have to come here prepared to feel "ground down" by the overabundance of cutlery shops that dominate the narrow, sloping streets of this rather dismal town.

You'll notice that the town has been built along steep hillsides, precipitous terrain that borders the Durolle River. People realized as early as the fifteenth century that the natural succession of waterfalls of this rapid waterway could generate the necessary power for the turning of the grinding wheels, the essential element of the knife-making process. Today much of this history is retraced at the **Maison des Coutelliers**, or Cutlers' House, at 23 and 58 rue de la Coutellerie, certainly the best place to begin your visit at Thiers. Different facets of the cutlery industry, particularly those of the past, are divulged here by exhibits and a few actual demonstrations.

The conditions that many of the workers had to contend with were harsh, particularly during the grinding process, the crucial step in the creation of the blade's cutting edge. Until relatively recently, a worker would lie facedown on a board to apply more pressure to the blade as he ground it over the wheel that was turned by the waters that passed beneath him. This position allowed the grinder to apply more leverage to a maneuver that already required a tremendous amount of force and resilience, in fact, dogs were trained to lie on the backs of the grinders' legs to warm them from the chill of the icy river.

Many of the exhibits upstairs in this building, and farther down the street in the second section of the museum, handsomely represent some of the finest examples of this trade. I stood in rapt attention in front of a 1911 storefront that displayed the variety and sheer beauty of carving instruments from that time; a few extraordinary knives, measuring as much as six feet long, and smaller ones with handles carved out of ivory, ebony, and horn, were most certainly eye-catching enough to lure customers inside.

Unfortunately, today's shopfronts are more bazaarlike than the spectacular window presentations of yesteryear. From the more than twenty cutlery stores in Thiers, it's hard to name the best because they all sell similar merchandise at competing prices. You will see the name "Laguiole" throughout because these knives have become *très à la mode* over the past five years or so. It is important to realize that Laguiole refers to a particular form, and in Thiers there are about forty different houses, of varying quality, that make these knives. If I wanted to buy true Laguiole knives, I would probably buy them in the town of Laguiole (see "The Southwest," page 308) or in the Laguiole boutique in Paris, where you can be more sure of the quality and the shopping scene is more selective and less commercial than the one at Thiers.

You can indeed ferret out some beautifully crafted knives in this city, however, both industrially made models and others of more artisanal creation. The range extends from world-famous culinary knives the likes of Sabatier and 32 Dumas to lesser-known cutlery such as "Le Thiers," the sleek, contemporary-looking knives that were released in 1995 to rival those of Laguiole. **J. P. Treille** (7 rue de la Coutellerie), **Coredif** (19 place du Palais), and the all-encompassing **Coutellerie Chambriard** (2, 3, and 8 place de l'Hôtel-de-Ville) are a few of the most appealing shops.

A hearty lunch of Auvergnate specialities at **Le Coutelier** (4 place du Palais; tel.: 04.73.80.79.59), surrounded by all of the tools of the cutlery trade, will sharpen your impression of Thiers considerably. And if you're looking to pick up a few provisions for a walk around the not-so-distant craters, go to **Produits Regionnaux** at 3 rue Alexandre-Bigay, just a few steps from the post office. Although scantily stocked, their regional foodstuffs are of excellent quality.

BRITTANY
Bretagne

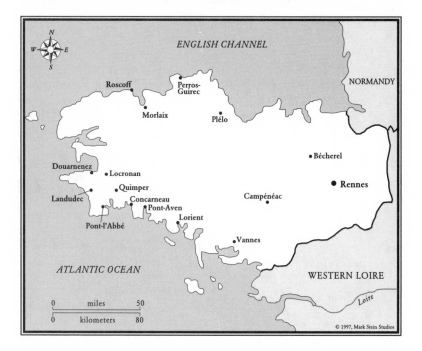

butter cookies • model ships • old books and manuscripts • faience • cider • wool sweaters • heavily sculpted furnishings • seascape dioramas • seaweed-based products • chouchenn • grandmotherly breakfast bowls • old paintings and engravings • Gallic beer • quatre butter cakes • canned scallops • posters of fish • seaside paintings • marine hardware • coifs • table linens • *confiture de lait* • Kouign Amann • Celtic-inspired jewelry • chocolates • crêpe utensils • *vareuse* • seaweed-tinged chocolates • old lighthouses • canned sardines • Celtic books and music • ships-in-a-bottle • embroidered wall murals • harp and bagpipe tunes

USUALLY WHEN I try to describe Brittany I start out by comparing it to the state of Maine. Lobsters, cold water, and ferry crossings are just a few of the similarities, and my hunch is that there may be a handful more, particularly with regard to the robust nature of the hard-working residents and their link to the sea.

The history and tradition of the people of Brittany is, of course, much older than Maine. And if I compare the *penty*, the old stone houses of Brittany, to the sweet, wooden ones of New England, it is easy to see who has endured the Atlantic winds longer. The Parisians love to sneer at the inclement weather patterns of Brittany, but despite this, so many of them venture off to the farthermost western section of their land for *un grand bol d'air frais* (a big bowl of fresh air). It is true that the climate often is variable; it is always a bit cooler and more overcast in the northern part of the region than in the south. The houses reflect this difference; in the north, they are mostly made of slate and stone, whereas in the south, it is not uncommon to see a roof in *chaume* (thatch).

The products of Brittany are very much a reflection of the land: simple, pure, and free of any frivolities. Many of these goods are associated with the sea, for this is *the* region of France almost entirely surrounded by water. Historically, the life here has been hard, and what better way to comfort one's spirits than with a slice of rich butter cake or a handful of salty caramels.

Before I leave you to discover some of the most interesting *villes* and *villages* of Brittany, I must remind you that some of the best finds in France are found between destinations. To broaden your geographic sphere just a bit more, be sure to take in at least one or two of the magnificent islands that lie just off the shores of this great land. Beautiful Belle-Ile is the largest and probably the best known, but you don't have to go far from the shore to explore many, many more.

NORTHERN BRITTANY

Becherel (Ile-et-Villaine)

Imagine twelve bookstores for only 600 inhabitants. Either the people of Becherel are incredibly prolific readers or the town is stridently attempting to become the unofficial book capital of France. The latter is closer to the truth; in 1989 the town decided to create a center of attraction that would encourage people to visit this handsome medieval town. They must have picked the right conduit, because this beautifully preserved setting is attracting just the right kind of quiet, culturally enlightened visitors.

Everything that is old is greatly revered in this town, from the slate-roofed stone houses of Becherel to the many *librairies* or bookstores, most of which specialize in antique books and manuscripts. I stepped into **Saphir** on the main street at 5 rue du Faubourg Bertault and turned up some rare works that included first editions by the eighteenth-century novelist Chateaubriand, and poetry of Victor Hugo that had been put to music with his full approval. Whether you are interested in thirteenth-century parchments or letters by France's writers of today, if you like to rummage about, this is a shop for you. Prices range from two to 60,000F!

The other booksellers of Becherel are of the same genre, and most of them are open daily year-round. For a picturesque yet rather athletic walk, head down the pathway across from Saphir to take in the delightfully rural fringes of town. Walk down toward the valley past the old *lavoir* (where the women used to do their laundry), then up beyond the cemetery toward the town's church to fully appreciate the more bucolic aspects of Becherel.

Morlaix (Finistère)

Each town in France has distinct characteristics that distinguish it from the rest. You might think that Morlaix's distinguishing feature is the omnipresent nineteenth-century aqueduct that towers over the city like an icon to the industrialization of France. Even more typical, however, are the old houses that bear testimony to the city's past as a prosperous seaport during the fifteenth to seventeenth centuries. Among the most attractive are the *maisons à lanterne*, or lantern houses, named for the way huge chandeliers illuminated the often triple-tiered, mezzanine-like interiors of these structures. Glass roofs and natural lighting later transformed these once shadowy inner courtyards into more atrium-like spaces. The most exquisite example of this type of architecture is the Duchesse Anne, a sixteenth-century lantern house in the center of town.

In centuries past, the ground floor of a Morlaix house was reserved for commerce and the upper levels for habitation. Since then, some houses have become entirely commercial, such as **La Maison des Vins** (place des Viarmes; tel.: 02.98.88.07.82). Behind each of the wood-railed balconies of the upper floors lies a stock of wines that the owner, Monsieur Feunteuna, has carefully honed from all over France. Although Brittany is not a wine-producing land, regional beverages include *chouchenn* (a sweet drink made from honey and fermented fruit), a special whisky de Bretagne, and the ever-so popular *cidre breton,* a sort of hard cider.

If regional antiques interest you more, try stopping in at **Antiquités Tréanton** (40 rue de Paris; tel.: 02.98.88.07.82). Although closed the day I came by, they are reputed to have an eclectic assortment of interesting goods.

Perros-Guirec (Côtes-d'Armor)

Market: place du Marché
Friday 8 A.M.–1 P.M.

You might find yourself passing through this port city on the way to other more charming or fascinating destinations along the coast, such as the old fishing village of Paimpol, the pretty hydrangea-covered island of Bréhat, or the wondrous rose-colored granite formations at Ploumanach. If boating is your thing, you could very well find yourself pulling into Perros-Guirec for a few days' mooring. If this is the case, **Ship Marine** (tel.: 02.96.91.11.88) just across from the port stocks everything you might need for your excursion, from electronic navigation equipment and fish finders to maps, thermal socks, and made-in-France boating attire by Saint James, Anne Ar Breiz, and Aigle—guaranteed to protect you from the worst weather that may blow in off the Channel!

Unless you're in shape for a hike, you'll need a car to go to the next string of shops that are situated on the rue Maréchal-Joffre, a bit out of the center of town. The bright yellow and blue façade of **L'Art Breton** is hard to miss and as the name indicates, here you can expect to find art from Brittany, primarily in the form of faience from Quimper. The shop looks borderline touristy, but sells many items from the Henriot collection as well as other, lesser-known, more heavily designed pieces from Faiencerie P. Fouillen, also of Quimper. Each of these strongly colored works—vases, pitchers, and bowls—could stand alone as an interesting *objet*.

Antiques hold an important place in the shopping landscape of Perros-Guirec, perhaps because there are so many estates in the region occupied by people in search of a new piece to add to their décor, or looking to sell what the family no longer wants to keep. Two shops, **Jannou Antiquités** (at 112 rue Maréchal-Joffre; tel.: 02.96.91.02.33) and **M. & Mme. Stéphan** (at 66 rue Maréchal-Joffre; tel.: 02.96.23.38.63), buy and sell regional pieces, many of which focus on the theme of the sea. If you are driving, park at Jannou Antiquités and then walk down to the other shop, because navigating this busy thoroughfare can be a bit dangerous. Both shops have a small selection of model boats, seascape dioramas, and ships-in-a-bottle in addition to paintings and drawings of the region; Jannou, the larger of the two, also features some generously proportioned pieces of regional furniture.

Plélo (Côtes-d'Armor)

Le Char à Bancs

This was my one and only time at a *ferme auberge*, or inn on the farm, and if the others are anything like this one, I highly recommend you try them whenever possible! This was also my only taste of farm life in Brittany, whose interior is as embedded with tradition as the coast. You'll need a detailed map to find Plélo;

once there, follow the signs for Le Char à Bancs, an old mill snuggled in the countryside just outside of town. I arrived here on a busy Saturday evening where it seemed as though all of the neighboring townfolk had turned out for a hearty helping of *potée*, a country dish of pork, cabbage, potatoes, and carrots, the true speciality of this farm auberge. Authenticity reigns in everything from the rustic furnishings to the huge cauldron that simmers in the immense fireplace (the *potée* is cooked here over a well-stoked fire for about four hours before the guests arrive). After such a copious meal, I declined from indulging in a crêpe, the other mainstay of the house, and decided to retire to my *chambre*.

Spend a few nights at this farm if you want to disconnect from the rest of the world. There are no TVs or phones—the only noises you have to contend with are the early morning chirpings of birds or the occasional moo from a cow far off in the fields. The comfort of crisp white sheets and a thick eiderdown rival that of a four-star hotel, and the tastefully displayed country furnishings and bric-à-brac are delightful. The interiors of all four guest rooms were lovingly orchestrated by one of the owners' daughters, who, in addition to her chores on the farm, has spent time studying interior design.

Appropriately named Lamour (*amour* means love in French), this family is passionately involved in the workings of the farm and that love is transmitted to every person who passes through here. The family has even transformed one of its farmhouses into a mini-museum that shows how people lived in this rural environment one hundred years ago. Madame Lamour also has opened a small antique business on the side. She explained that her goods should be referred to more as *brocante*, or bric-à-brac, "little things from grandmothers." There's no doubt that all of these utilitarian pieces from days gone by provide just the sort of "down home" touches that would enhance a country kitchen or cozy interior. Displayed according to color and pattern, the folksy tabletop presentations tempted me so much that I purchased the first piece of what I hope will become a collection of enameled coffeepots, reasonably priced between 70F and 120F.

- Moulin de la Ville Geffroy, 22170 Plélo; tel.: 02.96.74.13.63; fax: 02.96.74.13.03
  Bed-and-Breakfast/Restaurant: Inexpensive
  Open daily during the summer except for Tuesday; off-season the auberge is open Saturday evenings and Sunday lunches; call ahead for rooms

Rennes (Ile-et-Vilaine)

TGV: 2½ hours
Main shopping streets: rue Bastard, rue d'Estrées
Market: place des Lices and the surrounding streets
Saturday 7 A.M.–1 P.M.

Although known as the capital of Brittany since the sixteenth century, Rennes does not possess many of the typical traits or charming facets that one normally associates with *la Bretagne*. There are, however, some lofty half-timbered dwellings in the medieval quarter, many of which house bistros and bars that become particularly animated in the evenings when members of the city's large student population head out for a good time. I chose the **Café Breton** (14 rue Nantaise; tel.: 02.99.30.74.95), a more discreet address, for my night out on the town and was pleased to find myself among sophisticated types whose quiet conversations left plenty of room for the soft, jazzy tunes that filled the air. Their bistrotlike fare does not usually feature regional specialties, but the warm, inviting décor more than makes up for it with its regional accents of marine blue and charcoal drawings of *bigoudens*, the traditionally costumed people of Brittany. The owner, who lived in London for a couple of years, has done a terrific job of transforming this turn-of-the-century grocery store (hence the explanation for the abundance of wooden shelves and drawers) into a very "happening" place. Open most days for brunch, tea, and dinner, you may want to call ahead, particularly on Saturdays, when people from the neighboring market come by in droves.

Michel Flageul

Michel Flageul is a local craftsman whose wonderous marine-scape dioramas and ships-in-a-bottle are unexpected finds in the landlocked city of Rennes. I saw many of this artist's works throughout my travels in Brittany at prices that were almost double what you would pay here. Monsieur Flageul's modest locale is only a few minutes from the center of town.

At this atelier/boutique visitors can learn how each of these marine-inspired works is made. The attention to detail is incredible; the thick swells of putty used to represent the sea in the wood-framed, glass-encased dioramas, for example, are painted either blue-grey for the Atlantic or grey-green for the Channel. The boats, exact replicas of those that sail on the nearby seas, are lovingly assembled out of handcrafted wood hulls and hand-sewn silk. Seagulls, which appear to be suspended in space, soar as the Flageul signature trademark. Prices vary considerably depending on the importance of the piece: plan on spending about 1,800F for a two-boat diorama two feet long; 600F to 800F for a proud little ship in a Gordon's gin bottle; and 2,500F for a clipper ship in a bottle, which requires about thirty hours to make. Monsieur Flageul has shipped his creations all over the world.

- 3 rue Hamon, 35000 Rennes; tel.: 02.99.64.57.40
  No credit cards
  Call ahead

Roscoff (Finistère)

The people of Brittany have always relied upon the healing powers of the sea; local people once rubbed themselves with seaweed in the coastal inlets as soon as the tide went out as treatment for their assorted ailments. Today health-oriented facilities, called *centres de thalassothérapie*, bespeckle the coast like seagulls along the shore, and although people attend these centers for a variety of reasons, everyone is subjected to a flood of treatments, all of which revolve around the two most essential elements of *la thalasso*: saltwater and seaweed. **Roc Kroum**, the first of these such establishments, devotes itself today to the research, development, and application of this near science. For more information call 02.98.29.20.00 or fax 02.98.61.22.73.

Thalado

Probably no one is as dedicated to the research and development of products composed of the most beneficial elements of the sea as Bertrand de Kerdrel, the dynamic and most imaginative force behind Thalado, a boutique/exhibition room that extols the virtues of the big blue and the 800 different kinds of seaweed off the coast of northern Brittany. Monsieur de Kerdrel engages three different laboratories to produce his innumerable seaweed-based goods, which range from freeze-dried seaweed for marine-ameliorated cooking, to a seaweed-studded bar of creamy soap that delicately exfoliates and moisturizes your skin with every cleansing.

- rue Victor Hugo, 29681 Roscoff; tel.: 02.98.69.77.05; fax: 02.98.61.28.83
  Mail order available
  Open Monday–Saturday 9:15 A.M.–noon and 2:15–6:30 P.M.

SOUTHERN BRITTANY

Campénéac (Morbihan)

Abbaye la Joie Notre Dame

I first tasted the tiny, melon-ball-shaped butter cookies of the Abbaye la Joie Notre Dame during a stay at the Castel Marie Louise, a charming little luxury hotel at the seaside resort of La Baule in the Western Loire, just a stone's throw from Brittany. After a bit of doing, I traced them to Campénéac, a hamlet just outside of Ploërmel in the central part of the region. It is common throughout France to find monasteries that devote expansive spaces to the sale of goods produced by the monks, which might include honeys, cheeses, pottery, or music from their choirs. This is the first time, however, that I shopped at an abbey boutique where many of the goods were made by nuns. Maybe that is why all their butter cookies, cakes, and chocolates are so sweet! Their singing voices on the cassette that I purchased are nearly as mellifluous.

- BP1, 56800 Campénéac; tel.: 02.97.93.42.07; fax: 02.97.93.11.23
  Open Monday–Saturday 9:30 A.M.–noon and 2:30–5 P.M.; Sunday 2:30–4:30 P.M.

Concarneau (Finistère)

Market: avenue Pierre-Guéguin
Friday 7 A.M.–1 P.M.

Although the pleasure boats seem to outnumber the trollers, and the canning industry is not what it used to be, Concarneau is still the second-largest fishing port in France. A visit to the **Musée de la Pêche**, or Fishing Museum, is the best place to begin to gain a sense of the complexities of this trade, and even better, their displays are all so beautifully presented that you don't have to read a word of French to understand them! Housed in an eighteenth-century maritime cooperative, the structure itself, particularly with its high wooden ceiling, looks more like a church than a selling space from centuries past. A variety of boats, typical of the region, float inside and out as significant props in the recounting of the history, both past and present, of this fascinating industry. Unfortunately the museum's boutique is not nearly as comprehensive as the exhibitions, although you should be able to find a book or a poster that will remind you of your undoubtedly all-absorbing visit.

If you've made it to the Musée de la Pêche, you have entered *la ville close,* or the closed city, the picturesque old part of town that is really an island connected by a road to the mainland. The museum is just inside the entrance on your left. If you continue down the main street, you'll discover a number of other shops, touristy and otherwise. If you're looking for marine attire or equipment, go where the sailors go: to the **Cooperative Maritime**, situated on the mainland outside the *ville close* toward the far end of the quai Carnot on the rue des Chalutiers. The *vareuse*, a classic piece of sailors' garb originally made from sailcloth, has remained traditional in its color and form: a reddish-brown tainted over-the-head smock that is to French sailors as *les bleus de travail*, or blue workclothes, are to French workers.

Ets. Courtin

As you exit Concarneau in the direction of Quimper, you will pass Ets. Courtin, one of the city's original canneries that dates back to 1893. At one point Concarneau was the leader in canned sardines, and then the numbers dropped from thirty factories at the beginning of the century to only three today. Whether you purchase fresh or canned seafood at this clean and tidy fish market, the quality is top-drawer. Monsieur Courtin explained that his clientele is composed largely of restaurants, most far from the Atlantic, in such cities as Nancy or Lyons. The Courtin speciality is plump, fleshy scallops, both fresh and canned. Several seafood sauces, fish soup, and different fish pâtés—perfect for the apéritif—round out the selection of gourmet canned goods. And if you come at the right time, you might even be able to visit the cannery to see how all of these delicacies are prepared, pampered, and packaged!

- 3 rue du Moros, 29900 Concarneau; tel.: 02.98.50.62.86;
    fax: 02.98.97.22.57
    Open Monday–Saturday 8:30 A.M.–12:30 P.M. and 1:30–7 P.M.

Galerie Henry Depoid

Back within the walls of *la ville close* resides one of the most reputable art galleries of the region. Monsieur Depoid is the master behind this striking collection of tableaus from artists known as the "Groupe de Concarneau"—primarily painters who were attracted to the region for the same reasons as those of Pont-Aven: for the light, the seascapes, and a cost of living much lower than the big cities. These works, mostly oil paintings with a smattering of pastels and engravings, date from 1850 to 1950 with prices that range from about 15,000F to more than 100,000F. Look for names such as Guillou and Barnoin, two of the most celebrated painters of the region.

- 11 rue Vauban (Ville-Close), BP 311, 29183 Concarneau;
    tel.: 02.98.97.30.91 or 02.98.97.31.36; fax: 02.98.50.89.50
    Open Easter–September 10:30 A.M.–6:30 P.M.; by appointment in winter

Douarnenez (Finistère)

The **Musée du Bateau**, or boat museum (place de l'Enfer), is the main draw of this small intercoastal town, which also once survived primarily off of the canning industry before that business shifted to Mediterranean countries such as Italy and Morroco. With the museum installation closely resembling that of the Musée de la Pêche in Concarneau, and the actual setting not unlike that of a smaller Mystic Seaport in Connecticut, the little inland port of Douarnenez should read like a stunning success story. A shortage of funding however, means that the main attraction is the museum instead of the entire port. The only ships left in town are on permanent display within the museum's old warehouselike setting, a former cannery. The museum also has an impressive collection of boats from all over the world.

There is still a semblance of activity in the shipyard, mostly on brighter days, and the workshop of the Belgian woodsculpter **Emmanuel Bourgeau** takes front and center. The only craftsman in France to do this highly skilled work, Monsieur Bourgeau works exclusively by special order for his elaborately carved prow figures that distinguish him from the rest of the local artisans.

Menguy-Maguet

When I first walked up the gangplank and entered this little cottage just across from the musem, I thought that it was just your average souvenir shop. As I made my way toward the back of the boutique, however, I realized that I had entered a special world reserved for practitioners of the sea. Old wooden drawers were jammed with an array of bronze hinges, hooks, and other assorted accessories that only a true mariner would know how to use, but that appeal to weekend sailors who like to fuss and fiddle with their boats all year long. The uses of this terrificly authentic hardware (there's not a bit of plastic in sight) are limitless, and I could easily imagine someone buying a supply of knobs and handles to use in their home. The shop also sells portholes, lanterns, and buoys; a mail order catalogue, which, although rather archaic-looking, presents the extensive product range in great detail.

- place de l'Enfer, 29100 Douarnenez; tel.: 02.98.92.00.97;
  fax: 02.98.92.27.60
  Mail order available
  Open daily 9 A.M.–noon and 2–7 P.M.

Outside Douarnenez (Finistère)

La Grange du Ris

Hunkered down on the hilltop across from the deliciously unspoiled beach, *la plage du ris*, the large barn of *antiquaire* Alain le Berré is hard to miss. At first glance, the jumble of goods inside might look like the remnants of an old yard sale, but on closer inspection most of the pieces bear testimony to this young dealer's love for traditional furnishings and folkloric costumes from the region. All quite massive and mostly made of oak, some elaborately carved pieces date from the eighteenth century, such as a *lit clos*, a Breton bed characterized by wood panels that can be closed for privacy or warmth. This particular work had been cleverly transformed into a buffet with an asking price of 15,000F.

More transportable items include an assortment of finery and costumes that were part of the traditional dress of the *bigoudens*, the native people of Brittany. As I admired these museum-quality pieces, Monsieur le Berré quietly announced that he plans to open a museum devoted to the typical costumes of the Finistère region.

• plage du Ris, 29100 Kerlaz–Douarnenez; tel.: 02.98.92.86.26
Open Monday–Saturday 10 A.M.–noon and 2–7 P.M.

Locronan

The splendid grey-green granite houses with their traditional blue-grey slate roofs create a stately harmony within this beautiful village that is most pleasing to behold. Locronan, one of the most picturesque sites of Brittany, became rich during the seventeenth and eighteenth centuries primarily from its sailcloth and weaving industries. The **Musée de Locronan** traces some of this history, although if you want to see some of the actual weaving, you should check with the **Maison des Artisans** at the place de l'Eglise. Both this establishment and the boutique **Lizig** on rue des Charettes sell traditional Breton linens embroidered with Celtic-inspired designs as well as other craft items of regional significance. Not all are made in the region, however; some of the most beautiful Brittany linens I spotted were manufactured at Textiles Bochard in Picardy. The boutique **Quimper Faience** (2 rue du Prieuré) is a real must for Henriot fans. If you have not yet sampled a Kouign Amann, the famous butter-saturated pastry of Brittany, the bakery of **Monsieur Le Guillou** (place de l'Église) sells one of the best. Although it tastes best and certainly is far more digestible heated, you can buy a piece here and wash it down with a nice hot cup of tea in a nearby café.

Lorient (Finistère)

TGV: 3½ hours
Market: Halles de Merville
Daily 8 A.M.–1 P.M.

Always busy on the nautical front, this town was exceptionally crowded on the day I visited because of the highly publicized departure of the Lorient–St. Barts transatlantic race. If your passion is boating, or just feeling a part of its privileged world, you'll enjoy Lorient; aside from the port, however, the rest of the city is an eyesore. The majority of Lorient was destroyed during World War II, which ended the intense commercial activity that flourished here during the seventeenth and eighteenth centuries, largely with the *Compagnie des Indes*, or India Company. For more about this unique relationship between the Orient and Lorient (guess the origin of this city's name), I recommend a visit to the **Musée de la Compagnie de Indes**, located in the Citadelle at the Port-Louis.

Antiquités de Marine

As the name suggests, this store features marine-related antiques. It is worth coming to Lorient to see this big and burgeoning tribute to some of the more unusual finds of the seafarer's universe. Monsieur Chrestien, his son and godson, the captains of this treasure chest of goods from the sea, devote much time to fixing up their finds, and one of them said, "We restore more boats than Lorient's naval shipyard." Their boats are not necessarily toy-size, either; the day I visited they had been working for four months on an eight-foot cruise ship which was made in 1951 as a working model for a much larger vessel.

One wall of the store amused me with its lineup of at least fifty different lighthouses, affordably priced between 100F and 200F. These were exactly the kinds of *souvenirs de bord de mer* (seaside souvenirs) that people would snatch up toward the earlier part of this century. Monsieur Chrestien continued his tour, emphasizing that each of his boats had a story behind them. After looking at and asking about other items such as a skillfully carved wooden prow of a voluptuous woman, which would make any sailor proud to serve on her ship, I surmised that hidden within virtually all of the pieces in this store is a story just waiting to be told.

• 13 rue Vauban, 56100 Lorient; tel./fax: 02.97.21.01.02
Open Tuesday–Saturday 10 A.M.–noon and 2–7 P.M.

Pont-l'Abbé (Finistère)

Market: Place de la République and place Gambetta
Thursday 8 A.M.–1 P.M.

It's hard to talk about Brittany without giving mention to *les bigoudens*. *Bigoudens* or *bigoudines* refer to the people who are from *les pays bigouden*, the area largely situated above Pont-l'Abbé in the southwestern arm of Brittany. The town of Pont-l'Abbé is the capital of this so-called *bigouden* country, a micro-region of its own that has fortified its identity with its own set of traditions and customs.

I remember my astonishment and delight upon seeing some of the older women scuttling through the windswept streets in their traditional *bigoudine* dress the first time I came to this pretty little town a number of years ago. They seemed to balance their frightfully tall, snow-white coifs, or head-dresses, in sheer defiance of this windy land. It is still not so unusual to see the women dressed in these folkloric costumes on a daily basis. If you're thinking about attempting a coif, or any other necessary element of the traditional attire, take a peek *chez* **Madame Jean Tirilly** (15 rue Michelet; tel.: 02.98.87.26.39), where you can plunk down as much as 500F for one of the prettiest and tallest coifs in her specialized boutique.

The most captivating display of *bigouden* costumes, however, is at **Le Musée Bigouden**, the museum housed within the old château that stands as a beacon at the entrance of Pont-l'Abbé. The museum's collection of regional furniture is also engrossing, but if you're looking to buy, pay a visit to the antique dealer/woodworker **Jacques Aubry** (20 rue Hoche; tel.: 02.98.87.16.10), who is passionate about traditional Breton pieces that have been sculpted and tacked (*clouté*) to perfection.

Le Minor

A veritable institution in Pont-l'Abbé, the whole look of Le Minor's home and table arts collection is based on a modern interpretation of the *bigouden* tradition. After a visit to Le Musée Bigouden, you will have a greater appreciation for the heavy gold and orange embroideries that were painstakingly worked on to the thick black almost feltlike backgrounds of the essential pieces of the men's costumes. These ornate works required great physical strength, so in the *bigouden* tradition, these fashion statements for men were mostly carried out *by* men. The brightly colored tapestries at Le Minor are direct descendants of this centuries-old tradition; prices range from 6,000F to 40,000F.

Classic *bigouden* and *breton* motifs, which include stylized flowers, roosters, palm branches, and Celtic-looking patterns, run riot on the boutique's printed and embroidered table linens. Colors range from bright blues and yellows to more subdued tones of celery and winter gray. The spirit of their tabletops can be either bold or sober, and in some instances, matching services in Limoges china complete the picture. Faience from Quimper also is sold here, in addition to beach bags, toiletry cases, cotton scarves, and other perky accessories. The upstairs is devoted to casually chic, traditionally Breton fashions for men and women.

- 5 quai St-Laurent, 29120 Pont-l'Abbé; tel.: 02.98.87.07.22
  Open Monday 2–7 P.M.; Tuesday–Saturday 9 A.M.–noon and 2–7 P.M.

Pont-Aven (Finistère)

The little inland coastal town of Pont-Aven is known both for *L'Ecole de Pont-Aven*, the colony of painters who gathered here between 1886 and 1896, and for *les galettes*, the thin and crisp or thick and rich butter cookies that have become synonymous with Brittany. At **Le Musée de Pont-Aven** you can learn more about the innovative movement of painters which was spearheaded by the beloved Paul Gauguin, although most of these artists' major works are spread across the world in museums and private collections in Paris, New York, Chicago, and elsewhere. Like Barbizon, Honfleur, and other villages that have left their mark on the pages of art history books, this tiny town is loaded with art galleries, many of which sell works of questionable quality. If you are considering the purchase of a work from *L'École de Pont-Aven*, look at the **Galerie de la Place** (4 place Paul-Gauguin; tel.: 02.98.06.10.57) in Pont-L'Abbé or at the **Galerie Depoid** in Concarneau.

Galettes Penven

The choice of *galettes* in Pont-Aven is nearly as bewildering as the selection of art galleries. Tradition and comparative taste-testings rank this boutique as number one. The Penven bakers have been making these little butter cookies for the past three generations; in fact, they use the same recipe that the founder, Isadore Penven, invented in 1890. Their *galettes*, both thick like shortbreads and thin like crisp sugar cookies, make perfect gifts for cookie lovers back home; although they have no preservatives, they remain fresh in their pretty red or green tins for up to one year. These cookies have been sold in Japan and Hong Kong since 1914, but not in the U.S.–so why should we Americans deprive ourselves any longer? If you're looking for other *spécialités de la Bretagne*, you can choose among a collection of salted butter caramels, cider, faience, and more. You will find them across from the port.

- 1 quai Théodore-Botrel, 29930 Pont-Aven; tel.: 02.98.00.06.49;
  fax: 02.98.06.14.53
  Open daily May 1–September 30 10 A.M.–7 P.M.; off-season Monday–
  Saturday 10 A.M.–noon and 2–7 P.M.

Moulin de Rosmadec

The lulling sound of the passing of the river Aven alongside this old mill is as reassuring as the solid wood and stone interior of this intriguing fifteenth-century structure. Take the time to stop a while in the front entrance room where the remains of the inner workings of the mill await your solemn contemplation. Whether you find yourself inside within the snug dining room or outside on the secluded terrace, you can expect a dining experience with good taste in every respect.

• 29330 Pont-Aven; tel.: 02.98.06.00.22; fax: 02.98.06.18.00
  Restaurant: Expensive
  Open year-round except during the months of February and November; closed Wednesday and Sunday evening in off-season

Quimper (Finistère)

TGV: 4½ hours
Main shopping streets: rue Kéréon, rue St-Mathieu,
quartier des Halles
Market: Les Halles
Daily, 8 A.M.–1 P.M.
in the streets surrounding Les Halles
Wednesday and Saturday, 8 A.M.–1 P.M.

One of the largest and liveliest cities of Brittany, Quimper emanates stylishness and Old World charm simultaneously. This, of course, makes the shopping scene far from shabby on all fronts. In terms of regional products, all of Brittany is well represented here, and the only real disappointment is the shortage of antique shops. In this region of France, it's better to hunt for antiques outside the major cities, where the prices can be better as well. One shop, however, that is particularly alluring as much for its rustic regional furnishings, old faience, and assorted *objects* as for the warm glow of its interior, is known simply as **Antiquités** (24 rue des Gentilshommes; tel.: 02.98.95.47.22). On the other side of town, in an area referred to as the quartier Rive Gauche, Monsieur Le Meur of the **Galerie Le Cornet à Dés** (1 rue Ste-Thérèse; tel.: 02.98.53.37.51), showcases his collection of faience and paintings in a considerably more sophisticated setting. This highly respected dealer focuses primarily on Henriot faience and stoneware from the twenties, thirties, and forties, certainly the most artistic period of this venerable house. The creativity does not stop there, and other versions of traditional themes and regional scenes by painters such as Mathurin Meheut might just surprise you by their modernity.

If you head back toward the cathedral, be sure to stop at the **Musée Départemental Breton** (just off rue Elie-Fréron), a handsome museum devoted to the folklore, traditions, and popular arts of the people of Brittany. From *bigouden* costumes to wooden polychrome religious statues, this museum will bring you one giant leap closer to understanding the richness of this near-ancient culture.

Throughout Brittany, Celtic influences appear in everything from music and books to the motifs borrowed for the decoration of linens and home accessories. Celtic crosses, fleurs-de-lis, and triskels (designs that represent the four essential elements of life: water, earth, fire, and air) carry great symbolism in this land. Pierre Toulhoat, a craftsman who lives and works in Quimper, has taken these and other symbols and forged them into a collection of jewelry that is worthy of the knights of the round table. Their pewtery-like finish makes them look quite Spartan and therefore easily identifiable throughout Brittany. You can find them at **L'Iris d'Argent** (16 rue du Parc; tel.: 02.98.95.25.04), where prices range from 120F to 500F. The sometimes shrill sounds (it must be the bagpipes) of Celtic music are not for everyone, but if you feel like giving them a try, go directly to **Ar Bed Keltiek** (2 rue Roi Gradlon; tel.: 02.98.95.42.82; fax: 02.98.95.24.73). Music by the harpist Alan Stivell is currently grazing the charts, and if it's books, cards, or posters you're after, both in the Celtic language or about the people and their lands, this store has plenty of them, too!

In Quimper, it's easy to forget that you are close to the sea. **Jolie Brise** (10 rue des Boucheries; tel.: 02.98.95.10.45), a boutique that specializes in decorative items with classic marine themes, can serve as a good reminder. Almost next door at **Boule de Neige** (14 rue des Boucheries), the acclaimed *pâtissier/chocolatier*, Georges Larnicol, pays tribute to *la mer* with his seaweed-tinged chocolates, which are said to reduce cholesterol while helping you slim down. I instead chose a creamy and certainly less healthful pastry to consume in this busy *salon de thé*.

I have not talked much about *crêpes* or *crêperies* because you will undoubtedly find enough of them on your own. If you are interested in buying classic crêpe-making utensils, however, try **Jacques Biolay** (8 rue Elie-Fréron; tel.: 02.98.95.33.84), a cookware shop just up the street from the cathedral. Situated on a tiny street not too far from here is **Crêperie au Vieux Quimper** (20 rue Verdelet; tel.: 02.98.95.31.34), one of the warmest and most authentic places to sample crêpes in all of Quimper.

François Le Villec

Before I ever went to Quimper, I learned about François Le Villec's table arts and home décor collection from my upstairs neighbors in Paris. My neighbors happened to be the children of the dynamic couple behind this store's name, and since they knew that I was interested in French products, they decided to slip one of their parents' catalogues into my mailbox.

I was immediately impressed with Le Villec's bright, fresh interpretations of traditional Breton prints. Their selection of 100-percent cotton tablecloths and placemats looks stronger and more colorful every year; and this is where they have the advantage over Henriot, whose commitment to coordinating its textiles with its faience has been minimal. In addition to all of the beautiful prints, Le Villec has created several different services of hand-painted faience which form a perfect marriage with their table linens. A few accessories round out the collection, so if you're really drawing a blank about what to bring home for your favorite aunt, why not consider one of their cheery blue-crested umbrellas (387F), appropriately bordered with the folkloric images of *le breton* and *la bretonne*?

• 4 rue du Roi-Gradlon, 29000 Quimper; tel.: 02.98.95.31.54;
   fax: 02.98.64.30.86
Mail order available
Open Monday–Saturday 9:30 A.M.–12:30 P.M. and 1:30–6 P.M.

Faïenceries HB Henriot

When people talk about Quimper faience, they are generally referring to this company, HB Henriot. Although founded in 1690, the Quimper explosion truly began in the 1980s when Paul and Sarah Janssens purchased the then bankrupt Henriot and turned it into a booming empire. The Janssens already had a good handle on the U.S. market: not only did they own a boutique in Connecticut that featured Quimper faience, but they also had become the sole importers for Henriot in the U.S. Today about a quarter of the Henriot production is sold stateside, which largely explains why Americans are so familiar with this brand of French faïence.

The motifs are easily recognizable, not only by the little folkloric Breton men and women that serve as the focal point of the various pieces, but particularly for the light, almost feathery brushstrokes, called *le coup de pinceau*, that breathe life into the stylized flowers and leaves that typify their many designs. Each piece is hand-painted with this technique in a classic range of colors that primarily includes red, green, yellow, and blue (the country blue shade is so well known that the French sometimes identify a color as *bleue de Quimper*). A visit through the workshops is a must, and if you are at all like me, you will instantly be surprised by how quiet it is here. Virtually no machinery is involved in the fabrication of the pieces, and the more than fifty decorators require a certain amount of tranquility for their concentration. *Mais bien sur!*

The guided tour lasts about thirty to forty-five minutes, but you'll need to spend more time at the entire Henriot complex to see everything on view. Before you head off to their boutique (once you enter, it's even harder to leave), don't miss the beautifully installed exhibitions at the **Musée de la Faïence** next door. The museum traces the history of faience and exhibits the various steps of the manufacturing process, but its real strength is in its tremendously rich collection of ceramic works from Quimper and other corners of the earth.

Next, lose yourself in the Henriot boutique, an immense but warm space that opened just a few years ago under the watchful eye of Sarah Janssens. Rustic furniture and stone walls contribute to the French country look that Quimper faience epitomizes so well. Many of the tables have been dressed with Provençal tablecloths and set with faience—a successful pairing indeed. Most of the Henriot collection is sold here, including a number of pieces that are rarely found elsewhere. The supply is enormous, and you are sure to have a field day running back and forth between the regularly priced pieces and the seconds, most of which have been marked down by 20 to 30 percent!

• rue Haute, BP 1219, 29102 Quimper; tel.: 02.98.90.09.36;
  fax: 02.98.90.16.02
Open Monday–Saturday 9:30 A.M.–12:30 P.M. and 1:30–6 P.M.
Visits from March to October, Monday–Thursday 9–11:15 A.M. and
  1:30–4:15 P.M.; Friday 9–11:15 A.M. and 1:30–3 P.M.

Le Minor

• 7 rue St-François, 29000 Quimper; tel.: 02.98.95.15.55
Open Monday 2–7 P.M.; Tuesday–Saturday 9:30 A.M.–noon and 2–7 P.M.
See Pont-l'Abbé description on page 76.

Outside Quimper (Finistère)

Château du Guilguiffin

The location is ideal. The setting is grandiose. The château is majestic. The rooms are exquisite. The host is charming. What more could you ask for for a bed-and-breakfast? Spending a night or more at the Château du Guilguiffin means discovering another side of Brittany, one that often remains hidden behind the rusticity of the old stone houses or lost amongst the quaintness of the coastal villages. This side of Brittany is one of elegance and refinement.

- 29710 Landudec; tel.: 02.98.91.52.11; fax: 02.98.91.52.52
  Château-Hôtel: Moderate–Expensive
  Best to call ahead

Vannes (Morbihan)

TGV: 3¼ hours from Paris
Main shopping streets: rue des Halles, rue du Méné
Markets: place des Lices
Wednesday and Saturday 7 A.M.–1 P.M.

Vannes is perhaps the prettiest port city in all of Brittany. It resembles La Rochelle in the Poitou Charentes region, and both cities do a splendid job of juggling their dual identities of busy urban centers and active ports. Most of the port activity in Vannes comes from the leisure boats, both big and small, privately owned or otherwise. Many excursion boats leave from Vannes for visits to the numerous islands that punctuate *le Golfe du Morbihan*, so it's convenient that the city has much to offer, particularly if you need to kill a couple of hours before the next departure. For antiquing, head toward the cathedral to the rue St-Guenhael or the rue de la Bienfaisance, where poking around could result in a few unusual finds *intra muros*, within the old city walls, in the heart of the historic quarter.

Also in the old section and only a short walk from the *antiquaires* is the jeweler **Pierre-Yves Ouisse** (26 rue des Halles), a good address for the Celtic pieces of Pierre Toulhoat, particularly if you missed them in Quimper or in Pont-l'Abbé at Le Minor. At 9 rue St-Nicolas, a bit farther away but definitely worth the walk (particularly if you are known to display chocoholic tendencies), is the nearly 100-year-old *chocolatier*, **Desplousse**. Their *bourriches* (round crates) contain one of the most appreciated delicacies of the Gulf, oysters, but here their glossy sheen comes from the darkest, finest chocolate, and instead of resting upon seaweed, they have been placed on green Easter grass. The interior of these chocolate oysters is to die for: a sort of melt-in-your-mouth praline center that makes Reese's cups taste like cardboard!

Clipper

As the name indicates, this small boutique displays clipper ships along with a ship's cargo of other model boats, many of which are typical of Brittany, and even more that once circulated around *le Golfe*. The *sinago*, a flat-bottomed boat whose blood-red sail made it hard to miss in the Gulf, is one such boat; originally used for fishing, today only a tiny fleet remains for touring, but here you can purchase one in miniature as a model boat or in watercolors and prints. Prices in this shop range from 49F for a brightly painted rowboat (perfect for a little boy's room) to 2,200F and beyond for bigger, more detailed models such as Atlantic fishing boats. Some of the models are free-standing, although most have been encased in glass boxes, quite suitable for mounting on the walls. Other items include half hulls, tableaus of the various nautical knots, posters, and assorted other trinkets with a marine theme.

- 16 rue St-Salomon, 56000 Vannes; tel.: 02.97.54.17.24; fax: 02.97.47.59.56
  Open Monday–Saturday 9:30 A.M.–12:30 P.M. and 1:30–6 P.M.

La Tapénade

The name of this shop rings very *provençal*, but it is in fact an excellent place to find the best comestibles of Brittany. Almost every corner of the region is represented here, and one quick look around tells you that the food and drink specialties of *la Bretagne* are indeed plentiful. *Confiture de lait*, or milk jam, from the Morbihan is so yummy that you might want to eat it by the spoonful, directly out of the jar. Other favorite sweets include salted butter caramels from Quiberon, rum-soaked crêpes in a jar, and *oeufs de mouettes*, or seagulls' eggs, which are candy-coated speckled eggs filled with a tender chocolaty praline center. Heartier types might opt for canned sardines, wild boar pâté, or a pint of Cervoise Lancelot, a regional beer made from buckwheat according to the original recipe of the Gauls.

- 23 rue des Halles, 56000 Vannes; tel.: 02.97.42.69.65
  Open Monday 2–7:15 P.M.; Tuesday–Saturday 9 A.M.–12:15 P.M. and 2–7:15 P.M.

BURGUNDY
Bourgogne

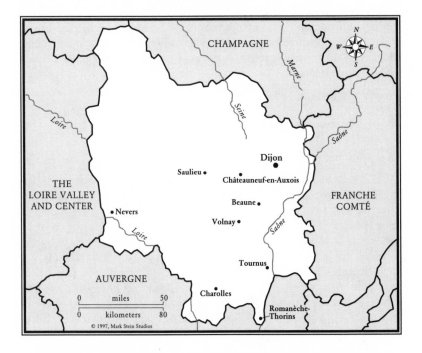

wines • mustard • pottery • wine posters and books • Gothic and
Renaissance furnishings • faience • gingerbread • *crème de cassis* •
wine bars and bistrot accessories • *pastilles de l'Abbaye de Flavigny*
• antiques • cheeses • Morvan crafts • ceramic mustard pots •
medieval tapestry–patterned pillows • wine accessories • pewter
cups • old vintages • *escargots* • Côte d'Or tea towels • apothecary
jars • snail-shaped chocolates • royalist puzzles • religious im-
agery greeting and playing cards

UNEQUIVOCALLY ONE OF the most genteel provinces of France, Burgundy se-
duces visitors with its lush, green, and ever-so-gentle countryside long before
they begin to explore the complexities of its wine. When I think of Burgundy,
the region, I first envision varying shades of brown–then comes the deep,
glossy, crimson red of the local wine. Brown has never been my favorite color,
but in Burgundy it is deep and rich, not dull. Even the subtle browns of the
cows that graze in the pastures take on a tony hue that instantly seems to clas-

sify them as elegant animals instead of stupid beasts. The golden brown stones of the Côte-d'Or *département* can be uplifting even on the greyest days. I've come to the conclusion that as much as the color burgundy maintains real continuity throughout this region, the color brown serves as a metaphor for the innumerable nuances and riches of this bountiful land.

One could languish in the cultural aspects of the region as much as in its wine. Tourists flock to the near-subliminal Romanesque basilica at Vézelay, but few travelers discover the mysteries of the Burgundy wines. Neophytes (like me) might be amazed that the size and repartition of the Burgundy vineyards have nothing to do with those of Bordeaux, for example. One blink of the eyes and you've already passed through Puligny-Montrachet, Meursault, Gevrey-Chambertin, and many, many other *appéllations* where each acre of land counts among the most prized in all of France. It turned out to be an exhausting and highly aggravating challenge for my traveling companion and me to locate the renowned Michel Lafarge winery in Volnay, but it occurred to us that the lack of readily visible signs to *le village* and *le vigneron* was both deliberate and understandable, because after all, the vintners have their work to do, too!

Beaune (Côte-d'Or)

Main shopping streets: rue Carnot, rue Monge,
Market: town center
Wednesday and Saturday 7 A.M.–12:30 P.M.

Beaune's key location in the heart of the Côte-d'Or department predestined its role as a major trading place for Burgundy wines. Every other establishment, situated both inside and outside the sixteenth- and seventeenth-century walls of this fortified city, seems devoted to the selling of wine. You can make a day of stopping into these merchants' showrooms, and sometimes even sample wines from the few vineyards that each of them represents—but don't expect to find many all-inclusive cellars that represent all of the region's wines.

Before you plunge into the wine world of Beaune (pronounced like *bone*), I suggest you start with a culturally enlightening visit to the **Hôtel-Dieu**, a gem of medieval architecture initially constructed as a hospital for the poor in 1443. The Gothic façade, as well as each of the sparsely yet handsomely furnished rooms, have been impeccably preserved, thanks largely to the annual Hospices de Beaune wine auction, the famous sale, held on the third Sunday of November at which the public may taste, but not buy. The Hôtel-Dieu gift shop is better stocked than the norm, and if you're a card collector you can pick and choose images to your heart's delight. Other items include embroidered pillows inspired by classic medieval tapestries; reproductions of pewter pieces that were set upon the patients' bedstands; and books, prints, playing cards, and puzzles that draw primarily upon religious or royalist themes.

My search for regional antiques proved to be a bit disappointing in this medieval town, although two well-known shops worth a look are just a few steps from the Hôtel-Dieu: **Jean Berger** (10 place de la Halle; tel.: 03.80.22.09.79) and **Tri'antique** (3 avenue de la République; tel.: 03.80.24.20.90). On a far more modern note, the store **Athenaeum de la Vigne et du Vin** (tel.: 03.80.22.12.00), just across from the Hôtel-Dieu, specializes in books and travel guides of the region, many of which may be hard to find elsewhere.

Cave Sainte-Hélène

The dim interior of this thirteenth-century wine cellar might not entice you to enter—unless, of course, you interpret the dimness as a sign that the fine vintages inside need to remain in their sleepy state. Owner Pierre Escoffier joked that he should wear a miner's hat to illuminate his various wines when necessary, but he knows his collection of *vieilles millesimés* (old vintages) so well that he can easily put his hand on just the rare vintage that a visitor seeks. Pierre's business took off a number of years ago thanks to an American in search of fifty cases of specific Burgundies; today people mostly come to him for vintages whose years correspond with birthdays or anniversaries that they plan to celebrate. Go directly to the product list to see what is available in wines from Burgundy, Bordeaux, and Côtes du Rhone; from this point, Pierre and his wife, Fabienne will advise you with great expertise.

- 24 place Carnot, passage Ste-Hélène; 21200 Beaune; tel.: 03.80.22.30.22; fax: 03.80.24.99.79
  Open daily except Wednesday and Sunday 9:30 A.M.–noon and 3–6 P.M.

Charolles (Saône-et-Loire)

Manufacture de Faïence Jacques Molin

Although it may not warrant a detour, if you find yourself in the vicinity of Charolles, you may want to check out the goods of this more than 150-year-old faience manufacturer. Molin continues to produce many of the traditional French country décors of bright flowers on scallop-edged dishes, but most of today's creations are more contemporary in color, shape, and design. Colorful, crackled glazes on more streamlined forms emphasize the current trend toward pieces that achieve greater definition by their overall look instead of the motifs that were once used to adorn them.

- 71120 Charolles, tel.: 03.85.24.13.46; fax: 03.85.88.33.85
  Open Monday–Friday 8 A.M.–noon and 2–6 P.M.

Châteauneuf-en-Auxois (Côte-d'Or)

Hostellerie du Château

Almost equidistant between Beaune and Dijon near Pouilly-en-Auxois, the medieval village of Châteauneuf-en-Auxois embraces you with its bucolic charm, its unspoiled nature, and its spectacular panoramic views of the valley. And if you're a cat lover, you'll delight in the abundance of barnyard mousers! There's not much to see here except for the sheer beauty of the site and its château, but if you are looking to restore yourself, the Hostellerie du Château will surely provide you with the right formula. Florence and André Hartmann, the young couple who recently took over this hotel/restaurant, master the dining room and the kitchen so smoothly that you'd think they've been in this business for many years. André exercises his skills in the kitchen, producing results that rival some of the finest tables of the region. The rooms are modest, although certainly adequate for a few nights' stay.

- 21320 Châteauneuf-en-Auxois, tel.: 03.80.49.22.00; fax: 03.80.49.21.27

  Hotel/Restaurant: Inexpensive–Moderate

  Open daily throughout the tourist season; closed Monday evening and Tuesday during off-season

---

Dijon (Côte-d'Or)

TGV: 1 hour and 40 minutes
Main shopping streets: rue de la Liberté, rue Musette,
rue des Forges, rue du Bourg
Market: in the streets surrounding Les Halles
Tuesday, Friday, and Saturday 7:30 A.M.–12:30 P.M.

One quick tour through Dijon shows you that the city has not only maintained, but more importantly enhanced, the architectural riches that were erected under the reign of the *ducs de Bourgogne*. The city's importance as a parliamentary center during the seventeenth and eighteenth centuries created even more resplendent buildings, and today, Dijon is recognized both as the capital of Burgundy and as a premiere cultural center, bursting with historic buildings and significant museums. Vestiges from the city's diverse heritage can be spotted on virtually every street, which makes browsing around its busy commercial district all the more interesting. Antiquing in Dijon can also yield some real treasures and your best bet is to weave in and around rue Verrerie and rue Vannerie.

Maille

Dijon, of course, means mustard, and the granddaddy of Dijon mustards is uncontestably Maille, a house founded in 1747. The Maille boutique, established in 1777, should be viewed from across the street to fully appreciate the distinguished appearance of its bottle-green storefront. Gold lettering accentuates the prestige of this world-famous name, and the window display of centuries-old mustard jars also indicates that you are about to enter a space of deep-seeded (as in mustard) tradition! Before you go in, scan their current collection of ceramic *pots à moutarde*, which is also featured in their shopwindow; they come in an array of shapes and sizes, most of which have been decorated with country kitchen motifs. Prices range from 150F to 1,500F.

- 32 rue de la Liberté, 21000 Dijon; tel.: 03.80.30.41.02; fax: 03.80.50.09.46
  Open Monday–Friday 9 A.M.–noon and 2:15–7 P.M.; Saturday 9:15 A.M.–12:15 P.M. and 2:15–7 P.M.

Mulot & Petitjean

Another venerable institution of Dijon, Mulot & Petitjean began making their now-famous gingerbread in 1796. From the looks of Mulot & Petitjean's three establishments, the *dijonnais* fancy this healthy treat almost as much as the Alsatians. The half-timbered façade of the boutique at place Bossuet announces the Old World charm that warms you as soon as you step inside. Exquisitely carved woodwork, complete with rich gilding and decorative accents such as the coat of arms of Dijon, create the ideal setting for the prettily wrapped spicy brown breads that look almost too good to eat. Favorite forms include snails, Burgundy bottles, and crowns garnished with candied fruits fit for a king. This is a great place to collect booty from Burgundy, because in addition to the multiflavored gingerbreads, the shop also tempts you with *escargots en chocolat*, tiny candies from l'Abbaye de Flavigny, all kinds of mustards, *crème de cassis*, and a small, but select, sampling of Burgundy wines.

- 13 place Bossuet/16 rue de la Liberté/1 place Notre-Dame; 21000 Dijon; tel.: 03.80.30.07.10; fax: 03.80.30.18.03
  place Bossuet and Notre-Dame stores open Monday-Saturday 9 A.M.–12 P.M. and 2–7 P.M.
  The rue de la Liberté boutique is open Monday 8:30 A.M.–noon and 2–7:30 P.M.; Tuesday–Saturday 8:30 A.M.–7:30 P.M.; Sunday 9 A.M.–noon and 2–7 P.M. during summer and until 6 P.M. during winter

Nevers (Nièvre)

Just about an hour south of Gien, the centuries-old faience manufacturer that has gained worldwide recognition over the past ten years, sits Nevers—practically in the middle of nowhere, but nonetheless home to about four different *faïenceries*. Collectors and people in the know appreciate the value of Nevers ceramics, but they remain somewhat of a rarity in Paris, let alone outside of France. The production at Nevers does in fact tend to be small since virtually every step is still carried out by hand; consequently, prices here run higher than those at the more industrially oriented Gien.

Begin with a visit to the **Musée de la Faïence** at 16 rue St-Genest (tel.: 03.86.23.92.89; fax: 03.86.68.45.99) to become familiar with the distinctive look of pieces from Nevers. The museum's collection of apothecary jars characterizes the Nevers style quite well, particularly with the often heavy-handed applications of color, design, and inscriptions that the French might refer to as *chargé* (loaded). If you want to see more old pieces, visit **L'Echauguette** (1 rue de la Cathédrale; tel.: 03.86.59.50.62) where you can admire and perhaps buy any of Madame Mallet's superb eighteenth- and nineteenth-century pieces, handsomely priced between 1,500F and 8,000F.

Christine Girande

The only woman among many men in her field, Christine Girande's creations radiate a lightness of design and a fresh, feminine spirit atypical of traditional Nevers faïence. Although she works primarily with classic designs, Christine opens up the patterns and gives them an airy feeling well suited to interiors of all kinds. Innovative color combinations include royal blue and leaf green, a harmonious association that rarely stands alone in typical Nevers pieces. Prices run high, but that's the cost of *la création*.

• 26 rue du 14 Juillet, 58000 Nevers; tel.: 03.86.36.42.08
  Open Tuesday–Saturday 9 A.M.–noon and 2–7 P.M.

Montagnon

During its heyday, Nevers was one of the top five cities toward which France turned for most of its earthenware. This was long before the days of porcelain, and although pewter existed, its usage was not multipurpose. It took two Italians to really fire up the French faience industry, and they did so by settling in Nevers in 1566. The faïence workshop that is known today as Montagnon came into existence about a cenutry later in 1648. Its reputation has by no means faltered over the past 350 years; all the pieces are still entirely hand-turned and hand-painted at this boutique. A look around the showplace provides a survey of the most representative Nevers patterns from centuries past: Italian Renaissance scenes; Chinese motifs; birds; flowers; pastoral themes;

and historical and patriotic adornments all capture the tastes and tendencies of those diverse times. Cobalt blues, orangey yellows, and ruddy browns dominate, and the sizes and prices vary as much as their designs.

• 10 rue de la Porte-du-Croux, 58005 Nevers; tel.: 03.86.57.27.16; fax: 03.86.21.51.26
  Open Monday–Saturday 9 A.M.–noon and 2–7 P.M.
  Workshop visits the first Wednesday of the month at 2:30 P.M.

Romanèche-Thorins (Saône-et-Loire)

Le Hameau du Vin

The name of this little speck of a village at the southernmost tip of Burgundy probably means nothing to you, but I'm sure that Georges Duboeuf does. If not, it will by the time you leave this enormous complex, entirely consecrated to the wonders of wine and, *bien sur*, those of Monsieur Duboeuf! You shouldn't leave Burgundy–or France, for that matter–without stopping here, but allow some time. You'll need to spend at least a couple of hours touring the winemaking museum, and more time to savor a few glasses of Beaujolais and absorb all of the wine-related information (explanations are in English and admission includes a glass of wine).

The term "museum" does not effectively describe the scope of this multimedia center, whose purpose is to entertain visitors as it educates them about the history and the making of wine. Think of it as the Disneyland of the wine world; "the hamlet" opened in 1993, and its spic-and-span appearance should be glistening far into the next millennium. Everything you need–from a turn-of-the-century café to an expansive department-storelike shop–has been designed for your convenience and pleasure. Now it's up to you to pull into the old Romanèche-Thorins train station to embark upon your journey through *le monde du vin*!

• La Gare, 71570 Romanèche-Thorins; tel.: 03.85.35.22.22; fax: 03.85.35.21.18
  Open daily 9 A.M.–9 P.M.

Les Maritonnes

After an exhausting visit *chez Duboeuf,* you'll appreciate even more the few steps it takes to tuck yourself into this quaint auberge brimming with country charm. If you are lucky enough to visit in the spring, you'll enjoy the garden shrouded by pale lavender blooms of wysteria; in the summer, guests like the hotel's delightful pool and inviting terrace. The dining room, splendorous with rustic furnishings and paintings from the region, seems to have been designed with chilly weather in mind, and the all-female waitstaff (highly unusual in France) is so friendly and accommodating that you may find it difficult to press on. The guestrooms are clean and adequate in size, although they could use a few renovations.

- 71570 Romanèche-Thorins; Tel.: 03.85.35.51.70; fax: 03.85.35.58.14
  One-Star Michelin Restaurant: Moderate–Expensive/Three-Star Hotel: Moderate
  Open year-round except from December 15–January 31; restaurant closed Monday, Tuesday lunch, and Sunday evening during off-season

Saulieu (Côte-d'Or)

Boutique Bernard Loiseau

You don't have to intimidate yourself by entering the inner sanctum of celebrity chef Bernard Loiseau's famed restaurant, La Côte d'Or; the boutique, which is separate from the restaurant, resides in a recently renovated space built to resemble an old grocery store. As hotel/restaurant shops go, this is among the most attractive—not only for its handsome wooden display cases, butcher-block tables, terra-cotta floor tiling, and bulbous brass ceiling lamps, but also for its broad range of products. Goods range from linens and china, made especially for the restaurant, to works by local craftspeople from the neighboring forest of the Morvan. You can pay as little as 20F for a beige kitchen towel, marked "La Côte d'Or/Bernard Loiseau" in brown lettering, or as much as 800F for a rosy clay cherub, hand-molded by a woman from Saulieu. And what would an old Burgundy grocery store be without a wine cellar? To find out, walk down to the *cave* and peruse the hand-picked selection of wines from the region and beyond.

- 4 rue d'Argentine, 21210 Saulieu; tel.: 03.80.90.53.50; fax: 03.80.64.24.22

Open Monday–Saturday 10 A.M.–noon and 5–7 P.M.; Sunday 9:30 A.M.–
12:30 P.M. and 3–7 P.M.

La Côte d'Or

When my traveling companion quietly suggested that we splurge
for dinner and a night's stay at this *haut lieu de la gastronomie
française*, how could I refuse? Luxurious it was, ostentatious it
was not. The meal was delicious, but what impressed me the
most was the way the inn has gathered all of the raw materials
of this land into one sumptuous tableau. From thick, wood
beams to smooth, stone walls, warm and rich variations of the
browns of the Burgundy countryside discreetly endear you to
this old postal inn—so much so, in fact, that you might find
yourself with a dangerous yearning to go back.

• 2 rue d'Argentine, 21210 Saulieu; tel.: 03.80.90.53.53; fax:
  03.80.64.08.92
  Three-Star Michelin Resturant and Relais & Châteaux Hôtel:
  Very Expensive
  Open year-round

Tournus (Saône-et-Loire)

Market: Town Center Saturday
8 A.M.–noon

This glorious little Romanesque town is high on the list of well-kept secrets,
and the townspeople have made a concerted effort to protect themselves
from an influx of run-of-the-mill tourists. Marvels of Romanesque architecture punctuate Tournus, although if you're interested in more in-depth visits,
begin with the pinky-brown stone **Abbaye,** and then leave yourself time for
a quick tour through the **Musée Bourguignon**, a museum featuring the arts
and traditions of the Burgundy people. If you're looking for a long and
highly gastronomic break from all of this cultural enlightenment, consider
the centrally located **Restaurant Greuze** (1 rue A.-Thibault; tel.:
03.85.51.13.52), a two-star Michelin establishment best known for its *cuisine
traditionelle* and elegant interior.

Bruno Perrier

Master *antiquaire* Bruno Perrier waited patiently for a number of years before
taking over the twelfth-century church of St-Valérien for the presentation of

his rare and unusual pieces from the *Haute Epoque*. Outside, the golden-tan stones of this jewel of Romanesque architecture signal the warmth that envelops you once you step into this magnificent space. With Gregorian chants as background music, this church seems to have been designed for the Gothic and Renaissance furnishings, sculpture, tapestries, and other assorted *objets* that embellish it so divinely. Monsieur Perrier did well to wait, because I cannot imagine a more spectacular setting for his collection of unique works, most of which would inspire the envy of many a museum curator. Monsieur Perrier's clients do in fact include museums, private and public institutions, and, of course, highly discriminating collectors. And it's no wonder, since prices can easily reach six figures (in French francs)– but the best part is that it doesn't cost you a *sou* to take a look around!

If you're interested in antiques of an entirely different nature, ask Monsieur Perrier about his brother, another very enterprising connoisseur, who specializes in turn-of-the-century bistrot furnishings and accessories the likes of *bars à zinc*.

- rue Alexis-Bessard, BP 85, 71700 Tournus; tel.: 03.85.51.13.59;
  fax: 03.85.51.36.29
  Open daily except Tuesday, 10 A.M.–12:30 P.M. and 3–7:30 P.M.

Outside Tournus (Saône-et-Loire)

Pascal Pauget

"You have to have a love for wine to distinguish yourself from the others." Well-stated, Pascal–it took me about thirty seconds to surmise that this young vintner does indeed possess this *amour du vin*. I became more interested in this winemaker's cellar when I heard great accolades about the quality of his products. Not only do most of the big Burgundy wineries ward off visits from errant wine enthusiasts, but sometimes, even if you do manage to worm your way into one of their sacred cellars, you leave with the impression that your presence was more of a bother than a pleasure. Although the wines (mostly Mâcon) of Pascal Pauget are not in quite the same league as those of Côtes de Nuits or Côtes de Beaune, his passionate approach to winemaking has already begun to yield some startling results. What is most fun, though, is to watch him articulate his prodigious knowledge of Burgundy wines. If you do not understand French and have no one to translate for you, you will have to let his wines speak for themselves. The day I visited I was particularly pleased by his Mâcon '94, a rather fruity Chardonnay that left a hint of lemon on the palate. Cost per bottle: 40F.

- La Croisette, 71700 Tournus; tel.: 03.85.32.53.15
  Call ahead or try stopping by

CHAMPAGNE
Champagne

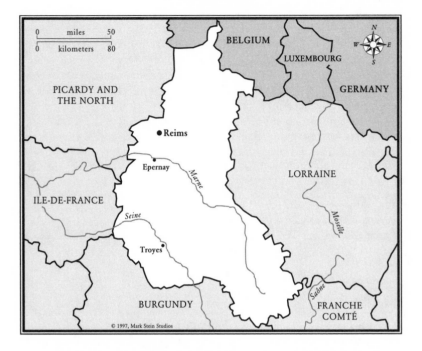

factory discount shopping • Champagne • contemporary glass creations • *biscuits rose de Reims* • books and posters on Champagne • Bayel crystal • old Champagne-related memorabilia • chocolates • Champagne accessories and assorted items emblazoned with the names of the Champagne houses

WHENEVER PEOPLE TELL me that they are heading to Paris and would like to work in a quick sidetrip to the wine country, I always give the Champagne region, within a two-hour drive of the capital, my highest recommendation. As much as each Champagne house has its own ambiance and approach, from conducting tours on a little train or enforcing a rigid appointments-only policy for visits, they all impress visitors with their grandeur, prestige, and consummate style. You can pick up a list of the cellars from the tourism office in Reims, which provides information about visits: note that all of them have boutiques. Some travelers do the Paris–Reims trek by train, which is fine if you don't have a car, but one of the best parts of visiting the

Champagne region involves cruising through the impeccably manicured countryside, particularly along the stately stretch between Reims and Epernay.

Having a car becomes a true necessity for factory discount shopping in Troyes at the southern end of the Champagne region. Yes, this is still Champagne, and you might be amazed to see that the vines extend way into the depths of the Aube department. In view of this, it would not be considered at all strange to celebrate a successful day of bargain-hunting with a self-congratulatory glass of Champagne in the picturesque old town of Troyes!

THE CHAMPAGNE REGION

Epernay (Marne)

Moët et Chandon

If I had to chose between visiting the cellars of Moët et Chandon or browsing through their boutique, you can bet that I would insist upon the latter. A tour through the Champagne-stacked subterranean galleries will, of course, inspire you to sing the praises of Dom Perignon, named after a well-intentioned monk who concocted this light, fruity nectar with a distinctive fizz that tantalizes virtually all of our senses with each delicious mouthful.

On the shopping scene, you'll be happy to see that Moët pays its products the homage they rightfully deserve. Truly the most beautiful Champagne boutique in all of Champagne, if it were not for the absence of mirrors or excessive gold trim, this glamorous selling space would look more like a Cartier boutique than a fancy Champagne emporium. The influences of the high-powered, high-profile luxury group, LVMH (Louis Vuitton Moët Hennessy), the owner of Moët et Chandon, show in the opulent glass showcases that serve as individual *presentoirs* for the exclusive goods displayed inside. It takes much willpower to resist purchasing items such as the abbey gift package (650F), which includes a bottle of Dom Perignon accompanied by two crystal flutes in a laquered wooden box; a gift set of hollow-stemmed crystal flutes by Bayel (700F), the leading crystal-maker of the region; or a more modest purchase of a forest green apron marked Moët et Chandon in gold lettering (100F). Who ever thought that Champagne shopping could be so arduous?

- 20 avenue de Champagne, 51200 Epernay; tel.: 03.26.51.20.00; fax: 03.26.51.20.10
  Open year round Monday–Friday 9:30–11:30 A.M. and 2–4:30 P.M.; and from Easter–mid November Saturday 9:30–11:30 A.M. and 2–4:30 P.M., Sunday and holidays 9:30 A.M.–noon and 2–4 P.M.

Reims (Marne)

Main shopping streets: rue de Vesle, place d'Erlon
Market: place du Boulingrin
Wednesday and Saturday 8 A.M.–1 P.M.
Flea market: boulevard Jamin
Friday and Monday 2–6 P.M.;
Saturday and Sunday 10 A.M.–7 P.M.

It wasn't until I came to Champagne as a "reporter" instead of a tourist that I was able to observe some of the prominent players of this very select and closed world. It all began when my guide, Olivier, a particularly well-connected person in Champagne, suggested we have lunch at the **Brasserie Boulingrin** (48 rue de Mars; tel.: 03.26.40.96.22). What first appeared to be a typical *brasserie* turned out to be *the* gathering place of the muckety-mucks of the Champagne world. Olivier felt compelled to mention right off that you never make the *faux pas* of ordering a *kir royal* (a mixture of *crème de cassis* and Champagne) in Champagne. Okay, I wasn't counting on doing that anyway. The second oh-by-the-way he added was that you always wait for the apéritif to have your first *coupe de champagne* of the day, to maintain a certain decorum. It didn't take me long to discern that after that first *coupe*, the *champenois* really let 'er rip!

It's true they drink Champagne the way many people drink Coca-Cola, and after Olivier pointed out to me exactly who the other luncheon regulars happened to be, it wouldn't have surprised me to learn that they were nursed on this heavenly juice. With the majority of the big Champagne houses based in Reims, the *reimois* appear to know a thing or two about having a good time. *Mais, c'est normale, nous sommes en Champagne!*

Biscuiterie Remoise

Most foreigners would never think of serving cookies with Champagne, but in France one type of crunchy sweet, called *le biscuit rose de Reims*, is frequently associated with *le champagne*. Similar in shape to ladyfingers, although much harder in consistency, these sugar-dusted, cotton candy-colored treats form a delightfully pretty picture when piled high on a silver dish next to a tray of flutes filled with freshly poured bubbly. Their light meringuey taste produces a Champagne-laced tang with every sip and nibble—just the sort of sensation that would make a big hit at a ladies' luncheon, a bridal shower, or other similarly festive occasion. Although cumbersome, *les biscuits* are light enough for travel or shipping, and their longish shelf life will give you plenty of time to plan your next party!

- 11 rue Périn, 51100 Reims; tel.: 03.26.40.67.67; fax: 03.26.47.04.48
  Open Monday–Friday 8 A.M.–7 P.M.; Saturday 9 A.M.–noon and 2–6 P.M.
  Visits Monday–Friday 9 A.M.–noon

G. H. Mumm & Co.

Before you enter the elegant portals of this *grande maison*, may I suggest you first practice the correct pronunciation of their name. It's almost too easy—just say *moom*, like moon but with an "m" at the end. This way if you ask any questions during the awe-inspiring tour that leads you through a portion of more than sixteen miles of cellars, or when shopping around in the boutique, you will automatically make a fine impression—even if you don't know a thing about these world famous wines.

The boutique offers a dazzling selection of Champagnes, many of which you might never have seen elsewhere. Even *les grands classiques* often sell here in packages unique to *la maison mère* or mother house: I bought a bottle of Mumm Cordon Rouge (107F) primarily for its confetti-covered container, a festive red tin perfect for the storage of Christmas cookies. Other shopping musts include a magnum of their *cuvée de prestige*, Grand Cordon 1985, also presented in a gift box (610F) and the Cordon Rosé, a 1985 rosé vintage whose pink rosebud label was designed by the great Japanese painter Foujita. If you have already acquired more than enough Champagne to bring home or to consume before leaving the country, pick up *Mumm, un Champagne dans l'Histoire*, a book in French about Mumm and the history of Champagne, filled with many beautiful images of the house and the champagne-making process.

- 34 rue du Champ de Mars, 51100 Reims; tel.: 03.26.49.59.70; fax: 03.26.49.59.01
  Open Monday–Friday 9–11 A.M. and 2–5 P.M., also on weekends and holidays from March 1 to October 31

Le Vintage

Just behind the famous Reims cathedral, Le Vintage offers one-stop shopping for the various Champagnes of more than twenty major houses in the region. Big names such as Krug, Roederer, Taittinger, and Veuve Clicquot stand among other wines and spirits of France that the *champenois* have been known to sample from time to time. Other fun gift ideas include packaged sets of quarter bottles of champagne from a sampling of big names, and chocolates in the form of champagne corks filled with marc de champagne, the strong local brandy.

- 1 cours Anatole-France, 51100 Reims; tel.: 03.26.40.40.82
  Open daily 9 A.M.–12:30 P.M. and 2:30–7 P.M.

Le Vigneron

Some of my best discoveries have occurred late in the evening. This was exactly the case at this enchanting restaurant, which was presented to me just after I had lamented that, except for the cellars, so much of Reims looks new and void of charm (a good part of the city was destroyed during World War II). The heartwarming interior of Le Vigneron more than makes up for all of the rest and, better yet, it serves as the unofficial Champagne museum for the entire region. Monsieur Hervé Liégent, the proud owner of this unique establishment, has traveled as far as Buenos Aires for that extra-special piece of artwork or memorabilia that he deems worthy of adding to his superb collection of Champagne-related objects. Turn-of-the-century publicity posters by such illustrious artists as Mucha and Gruau, prototypes of labels, bottles, buckets—you name it, everything and anything of significance that has touched *la vie de champagne* has been put tastefully on display for the diners' delight. There's even a cellar stocked with old vintages, of which Monsieur Liégent may be coaxed to part with a bottle or two. As for the sale of an old poster, I'll leave the negotiating up to you!

• place Paul-Jamot, 51100 Reims; tel.: 03.26.47.00.71; fax: 03.26.47.87.66
  Restaurant: Moderate–Expensive
  Open daily except Saturday lunch and Sunday evening

FACTORY DISCOUNT SHOPPING IN AND AROUND TROYES (AUBE)

Barely two hours from Paris by *l'autoroute*, Parisians would do well to plan more shopping excursions to Troyes, *the* haven of factory outlet stores in France. This kind of shopping has never really been part of French *habitudes*; the recent economic crisis, however, has forced many of the French to alter their buying habits considerably. The notion of "groveling" for bargains has since become far more acceptable, and although discount shopping outlets in France is not nearly as widespread as in the U.S., there have been great advances in recent years.

The textile industry has been a strong presence in the city of Troyes for centuries, and today nearly 150 factories still produce a quarter of the knitwear sold under French labels. *Magasins d'usine*, or factory stores, have existed here for decades, but only within the past few years have some begun to reach U.S. standards of appearance in both the stores and the shopping centers. As you drive in and around Troyes, you will be bombarded with billboards announcing the names of the dozen or more discount shopping complexes and individual factory stores located on the fringes of the city. If you plan to take it all in, go first to the tourism office at 16 boulevard Carnot to pick up a map and listing of the various stores within the area.

If it's close to lunchtime and you're not too pressed for time, you may want to consider a reasonably priced repast (menus at 105F–150F) next door at the **Royal Hôtel** (22 boulevard Carnot; tel.: 03.25.73.19.99). Fine cuisine might sound like too much of a contrast to your discount shopping program, but after all, this is France; not only is the midday meal close to sacrosanct in this country, but the French also don't have nearly as many eateries or food courts in their malls as Americans. If you do go to the tourism office or restaurant, park nearby at the train station; the outlet shopping may not be within walking distance, but the handsome, medieval quarter of Troyes lies just a few city streets and a row of half-timbered houses away.

I spent a whole day scurrying around to nearly all of the outlets and outlet malls to find the ones that, in my opinion, most merit your attention. The mall, **Marques Avenue**, and the shopping center, **Mc Arthur Glen**, distinguish themselves from the others by their selection of merchandise and store layouts. Highlights of the thirty-five factory stores at Marques Avenue include the fashion-forward womenswear label **Apostrophe**, French knitwear biggies **Caroll** and **Alain Manoukian**, zippy sportswear manufacturers **Creeks Liberto**, **Usine Plus-Chipie** and Banana Republic-ish **Bensimon**, and the boutique **Cuir Collection**, which includes a wide selection of leather bags and accessories by trendsetters Soco and Upla.

Newcomer Mc Arthur Glen actually wins the best discount shopping complex of France prize hands down—at least in my opinion, and I've shopped around! This village of forty boutiques, which opened in the fall of 1995, was the brainchild of an American businessman. Its neat, organized setup instantly puts most shoppers at ease, and of course, when shoppers feel safe and secure they feel ready to buy. Spoiling babies and children poses no problem here in the company of top selling French brands **Naf Naf**, **Chevignon Kids**, **Catimimi**, and the oh-so-adorable **Petit Bateau**. **Kenzo**, **Ted Lapidus**, **Bally**, and would you believe **Polo Ralph Lauren** vie for attention among the clothing for adults. Discounts run as much as 40 percent off on mostly the previous year's collections at the majority of stores in this shopping plaza.

• **Marques Avenue**: 114 boulevard de Dijon, St-Julien/Troyes; tel.:
  03.25.82.39.19

Open Monday 2–7 P.M.; Tuesday–Friday 10 A.M.–7 P.M. and Saturday 9:30 A.M.–7 P.M.
• **Mc Arthur Glen**: Voie du Bois, 10150 Pont-Ste-Marie; tel.: 03.25.70.47.10
Open Monday 2–7 P.M.; Tuesday–Friday 10 A.M.–7 P.M. and 9:30 A.M.– 7 P.M.

Outside Troyes (Aube)

Soleil Verre

It may take some doing to locate this glass-making workshop, but if you have a penchant for colorful contemporary glass creations, it will be well worth your search. If you head east out of the city center toward Paris, look closely for the little roadway that leads you to this funky atelier. As you enter the dust and smoke-filled space, many of the works might look familar to you because certain Soleil Verre pieces sell for nearly double the price at stylish U.S. outposts such as Barneys. Here you can buy directly from any one of the four artists who you are apt to meet toiling away at their design tables. Prices range from 100F to 2,000F for decorative pieces in the form of bowls, plates, ashtrays, and cups—many of which have been limited to series of ten to twenty examples.

• 3 Chemin des Hauts-Cortins, 10000 Troyes; tel.: 03.25.76.19.77; fax: 03.25.76.19.78
No credit cards
Open Monday–Friday at varying hours

CORSICA
Corse

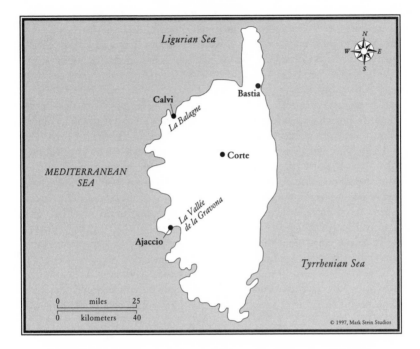

handcrafted knives • pottery • olive oil • chestnut cakes, cookies, and flour • *stylets* • wines • goat and ewe's milk cheeses • antique chestnut furnishings • alabaster busts of Napoleon • fig jam • regional landscape and seascape paintings • Cap Corse • confections of exotic fruits from the *maquis* • chestnut beer • Moorish music boxes • Corsican citterns • homemade sausages and hams • freshly colored engravings of old images • moving music • *muscat Corse* • books and posters

MY FIRST TRIP to Corsica took me to Bonifacio and Porto-Vecchio (and a few points in between), two tempered destinations on an island best known for its rugged spirit and jagged terrain. The beaches and seascapes along this southern tip stun visitors with their raw beauty; the water ripples with the brightest and purest of blues, signaling the renowned cleanliness of this part of the Mediterranean Sea. If you take a cruise around this spectacular coastline, you can count on being dazzled by an array of sumptuous villas whose owners include prominent French celebrities, controversial local politicos, and millionaires.

The setting is manageable and even rather gentrified until you climb into the mountains. Here you discover the real Corsica, the true *île de la beauté*, or the island of beauty, made up of about fifty summits, where the rural life takes you 50 to 100 years back in time. Historically, most Corsicans have lived in the mountains. Whether you find yourself creeping through the thick of the lush, green peaks or edging along barren coastal roads whose cliffs plummet spectacularly below to the Mediterranean, the views are nothing less than breathtaking.

The people, of course, typify Corsica just as much as the land. I descended upon this sprawling island just two days after a trip to Alsace. Physically, the people couldn't look any more dissimilar, although in terms of pride for their land, heritage, and culture, they struck me as astonishingly alike. After fighting off the Moors and the Genoese for centuries, it is not surprising that Corsicans tend to be virulent by nature. Many of them have continued to act out aggressively toward the French government, but it doesn't take long to realize that their main objective is to preserve their own identity. One of the most important components of their *identité corse* is *la langue corse*, a language with sounds not unlike those of Italian that you will hear spoken in rapid spitfire throughout the land.

The arts, crafts, and food products of Corsica have been influenced by the wild aspects of this island and the fiery nature of its people, a dynamic combination that makes shopping and touring in this region anything but dull.

Ajaccio (Corse-du-Sud)

Main shopping street: rue Bonaparte
Market: place due Marché
Tuesday–Sunday 8 A.M.–12:30 P.M.

Although Ajaccio does not serve as the best introduction to Corsica, with so many cruiseships and ferries disembarking in this busy port city, this is exactly where many visitors begin. I recommend you make this just a stopover on your way to the mountains or the coast. A few hours leaves you plenty of time to take in the two main sights in Ajaccio: the house where Napoleon was born and the cathedral where he was baptized. You don't have to be in Corsica or among the Corsicans for long to recall that Corsica is indeed the birthplace of Napoleon—and not where he was exiled (so many people confuse the two). Not only will you find yourself assailed by Napoleon memorabilia as soon as you step onto the streets of Ajaccio, but as you look around, you also can't help but notice that the physique and attitude of many a Corsican man bear an almost startling resemblance to that of France's greatest leader.

A visit to **La Maison Bonaparte** is a must, not so much for what you'll see inside but for the been-there, seen-that value that you derive from it. As I trudged up the tiny street that leads to the house just off the rue Bonaparte, I was amazed by the amount of footage that an American tourist was taking up on his Camcorder just to capture the indisputably plain façade. You'd think that he was filming the hundreds of statues on the front of Notre Dame! The mini-boutique inside showcases some souvenir items of a far better quality than what you encounter on the street. Playing cards, puzzles, books, and china emblazoned with the Emperor's bust keep very high-tech company with a CD-ROM that stars Napoleon in a multimedia presentation.

Step into the honey-colored cathedral just up the street to experience a few contemplative moments away from the fray. The cathedral's exquisite trompe l'oeil frescoes make stopping in Ajaccio all the more worthwhile. A couple of *antiquaires* have set up shop around the cathedral, but the really good stuff is back down on the rue Bonaparte. Be careful if you buy, however, because prices tend to run higher than those on the Continent, particularly since most of the goods originated there. Stick with the local offerings, such as a painting of Bonifacio or an unusual *objet corse*. Two stunning addresses to visit are **Arte e Oprara** (16 rue Bonaparte; tel.: 04.95.21.22.54) and the highly decorative collection of **Marie France Maudrux-Miniconi** (23 rue Bonaparte; tel.: 04.95.21.20.00), a dealer who also has a stand at the Village Suisse in Paris. A Corsican version of the rue Bonaparte in Paris, the rest of the street buzzes with several smart and up-to-the-minute fashion boutiques for women.

The bookstore/gallery **La Marge** (4 rue Emmanuel Arène; tel.: 04.95.21.53.01; fax: 04.95.21.57.21) displays many other sides of Corsica through books, posters, maps, and music. Napoleon titles reign supreme, but don't overlook all of the beautiful coffee-table books as well as one of the bestsellers for the anglophone market, *Granite Island*, a history of Corsica recounted by Englishwoman Dorothy Carrington. For music, you can't beat the throaty, heartfelt songs of I Muvrini, one of the best-loved groups of the island.

Bastia (Haute-Corse)

Main shopping streets: boulevard Paoli, rue Napoléon,
rue César-Campinchi
Market: place de l'Hôtel-de-Ville

Saturday and Sunday 7 A.M.–1 P.M.
Flea market: place St-Nicolas
Sunday 8 A.M.–1 P.M.

The Citadelle marks a good starting point for your tour around Bastia. You're likely to feel closest to the Mediterranean within the tight network of streets in this old quarter. By Mediterranean, I'm not necessarily referring to the sea, but rather to a whole ambiance, a feeling in the air, a look that instantly connotes an otherworldly charm in what lies before you. Bastia is said to be the most Italian of all of the Corsican cities, and this, along with the Tuscan-colored, stucco houses along the port, must partly explain the profoundly warm connection that many travelers feel with this city. Lunch or dinner at the restaurant, **A Casarella** (Stretta di a Santa Croce citadella; tel.: 04.95.32.02.32), reinforces these sentiments even more. I can't think of any better way to take refuge from the beating midday sun than to sit in the cool, pastel-colored interior of this centuries-old house while feasting on the freshly grilled catch of the day with a chilled glass of Patrimonio, a fine white Corsican wine.

If you are still interested in boutique browsing, find your way to the other side of town. If you decide to walk, you'll pass through the oldest (and ugliest) part of Bastia behind the old port. If you're interested in fine Corsican craftsmanship, or more specifically a sort of dagger called a *stylet*, duck in to see the highly skilled *artisan* **Joseph Antonini** on the tiny rue Droite (tel.: 04.95.32.16.71).

As I was walking on the back streets toward the new port I stumbled upon **Antiquités** at 15 rue Napoléon (tel.: 04.95.31.54.62), a lovely little antique shop owned by veteran antique dealer Claude Taccola. I told Monsieur Taccola that I was most interested in hearing about his regional pieces, so we focused on some eighteenth-century Corsican furnishings in chestnut, of which the most beautiful typically come from churches. The shop has many fine engravings, lithographs, and oil paintings of Corsican people and scenes, and readily handles shipping abroad.

If you're more interested in regional food items, the **U Montagnolu** (15 rue César-Campinchi; tel.: 04.95.32.78.04) is filled with the products of this land: Corsican hams, sausages, and cheeses. This small, inviting shop also has a fine selection of Corsican wines, honeys, jams, and even a highly regarded, regionally made moisturizer called Oliambru. For true devotees, the store frequently mails its products throughout Europe.

Just across from the cruise ships on the expansive place St-Nicholas, the **Cap Corse Mattei** emporium is hard to miss. This is the kind of selling space that instantly launches me into dreamland; there's something about a turn-of-the-century colonial décor resplendent with red lacquered display cases, cool white walls, potted palms, and creaky wooden flooring that makes me feel as though I'm in an exotic land. What exactly is Cap Corse? Most frequently served as an apéritif, it's a wine made from oranges; the red is the most popular kind, and in several different vintages progressing up to ten years. The name refers to the fingerlike projection of the island just north of Bastia.

As you can tell, the shopping scene in Bastia is plentiful, and as you take it all in, be sure to go a bit farther north to 2 avenue Emile-Sari to the boutique **Giramondu** (tel.: 04.95.32.50.49), one of the *grand spécialiste* of Corsican pottery. See Corte description, page 109.

Calvi and La Balagne (Haute-Corse)

Travelers from Britain and artists from many regions began to flock to the port city of Calvi and its environs, La Balagne, toward the beginning of the twentieth century for its pleasant climate and easy access. The port activity has not been built up nearly as much as that of Ajaccio or Bastia, and consequently Calvi has remained an alluring seaside town. Even if you're just passing through, stop for a drink or a coffee in one of the little cafés facing the Mediterranean. The town has few shops, but two excellent sources of regional food products are **A Casetta** at 16 rue Clemenceau (tel.: 04.95.65.32.15) and **Histoire Simple**, situated just across from the Citadelle.

Conveniently located just outside of Calvi, **La Signoria** (tel.: 04.95.65.23.73; fax: 04.95.65.38.77) could easily serve as your base for a few days' stay because there are so many excursions to take from here. The only trouble is that you might feel so comfortable within the peaceful and luxurious surroundings of this three-star hotel that you won't want to leave. The dining room, which features the innovative talents of chef Christian Sirurguet, may keep you equally enthralled, and if you become hooked on the delectable selection of local cheeses, served with fig jam and a glass of Grappa, then you're likely to become *un habitué*!

La Balagne encompasses a pastel-colored collage of typical Corsican villages, many of which sit perched on the hillsides high above the sea. During much of the year, parts of the craggy landscape shimmer silvery green from the leaves of the olive trees that served as the main source of revenue for the region. Although the olive oil trade petered out toward the early 1900s, in recent years there has been a concerted effort to revive this tradition. Untouched by frostbite, some of the trees are more than 1,000 years old. Their shade provides the perfect setting for the olive festival that takes place just outside of the little village of Montemaggiore every year toward the end of July.

If you're hungry for a no-frills, Corsican meal in Montemaggiore, **Chez Françoise** (tel.: 04.95.62.81.02), in the center of the village, is a favorite among the locals. Heading toward Lunghignano on the curvy D451 beyond

Montemaggiore, a folkloric experience awaits you at the hundred-year-old olive oil mill, **U Fragnu** (tel.: 04.95.62.75.51). About once every two weeks from April to June, a sweet little donkey obediently turns around and around to crush the black olives from U Fragnu's own harvest. This olive-oil making *à l'ancienne* also plays year-round on the shop's video, and if you listen carefully, you may even hear the donkey crying ee-o-ee-o in the neighboring fields. Since U Fragnu eeks out only a limited quantity of olive oil, the goods at the shop consist mainly of oils from other mills as well as honeys, jams, and wines from all over Corsica.

For regional products displayed in a truly spectacular setting, go directly to **Domaine Orsini** (tel.: 04.95.62.81.01; fax: 04.95.62.79.70), a 150-year-old estate overlooking the valley just off of the D151, outside of the village of Calenzana. Here you might be greeted by Monsieur Orsini himself, a true Corsican who reminded me of the young Marlon Brando. Two large vaulted cellars serve as tasting rooms for the wines, liqueurs, and *eaux-de-vie* produced on the Orsini domain. Each space has been tastefully and impeccably decorated in a California sort of way with cushiony, caramel-colored seating and stylish accents of local craftsmen's works.

Pigna tops the list of Balagne villages, both for its towering height above the Mediterranean and for the quality of its arts and crafts. Its unspoiled setting offers an additional bonus, and I felt relieved for its fifty inhabitants that the tourists were limited to a respectful few. Insufficient road signs must help their cause. As you follow the ceramic plaques throughout this tiny village, you'll find the ateliers and showplaces of several different craftspeople including that of **Marie-Claire Darneal** (tel.: 04.95.61.77.34; fax: 04.95.61.77.81), who creates colorful music boxes with the Moorish influences of Corsica, as well as that of **Ugo Casalonga** (tel.: 04.95.61.79.18; fax: 04.95.61.77.81), a violin-maker who handcrafts Corsican *ceteres*, a sort of cittern, the essential instrument behind the traditional music of the island. Jacky Quilichini's little shop, **Ceramica di Pigna** (tel.: 04.95.61.77.25; fax: 04.95.61.77.25), charmed me with its mustard yellow and seawater-blue pieces of handmade pottery, all minimally decorated with locally inspired designs of fish, grapes, olives, chestnuts, and goats' heads.

Works of an entirely different theme and medium quietly beg for attention next door at **Atelier de Taille-Douce** (tel.: 04.95.61.77.08). Gilles Casalonga has been printing in the old method with zinc and copper plates for over twenty years, and today his works represent more modern versions of sixteenth to nineteenth-century engravings. The fresher, more amusing look comes with the use of color on white paper; a sixteenth-century map of Corsica in sun yellow or a cherry-red view of Pascal Paoli (a great Corsican leader revered here far more than Napoleon) instantly brighten images that otherwise might have become dust collectors in the attic. Prices range from 80F to 300F per print, and it's easy to pick up a few to compose a colorful grouping for any type of interior, whether modern or traditional.

I stopped into **Casa Musicale** (tel.: 04.95.61.77.81; fax: 04.95.61.74.28) for a simple lunch of *soupe Corse* (similar to minestrone) and regional cheeses, and ended up being serenaded by nearby customers who repeatedly broke into song. Concert presentations upstairs take on a more formal approach, but in any case, if you like music you'll love Casa Musicale. Depending on the weather outside, the old olive mill interior alternates between cozy and cool; the terrace is perfect for sunseekers by day and those looking to wish on a shooting star by night. The basic yet freshly decorated rooms are almost too much of a scoop for the average tourist—particularly the Sulana, which has its own private patio complete with a panoramic view of the Mediterranean.

Corte (Haute-Corse)

Locked within the heart of the island, there's no way around it—you have to drive along a treacherous mountain road to reach Corte. Once there, however, you'll discover an ambiance quite unlike that of the other major Corsican cities. Most of the animation at Corte comes from students rather than tourists. The government's efforts to revitalize this once primarily pastoral community did not stop with *l'université* Pascal Paoli, either, because they chose the Citadelle of Corte as the site for the **Musée de la Corse**, a newly opened museum devoted to the history and traditions of the Corsican people.

Almost right next door at the place Gaffory in this old section of town, it's hard to miss the colorful tile and sponge-painted façade of **Terraghja** (tel.: 04.95.46.10.17), one of the best places in Corsica to buy the much loved pottery of F. F. Griffi. I say "one of" because the boutique, Giramondu, in Bastia, also showcases this collection of vividly colored ceramics whose dynamic designs and heavy-handed glazes are a veritable metaphor for the rebellious spirit of the Corsican people. Both beautiful and utilitarian, the pottery is honestly priced, particularly the larger pieces. About 500F will buy you a magnificent vase large enough to make a statement yet small enough to cart home!

If you walk out of the boutique and down to the right, you'll find yourself in front of Corsica's most celebrated grocery store, **Epicérie du Vieux Marché**. I had seen postcards of the fully stocked interior of this traditional Corsican *epicérie* before being escorted here by Monsieur Griffi. The pungent smells of fresh cheeses and aged sausages nearly overwhelmed me with memories of the little Italian food shop that I often went to as a child. Clad entirely in black in the true Mediterranean tradition, even the *mama* who helps to serve the customers along with her son, Jean-Marie Ghionga, looks as Italian as my ancestors, but like most of what is sold in every little nook and cranny of this shop, she is Corsican through and through. A gold mine of Corsican food products such as olive oil, chestnut cakes and flour, hard candies made with exotic fruits from the *maquis*, wines, liqueurs, and much more share shelf space with more familiar-looking sundries—all just as vital to daily Corsican life as the rest!

La Vallée de la Gravona (Corse-du-Sud)

I don't recall seeing any signs guiding me to *la vallée de la Gravona*, but then again, that's not at all unusual for Corsica. On your map you should see the Gravode river just northeast of Ajaccio. I'm taking you to its valley and then up the hillsides to experience life in the Corsican hinterlands—*la vraie vie corse!* From Ajaccio, take the N193 toward Corte (remember, don't look for road signs—just ask yourself if this looks like a main road). The first stop is **Didier Raffalli**, a *berger/fromager* (shepherd/cheese maker) located in the little community of Sarrola Carcopino on the D161 at the intersection of N193. If you come by here around noon, it's hard to miss this little establishment: although there aren't any signs, you'll see the locals stopping by for a fresh helping of *brocciu*, the most common Corsican cheese, similar to ricotta). And fresh it is: Didier wakes up every morning by 5 A.M. to milk his more than 150 ewes, then makes his cheese in time for the lunch-hour rush. If the earthy *brocciu* does not appeal to you, try Didier's other cheese that has been aged for about a month, giving it a less milky taste and texture.

Driving up the D1 to the tiny mountain village of Cutuli-Curtichjatu can be somewhat harrowing, especially if you've just arrived in Corsica. You might have the feeling that you have landed in a place where no man has traveled before, but rest assured: some of the products from this tiny village have gained recognition as far away as Paris and beyond. The renowned Parisian chef Guy Savoy bestowed **Jerome Pierlovisi** with his full approval after having tasted his homemade *charcuterie* (mostly hams and sausages). Jerôme raises his owns pigs (which are apt to cross your path on the roadway), and, dare I say, executes everything from start to finish. His personal touch may be the secret to the rich, aromatic flavor of these highly reputed pork products. To visit, ask for Jerôme (Casa a Torra) in the village or call ahead to 04.95.25.61.49 (tel. and fax).

Although you may also find him with a knife in hand, stopping in to see the cutler **Jean Biancucci** (tel./fax: 04.95.25.64.72) in the same village, is anything but a scary experience. Walking into this big, old, dusty atelier might make you feel as though you've stepped back into another era. Originally a cabinetmaker, Monsieur Biancucci devotes most of his time these days to carving the wooden handles of his traditional Corsican knives. His son works the forge out back, and together they give life to pieces that are not only beautiful to have and to hold, but that also become a near necessity for cutting *la charcuterie corse!* Prices range from 520F to 2,500F for these one-of-a-kind pocketknives whose forms are inspired by models originally made from goats' horns.

Almost halfway between Ajaccio and Corte, the village of Bucugnanu is considerably easier to find. Plan to pass by here around lunchtime to savor a typical Corsican meal of *charcuterie*, cannelloni, and sweetened *brocciu* at the *ferme auberge* **A Tanneda** (tel.: 04.95.27.42.44; fax: 04.95.27.40.33). *Bon appétit!*

THE CÔTE D'AZUR
La Côte d'Azur

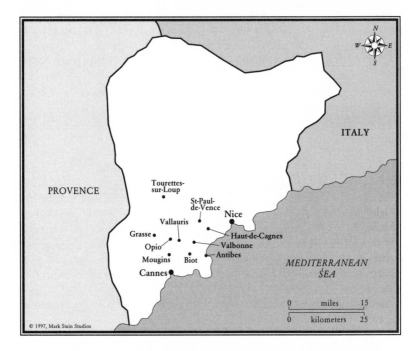

orange marmalade • olive oil • perfume • ceramics • *pétanque* balls
• antiques • weavings • olivewood bowls • herbs • rosewater • *fruits
confits* • handblown glass • Majolica • Provençal prints • pottery
• honey • bronze sculptures • *fleurs d'oranger* • art • leather bags
and jackets • pillows • table throws • jams • bedspreads • wine •
topiaries • ceramics signed by Picasso • pastis • artful posters

CALL IT LA *Côte d'Azur* if you can pronounce it with confidence. Otherwise,
everyone understands the Riviera just as well—even if you don't bother to
roll your Rs. When in doubt, just refer to it as the south of France and
people will conjure up Miami-esque images of palm trees swaying in the
breeze and beautiful people sunning on brightly colored *transats* (short for
transatlantiques, the kind of lounge chairs that were used on the cruise ships
that crossed the Atlantic before plastic chairs came into vogue).

Then comes the Mediterranean: if its deep blue waters don't intrigue you,
then the spectacular views of the rugged slopes above the sea most likely

112

will. The Côte d'Azur translates into fine cuisine, rich culture, and terrific shopping.

Sure, it was "the" place to vacation back in the 1950s, '60s, and '70s before people discovered the supposed allure of Ibiza, Positano, and St-Barts, but *la Côte* still has its place in the sun—even on grey days. If you are looking for a steady diet of R&R, you may be better off elsewhere because, as is the case with so many other areas of France, here there are countless things to see and do. The art offerings are fantastic—whether you're touring or buying; some of the best collections have found their final resting place in the region, and many of the galleries here receive international acclaim as well. Don't be discouraged, though, if you find that you have to wade through arts and crafts of inferior quality to find the good stuff. Well-directed searching only adds to the hunt!

Late spring or early fall are the absolute best times to come here if you're looking for good weather without the hordes of tourists. You'll find it a lot easier to get around during these seasons as well, which is important because the touring can involve a fair amount of driving both along the coastal highways and in the *arrière pays* or the so-called back country. The *villages perchés*, or perched villages, are enchantingly beautiful—particularly at the end of the day when the light turns the stone houses into warm, golden, sun-kissed loaves. These villages were built on hilltops during feudal times, and today many of them house quaint restaurants and shops for the pleasure of the visitors and residents alike. My favorite villages are Haut de Cagnes (mostly for the beauty of its château) and Mougins for the tony crowd that it attracts.

Antibes (Alpes-Maritimes)

Main shopping streets: rue Aubernon, rue Géorges-Clemenceau
Markets: Cours Masséna
Tuesday–Sunday 6 A.M.–1 P.M.; daily in summer
Flea market: place Audiberti
Thursdays and Saturdays 7 A.M.–6 P.M.

Antibes is probably best known for its *Jazz à Juan*, a musical "happening" that brings together international artists of the highest order every year during the second half of July. Started in the early 1960s, this event has become one of the most reputed jazz festivals in the world and certainly one of the highlights of the summer season in the Midi. Antibes also has gained worldwide recognition for its **Salon des Antiquaires**, one of the best assemblages of superior-quality antiques in all of Europe. This show takes place every spring, generally around Easter. Contact the tourism office (11 place Général-de-Gaulle; tel.: 04.92.90.53.00; fax 04.92.90.53.01) ahead to obtain specific dates.

The boutique browsing in old Antibes is the most fun, and the area around the place Audiberti is particularly plentiful in *brocantes* (far-from-high-end antiques). Many of these streets are reserved for pedestrians, so it's easy to poke around without the worry of colliding with a speedy Citroën. The rue James-Close houses some lovely little shops, including **Crème d'Olive** at number 29. At first glance you may think this is just a typical Provençal food shop, but in addition to a classic assortment of olives, olive oil, and *tapénade*, it stocks a variety of herb mixtures that have been specially prepared with the savory instincts of the owner, Monsieur Lagier. Whether you add them to pizza, pasta, or a simple *poisson*, these herbal accents will turn you into a Mediterranean cook in no time! Before you leave, be sure to pick up some *poivre aux roses*: although intended for cooking purposes, this pepper-and-rose combo is pretty enough to use as a kitchen potpourri.

If you like upmarket fashion boutiques, drive over to the neighboring Juan-les-Pins. Take the long way around by encircling the Cap d'Antibes for handsome views of prime real estate and majestic homes.

Gismondi

This is not the kind of place for casual browsers, but the welcome for me was far from frosty. Although I was not interested in spending six figures on an exquisite piece of seventeenth-century furniture, Suzanne, the salesperson (or should I say art technician?) was more than happy to speak with me about the gallery and the treasures that one expects to find here.

Monsieur Gismondi is originally from Antibes, and it is not surprising that he started the *Salon des Antiquaires* a number of years ago. Of course, many people who reside on the Cap sometimes buy from Gismondi, but his reputation far exceeds the Riviera. Connoisseurs call from all over the world to purchase pieces of museum quality. The gallery is most known for *marqueterie* (inlaid) Boulle pieces as well as for seventeenth-century cabinets. As is the case with works of such high artistic brilliance, each one has its own story to tell.

- Les Remparts, 06600 Antibes; tel.: 04.93.34.06.67; fax: 04.93.34.35.84
  Open Monday–Saturday 9:30 A.M.–12:30 P.M. and 2:30–6:30 P.M.

Biot (Alpes-Maritimes)

La Verrerie de Biot

The first thing to learn is how to correctly pronounce the name of this quaint little village. There are already so many tourists here that you don't want to sound like even more of an *idiote* (rhymes with Biot) by not getting the name right. Try *bee-ut* (*ut* as in utterly), but say it fast so that both syllables glide into one.

Do not (and I repeat, do not) visit Biot in August. I was lucky to visit Biot at two very different times. The first time was indeed in the heat of the summer; the second was in early fall during a torrential downpour. I will take being drenched to the bone any day to being engulfed by masses of pushy tourists clad in little more than clingy shorts, skintight T-shirts, and rubbery thongs. Call me a snob but I really am a firm believer in seeing goods in the right context.

I had heard about the artisanally made glassware of Biot long before I visited the town's large glass-making complex, but I didn't really appreciate the chic that these fine products possess until I saw them as part of a handsomely set table at a stylish garden party in St-Tropez. What seemed highly sophisticated to me at the time was in fact a typical gathering of *le beau monde de St-Tropez*. The tables were draped in canvaslike tablecloths of a thick blue and white stripe that offset the pretty Provençal pottery in a way that totally embodied the uniqueness of St-Tropez—that of a mix between the Côte d'Azur and Provence. And certainly the focal point of each table was the thick-rimmed, bubble-filled glassware of Biot that simply, yet distinctly, spoke of a rare marriage between elegance and rusticity.

• Chemin des Combes, 06410 Biot; tel.: 04.93.65.03.00; fax:
  04.93.65.00.56
  Open Monday 2–6:30 P.M. and Tuesday–Saturday 9 A.M.–6:30 P.M.
  (until 7:30 P.M. during July and August); Sunday and holidays 10 A.M.–
  1 P.M. and 2:30–6:30 P.M.; closed December 25 and January 1

Galerie des Arcades

This bar/restaurant/hotel/art gallery is a must! The Biot glassware center is at the base of the village, but the Galerie des Arcades gives you another good reason to visit this picturesque small town. The place des Arcades is in itself a work of art, and every facet of the Galerie des Arcades catapults you into the contemporary art world of the Côte d'Azur. You can buy here (ask to see the adjacent and lower galleries), dine here, sleep here in a theateresque décor, or just have a drink on the terrace (in the same place as where the negotiations took place for the sale of Duchamp's *Nude Descending the Staircase*)—but whatever you do, be sure to absorb as much art as time will permit.

• 16 place des Arcades, 06410 Biot; tel.: 04.93.65.01.04; fax:
  04.93.65.01.45

> Hotel/Restaurant/Boutique: Inexpensive–Moderate
> Open daily except Monday all day and Sunday evening

Around Biot (Alpes-Maritimes)

Fenouil

In my travels I discovered that Majolica, both old and new, seems to be a favorite among many people on the Riviera. Decidedly it must be that tie to the Mediterranean via the ceramics of the greatest Majolica-producing countries: Spain, France, and Italy. Here you can expect to discover one of the finest and most carefully honed collections of *barbotines* in all of the country. The owner, Sophie Lehr, is *une passionné* and her collection of Majolica reflects her expertise for the old and the new.

• Au Golfe de Biot, 06410 Biot; tel.: 04.93.65.09.46
  Best to call ahead.

Mougins (Alpes-Maritimes)

Les Boutiques du Moulin

For most discriminating travelers, the restaurant Le Moulin de Mougins needs no introduction. It is certainly considered one of the finest in the south of France, and whether this is due to proximity or fame (or a little of both), its association with stars and thus the Cannes Film Festival is renowned.

Much has been said about Roger Vergé, but, as is usually the case in France, behind every prominent chef lies a very influential woman. It's clear that Madame Vergé is most definitely a woman of taste. Her shop, La Boutique du Moulin (the other boutique refers to the wine cellar) is a reflection of her likes and loves.

Madame Vergé told me, for example, that "writing is always present in my life," so it is not surprising that amidst her collection of *objets* and fine table accessories one might uncover a choice selection of writing paper and guest books as well. You also will find the same service of Haviland china as was made exclusively for the restaurant, in addition to countless jars of jams and mustards—all of which bear the Moulin de Mougins label. The real treat here, however, lies in the small yet highly ecclectic mix of items—whether antique or not—that have obviously caught the fancy of style-setter Denise Vergé.

• 06250 Mougins; tel.: 04.93.75.78.24; fax: 04.93.90.18.55
  Open daily 9 A.M.–8 P.M.

Cannes (Alpes-Maritimes)

Main shopping streets: boulevard de La Croisette,
rue d'Antibes, rue des Etats-Unis, rue Meynadier
Markets: Marché Forville
Open daily 5 A.M.–1 P.M.

The shopping in Cannes is worthy of star billing. The big name stores on the Croisette are lined up as prominently as the parade of shiny new luxury cars that slither around this resort town. **Chanel, Dior, Nina Ricci, Hermès, Jean Louis Scherrer, Van Cleef & Arpels**, and many, many more showcase boutiques reign here in great force. The population in Cannes triples during the Film Festival, and with all of the other important events that are held here throughout the year, the city draws lots of visitors with time (and obviously a bit of money) on their hands.

A mall called **Les Boutiques de Gray Street** or **Le Gray d'Albion** connects the rue d'Antibes to La Croisette (officially, boulevard de la Croisette) and houses a slew of prominent boutiques such as **Façonnable, Stéphane Kélian**, and **Chantal Thomass**. The **Souleiado** boutique here is one of the most attractive in all of the south of France.

If you are weak by now from all of this shopping, stop in to **Maiffret** (31 rue d'Antibes) for a quick pick-me-up in the form of a buttery caramel chocolate (eat it all in one bite so the liquid caramel does not drip down your chin). If you are feeling more haggard than *gourmand*, consider having yourself coiffed at **Jean Louis David** (21 rue des États-Unis), the official *coiffeur des stars*.

If you are looking for a simpler way of life with considerably less "glam," head over to Le Suquet, the old part of town where you can lose yourself in the labyrinth of streets. The antique shop **Le Passé Simple** (76 rue Meynadier) presents an enormous collection of traditional knickknacks from the simple past that could keep your eyes dancing for hours.

Cannolive

The little street where you'll find this delightful *épicerie* might not even appear on your map, but the rue Meynadier actually leads right into it (just across from the train station). Plan on stopping here on your way to or from the Suquet, particularly if you don't head out until the afternoon, when the Marché Forville is closed. Cannnolive offers an extensive selection of popular Provençal products such as olive oil, lavender, and honey.

Don't miss their bittersweet, citrus fruit jams from the neighboring town of Vallauris, which rival the thick-cut English marmalades. Their stock of regional wines is also impressive, as is the apéritif pastis. Instead of settling for a run-of-the-mill brand, I suggest you choose one from Henri Bardouin–

all are artisanally made and quite aromatic (various mixtures of Provençal herbs have been added to enhance the already distinctive anise flavor). Prices run about 100F per bottle.

• 16 rue Vénizelos, 06400 Cannes; tel.: 04.93.39.08.19
   Open 8 A.M.–noon and 2:30–7 P.M.

Double V

I have often been accused of being "the queen of ambiance," so it is no wonder I felt an instant attraction toward this boutique. The window display grabbed me first—an eclectic mix of antique furniture and *objects d'art* positioned rather incongruously alongside the shop's fashions for women. This is an unusual juxtaposition for a town like Cannes, where most stores portray a very streamlined appearance instead of spinning off into the uncertain land of the original.

Madame Danel is the *tour de force* behind this unusual sales approach, and she coyly admitted that although she mostly enjoys flaunting furs, exotic evening attire, and other assorted titillating frocks, she sells antiques here as well—mainly to attract the men (surprisingly enough!).

It really is fun to look around here because the contrasts are indeed so strong. Just imagine some of the most turned-out women of Cannes rifling through racks of bargain basement-priced clothing (much of it is second-hand) and fighting over finds like this season's Thierry Mugler suit (originally marked at 18,000F but sold here for a third the price) as the melodious tunes of *Radio Nostalgie* and the heady scent of incense fill the air.

• Galerie du Gray d'Abion, 17 boulevard de La Croisette, 06400 Cannes;
   tel.: 04.93.99.78.29
   Open Monday–Saturday 10 A.M.–7:30 P.M.

Mis en Demeure

If you do not have the good fortune to be invited to someone's villa on the Riviera, then you have one more reason to stop in and absorb the many home décor ideas presented in this handsome store. Jean Loup Daraux is the design genius behind Mise en Demeure, and in addition to these two shops in Cannes he also has a showcase on the Left Bank in Paris. Monsieur Daraux's own creations, which consist largely of fabrics, furniture, and table linens, are featured in his shops, along with a very rich collection of English, Spanish, and Italian textiles. In fact, Monsieur Daraux promotes a whole *style de vivre* that might best be described as part Ralph Lauren *à la française*, part *provençal sophistiqué*, all with a dash of English spirit—just enough to assure comfy chairs and heartwarming motifs.

• Gray d'Albion, 17 boulevard de la Croisette, 06400 Cannes; tel:
  04.92.99.22.80; fax: 04.92.99.22.94
  Other address: rue des Etats-Unis
  Open Monday 2:30–7:15 P.M.; Tuesday–Saturday 9:30 A.M.–12:15 P.M.
  and 2:30–7:15 P.M.

Owo

I stumbled upon this shop by accident, which is sometimes how I make my
best discoveries. Claudie Tosi has been arranging dried flowers for over ten
years, and she recently began to work with a different type of preserved
flower called *fleur stabilisée*. The result is magnificent because the flowers and
greenery have been treated so that they maintain their original color and
much of their lifelike texture.

These real, preserved flowers look almost freshly cut, and apparently the
color lasts about two years before it begins to fade. Nearly all of the blooms
come from the surrounding region, and Madame Tosi has a true talent for
arranging them into adorable compositions of varying sizes. My favorite was
the standing nosegay bouquet made of elegant roses and deep forest green
leaves (priced at 60F; larger ones sell for 90F and 180F).

I later saw nearly the same arrangements, this time designed by Parisian

---

La Palme d'Or

If you really want to feel like a star in Cannes, try doing something spectacular like dining at La Palme d'Or. Sure, you can
stroll along La Croisette or even have a drink at the Carlton,
but if you want to feel otherworldly, you should experience the
finest restaurant in town. Whether you choose to bask in the
sun on the terrace or sit ensconced in the handsome Art Deco
décor of the dining room, your eyes will be drawn to the pen-
etrating blue green of the Mediterranean, interrupted only by a
few yachts on its horizon. This breathtaking view will transfix
you only until your meal arrives to compete for your full attention. Incidentally, La Palme d'Or is not named for the golden
palm trees on the Croisette, but instead for the prize awarded
annually to the top-ranking flick of *le festival*!

• Hôtel Martinez, 73 La Croisette, 06406 Cannes; tel.:
    04.92.98.74.14; fax: 02.93.39.67.82
  Restaurant/Hotel: Very Expensive
  Open daily except Monday (full day) and Tuesday lunch

florist Christian Tortu, selling for more than double these prices at certain locations in Provence, Paris, and New York!

• 7 rue Lafontaine, 06400 Cannes; tel.: 04.93.99.04.25
  Open daily 9:30 A.M.–12:15 P.M. and 2:45–7 P.M. except Monday in October and November and holidays

---

First Class

Since I once ran a shopping service in Paris that focused on off-the-beaten-path boutiques and behind-the-scenes visits at the big-name stores, I developed an instant appreciation for First Class and its wide range of services. If you are looking to be shown around town or have an unusual request to be filled, try contacting Philip Brest, a charming man who is certainly well-connected in Cannes. Their fees range from 700F for a half day to 1,100F for a full day, without transportation.

• Résidence Cannes 2000, 29 boulevard Ferrage, 06414 Cannes; tel.: 04.93.99.26.26; fax: 04.93.99.77.88
  All-around service provider

Grasse (Alpes-Maritimes)

Market: place aux Aires Tuesday–Sunday 8 A.M.–noon
Flea Market: place aux Herbes Wednesday 8 A.M.–noon

Grasse: the name itself evokes endless fields of fragrantful lavender, roses, and orange blossoms. It is said that the jasmin in Grasse still is picked entirely by hand in the wee hours of the morning when the flower is at its fullest and freshest. Although more and more extracts and essences are produced in the far-off corners of the world where high costs of labor are not an issue, it is no secret that most of the world's best-loved fragrances are in fact concocted in laboratories outside of Paris by skilled technicians who take orders only from "the nose" (the person who actually creates the perfume). These highly complex compositions currently tend to consist more of synthetically made essences than of natural ones. This further explains why Grasse does not have the importance that it once did for the perfume industry of France, and from a shopper's point of view there is not much to buy, so don't come here with great expectations. Instead, come to learn about the *history*, which can best be experienced and retraced in a visit to the **Musée International de la Parfumerie** and the adjacent **Musée Frago-**

nard—both in the center of town. Plan to spend a half day here and you'll walk away with an entirely different concept of fragrances and their origins. Care for a perfumed glove, anyone?

Haut-de-Cagnes (Alpes-Maritimes)

Terraïo

I first came to the medieval village of Haut-de-Cagnes over ten years ago to visit friends, and our friendship has given me reason to return somewhat regularly ever since. Each time that we head up to the village along the same old winding streets, I am always grateful to make it through without a scrape.

The last time I was there I paid even closer attention to my surroundings because it was the first time that I had to both navigate and drive by myself. This familiar roller-coaster ride took on a new perspective, and this time my eyes focused even more on the richly lighted storefront of Terraio, an exclusive-looking shop just across from the château. I had passed it countless times before, but never had entered. I asked my friends about it, and after visiting the shop, I quickly concluded that I now had two good reasons to visit Haut-de-Cagnes: to see my dear friends and to admire the exquisitely made pottery of Terraïo.

Terraïo is the name of the shop, but the master behind all of these works is a humble man named Claude Barnoin. Unlike many of the other inhabitants of this picturesque village, Monsieur Barnoin is a native of Haut-de-Cagnes, and thus it is not surprising that his pottery is created in a true Mediterranean spirit. With the exception of a few bluish-white pieces, nearly all of the works here are of the richest azurite blue. The forms are simple, classic, and mostly rather large. Although Monsieur Barnoin has created entire place settings for a few very privileged people (traveling royalty and the like), most clients content themselves with one or two magnificent bowls or platters. Prices range from 250F to 4,000F.

• 12 place du Docteur-Maurel, 06800 Haut-de-Cagnes; tel.: 04.93.20.86.83
Open daily in the afternoon

Nice (Alpes-Maritimes)

Main shopping streets: avenue Jean-Médecin, rue de France, rue Masséna
Markets: Marché aux Fleurs/Cours Saleya
Tuesday–Sunday 7 A.M.–1 P.M.
Flea market: Marché aux Fleurs/Cours Saleya
Monday 7 A.M.–1 P.M.

I have never come to Nice to spend time on the beach—there's just too much to do here. Start out early in the morning and visit the **Marché aux Fleurs**. They sell a lot more than just flowers. Be sure to try one of the *specialités niçoises*, *la socca*, a big pancake made with chickpea flower and olive oil. The ones from the market stand of **Chez Thérèsa** are the best—particularly if you like ample dashes of pepper.

To continue in the spirit of local color, head in toward *le vieux Nice*, the oldest and most beguiling part of town. The shops here are on a more intimate scale than those in the newer section of the city; one such example is **St-Réparate-Provence** (next to the cathedral of the same name), which sells traditional Provençal fashions for women alongside classic Austrian boiled-wool jackets by Geiger.

The possibilities for antiquing in Nice are numerous. If you have a considerable budget, stroll down the promenade des Anglais to the **Galerie des Antiquaires** at number 7 (closed Sundays and Mondays), where about thirty dealers sell upmarket pieces. While you're here, go around the corner to the **Galerie Ferreo** at 2 rue du Congrès to admire works by France's foremost contemporary artists, including César, Arman, and Ben.

The area across from the port, called **Les Puces de Nice** (open all day except Sunday and Monday), is more fun and within most peoples' budgets. From here walk up the rue Catherine-Ségurane to the rue Antoine-Gauthier and the rue Emmanuel-Philibert for more antique hunting and browsing.

Just one more shopping tip for Nice: the city has some very fine modern art museums such as the **Musée Matisse** and the **Musée Chagall**, and you can always raid their gift shops for more art-oriented souvenirs!

Aliziari

Lesson Number 1: Never buy olive oil without tasting it. If you hang around here long enough, and particularly if you have the opportunity to talk with Monsieur Draut, the owner of this venerable house, you will learn a lot about olive oil and its wonderous properties. And in case you didn't know, it is best to cleanse your palate first with a slice of apple before tasting the oil.

The walls of this old establishment (circa 1930) appear to have been built around the three huge metal vats that face you as you enter the shop. These cylinders are not here just for decoration, because they serve as a sort of olive oil filling station for regular customers who faithfully make the trek here, armed with containers of varying sizes and shapes, in quest of their weekly supply. You can choose from two types of olive oil, both of which are *1er pression à froid* (first cold-pressed and unfiltered) and made at the store's nineteenth century mill in the center of Nice. Although the *vierge extra* (much like a *tête de cuvée*) is considered to be the finest, the fruitiest, and the smoothest, whether it is the best really is a question of personal preference. The *vierge fine* is robust and more bitter, but many people savor it for its distinctive flavor.

The olive oil tasted delicious, but I was even more thrilled about the shop's old-fashioned metal canisters painted in exaggerated hues of Mediterranean blues and Provençal greens and yellows. They come in a range of shapes and sizes, and also look handsome in the kitchen back home.

The range of inexpensive regional gift ideas is vast. In addition to local speciality foodstuffs, you will also discover a realm of bath and beauty products, including soothing waters made from roses and bachelor buttons as well as soaps and creams made with olive oil.

- 14 rue St-François-de-Paule, 06300 Nice; tel.: 04.93.85.76.92
  Open Tuesday–Saturday 8:15 A.M.–12:30 P.M. and 2:15–7:15 P.M.

Auer

Like Alziari, the Maison Auer is conveniently located on the rue St-Francois-de-Paule, the pedestrian street that leads into the marketplace at the Cours Saleya. And also like Alziari, Auer will seduce you with the authenticity of its décor. Its rich Rococco embellishments have not changed much in the past 170 years, and the creamy lacquered *presentoirs* still serve as luxurious showcases for the house's fine selection of sweets.

Auer is most known for its *fruits confits*, or candied fruit, and I was told that this is the last place in France to make them on the premises. I had the pleasure of visiting the *laboratoire* behind the store and was tremendously impressed not only with the beauty of the copper cauldrons, but also with the time-consuming labor required for each step of the sugaring process. Monsieur Thierry Auer emphasized that the freshness of the fruit is also of the utmost importance. The result is divine, and if you have never indulged in *fruits confits*, you must try them here. Although they are full of sugar they don't taste too sweet. They also travel well and keep for months.

For a unique treat, pick up a jar of *confiture de fruits confits* (jam made from candied fruit), 35F worth of scrumptious pleasure. Chocolate lovers, don't despair—Auer can provide a fix for you, too.

- 7 rue St-François-de-Paule, 06300 Nice; tel.: 04.93.85.77.98;
  fax: 04.93.62.07.17
  Open Tuesday–Sunday 8 A.M.–12:30 P.M. and 2:30–7 P.M.

G. Poilpot

If you don't have time to go to Grasse, this is the next best thing. Actually, in all of Grasse I did not find a shop that reeked (literally) with as much Old World charm as this one. As Monsieur Poilpot explained, it is in *le vieux style*, quite appropriate for *le vieux Nice* and certainly a refreshing change from the polished perfume emporiums throughout the world.

Most of the Poilpot fragrance collection is contained within the hundreds of small vials displayed on tables outside the shop. There are about eighty compositions in all, made of both natural and synthetic essences from Grasse. Trust your nose and don't judge them by the names (the one called "Jogging," for example, happens to smell like Chanel No. 19). The more you sniff around, the more you are apt to find some favorite and familar fragrances.

What you lose in the packaging, you gain in the pricing. Most of the vials cost about 15F. If you are more interested in achieving a certain look for your bathroom, check out the tall one-liter glass bottles inside. I found that the jewel-like colors of the toilet waters set off the medicinal-looking bottles' appearance quite handsomely.

• 10 rue St-Gaëtan; 06300 Nice; tel.: 04.93.85.60.77
  Open Tuesday–Saturday 9:30 A.M.–noon and 2:30–6:30 P.M.; closed first two weeks of November.

Salon de Thé Auer

In nearly every town I visit I ask about the tea salons. They are harder to find in the provinces than in Paris, and the possibility of finding them on the Côte d'Azur is practically nil, so you can imagine my delight when I spotted this demure *salon de thé* toward the back of the Maison Auer. It has everything one expects from a tearoom: an elegant and traditional setting away from the hustle and bustle of the street; and of course a refined selection of teas and sweets. Breakfast is quite delicious here as well!

• 7 rue St-François-de-Paule, 06300 Nice; tel.: 04.93.85.77.98; fax: 04.93.62.07.17
  Tea Salon: Inexpensive–Moderate
  Open Tuesday–Saturday 8 A.M.–noon and 2:30–7 P.M.

Opio (Alpes-Maritimes)

Moulins de la Brague Huilerie d'Opio

If you do find yourself heading off to Grasse, plan to make a stop at this old olive mill (est. 1848). You will have a different experience here than at Alziari in Nice. First, at this mill you are out in the country amid the twisted, silvery-green leaf trees of the olive groves. Most important, a visit to this mill will help you to better understand the glorious process of turning the hard, ripe fruit into liquid gold for an entire community. (People from the surrounding area bring their olives here to be pressed as well.)

Unfortunately I toured the mill when there was no activity—the harvest is from mid-November through March—but with the help of a few explanations, a short video, a quick look at the presses and more modern machines, I was able to gain a better understanding and appreciation for the amount of love and labor required to make olive oil of the finest quality.

The store, housed in the old mill, is stocked with a selection of olives, olive oil, *tapénade* (a thick, rich olive spread), and a range of Provençal goods.

• 2 route de Châteauneuf, 06650 Opio; tel.: 04.93.77.23.03;
    fax: 04.93.77.39.17
  Open Monday–Saturday 9 A.M.–noon and 2–6:30 P.M.

Hotel la Pérouse

I could recommend this hotel for many reasons. The location just next to *le vieux Nice* and la promenade des Anglais is excellent. The rooms have the sort of comfort that many people, particularly Americans, expect from a superior-quality hotel. The staff is friendly and service-oriented. The patio and pool area resembles a theater set with the jagged rocks of the hillside of Nice as its backdrop. You can take a dip in the hot tub under the stars or have breakfast on your balcony. Ask for a room with a view and you'll leave with the lasting impression of the vast Baie des Anges.

• 11 quai Rauba-Capeu, 06300 Nice; tel.: 04.93.62.34.63; fax:
    04.93.62.59.41
  Four-Star Hotel: Expensive
  Open year-round

St-Paul-de-Vence (Alpes-Maritimes)

Whenever I come to a village like this, I have the same pervasive thought: Oh, how I'd love to be here alone—or at least not with fifteen busloads of tourists. It wasn't until the end of my visit to St-Paul-de-Vence that I discovered how to enjoy this spectacular yet overrun medieval village.

The trick is to avoid the masses of daytrippers that peak between 11 A.M. and 4 P.M. There are only a few hotels in St-Paul, so the village is extremely quiet during off hours. I suggest that you arrive *very* early to take a quiet stroll on the ramparts and through the tiny streets, then plan to do the following during the onslaught: take lots of time to browse in the very untouristy shops listed below, and/or plan a leisurely lunch at either of St-Paul's prestigious restaurants, the famed **La Colombe d'Or** (place des Orneaux; tel.: 04.93.32.80.02; fax: 04.93.32.77.78) or the more recently opened **Le Saint-Paul** (86 rue Grande; tel.: 04.93.32.65.25; fax: 04.93.32.52.94).

Although a bit of a hike by foot, a visit to the **Foundation Maeght**, one of the most important modern art museums in the world, is worth the effort. The gift shop is also quite nice, but not as well stocked as the Museum of Modern Art shop in New York. The selection of books and catalogues is considerable, although nearly all of them are in French. How about a Miró printed tote bag instead?

Da Cavanna

Annie and Daniel Da Cavanna have combined their talents of colorist/stylist and leather craftsman to yield creations of an *indémodable* chic. Madame designs and Monsieur works the leather in the tiny workshop in the back of this boutique. All of their clothing and accessories are entirely handmade, and almost all of them are unique pieces. The true uniqueness of their fashions lies in the unusual mixing and matching of fabrics with leather. A typical jacket (priced at 3,600F), for example, might feature several different colors of suede offset by contrasting yet coordinating textiles. Some of the fabrics resemble eighteenth- and nineteenth-century upholstery materials; others, such as the ones from Rubelli and Missoni, are more contemporary. I found the look to be striking, and oddly enough, quite Californian.

Customers can buy off the rack or order a tailor-made model. Nearly all of the fashions are for women, and most of the major pieces consist of jackets of varying styles accompanied by coordinating skirts. In the summer they show a lot of linens in the same spirit. If you are not ready for a big splurge, take a look at their whimsical selection of bags, most of which are priced at about 590F.

• 65 rue Grande, 06570 St-Paul-de-Vence; tel.: 04.93.32.77.60
Open daily except Tuesday 9:30 A.M.–1 P.M. and 2:30–7 P.M.

L'Ile en Terre

L'Ile en Terre, loosely translated as the island of earth, seemed more like an oasis in the middle of the desert to me. By the time I arrived in St-Paul, I had been bombarded with so much mediocre *poterie* that I was truly in need of the real thing. I found it here, and in large quantities to boot! This gallery-like shop represents about fifteen artists, all of whom work locally with clay.

The pieces are exquisite; much of it is raku, and nearly every one is a work of art. Some of the pottery is utilitarian, such as bowls that evoke the artist's own rendition of the Provençal spirit. They have great jewelry, too, entirely handcrafted out of ceramic beads. Prices throughout the store range from 100F to 20,000F.

- 5 rue Grande, 06570 St-Paul-de-Vence; tel.: 04.93.32.86.91;
    fax: 04.93.58.77.00
  Open daily 10 A.M.–7 P.M. (except for an hour lunch break in winter)

Tourettes-sur-Loup (Alpes-Maritimes)

Market: place de la Madeleine
Wednesday 7 A.M.–1 P.M.

Although only nine miles inland from the coast, the narrow, curvy roads that lead up to this ancient village deter flocks of tourists. Also, unlike St-Paul-de-Vence, most of the artists and craftspeople who exhibit here actually do call Tourettes home. The overall spirit of the village is quite down-to-earth, and it's obvious that the people achieve a delicate balance of art, trade, and tourism.

According to my guide (who happens to run his own restaurant in town and graciously volunteered to take me around for a few hours on his day off), this unpretentious little town happens to be a favorite of Gene Wilder, Mel Brooks, and his wife, Anne Bancroft. Apparently they enjoy it so much that they come back every year.

As I walked through the little shop-filled streets, I wondered which artisans were their favorites. One vendor sells goods made from the wood of the olive tree, and although the presentation appears a bit touristy, a closer look reveals the beauty and durability of the handcrafted salad bowls.

Tourettes is primarily known for its weavers. They are all female, and they are all easy to find along the little back streets that typify this *village*. Most make fashions for women with the exception of **Cha Tsouo**, who focuses on elegant bedspreads and throws for the home. I fell for some of Michèle Badets's fashions at her **Atelier Arachnée**, such as a very tailored, Chanelish suit woven from a wonderful palette of reds (some of which were Harris tweeds), silk lined, that rang in for just under 3,000F.

Entering the gallery and workshop of the sculptor **Yvette Lamoureux** is like walking onto a stage: the foreground is populated with players in the form of bronze sculptures that appear to dance and strike poses as though they were acting out a role in *La Bayadère* or *Don Giovanni*. The backdrop is cast by the workshop of Madame Lamoureux, who is the maestro, the composer, and the director all in one. Her pieces speak of her passion for the performing arts; the dramatic lighting, the classical music, and the combination of smells of burning wood and melting wax create a performance in and of themselves. Each piece, which costs between 11,000F and 70,000F, is cast in eight models and several different patinas.

Plan to spend at least a couple of hours exploring the village. Most of the shops and artisans are along the main walkways. It's fun to wander off the beaten path, however. If you like trompe l'oeil, pay a visit to **Martine Corbin**, who has some sweet gift items of varied prices. (She also paints particularly real-looking portraits of putty tats.)

Those who revel in stylish furniture of collectors' quality should visit **Jacqueline Morabito** at the nearby village of La-Colle-sur-Loup (tel.: 04.93.32.64.91; fax: 04.93.32.54.94).

David-David

I first saw the fine works of Hélène and Jeanine David about five years ago when I recognized many of their pillows, having seen them before in some of the finest home interior shops of Paris.

Their success continues to flourish, and now the David sisters' creations can be found in high-end stores throughout the world, such as Bergdorf Goodman in New York. Obviously success has not gone to their heads, because the look of their Tourettes shop fits the style of their products. From cushions to house linens, the look is understated. Their works speak of quiet elegance, much like in Calvin Klein's home collection. Mostly solid, earth-toned linens, cottons, and even some hemp are fashioned into minimalist pieces that transcend all geographical boundaries.

- 61 Grand Rue, 06140 Tourrettes-sur-Loup; tel.: 04.93.24.17.33
  Open daily 10:30 A.M.–1 P.M. and 3–6 P.M.

Valbonne (Alpes-Maritimes)

Market: Place des Arcades
Friday 8 A.M.–1 P.M.

Although many people drive directly through here on their way to or from Opio or Grasse, Valbonne is one of the most overlooked towns on the Côte d' Azur. This is a blessing for those of us who prefer visiting a historic village unspoiled by heavy tourist traffic. There is not enough for you to see and do here for hours on end, but the quaintness of Valbonne provides a wonderful respite from the more crowded attractions in the area.

The gridlike pattern of streets in this sixteenth-century town sets it apart from the *villages perchés* throughout the region. The rectalinear configuration of streets provide architectural and historical interest, and there is little chance of becoming lost. The shops on the main street are quite touristy, but if you turn off onto the side streets you are likely to experience a bit more local flavor.

The English-speaking bookstore is not here just for the tourists: it attests to the large concentration of British and other English-speaking people who reside within the outlying area. Called Valbonne Sophia Antipolis, this high-tech megalopolis is often referred to as the Silicon Valley of France.

Ruchers Mazzini

Longtime beekeepers Monsieur and Madame Mazzini can understand their bees' habits, likes, and desires faster than you can say WorldWide Web. The love, care, and devotion they give to their buzzing babies only enhances the quality of the honey that they produce. During the cool days of spring, the bees are carefully transported to the mountains; those that stay throughout the summer produce a rich, robust honey of the darkest color. Others are brought to the lavender fields from which they create a honey of the most refined and subtle flavor. If you are torn between the two and only have room for one jar, try *toutes fleurs*, a honey made from bees that sucked the sweetness out of flowers from several different parts of Provence. Or pick up a jar of *pollen de fleurs*, which costs about 28F for a two-week supply. These golden grains are said to have healing qualities and work wonders on your liver and digestive system. It may be just what you need to get you through the rest of your trip in France!

• 12 rue Emile-Pourcel, 06560 Valbonne; tel.: 04.93.12.05.18
  Open daily except January 1

Verrerie Loumani

If it weren't for the fact that I wanted to take a quick look at the village church, I might never have discovered this glass workshop located next door. Decorated in a rather painterly manner, the pieces here are extremely well executed. I was not surprised to learn that the brothers, Ahmed and Ada Loumani, who created this studio, learned much of their craft from another brother who happens to be one of the master glassblowers at Biot. The fact that they are all originally *biotois* helped me to better understand this family passion for glassmaking of superior quality.

• Moulin des Artisans, 06560 Valbonne; tel./fax: 04.93.12.23.23
  Open Monday–Saturday 11 A.M.– 7 P.M.; Sunday 3–6 P.M.

Valluris (Alpes-Maritimes)

Market: Place de l'Homme aux Moutons
Tuesday–Sunday 8 A.M.–1 P.M.

Vallauris is known for its ceramics, but my expectations regarding their quality were low. As I drove down the main street, my anxiety about finding an overabundance of pottery shops increased. I started to think that, like so many other towns, Vallauris was resting on the laurels of its past and that today most of the pottery sold here is for tourists. Happily, my worst fears began to dissolve as I looked more closely and found several galleries that featured works of museum quality.

Although the people of Vallauris like to boast about the presence of pottery in the city over the past 2,000 years, it wasn't until the late 1940s that the city began to attract prominent artists. Picasso was the first to arrive, followed by Matisse, Miró, and Chagall, and by the 1950s, this sleepy Mediterranean town was in full swing.

In order to better understand the creative boom that Vallauris experienced during this Golden Age, begin with a visit to the **Château Musée de Vallauris**, located at place de la Libération in the heart of town. The extensive ceramic collection can capture your attention for a good while, particularly since many of the pieces are winners of *La Biennale*, an internationally acclaimed ceramic show that has been held in Vallauris every two years since 1966. Allow plenty of time to contemplate Picasso's rapturous painting, *La Guerre et la Paix*, which is housed within the thirteenth-century Romanesque chapel in the oldest part of the château.

You may want to pick up a complete listing of the various galleries and potters from the tourism office (square du 8 Mai) because many of them, such as **Roger Collet** (Montée Ste-Anne), are off the main streets. This section lists the ones I consider the highlights of Vallauris, but the selection is highly personal. The **Galerie Jean Marais**, which is named after and shows the works of this famous French actor, is also highly reputable, as is the **Galerie Sassi-Milici**. For more traditional or utilitarian pieces, **Foucard-Jourdan** is your best bet. All three of these galleries are near one another in the city center.

If you're looking for a quick diversion from ceramics, stop at **Fraber Pétanque** (1193 chemin de St-Bernard), one of the few workshops that still crafts the shiny silver *boules de pétanques*, the essential element of that quintessentially Provençal game played throughout most of France.

Creations Robert Picault

If there is one pottery that is most representative of the traditional ceramics of Vallauris, it is that of Picault. Although the inspiration for their signature geometric motifs originates from an ancient Chinese dynasty, the overall feel is very Mediterranean due to the use of sea blue, emerald green, and burnt sienna on pieces that are traditional in their form and function. A typical piece would be a V-shaped bowl glazed on both the inside and outside with bold designs in marinescape colors.

• avenue P-Picasso, 06220 Vallauris; tel.: 04.93.63.75.44; fax: 04.93.63.76.44

Open Monday–Friday 10 A.M.–noon and 2–6 P.M.

Galerie Madoura

The granddaddy of them all, Galerie Madoura is known throughout the world. Picasso came here in 1946 to create a few pieces with Suzanne Ramié in her atelier, and the rest is history. The day that I stopped in, I had to dodge a Japanese TV crew in order to properly appreciate this handsome stone and wood-beamed space that was built as a ceramic workshop in the eighteenth century. (Make sure you go to the gallery and not just to the Madoura Boutique, which, although easier to find, serves more as a store-front than a showplace.) The pieces speak for themselves, and just the idea of so many Picasso ceramics assembled together for sale is thrilling in itself.

Nearly all of the works are from limited and numbered editions of 50 to 500 pieces, so the supply is decidedly on the wane. Prices range from 1,250 to 25,000F, and a mini-museum upstairs displays some truly exquisite creations, some of which have been sold out for over thirty-five years.

For unique pieces instead of those in a series, look around in the front room by the entrance. Although not signed Picasso, these one-of-a-kind works are from the gallery's own production and their attention to color, glaze, and form is exceptional.

• avenue des Combattants d'AFN, 06220 Vallauris; tel.: 04.93.64.66.39

Open Monday–Friday 10 A.M.–12:30 P.M. and 2:30–6:30 P.M.;

Closed November 1–mid-December

Mosaique Gerbino

When you walk into this shop, try to look at each piece one by one and imagine them in your home away from the hundreds of other creations of the same kind on view here. These rich and decorative mosaic-inspired ceramics fit in with a number of interiors, but it may take a bit of imagination in this convenience-store-like setting.

I encourage you to buy here for the broader selection and lower prices than you would find in a tastefully decorated retail space. Yvan Koenig has carried on the unusual and painstaking technique that Jean Gerbino developed in 1930 which involves the piecing together of bits of clay in a style Monsieur Gerbino learned during a short stay in Algeria at the beginning of his career as a ceramicist. The prices are as varied as the forms, starting with ashtrays selling for 66F and going upward to 4,000F for a more contemporary piece of geometrically constructed sculpture.

• 4 avenue du Stade, 06220 Vallauris; tel.: 04.93.63.77.18

Open Monday–Saturday 10 A.M.–noon and 1–6 P.M.

La Colombe d'Argile

The name means clay dove—appropriate for this unpretentious address where you can enjoy a good lunch at an honest price. The huge old kiln toward the back of the dining room is evidence that the space formerly housed a pottery workshop. If you want to stick with Vallauris tradition, order the special fish cooked in clay. The carefully designed earthy mask not only makes for a beautiful presentation but also keeps the fish moist when "fired."

- avenue de Tapis-Vert (corner of the rue Hoche), 06220
     Vallauris; tel.: 04.93.64.30.64
  Restaurant: Moderate
  Open year-round; closed Sunday evening and Monday

FRANCHE COMTÉ
Franche Comté

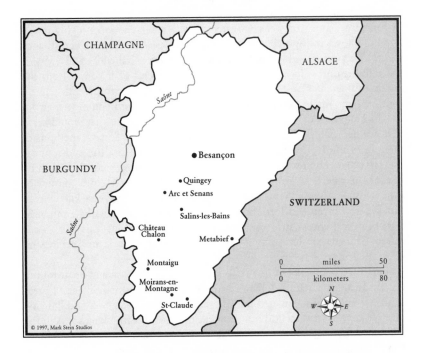

wooden toys and games • *vin jaune* • watches • faience • wines • antique pine and oak furniture • posters, postcards, books and magazines on architecture • dark chocolate disks • pipes • model houses and monuments • diamonds • hams • jewelry

FEW NORTH AMERICANS have heard of this region of France, although the Jura, which is the name of both the most widely known province in Franche Comté and of the local mountains, might sound familiar. No six-lane highways interfere with the bucolic quietude of the passing scenery, and the geographical remoteness has preserved the region's rural vistas while protecting the towns from massive tourist invasions.

The panoramas are indeed bountiful as the terrain leads you from short stretches of plains to rolling hillsides, and if you dare, to steep mountains whose hairpin turns might just leave you swerving and careening in your sleep. As the roadways change, so do the houses. Long, low half-timbered dwellings, constructed in brick, freckle the farmlands; houses in the Haut

133

Jura, the higher part of the mountains, are massive, squarely proportioned stone edifices big enough to shelter both families and their animals.

In the past, the local people spent most of their time indoors during the long and harsh midwinter months—a sort of hibernation that spawned a number of vocations for which the region later became known. The crafting of timepieces and toys were two such activities, but the most highly developed of all was indisputably the making of cheese, and in particular, that of comté. This cheese, which tastes like a cross between Cheddar and Swiss, is the number-one seller in all of France, and the best of it comes from the region of Franche Comté. The tradition began during the fourteenth century when the mountain people decided to join together and combine their individual supplies of milk to make huge wheels of cheese that would serve as a nonperishable food source throughout the winter. Today's methods of manufacturing are greater in scale, but in many instances, the end result is the same. The comté of the **Fromageries Marcel Petite** is considered to be one of the finest, and after a visit here you will appreciate the amount of time, effort, and milk that is poured in to each of their thirty-five kilo wheels. Housed within an old fort about 20 kilometers from Pontarlier, this near state-of-the-art cheese stronghold usually admits visitors just one day a week (often Thursdays) during July and August. Call ahead for specifics at 03.81.39.07.54.

Before you embark upon your journey through the Jura and its surrounding lands, mark Château Châlon on your map. This small village of great character and charm, situated midway between Lons-le-Saunier and Poligny, near Voiteur, is hard to find but provides the most breathtaking views in the region. Skirted by hillsides of noble vines, this peaceful medieval village roosts high above plains that stretch as far as the eye can see.

Arc et Senans (Jura)

Saline Royale d'Arc et Senans

In order to better understand the Royal Saltworks of Arc et Senans, I suggest you first visit, or at least read my description of, Salins-les-Bains (see page 139). Built toward the end of the eighteenth century by the highly acclaimed architect, Claude-Nicolas Ledoux, these Royal Saltworks are as grand and statuesque as those of Salins-les-Bains are functional, basic, and void of the slightest artifice. The Saline Royale complex was erected over five hundred years after Salins-les-Bains to better process the salt that was piped in from the original source via lengthy stretches of hollowed-out trees. All of this was accomplished during an age when aesthetics meant a great deal more than "just getting the job done." Classified as a historical monument on the UNESCO world heritage list, a tour of the Saline Royale is a must not only for its architecture but also for the unique approach to the work environment that Ledoux attempted to install here. Thousands of tourists visit this unique cultural center from as far away as Japan.

A stop at the gift shop/bookstore itself is worth the detour. Visitors particularly interested in architecture will marvel at the comprehensive selection of books and magazines, in French and English, that are sold on the subject. Other less specialized gift items include posters, puzzles, watches, and clay and cardboard models of the Saline Royale and other celebrated monuments. A selection of children's books that illustrate the building of a house, a cathedral, or a fortress also are great finds, and the generous collection of regional maps and guidebooks will help to set you on your way!

- 25610 Arc et Senans; tel.: 03.81.54.45.45; fax: 03.81.54.45.46
Cultural Center/Museum/Boutique
Open January 1–March 31 and November 2–December 31 10 A.M.–
    noon and 2–5 P.M.; April 1–June 30 and September 1–November 1,
    9 A.M.–noon and 2–8 P.M.; July 1–August 31, 9 A.M.–7 P.M.

Besançon (Doubs)

Main shopping streets: rue des Granges, Grande Rue
Market: place du Marché Friday 8 A.M.–1 P.M.
Flea market: Micropolis at the Palais des Congre's
every second Sunday of the month 8 A.M.–6 P.M.

Most people associate watchmaking with the Swiss or the Asians, who have gained even greater market share within the past couple of decades. France also has its own watch and clockmaking industry, however, which has its center in and around Besançon–a town just a short distance from Switzerland. Historically, watchmaking, or *l'horlogerie*, took place in these mountainous regions because so much of the manual work could be quietly carried out independently at home. A cottage industry of sorts, it occupied many of the mountain people's time and brought in extra money during the long winter months.

Akteo ranks among the best known and best-selling watch brands of Besançon, and the shop **Kanai** (6 Grande Rue) brightly displays a large part of the Akteo collection. Swatch-like in design, the Akteo look tends to be more sophisticated and of superior quality. Prices range from 400F to 600F. If you want to take a giant step in caliber (and price), head to the opposite end of the street where **Van Brill'** (83 Grande Rue), a reputable jeweler, sells watches by Michel Herbelin and E. P. Pequignet, both of which are based in the region but have Paris- or Swiss-made faces.

Another shop that sells products highly typical of the region is **La Paillotte** (108 Grande Rue), a merry little boutique that features boldly painted toys and games crafted entirely out of wood.

On a visit to the town in December, the chill in the air reminded me that I had passed in front of a chocolate *salon* earlier that seemed inviting. I traced my way back to **J. Belin** (23 rue de la République) and was relieved to see that this little side trip took me just far enough away from the fray. Inside, all was peaceful and serene: apricot walls accented by wood paneling created a warm interior that made sitting down at one of their small tables all the more tempting. As the gentle sounds of classical music soothed my ears and the strong, robust smell of chocolate teased my palate, I knew if I stayed I might never leave, so I purchased a few exquisitely shaped *palets amers* (dark chocolate disks) to go.

A few boutiques later, I hit upon **Barthod** (22 and 25 rue Bersot), one of the best wine shops around. The store sells wines from all over France, but I was most interested in finding out about those of the Jura. The extensive selection includes a number of wines that can be consumed right away, such as the reds of Arbois, as well as the region's most characteristic wine, *le vin jaune*, or yellow wine. Often used in cooking, the wine becomes more golden with age, and the perfect age is said to be about twenty years old.

Next door to the boutique is the **Barthod wine bar**, a rather chic address where you can make a dinner of such regional specialities as cheese, ham, and potatoes while trying different types of wine. It is best to call ahead to reserve: 03.81.82.27.14.

Moirans-en-Montagne (Jura)

Musée du Jouet

Certainly the main attraction in this rather dreary little town is the Musée du Jouet, or the Toy Museum. Toymaking, originally artisanal and now primarily industrial, has been an important activity in the area since the fifteenth century, during which time local monks began to make rosaries, and later toys, for the people who passed through the mountains on pilgrimages. The museum traces the history of the different toy manufacturing processes, but its real strength is the colossal collection of old toys (about 5,000 in all). Organized according to theme, each glass showcase displays toys that served as props for the roles children like to play. The window that illustrates the child's desire to play house, for example, features an assortment of play household items—dishes, irons, ovens, and much, much more—from different eras and countries. This FAO Schwartz–like display of goods enchants children while conjuring up nostalgic sentiments for grown-ups—and toy collectors will rejoice! My only regret is that as much as each individual display is attractively presented, the cavernous space lends itself more to an air and space museum than a rich collection of playthings.

Most of the toys in the museum's boutique are made at Moirans-en-Montagne; some are molded out of plastic, although the most traditional ones have been crafted out of solid wood, mostly boxwood, and then lacquered in circus clown colors. These are the kinds of toys that parents like to give to their children. The building blocks (189F) come complete with medieval turrets, and the pull toys are as well suited for display as for yanking around. Animal lovers will instantly be charmed by the purple dog (99F), and I couldn't resist the bright yellow jump rope with the green, frog-faced wooden handles (59F) for my little red-headed godchild. Dads who collect model cars are apt to snatch up one of these slick wooden ones in a heartbeat. How about a 1957 Ferrari Testa Rossa (859F) in racer red?

• 5 rue du Murgin, 39260 Moirans-en-Montagne; tel.: 03.84.42.38.64; fax: 03.84.42.38.97
  Museum/Boutique
  Open daily February–May and September–December 2–6 P.M.; June 10 A.M.–noon and 2–6 P.M.; July and August 10 A.M.–7 P.M. and during school vacations 10 A.M.–noon and 2–6 P.M.

Montaigu (Jura)

Cellier des Chartreux

You'll need a detailed map, or at least good directions, to find this small, little known village perched on a hilltop, not far from Lons-le-Saunier. The only winemakers of Montaigu, the Pignier family has resided here for the past seven generations in a unique setting that is in itself worth the search. It is not until you descend the short, steep steps of the narrow, stone staircase that leads down into the cellar that you are seized by the sheer magnificence of this thirteenth-century *cave*.

Built by the Chartreux monks, this soulful space, resplendent with a skillfully constructed vaulted ceiling of early Gothic style, seems better suited for prayer than for aging wine. My brief visit was conducted by one of the Pignier daughters, who suggested I taste a few of their Chardonnays before moving on to their *vin jaune*. Quite different from the wines of California or Burgundy, these Chardonnays are reminiscent of a very dry sherry and are best consumed after three to five years.

• Montaigu, 39570 Lons-le-Saunier; tel.: 03.84.24.24.30; fax: 03.84.47.46.00
  Open daily 8 A.M.–7 P.M. except Sunday afternoon

Quingey (Doubs)

Jacqueline Monnier Antiquités

Traveling down toward the Jura on the N83 from Besançon, I spotted this old farmhouse just on the outskirts of Quingey and wondered if it would meet my goal to find the one antique shop most representative of the local traditions and style. At first glance, I was overwhelmed by the quantity of items but didn't notice too many regional pieces. After I had worked my way through the two antique-filled floors of this farmhouse, however, I ended up downstairs in the old stables. Here I unearthed a wealth of furniture, mostly from the eighteenth and nineteenth centuries, quite characteristic of the rugged spirit of this mountainous land. Crafted primarily out of oak and pine from the nearby forests of the Jura, these rustic pieces warmed me with their simple designs. As I admired a huge, 100-year-old, solid pine kitchen table from the Haut Jura, I couldn't help thinking this is what French country is all about. Priced at 6,500F, it would fetch at least four times that price sold outside of France.

- Faubourg Ste-Anne, 25440 Quingey; tel.: 03.81.63.63.52;
  fax: 03.81.63.63.52
  Open daily 2:30–6:30 P.M.

St-Claude (Jura)

Pipes and diamonds, diamonds and pipes—certainly a funny mix of two very different products. The two things they have in common is that they require a certain amount of craftsmanship and they both have been closely linked with St-Claude. The town itself might not merit a detour, but if you have a special interest in either of these products, you should definitely plan a stop here. For fancifully carved pipes, stop in to see **Jean Masson** (24 route de la Faucille; tel.: 03.84.45.24.09), whose atelier is situated about 2.5 kilometers from town on the route to Geneva.

Bailly

Appropriately located near the police station, this diamond cutter's small atelier nonetheless requires a little investigative work to find. Once here, you can stand and watch the precision cutting technique that shapes each diamond into a sparkling stone of distinction. Diamond-cutting became big business in Antwerp during the mid-nineteenth century; then around 1870, many of the artisans moved to Geneva because of religious persecution. A short time after that, the nearby town of St-Claude became attractive for the hydraulic force that its rapid river could generate. By 1880, four to six times as many diamonds could be cut with this technique, which resulted in a near diamond-cutting boom for this sleepy little town. Today most of the world's diamonds are cut in India or the Far East, and here in St-Claude, the diamond cutters who remain use electricity.

Enough of the bare stones. I wanted to see a few set. Say no more—the owner of the shop quickly produced a couple of black leather briefcases whose interiors dazzled me with an array of tastefully mounted stones. My travel companion and I were most interested in the rings, so we selected one ruby and one emerald, each bezel set and exquisitely enhanced by an inlay of diamond chips. The ballpark price of about 5,000F seemed fair enough, and our only regret was that neither of us came accompanied by an attentive *monsieur*.

• 2 chemin de la Rochette, 39200 St-Claude; tel.: 03.84.45.19.23; fax: 03.84.45.08.45
  Open Monday–Friday 8 A.M.–noon and 2–6 P.M.

Ets. Vincent-Genod

It would be nice for Monsieur Genod if pipe smoking took off in the same trendy direction as cigar smoking has done in recent years. An affable man who talks about his craft with a little twinkle in his eye, this master pipe-maker has been in the business for nearly forty years. Although he once had as many as twenty workers under his command, today his scrappy atelier is down to a staff of three.

How did pipe-making start in St-Claude? Once again, the answer lay in the tremendous source of power required to turn the lathes. As with diamond cutting, the pipe-making industry began here in the mid to late nineteenth century when craftsmanship was less of an art and more of a way of life. Today all of these elegant pipes are still entirely made by hand *chez* Monsieur Genod out of Mediterranean brier, a heath whose roots seem to grow for this very purpose. Ranging from 80F to 800F in price, many of the pipes have been stained to a malachite green or a chestnut brown, but the most beautiful of all are those of the natural, faintly marbleized caramel color of the brier. The styles range from short to long, heavy to light, and straight to bent, topped off by a choice of mouthpieces almost nearly as diverse.

• 13 faubourg St-Marcel, 39200 St-Claude; tel.: 03.84.45.00.47
  Open Monday–Friday 9:30–11:30 A.M. and 2–6 P.M.
  There is also a boutique at 7 place de l'Abbaye; tel.: 03.84.45.53.59
  Open year-round Monday–Saturday 2–7 P.M.; July and August daily 9 A.M.–noon and 2–7 P.M.

Salins-les-Bains (Jura)

I first heard about this tranquil little town when I was conducting my preliminary research for this guidebook. Somewhere along the way I learned that Salins had a faience industry, so I circled the name on my already considerably marked-up map. Unfortunately, the supposed earthenware factory left me disappointed. Salins once had an important faience manufacturer that stemmed from the use of salt for the glazes, but the factory stopped producing tableware in 1992 and instead chose to specialize in toilets and the like. There is, however, a factory discount store at 18 avenue Aristide Briand (tel.: 03.84.73.01.45) that offers 30 to 50 percent discounts off on seconds that are characteristic of Quimper, Moustiers, and Lunéville.

My stop here was by no means a total loss. First, the town, with the Jura foothills as a backdrop, is picturesque; second, I learned much about the two primary activities for which the town is named: the saltworks and the salt baths. My education began in the bowels of the earth, far below the original salt-processing operations, where saltwater was pumped up from depths of up to 250 meters. More than 800 workers toiled away here in these subterranean, vaulted cellars during the Middle Ages, and a similar archaic-looking water pump still functions today. Salt in centuries past was, of course, a highly precious commodity. Today the water that is extracted from the springs is used solely for the adjacent thermal baths.

My ears perk up at any mention of a spa, so it didn't take me more than two minutes to "play hooky" and to slip in for a quick treatment. After a delicious, hearty *salade comtoise* next door at the delightfully charming bistrot, **Le Petit Blanc** (call ahead to reserve at 03.84.73.01.57), I waited obediently at the door of the **Centre Thermal et Remise en Forme** along with the rest of the eager spa-goers who had gathered for the opening of the afternoon session that was to begin promptly at 3 P.M. One hydrojet and bath later (93F plus 15F for a towel and a bathrobe), I walked out feeling like jelly, virtually free of the knots that had developed from a rigorous program of shopping, eating, and discovery.

• place des Salines, 39110 Salins-les-Bains; tel.: 03.84.73.04.63;
  fax: 03.84.73.28.32
  Open Monday and Friday 3–8 P.M.; Tuesday, Wednesday, Thursday, and
  Saturday 3–7 P.M.

ILE-DE-FRANCE
Ile-de-France

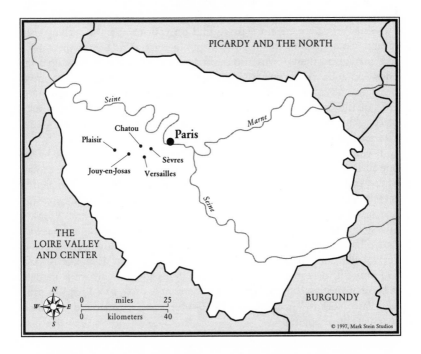

PICARDY AND THE NORTH

Seine

Marne

Chatou

Paris

Plaisir

Sèvres

Jouy-en-Josas   Versailles

Seine

THE
LOIRE VALLEY
AND CENTER

N

W   E

S

0   miles   25

0   kilometers   40

BURGUNDY

© 1997, Mark Stein Studios

**factory discount goods • copper pots • antiques • china • straw
boatmen's hats • home and personal accessories in *toile de Jouy*
and *indiennes* • Impressionist books, cards, and posters**

THE NAME OF this region, translated as island of France, comes from its
geography: the central plains are surrounded by four great rivers, *la Seine*,
l'Aisne, *l'Oise*, and *la Marne*. With fertile lands and close proximity to Paris,
the Ile-de-France is one of the richest regions of France economically and
culturally.

The entries in this section focus on lesser-known shopping-oriented addresses. These environs of Paris are highly popular with tourists, due largely
to a wealth of magnificent castles and historic sites such as Vaux-le-Vicomte,
Malmaison, Maintenon, Rambouillet, and much, much more. Some of these
landmarks have small gift shops, but I will leave you to discover these on
your own.

Painters from the Barbizon school and the Impressionists were greatly moved by the lush landscapes of the Ile-de-France, and leisurely day trips to towns such as Barbizon and Auvers-sur-Oise are a great way to gain a sense of the artists' love for the region—and to do a bit of artful shopping, too.

Many of the shops in the chic suburban enclaves such as Neuilly-sur-Seine, St-Germain-en-Laye, and Versailles are either the same or similar to those of Paris: they are also easy to find on your own, and travelling there means just a short métro or RER (commuter train) ride from the capital. The markets in these towns also make for colorful places to pick up a few odds and ends, and if you have the opportunity, be sure to take in one of the many *foires*, or festivals, which usually feature antiques or local crafts. One of the best of these is *la foire aux jambons*, a ham festival that takes place in the western suburb of Chatou twice a year, in September and March. The selection of antiques and bric-à-brac far outnumbers the hams!

If your goal is to accomplish a bit of reduced-priced shopping, try hitting one of the huge factory discount centers, located just outside of the capital, where you'll see many a Parisian plodding along in search of inexpensive accoutrements for themselves and their urban interiors. **Usines Center**, just 6 kilometers west of Paris at Vélizy (exit at Villacoublay on the N118), is one such complex; choose from 140 familar and not-so-familar boutiques that sell a broad range of reduced-priced goods from the current and previous year's collections. If you're on your way to the Charles-de-Gaulle Airport, and you still have room for a few more items to stuff into your luggage, stop off at another **Usines Center** in the *zone industrielle*, or Z.I., of Villepinte (exit Paris Nord II/Villepinte off of A104) for one last go around of French-style bargain shopping!

Chatou (Yvelines)

Market: place du Marché
Wednesday and Saturday 8:30 A.M.–12:30 P.M.

La Maison Fournaise

It takes only about fifteen minutes from the place de l'Etoile in Paris for you to find yourself seated on the same balcony as the one where Pierre-Auguste Renoir painted *Le Déjeuner des Canotiers* (*The Luncheon of the Boating Party*), one of the most important tableaus of the Impressionist period. A favorite gathering place for the Impressionists between 1870 and 1905, La Maison Fournaise meant long, languorous afternoons of boating along the Seine and feasts of eel marinated in white wine.

Eel is no longer on the menu, and today this landmark restaurant has become a chic address for business lunches and romantic evenings *à deux*. The views along the Seine have unfortunately changed for the worse, although the look of the restaurant has improved—particularly in the *salle des fresques*, a room whose original frescoes of dense, vivid shades of mustard, moss, and aquamarine reach from wall to ceiling. It is refreshing to see that exuberance and artistic flair can indeed be kept alive over the past one hundred years.

Even if you don't dine here, visit the adjacent museum that recounts this chapter of Impressionist history through its collection of old postcards, prints (mostly originals), some oils by Maurice Leloir, and a must-see video that recreates many scenes from this era. You might feel moved to buy one of the straw boatmen's hats, portrayed in the aforementioned painting, which sell for 65F in the small boutique. More traditional souvenir items include postcards, posters, and books.

- Ile des Impressionistes, 78400 Chatou; tel.: 05.34.80.63.22; fax: 05.30.53.39.03
  Museum/Boutique: Open Wednesday–Sunday 11 A.M.–5 P.M.
  Restaurant: Moderate–Expensive
  Tel.: 01. 30.71.41.91; fax: 01. 39.52.84.82
  Open daily year-round; closed Sunday evening October–April

Jouy-en-Josas (Yvelines)

Musée de la Toile de Jouy

One of my dreams in life is to have a room entirely dressed in *toile de Jouy*, the quintessentially French fabric that is often used to cover every nook and cranny of a room, including lampshades and footstools. These classic, monochromatic cotton prints are perfect for an old château or a country house.

Best known for their endearing bucolic scenes and loving depictions of gallant country people, these fabrics adorn each room in the museum. You may have to wait for your return home to order the yardage required to redo your chosen room (*toile de Jouy* motifs are easily found outside of France), because the museum's boutique sells mostly items that have been made from these prints. Frames, photo albums, desk sets, and a number of other home accessories, covered in a muted palette of *toile de Jouy* colors and patterns, mix easily with a variety of interiors. Reproductions of the *indiennes*, other multicolored prints of stylized floral or vegetal motifs that also were made in Jouy-en-Josas toward the end of the eighteenth century, sell here in the shape of smart travel bags, scarves, and pillows, to name a few. Expect Parisian-style prices.

- Château d'Eglantine, 54 rue Charles-de-Gaulle, 78350 Jouy-en-Josas; tel.: 02.39.56.48.64
  Open Tuesday-Friday 10 A.M.–6 P.M. (Until 5 P.M. in winter); Saturday, Sunday, and holidays 2–6 P.M (except November 11)

Plaisir (Yvelines)

J. Jacquetot

You don't have to travel as far as Villedieu-les-Poêles in Normandy to buy copper pots of outstanding quality, because this is exactly what you can expect to find at this off-the-beaten-path cookware supply house in Plaisir. About 25 kilometers from Paris on the N12 heading toward Dreux, take the Plaisir exit to the Z.I. Ebisoires and you're just about there! This is not your typical tourist destination, and you are not likely to encounter many tourists here. Instead you might find yourself rubbing elbows with a member of the kitchen staff of the Elysées Palace, the Senate, or the U.S. Embassy, because this is where they (and assorted other culinary professionals) come to buy new copper pots or to have their old ones retinned.

- Ferme des Ebisoires, BP 98, 78372 Plaisir Cédex, tel.: 01.30.55.50.72; fax: 01.34.81.07.81
  Open Monday–Thursday 8 A.M.–6 P.M.; Friday 8 A.M.–5 P.M.

Sèvres (Yvelines)

Musée National de la Céramique

If you take the Paris métro, get off at the Pont de Sèvres station and cross the bridge, you arrive almost directly in front of Le Musée de Sèvres, probably the most important ceramic museum in all of France.

Displays trace the history of ceramics, from faience to porcelain, through the centuries and across the continents. The collection is indeed alluring, and to appreciate it even more, I highly recommend the guided tours (call ahead to find out if you can join one of the visits arranged for groups).

Group visits also are permitted next door at **La Manufacture de Sèvres**, the first porcelain manufacturer in France, founded in 1740. The factory is government-owned, and to this day its production is reserved primarily for the state and French embassies throughout the world. With each near-subliminal piece almost entirely crafted by hand, you can understand why the yearly output amounts to only about 5,000 works. The good news is that La Manufacture also creates a small collection for sale to the public, most of which is on museum-like display within the *musée*. Beware: prices are high!

- place de la Manufacture 92310 Sèvres; tel.: 01.41.14.04.20; fax: 01.45.34.67.88
  Open daily except Tuesday and holidays 10 A.M.–5 P.M.

Versailles (Yvelines)

Main shopping streets: rue de la Paroisse, rue Royale, rue de Satory
Markets: place du Marché Notre-Dame
Tuesday, Friday, and Sunday 8 A.M.–1 P.M.

Passage de la Geole

Most of the visitors to the Château de Versailles skip over the actual town. Like the château, the city of Versailles exudes great distinction and true regal spirit, making it a delightful place to wander through the old streets without the hassles of dealing with crowds. Parts of the city have maintained village-like characteristics, especially the Passage de la Geole, whose Old World setting lends itself remarkably well to the sale of antiques.

The first time I came to this area I was perfectly content to poke around the various shops and stands that make up the charming assemblage of *antiquaires*. Then I spotted the couch of my dreams, a perfect little Louis Philippe loveseat with charmingly curvaceous lines. This is exactly the sort of *coup de foudre* (thunderbolt) you are apt to experience as you explore this village made up of more than twenty unique selling spaces. The offerings are ecclectic, but the dealers are reputable and the prices are fair.

• Enter off of place du Marché Notre-Dame
  Open Thursday 2:30–7 P.M. and Friday–Sunday 10:30 A.M.–7 P.M.

Trianon Palace

The best way to experience the Château de Versailles. Come here and live like a king in this palatial hotel which borders the grounds of the immense Parc de Versailles. You can zip up on a rented bike to simply take tea on their terrace or delight in a traditional French repast in their Belle Epoque–decorated Brasserie La Fontaine. The ultimate, however, is to loll in luxury as a hotel guest and to treat yourself to glorious self-indulgences such as a day of pampering at the Trianon Spa or a candlelight dinner at their reputed gastronomic restaurant, Les Trois Marches.

• 1 boulevard de la Reine, 78009 Versailles; tel.: 01.30.44.38.00;
  fax: 01.39.49.00.77
  Two-Star Michelin Restaurant and Four-Star Hotel: Very
    Expensive; Brasserie: Moderate
  Open year-round
  Spa closed Monday and Tuesday

LANGUEDOC ROUSSILLON
Languedoc Roussillon

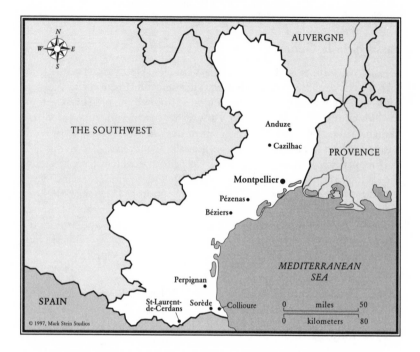

riding crops and Zorro-like whips • wines • trompe l'oeil ceramics • pottery • goat cheeses • old engravings • marionettes • chestnut jam • Molière-inspired gift items • *berlingots* • sweet wine from Banyuls • anchovies • Catalan cotton prints • muscat de Rivesaltes • heavily sculpted rustic furnishings • garnet jewelry • *touron* • traditional toiles of Catalonia • theater masks • Catalan music and books • antiques • honeys • Catalan clothing and home and fashion accessories

IN THE SOUTH of France, the world first discovered the sun-drenched glories of the Côte d'Azur, and more recently the aromatic charms of Provence. Certainly Languedoc Roussillon stands a good chance of becoming the next sunny French province to capture international interest. Little-known Languedoc has plentiful mountain terrain as varied as the craggy crests of the Cévennes and the verdant foothills of the Pyrénées, plus sweeping Mediterranean beaches, many of which have been spared the effects of tourism and provide picture-perfect views quite different from other parts of France. The history and culture can by no means be discounted, either. The eleventh and twelfth-century cloisters from the Abbey of St-Guilhem-le-Désert, a picturesque little village perched on a hillside at the base of the Cévennes, have found their second home at the famous Cloisters Museum, in northern Manhattan in New York City. France no longer sells its historic churches, monuments, or other dwellings, but it does sell pieces of its *tradition* in the shape of pottery, prints, fabrics, and many other products that reflect centuries' worth of knowledge and skills. The silk industry, once very important in the Cévennes, is explained at the silk museum/showroom in the little town of St-Hippolyte-du-Fort. Pézenas and Béziers bridge the contrasts between the northern part of Languedoc Roussillon and the southern swath. They lead you into the Mediterranean, and more precisely, the French side of Catalonia, the paprika-colored land flavored by zesty Spanish influences in everything from its food to its vibrant spirit.

THE CÉVENNES

Anduze (Gard)

Tucked into the gravelly foothills of the Cévennes mountains, the town of Anduze has been making pottery since the seventeenth century. The classically shaped *vase d'Anduze*, an urnlike planter said to have been inspired by a Medici vase, has become synonomous with Languedoc and Provence, where nary a stylish villa may be spotted without one. The Italian influence is visible in the form and regal ornamentations: draped garland and badgelike insignias grace the vases with enough pomp to befit a Roman emperor. Characteristic streaks of honey yellow, olive green, and manganese brown smoulder beneath the surface of their high-gloss glazes. The unusual color scheme that is not to everyone's liking, but the traditional shape in anything other than these colors is not considered a true Anduze vase.

Situated at Tornac just outside of Anduze, **La Poterie de la Madeleine** (tel.: 04.66.61.63.44; fax: 04.66.61.87.29) deviates a bit from *la tradition* by offering vases of less typical color combinations, primarily in solids of Mediterranean blues and greens and even a few chalky whites and sandy pinks, along with a classically glazed collection of vases. **Les Enfants de Boisset** (tel.: 04.66.61.80.86), also clearly indicated once in Anduze, is said to be the oldest *poterie*, and unquestionably the one that continues to work in the most artisanal fashion (most of the clay comes from a quarry out back). Items range in size from about one foot to well over three feet high. There's generally a good stock of smaller pieces, but most larger pieces must be ordered up to a year ahead. Customers rarely stop and shop and orders are usually planned well in advance just like a good garden. Both companies readily handle shipping, which explains why it's not unusual to encounter these distinguished pieces from Singapore to Monterey. In addition to the classic Anduze vases, more ordinary yet highly decorative vases sell in other classic Provençal and Mediterranean forms; the most common is the *jarre à l'huile,* or olive oil jar, traditionally in terra cotta copiously coated with a thick drizzle of emerald-green or mustard-yellow glaze. Keep in mind that most of this pottery sells at selective shops throughout the region. Not surprisingly, the most prized pieces are the older ones, exorbitantly priced at antique shops from Avignon to Paris to Georgetown–and beyond!

Just next door to Les Enfants de Boisset, the touristy outpost **La Vitrine Cevenole** (tel.: 04.66.61.87.28) features regional foodstuffs and knickknacks such as chestnut jam, mountain honey, lavender pillows, and olivewood bracelets. Cevenole and Languedoc wines are perfect accompaniments to the *pelardons des Cévennes,* aromatic goat cheeses preserved in herb-enhanced olive oil, ideal for local picnicking or back-home gifting. This is also a good place to pick up a cold drink.

Cazilhac (Hérault)

Aux 3 Cedres

You might find the rude and rugged scenery of the Cévennes so awe-inspiring that you will want to explore its hidden crevices and gorges. If you decide to leave rustic lodgings to the outdoorsy types, you will undoubtedly feel right at home within the comfy confines of host Nadia Isnard's poetically inspired bed-and-breakfast. The austere exterior of this old silk factory conceals many particularities inside: each of the spacious rooms distinguishes itself by a signature trademark such as a huge bamboo canopy bed or a décor of showy pink and black. The most enchanting *mise en scène* is in the antique green and salmon breakfast room, where guests enjoy bowls of homemade muesli and slices of buttery pound cake at an exquisitely set table, freshly dressed with crisp linens and adorned with Beatrix Potter–like figurines that add a note of whimsy. Little English is spoken here.

- 166 avenue des 2 ponts, 34190 Cazilhac (near Ganges); tel.: 04.67.73.50.77
  Bed-and-Breakfast: Inexpensive
  Call ahead

THE CITIES

Pézenas (Hérault)

Market: Cours Jeans Jaurès
Saturday 8 A.M.–1 P.M.

As you arrive in Pézenas on the N113, it's hard to tell that the center of town has such a complex configuration of centuries-old streets. As long as you're prepared to lose yourself at least a few times in this labyrinth of passageways (nearly all reserved for pedestrians), you'll be thrilled to discover the history, art, and quaint boutiques in this old town. A good part of its architectural heritage remains hidden within the inner courtyards of its seventeenth- and eighteenth-century buildings, so I encourage you to peek past some of the heavy door fronts to see the many wonders inside.

A source of energy for trudging through Pézenas's sometimes hilly streets is the *berlingot*, a tiny, pillow-shaped hard candy that comes in a variety of mouthwatering flavors such as licorice, coffee, raspberry, and bubble gum. Master candymaker **Lallemand** is the town specialist for these and other nougat- and caramel-flavored sweets. The shop is relatively easy to find, just across from the Maison des Métiers d'Art at 19 rue St-Jean (tel.: 04.67.98.81.98).

Annick Lansonneur

Molière lived here briefly with his theatrical troupe during the seventeenth century, and several of the town's shops have picked up on this bit of history. You're sure to be titillated by the theatrical spirit of Pézenas as you enter the boutique of Annick Lansonneur, master *créatrice* of the marvelously expressive marionettes that dance about her closet-sized but incredibly lively space. Annick is the sculptor technician and seamstress for every lifelike piece; this work is largely accomplished in the cupboard-sized corner toward the back where it's not unusual to find her plugging away at her sewing machine creating costumes worthy of a *grand couturier*. Annick expresses herself through the characters she invents, giving each of them a personality through their facial expressions, costumes, and accessories. The attention to detail is extraordinary, and I was not surprised to learn that the designer is known to fashion a puppet's buckle or miniature handbag out of a flea market find or even to make eyelashes out of hair collected from the local coiffeur's clippings. Familiar characters include Puss 'n Boots and a happy-faced clown; others spring from the depths of Annick's imagination. Prices range from 800F for a decorative doll molded out of plaster to about 12,000F for a marionette measuring five feet tall.

• 11–13 rue Mercière, 34120 Pézenas; tel: 04.67.98.07.18
Open most days 9 A.M.–noon and 2:30–6 P.M.

Gravures Anciennes

Monsieur and Madame Perraud possess some of the most interesting old engravings and drawings I have ever encountered, ferreted out from all over France. Prices begin at 200F and vary as much as the subject matter, which encompasses countless themes from the sixteenth to nineteenth centuries.

• 32 rue Conti, 34120 Pézenas; tel.: 04.67.23.04.32
Open most days 9 A.M.–noon and 2:30–6 P.M.

Béziers (Hérault)

Flower Market: allée Paul Riquet Friday 8 A.M.–7 P.M.
Flea Market: place du Champs de Mars Friday 8 A.M.–1 P.M.

Its subtle Mediterranean air, its basilica, its old Roman bridges, and above all, its strategic position on the Canal du Midi provide visitors with enough reasons to make a stop in Béziers. Constructed several centuries ago, the Canal du Midi, a man-made waterway that links the Atlantic to the Mediterranean, may well be one of the most stupefying architectural achievements of its time. Béziers marks the starting point for a two-hour boat tour that leisurely takes you through nine locks, one of the Canal's most renowned highlights.

Château de Raissac

Just about ten minutes from the center of town, out toward the vineyards of Languedoc, resides Norwegian-born Christine Viennet, an artist who demonstrates her passion for ceramics in a cornucopia of eye-catching and mouthwatering ways. As you enter the château you will be introduced to a large collection of old faïence, much of which Madame Viennet began to assemble well over twenty years ago. As much as I like museums, and particularly old faience, I found myself gravitating toward the sumptuous banquet of trompe l'oeil fruits, nuts, cookies, caviar, and other foods that looked as lifelike and luscious as a real epicurean feast.

Here lies the true talent of Madame Viennet, who had the ingenious idea to create colorful clay versions of favorite real-life edibles and to present them on antique plates. A plateful of cherries, for example, becomes instantly more alluring *and* convincing when displayed on an old piece of Nevers faïence than on an ordinary dish. The success was immediate, and today craftswomen in the adjacent atelier turn out works for a variety of stores throughout the world including Bergdorf Goodman and Gump's in the U.S. A large plateful of cherries can set you back as much as 900F, but smaller still lifes, such as a few chocolates in a pretty pink porcelain dish, cost as little as 150F. In general, prices at this shop are about 30 percent lower than cost of the same pieces elsewhere.

• Route de Murviel, 34500 Béziers; tel.: 04.67.49.17.60; fax: 04.67.28.51.82
  No credit cards
  Open Monday–Saturday 9 A.M.–12:30 P.M. and 2–7 P.M.; Sunday by
  appointment

CATALONIA

Collioure (Pyrénées-Roussillon)

Place Marèchal Leclerc
Market: Wednesday and Sunday 8 A.M.–1 P.M.

The Mediterranean coast of France includes a seashell-full of charming resorts that have been spared the spoils of tourism, and Collioure ranks among those chosen few. A historic fort towers over the quaint little port; the terracotta–roofed pastel houses appear to be piled on top of one another in a Picassoesque collage; and a half a dozen surrounding beaches draw bathers who delight more in the sea than in the idea of being seen! What more could you ask for from a village by the sea?

Cellier des Dominicains

Pay close attention or you'll miss this wine cellar, housed in the thirteenth-century church and cloisters of Dominican monks just on the edge of Collioure on the *nationale* leading toward Porte de Vendres. Stop here to prevent yourself from driving all the way to Banyuls for their sweet wine, because this cellar's selection of six different kinds, both red and white, of varying ages, provides a more than adequate representation of the nectars of this *appéllation*. Lesser known reds and rosés from Languedoc, and even many AOC Collioure, sell in great volume along with a couple of muscats de Rivesaltes, another preferred apéritif of the region.

• 66190 Collioure; tel.: 04.68.82.05.63; fax: 04.68.82.43.06
  Open during the season Monday–Saturday 8 A.M.–noon and 1:30–7 P.M.;
  Sunday 8 A.M.–noon; off-season Saturday 8 A.M.–noon and 1:30–
  7 P.M.

Les Anchoïs Desclaux

This is the land of anchovies. Normally this would make me cringe, but I found the anchovies in this town to be sweet, aromatic, and just fishy-tasting enough to remind me that these little filets do indeed come from the sea. Known for its salted anchovies since the Middle Ages, when Collioure was somehow exempt from the salt tax burden that befell many a neighboring village, this seaside town has managed to uphold its reputation for centuries.

Desclaux means quality, and to this day their anchovies are fished in the Mediterranean from June until September on nights when there is no moon, current, or wind; these tiny fish are cleverly coaxed toward the boats by the light of a single lamp on the calm waters. As soon as the catch is brought in, the anchovies are freshly salted and preserved in a briny mixture for at least three months. You can buy them in many forms, but the best ones for travel are those that have already been de-salted, fileted, and preserved in oil, which keeps them delectable for up to eight months. All kinds of fresh anchovy dishes are also prepared daily, an original take-out idea that comes in handy for local salad fixings or hors d'oeuvres.

- 3 route Nationale, 66190 Collioure; tel.: 04.68.82.05.25; fax: 04.68.82.13.24

  Open Monday–Saturday 9 A.M.–noon and 2–7 P.M.; Sunday 9:30 A.M.–12:30 P.M. and 3:30–7 P.M.

Sardane

Somewhat secluded within the backstreets of Collioure, this tiny boutique is worth seeking out for its exclusive collection of Catalan fabrics, most of which have been fashioned into a festive line of cotton casual wear for men, women, and children. In keeping with the relaxed spirit of the *Midi*, the simple and classically cut styles include roomy shirts, loosely fitted jackets, and short or long *paréo* skirts. The prominent regional note is the color-saturated prints, characterized by primarily small and repetitive motifs of meaningful symbols such as boats, fish, olives, grapes, and *la croix Catalane*, a cross composed of six elongated lozenges interspersed with garnetlike punctuations. Although made in Barcelona, the Sardane fabrics are of excellent quality and similar to those of Souleiado, the renowned textilemaker of Provence. A sampling of tablecloths and other home and personal accessories completes the *typiquement catalan* collection of reasonably priced goods.

- 4 rue Rière, 66190 Collioure; tel.: 04.68.82.34.90; fax: 04.68.98.01.40

  Open in season 11 A.M.–1 P.M. and 4–8 P.M.

Hostellerie des Templiers

Countless creative souls adopted Les Templiers as their hangout many years ago; nearly 2,000 works displayed throughout the bar, restaurant, corridor, and even some of the guest rooms prove that this establishment once buzzed with an artsy clientele that included Derain, Dufy, Picasso, Maillol, and Matisse, to name just a select few. Today Les Templiers is an excellent place to sip a chilled glass of Banyuls on the terrace or to feast over a fresh seafood dish in one of the more contemporary art-oriented dining rooms.

Void of any pretention and basic in comfort, the rooms are reasonably priced, particularly for such a centrally-located establishment. A must.

- 12 quai de l'Amirauté, 66190 Collioure; tel.: 04.68.98.31.10; fax: 04.68.98.01.24
  Café/Restaurant/Hotel: Moderate
  Open year-round

Perpignan (Pyrénées-Roussillon)

Main shopping streets: rue Louis-Blanc, rue des Augustins, rue Neuilly
Market: place de la République daily except Monday 8 A.M.–7 P.M.

Second only to Barcelona in Catalan cities, Perpignan burbles with a perceptible Spanish flair even as it maintains a distinctively French identity. Manageable in size and highly animated in spirit, Perpignan is a great city to explore on foot. The Castillet, an old pink brick citadel located near the heart of the shopping district, serves as an excellent landmark, making it virtually impossible to become lost. If you decide to spend a night or two in Perpignan, I recommend the four-star hotel and restaurant **La Villa Duflot** (tel.: 04.68.56.67.67; fax: 04.68.56.54.05); although located outside of the center of town, these rather *Dolce Vita*-esque digs surround a glorious pool that is sure to provide a welcome cool-down after a day's touring.

As you drive to or from Perpignan, you might want to check out **Comteroux** (tel.: 04.68.54.64.33; fax: 04.68.54.06.30), an immense home-decorating showroom situated on the route d'Espagne on the southern fringes of town. A huge selection of furniture and fabrics from leading French manufacturers is exhibited here to the delight of local residents in search of beautiful embellishments for their homes; as a visitor, you probably will want to focus more on their Catalan furnishings, both old and new, which are dispersed throughout the store. Constructed out of dark wood with heavily-sculpted *rosaces* or *fleurettes* (rose or flower-shaped ornamentations), traditional Catalan pieces evoke a seriousness of spirit more akin to Spanish styling than French. Look closely and be sure to ask questions, it's sometimes difficult to distinguish the store's reproductions from their antiques.

Gil & Jean Barate

So many regions of France possess their own distinctive jewelry, often in the form of a cross, the most prevalent symbol of the peoples' firm commitment to Christianity. The Catalan cross with *le grenat de Perpignan*, or the Perpignan garnet, is a stunning piece of jewelry, perfectly suited for any number of today's fashion statements. Garnets were viewed as prestigious, sacred stones in Catalonia as early as 1750, and were actually mined in the foothills of the Pyrénées until a short time ago. Today most garnets come from India, but what makes them unique to Perpignan is the manner in which they are cut. Whether round, oval, almond, or square in shape, the unique multifaceted convex nature of the cut brings a clear, scarlet brilliance to the stones, rarely duplicated elsewhere. The stones have finely crafted settings entirely fashioned out of eighteen-karat gold. It's no wonder that the women of Catalonia have been enraptured by these pieces for more than two centuries. This jeweler's selection of Perpignan finery ranges in price from 1,200F for a simple pair of earrings to 2,450F to 7,500F for the more ornately set Catalan crosses.

• 5 rue Louis-Blanc, 66000 Perpignan; tel.: 04.68.34.37.68
  Open Tuesday–Saturday 9 A.M.–noon and 2–7 P.M.

Maison Quinta

If you only have time to explore one store in Catalonia, go directly to Maison Quinta. Françoise and Henri Quinta should win an award for perpetuating and enhancing Catalan arts and traditions. Françoise is the creative dynamo who drummed up the idea, and most of all the energy, to open this exclusive emporium of Catalan goods; Henri is the driving force behind the aforementioned Comteroux; and together they breathed new life into an old manufacturer of traditional Catalan fabrics and renamed it Les Toiles du Soleil, or fabrics of the sun.

Here their color-drenched tablecloths, napkins, and fabrics "by the meter" take center stage, and a seamstress also works on site for custom orders. The traditional blood red/sun gold patterns accurately embody the vivacity and robust nature of this fiery land. These and other ethnic-tinged colors and patterns have also been crafted into vests, espadrilles, tote bags, and other accessories.

At Maison Quinta the regional theme spills over into CDs, books, arts and crafts, food and wine products, and more. There's even a mini sandwich bar where you can sample some of these savory delights while recharging yourself for a bit more browsing. Madame Quinta couldn't resist over-stepping her regional boundaries, and by doing so, she has added many beautiful home décor products from some of France's most creative design-ers. For one last treat, be sure to take a look upstairs in the small, exquisitely stocked room that serves as a bridal registry for the area's most fortunate brides-to-be.

- 3 rue Grande des Fabriques, 66000 Perpignan; tel.: 04.68.34.41.62; fax: 04.68.51.15.04
  Boutique/Sandwich Bar
  Open Monday 2:30–7 P.M., Tuesday–Saturday 9:30 A.M.–noon and 2:30– 7 P.M.

Casa Sansa

If you happen to arrive in town around lunchtime, stop here first. The snazzy yet traditional ambiance of this ecclectically decorated bistrot reflects the many faces of Catalonia—particu-larly the bidimensional aspect of the land and the sea. Sit back, order a *verre de muscat*, taste a few different tapas, and let yourself be seduced by the lively nature of this place and its people!

- 3 rue Fabrique Couverte and 2 rue Fabrique d'en Nadal, 66000 Perpignan; tel.: 04.68.34.21.84
  Open Monday–Saturday; closed Sunday and Monday at lunch
  Bistrot: Inexpensive–Moderate

St-Laurent-de-Cerdans (Pyrénées-Roussillon)

Les Toiles du Soleil

Far from the hubbub of the city, all of the ebullient Catalan fabrics show-cased at the well-appointed Maison Quinta are woven here in this old mill in much the same way that the first threads were drawn in 1860. The selec-tion at the factory store is far from sparse and tastefully presented in typical Quinta style. Prices on some items run a bit lower than elsewhere, although bargain-hunting should not be your prime reason to visit. The drive to this tiny town is at least half the fun, particularly if you like verdant, hilly countryside. You'll need a detailed map to find St-Laurent-de-Cerdans, cradled in the foothills of the Pyrénées, just a stone's throw away from the Spanish border. Plan to stop in Arles-sur-Tech at the little *pâtissier/confiseur/glacier* **Jean Touron** (tel.: 68.39.10.47) for an added sampling of Catalan culture in a chunk of *touron*, a chewy, gooey homemade nougat confection.

• 66260 St-Laurent-de-Cerdans; tel.: 04.68.39.50.02; fax: 04.68.54.06.30
Open daily 9 A.M.–noon and 2–6 P.M. Factory visits June–September.

Sorède (Pyréenées-Roussillon)

Les Micocouliers

Just inland from Collioure, this atelier of entirely handmade whips and riding crops has to be one of the most esoteric entries in this book!

The origins of this craft have been traced back to the thirteenth century in France, and in the little village of Sorède nearly 600 workers made these products until the early part of this century. The craft almost died out entirely in 1970, but this atelier opened up again in the early 1980s, and today its nineteenth-century lathes are turning full tilt to fill orders from clients around the world, including circuses, theater groups, and even Hermès, the big-name equestrian supplier to the elite. These products are fashioned entirely out of wood; leather is used only in the trimming. *Micocoulier*, or hackberry wood, explains the real raison d'être for this workshop; the craft was developed here not because of any increased demand for crops and whips in these parts, but instead because of the trees whose supple wood becomes even more pliable under the skillful manipulations (50 to 100 required for one crop) of these craftspeople. The atelier welcomes visitors and provides some explanations in English. A classic crop costs between 120F and 250F.

• 4 rue des Fabriques, 66690 Sorède; tel.: 04.68.89.04.50; fax: 04.68.89.35.79
Open year-round except for Christmas week, Monday–Friday 9 A.M.–noon and 2–4:30 P.M.

THE LIMOUSIN
Le Limousin

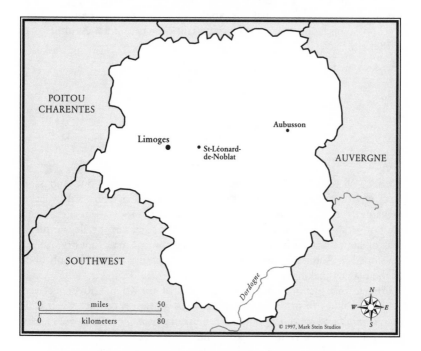

old tapestries • Limoges boxes • colorful fashions • antiques •
Limoges china • *lithophanies en porcelaine* • reproductions of old
tapestries • enamels • books, posters, and postcards of tapestries,
china, and enamels • regional foodstuffs • contemporary tapestry
creations • local crafts made of glass, metal, and ceramic • *cartons
de tapisseries* • bric-à-brac • brightly colored *objets*

SOME OF THE most overlooked parts of France are in the center of the
country, and are easy to pass through as you travel around France. Although
situated in France's heartland, *le Limousin* is often overlooked–and wrong-
fully so. Even the most dyed-in-the-wool city dwellers can't help but fall
under the charms of the Limousin countryside, known as one of the most
rural regions of the land. It is hard to remain indifferent to the region's
bucolic nature as you pass before poignant landscapes filled with sweet vistas
of brown cows grazing in fertile valleys, centuries-old bell towers piercing

early morning mists, and rustic stone farmhouses, constructed as if they were to last forever—and I'm sure that many of them will.

You will discover most of this along the route from Limoges, known for its china, to Aubusson, known for its tapestries, with only the handsome medieval village of St-Léonard-de-Noblat to bridge the gap between these lovely pastoral landscapes and the important centers of art and culture that bolster either end.

Aubusson (Creuse)

Market: place de l'Espagne
Saturday 8–12:30 A.M.

Hardly a château in France has not been adorned by at least one Aubusson tapestry. The original purpose of these celebrated wallcoverings was twofold: to warm the cold stone interiors while decorating the rooms with allegorical, mythological, historical, and later on, decorative scenes of the elegant pleasures of life portrayed by music, song, dance, and poetry. Tapestry-making developed in Aubusson during the eighteenth century as a natural offshoot of the blanket-making trade.

The town's manufacturers on the banks of the Creuse River received sizable subsidies from the state during the seventeenth century when Colbert, *le grand patron des arts*, dubbed Aubusson a *manufacture royale* (a factory that worked primarily for the king and his court). Unlike the other two tapestry giants, Les Gobelins and Beauvais, Aubusson is no longer state-run. Individuals can readily buy reproductions of old and contemporary works as well as more modern creations from the more than twenty ateliers that call Aubusson home. Grouped primarily within the center of this small town, many of these workshops/showrooms are open only during the tourist season. Pick up a list of the shops at the tourism office (rue Vieille); some of them conduct tours of their ateliers as well. Before you start shopping around, begin with a visit to the **Musée Départemental de la Tapisserie** (tel.: 05.55.66.33.06; fax: 05.55.83.89.87), a museum whose permanent exhibition of Aubusson masterpieces and temporary shows of related works pay tribute to one of the world's most respected art forms, the tapestry. The town of Aubusson offers little in terms of beauty, aside from its tapestries, but the surrounding countryside promises far more pleasing views, particularly along the N241, the route between Limoges and Aubusson. Located in St-Hilaire-le-Château about fifteen minutes outside of Aubusson on this road, the restaurant in the handsomely decorated **Hôtel du Thaurion** (tel.: 05.55.64.50.12; fax: 05.55.64.90.92) serves reasonably priced regional specialities, in portions hearty enough for the largest appetites.

Atelier Robert Four

They dye, they weave, they restore, they reproduce, they create—the only thing that this reputable manufacturer does not do is keep the Aubusson showroom open year-round! Apart from the months of July, August, and September, you may have to visit their rue Bonaparte address in Paris to see the best of Aubusson. Although the showroom has limited hours, however, the factory is open for tours year-round (except August). Originals and reproductions of old and more modern-styled tapestries sell in the showrooms; you can pay as little as 1,500F for a nineteenth-century remnant in *petit point* (perfect for working it up into a cushion) or as much as 210,000F for a sixteenth-century Flemish tapestry, big enough to cover an entire wall of a large-sized dining room. Top-quality rugs called *savonneries* (Aubusson's first rugs were created in a former *savonnerie*, or soap-making manufactory) also sell here in a range of *point noué* patterns. Prices for the often flowery nineteenth-century *cartons*, the gouachelike paintings of the proposed tapestry designs, run in the more accesible range of 3,000F to 8,000F.

- Grande Rue, 23200 Aubusson; tel.: 05.55.66.15.70; fax: 05.55.66.87.31
  Workshop open Monday–Friday 9:30 A.M.–noon and 2–4:30 P.M.
  Gallery open at varying hours during the summer.

Limoges (Haute-Vienne)

Main shopping street: boulevard Louis-Blanc, rue de la Boucherie
Market: Les Halles daily 7 A.M.–6 P.M.
Flea market: around the cathedral 8 A.M.–1 P.M.
the second Sunday of every month

Foreigners generally know that Bordeaux wines come from the area surrounding the city of Bordeaux. Few, however, know that Limoges is not the brand name of a certain type of china, but instead the city where the china is made. Some people are also under the impression that Haviland, one of the top manufacturers of Limoges china, is an English company because of the Anglo-Saxon ring to its name. Obviously there's a lot of confusion to clear up, and one way to start is by introducing you to a lovely city in the center of France called Limoges, whose fine white kaolin clay is the base for some of the world's finest china, *la porcelaine de Limoges*.

It helps to think of Limoges as a destination. Although the city is a good four-hour drive from Paris, it's worth a visit to learn about the history of Limoges china and, of course, to shop. *Le Limousin* also is a sensible stopping-off point for people en route to other regions such as the Dordogne or farther points southwest. Factory discount shopping for china can be a real hoot here, too; it's unlikely that you'll set out to buy (or even find) twelve place settings of one particular pattern, but you'd be amazed at the number of odds and ends you can pick up at bargain prices that you will cherish back home. Better yet, a good part of the reduced-price shopping takes place in stores that not only are manageable in size but also are amusing in their helter-skelter approach to presenting such fragile finery. Prices on china in the regular retail stores of Limoges run slightly lower than those of department stores in France; your best bet for sizable purchases of totally flawless china, however, is to shop at the rue de Paradis table arts stores in Paris, where prices run 25 to 30 percent less than those outside of Europe.

Before you hit the shops, visit the **Musée National Adrien-Dubouché** (closed on Tuesdays and at lunchtime) to see interesting examples of ceramics from all over the world and from across the centuries. The educational tour makes clear how heavily the French relied upon faience up until the early part of the nineteenth century, when the proliferation of porcelain began in Limoges. The ceramicists in the Orient had mastered the properties of this "hard" ceramic long before, and the museum displays many fine examples, some of which were imported by the *Compagnie des Indes* and most likely served as inspiration for the first creations in Limoges. Before you move on, look carefully at the Limoges china on display. The extreme whiteness and astonishing translucence of this porcelain has earned it the prestige and value it has today.

The recent Metropolitan Museum of Art exhibition in New York, *Les Emaux de Limoges*, helped to increase awareness that Limoges deserves kudos for another art form as well: enamels. The origins of these enamels have been traced back to the Middle Ages, when craftspeople created religious artifacts for distribution throughout all of Europe. Far more secular in subject matter, the best of today's Limoges enamels veer more toward contemporary art creations than sacred symbolism. Since the early sixties the city has organized an **Enamel Biennal**, a biennial international event that allows artists from all over the world the opportunity to show their works and share ideas about this unique medium. In the case of Limoges enamels, mixtures of glazes and powders appear to take on magical powers when applied to mostly metallic surfaces; after firing, an array of startling colors and textures emerges.

Speaking of startling colors and textures, no trip to Limoges is complete without a visit to **Jean Charles de Castelbajac**, the perrenial sweetheart of the fashion world who makes Limoges his home and headquarters. Stop into his gallery/boutique at 27 rue des Tanneries (tel/fax.: 05.55.32.23.05) for a look at his boldly colored, fun-loving accoutrements for you and your home—enameled boxes included.

With all of the wonderful riches of this city, the antiquing can be pretty hot. The rue de la Boucherie and the rue Elie-Berthet in the picturesque old section of town have a few interesting *antiquaires*, but the real fun takes place at the *foire à la brocante*, the second Sunday of every month in the streets surrounding the cathedral. People come from all over France to attend this *grand événement*. The day I was there, the area was hopping by 10 A.M. despite the cold, drizzling rain.

You can't leave Limoges without visiting its Halles, the food market *en permanence*, very much the focal point of the city center. For a real taste of local color, plan to have lunch in one of the many animated and totally nononsense bistrotlike eateries, which will serve you *un plat du jour* with *un coup de rouge*, or daily special with a glass of red wine, as if you're just one of their regular Joes (or should I say *Josephes?*)

ENAMELS

Galerie du Canal

Near the rue de la Boucherie in the old part of town, this large, loftlike space shows the works of half a dozen local artists, most of whom have chosen enamel as their medium. Some have strayed from tradition by applying the enamels to ceramics instead of metal, a likely adaptation for the porcelain-postured region of Limoges. This is the most arts-and-craftsy address in the city, and prices here vary as much as the quality of the work.

• 15 rue du Canal, 87000 Limoges; tel.: 05.55.33.14.11
  Open Tuesday–Saturday 10 A.M.–noon and 2–7 P.M.

Galerie Christel

You could make the trip to Limoges just to see the subliminal enamels of Christian Christel. Each work epitomizes a reflective study of color, form, and texture; the artist painstakingly carries out the innumerable processes required in the enameling of his forms in the quietude of his atelier near St-Léonard-de-Noblat. Whether round and matte red like the seat of an old leather armchair or tall and cylindrical, encircled by a glossy swish of multicolored Jupiter-like rings, every work is understandably *une pièce unique*. The gallery celebrates the creative genius of Monsieur Christel and several of his multitalented counterparts whose glass, ceramic, and metal creations also clamor for your attention. Prices range from 200F to 20,000F.

• 15 boulevard Louis-Blanc, 87000 Limoges; tel.: 05.55.34.23.36
  Open Monday–Saturday 9–12:30 A.M. and 2–7 P.M.

Georges Magadoux

This company produces some of the most reputed enamels of Limoges. The *bleus Magadoux*, a range of royal blues, are characteristic of this more than thirty-year-old house. Georges Magadoux is no longer alive, but his scenes of the old streets of Limoges, his religious symbols, and his contemporary designs inspired by Picasso and Chagall live on under the watchful eye of his son, who also oversees the little atelier in back of the shop. In keeping with *la tradition*, all of the pieces amass the most beautiful shades of blue, not unlike those of the Limousin sky on the brightest summer day. Prices range from about 400F to 5,000F.

- rue Cruche-d'Or and rue du Consulat, 87000 Limoges; tel.:
  05.55.34.18.80; fax: 05.55.32.95.47
  Open Tuesday–Saturday 9 A.M.–noon and 2–7 P.M.

PORCELAIN

The following stores are those I found most appealing. Keep in mind that there are many more factory outlets in and around Limoges.

Bernardaud

The dusty old barnlike interior of this leading porcelain maker's factory outlet contrasts dramatically with the pristine Bernardaud showcase boutique in Paris. Many of the same fresh, bold patterns that have boosted Bernardaud to most innovative *porcelainer* status decorate the scads of dishes and plates haphazardly stacked atop tables and piled high on the floor in this rustic space just across the street from the factory. The large selection here includes promising gift ideas galore! Prices have been reduced 20 to 70 percent; most of the goods sell for about half what you normally would pay in regular French stores. The items are mostly seconds, but the defects in many instances are virtually imperceptible; even so, all have been conscientiously marked with a red crayon. The store does not ship, but the staff does a good job with travel-ready wrapping!

- 30 rue Albert-Thomas, 87000 Limoges; tel.: 05.55.77.39.66
  Open October–March Monday–Saturday 9 A.M.–noon and 1–6 P.M.;
    April–September Monday–Saturday 9:30 A.M.–noon and 1–6:30 P.M.

Le Cygne Bleu

Conveniently located near the center of town, Le Cygne Bleu presents seconds and discontinued pieces from another Limoges frontrunner, Raynaud. The name may not be as familiar as the patterns, but once you see the 30 to 50 percent discounts, you'll take notice! No shipping.

- 6 place des Jacobins, 87000 Limoges; tel.: 05.55.32.45.81
  Open Monday–Saturday 9:30 A.M.–noon and 2:30–7 P.M.

Haviland/Pavillon de la Porcelaine

Founded by American-born David Haviland in 1842, this big-name Limoges porcelain maker is among the best known; patterns vary from a dainty flourish of eighteenth-century–inspired posies to more modern, color-concentrated interpretations of Oriental themes. Their newly renovated museum pays tribute to many exceptional pieces, particularly table settings created for famous places and people including Maxim's restaurant in Paris, the Empress Eugénie, and an impressive number of American presidents, to name a few. After seeing a video and a mini-workshop demonstration, you leave this museum with a much greater appreciation for all of the beautiful Limoges china that graces tables throughout the world.

The supermarket layout of the factory store challenges your china sensitivities for other reasons. Loaded with seconds and first-choice merchandise from Haviland and a couple of other brands of lesser quality, discounts are as high as 60 percent! Extra bonus: they also handle shipping.

- avenue J. F. Kennedy, Z. I. Magré, 87000 Limoges; tel.: 05.55.30.21.86; fax: 05.55.06.26.91

    Open daily 8:30 A.M.–7:30 P.M.; from November 1–Easter 9 A.M.–7 P.M.; closed December 25, January 1 and Sundays in January

Lachainette

Lachainette happens to be the name of the big table arts store in the center of town; of their three different addresses, I consider this seconds shop the most interesting. It looks like an old house that someone's grandmother left behind, chock full of a lifetime's worth of china collecting from many of the most distinguished houses of Limoges. Some of the services do in fact appear *passé*, while others consist of beauteous odds and ends from Robert Haviland & C. Parlon, Ancienne Manufacture Royale, Bernardaud, and more. Discounts are as high as 50 percent, and the store handles shipping.

- 27 boulevard Louis-Blanc, 87000 Limoges; tel.: 05.55.34.58.61; fax: 05.55.34.65.47

    Open Monday–Saturday 9:15 A.M.–noon and 2–7 P.M.

Laure Japy

This name may not mean much to you unless you pride yourself on being au courant about France's leading table arts *coloriste*, Laure Japy. Her Left Bank showcase in Paris ranks among my most favorite tabletop shops, and although some of her creations sell in upscale department stores abroad, she is known to only a select few. Her signature color-drenched designs have been applied to china, glassware, and table linens—all in a coordinating realm of hues and patterns. If you stop into her Limoges factory store, you're bound to find a porcelain tea service or two that you absolutely can't live without!

• 4 avenue de la Révolution, 87000 Limoges; tel.: 05.55.30.41.72
  Open Tuesday–Saturday 9 A.M.–noon and 2–6 P.M.

Outside Limoges (Haute-Vienne)

Ancienne Manufacture Royale

Created by the Comte d'Artois in 1737, Ancienne Manufacture Royale is indeed the oldest porcelain maker of Limoges, and as the name indicates, was once the manufacturer for the king. It's worth traveling the twenty minutes outside of Limoges to examine the elegant offerings sold in their factory boutique. The merchandise consists primarily of seconds and discontinued items reduced by approximately forty percent, although you may be more tempted to throw caution to the wind and splurge on one or more of their famous gold-encrusted pieces. You'd have to be an Arab prince to afford an entire service of these top-of-the-line creations, recognizable by their engraved glazes set in a thick band of gold. If you seek the ultimate and the most classic ex-

---

La Chapelle St-Martin

My travel companion and I discovered this elegant establishment after making several enquiries about where to sample some fine regional dining. Our hopes for *fine cuisine* turned into a true gastronomic experience as we found ourselves feasting on supremely tender and succulent *pièces de boeuf,* perfectly prepared in a light red wine sauce. The region's reputation for prized cattle nearly rivals that of its revered china, and here we were spoiled on both counts: every delectable morsel was served on a different pattern of *porcelaine de Limoges.* The layout of the house resembles that of a private mansion; the dining area is actually composed of a series of small rooms, each eloquently decorated in a different style. The affable hosts are Jacques and Viviane Dudognon; their son Gilles is the master chef of this reputable establishment.

• 87510 Nieul; tel.: 05.55.75.80.17; fax: 05.55.75.89.50
  Three-Star, Relais & Châteaux Hotel/Restaurant: Expensive
  Open year-round except January; restaurant closed on
     Monday

amples of Limoges lasciviousness, consider the ones with the crimson or midnight blue backgrounds, the most seductive of them all.

If you've already been shopping, you've probably encountered a sampling of Limoges boxes by now. I hope you haven't bought too many, however, because *les petites boîtes* happen to be another of the Manufacture's specialties; it is said that theirs are in fact the best in all of the region. No seconds on these, but the prices, between 250F and 310F, would have you thinking so! They usually carry a selection of about 100 different boxes, so unless you arrive on the heels of several busloads of tourists, you should be able to shop to your heart's content.

- 7 place des Horteils, Aixe-sur-Vienne; tel.: 05.55.70.44.82; fax: 05.55.70.45.00

  Open Monday–Friday 9:30 A.M.–12:30 P.M. and 1:30–6:30 P.M.; Saturday 9:30 A.M–noon and 2–6:30 P.M.

St-Léonard-de-Noblat (Haute-Vienne)

Jean Louis Coquet

When foreigners do see the name Coquet (pronounced *kokay*), they usually associate it with the word *coquette*. Only a few of the motifs that adorn the

---

Le Grand St-Leonard

This is the kind of place people think of when you mention a real French auberge. The interior of this old postal inn features country French accents of antique armoires and pretty displays of copper molds and flowery ceramics. Dressed with snappy white linens, poetic bouquets, and, of course, Coquet china, the tables set a cheery tone that can soften your soul even on the dreariest days of winter. Classically prepared cuisine completes this delightful picture of local vernacular, and it's good to know that if you feel too relaxed to move on, you can always request a room at the inn.

- 87400 St-Léonard-de-Noblat; tel.: 05.55.56.18.18; fax: 05.55.56.98.32

  Restaurant: Moderate;

  Two-Star Hotel: Inexpensive

  Open year-round except from mid–December to mid–January; closed also Mondays from September to June and Monday lunch in July and August

creations of this reputed Limoges porcelain maker could be referred to as coquettish; most embrace classic designs that stem from traditional patterns once used in both faience and porcelain. *Le Panier Fleuri*, or flowering basket, inspired by the centuries-old faience of Rouen in Normandy, represents one such example. The dishes from this pattern, as well as those from certain other services, are available in octagonal shapes or colored with celadon backgrounds. A Coquet trademark, this allows for many mixing and matching possibilities.

In this spacious and modern store, it's easy to pick up a few incongruous pieces that you can play with at home. Discounts run about 40 percent on items that generally have minimal flaws. I had a grand time picking out eight cobalt blue charger plates whose solid, glossy sheen did not leave much room for error!

• 87400 St-Léonard-de-Noblat; tel.: 05.55.56.08.28; fax: 05.55.56.13.97
  Open Monday–Saturday 9 A.M.–noon and 2–7 P.M.

THE LOIRE VALLEY AND CENTER
Centre Val de Loire

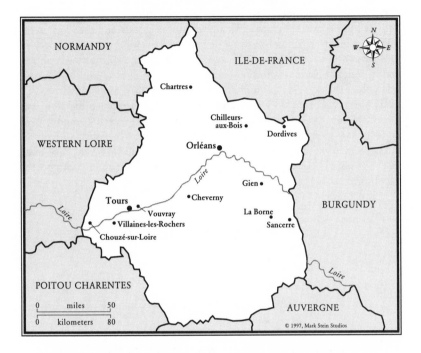

NORMANDY

ILE-DE-FRANCE

Chartres •

Chilleurs-
aux-Bois •

Dordives •

WESTERN LOIRE

Orléans •

Loire

Gien •

Tours • • • Cheverny

Vouvray

• Villaines-les-Rochers

La Borne •

BURGUNDY

Sancerre •

Chouzé-sur-Loire

POITOU CHARENTES

| 0 | miles | 50 |

| 0 | kilometers | 80 |

AUVERGNE

Loire

© 1997, Mark Stein Studios

wines • pottery • stained glass • contemporary art creations • goat
cheese • faience • chocolates • books on wine, perfume, stained
glass, and French kitchen arts • hand-painted Limoges boxes •
rillettes • handmade baskets • dog dishes • handwoven tapestries
• *rillons* • almond-flavored treats • silk upholstery fabrics • antiques • *pain à l'ancienne* • kitchen décor items • reproductions of
antique furnishings • *brioche* • perfume • estate sale bargains •
table arts at a discount

WHENEVER I MENTION *La Loire* people always seem to respond with expressions of delight, a quick nod of the head, and a comment like "Now,
that's where I'd like to go in France." If they haven't actually traveled to the
Loire Valley and its environs, they already seem to have been there many
times in their minds, in thoughts which prompt their eyes to flash with
excitement as they envision themselves visiting castles and countryside famous the world over. More informed travel enthusiasts know that the region

167

also stakes a significant claim in wine production, but aside from that, even the most well-versed francophiles usually draw blanks when it comes to citing products associated with this part of France.

Unlike many of the other French provinces, it's hard to point to one common cultural bond in this region that has affected the peoples' trade and traditions and consequent locally produced goods and arts and crafts. Instead, numerous influences have led to the development of a variety of products within the Loire. You'll notice that the mood of the towns, shops, and other establishments in the Central Loire section resonates with a considerably more down-to-earth din than the high-pitched tone set by the Châteaux Side. Part of these contrasts may be due to the strong connection with the earth that typifies the Center (local clay is an essential component of both the faience of Gien and the pottery of La Borne), and other differences might stem from the fact that the people of the Châteaux Side have lived in an important aristocratic sphere for centuries. Visit them both to see which one suits you the best!

CHÂTEAUX SIDE

Chartres (Eure-et-Loire)

Market: place Billard and rue des Changes
Saturday 8 A.M.–1 P.M.

When you hear the name Chartres, you automatically think of the mighty medieval cathedral, Notre-Dame-de-Chartres, of this lovely small town. And if you know anything at all about this astonishing architectural achievement, you probably have heard that it is best known for its jewel-like stained-glass windows, most of which date back to the twelfth and thirteenth centuries. I dare not tell you anything else about this *haut lieu d'art et de culture*, the subject of so many thousands of theses, books, and various other studies; any information that I could pass on to you would pale in comparison. One of the best ways to learn more about this mystical masterpiece is to take a tour with one of its foremost authorities, Englishman **Malcolm Miller**, who has made the Chartres Cathedral his passion for over forty years. He speaks daily from Easter until November at noon and 2:45 P.M.; wait for him in the front entry near the royal entrance or inquire ahead of time at the tourism office (place Cathédrale).

Once your stained-glass consciousness has been adequately elevated, you can segue over to the **Centre International du Vitrail** (5 rue Cardinal-Pie; tel.: 02.37.21.65.72; fax: 02.37.36.15.34), a complex dedicated to the exhibition, study, and research of *vitraux* (stained glass) from all over the world.

Temporary exhibitions of old and modern works rotate throughout the year, and if you're truly interested in this illuminating medium, you should contact them about participating in one of their workshops or conferences.

La Galerie du Vitrail

Now that you've done your homework, you may be eager to buy something that will remind you of Chartres's brilliant stained-glass treasures. Just across from the north side of the cathedral in a rustic eighteenth-century house, La Galerie du Vitrail tastefully exhibits an abundance of goods that pay homage to the glowing facets of this medium. The collection of more than 400 books in a half dozen different languages on this well-documented subject indicates right off that you are among people who take this art form quite seriously. The owners of this gallery/boutique, Monsieur and Madame Loire (their real name!), have continued the tradition of stained-glass–making in their atelier just outside of town, a business that was founded in 1946 by Monsieur Loire's father. Today the workshop still buzzes with ten craftspeople who fastidiously restore old pieces and create new ones.

The back of the boutique glows with their current production of works based on old themes and new designs. I instantly felt drawn to the room covered with luminescent panels from the *grande époque* of stained glass, the period from 1880 to 1930, when many a home and business was embellished with at least one decorative window or door. From the looks of things here, peoples' tastes changed dramatically over the course of those years, leaping from the heavy, color-charged designs of the Victorian era to the light, ethereal scenes of Art Nouveau. The adjacent space presents a more somber vision of life in the mostly abstract, contemporary creations of Monsieur Loire and other European artists. Prices range from 4,000F to 20,000F.

Take a look at the gallery's antique offerings, particularly since it's so rare to encounter sixteenth- and seventeenth-century pieces for sale (one seventeenth-century 8 × 10 stained glass work depicting the biblical flight from Egypt was priced at 6,000F). Turn-of-the-century flowery borders from churches or châteaux circulate more inconspicuously in the marketplace, demanding about 1,800F for a decorative stretch of trimming. Among the less pricey gift items, you can pick up a Chartres-inspired stained-glass ornamentation for 180F to 550F.

- 17 Cloître Notre-Dame, 28000 Chartres; tel.: 02.37.36.10.03; fax: 02.37.36.22.33

  Open Tuesday–Sunday from Easter to the end of October, and Tuesday–Saturday from November to Easter; closed January 15–February 8

  The atelier is open for visits Friday afternoons from Easter to November 1; ask a local for directions here or inquire at the tourism office on the place Cathédrale

Cheverny (Loir-et-Cher)

Château de Cheverny Auction

If you happen to be planning a springtime tour to the Loire Valley region, you must inquire about the Château de Cheverny auction so that your trip coincides with this big event. Even if you're not out to buy, a visit here promises to be nothing less than entertaining as you mill about in the company of local *châtelains* (château owners), fervent collectors, bargain-hungry dealers, and nonplussed visitors just out for a weekend stroll. Originated by the Marquise de Brantes, an enterprising former New Yorker affectionately referred to as Sue, this incredibly upscale sort of house sale provides the surrounding château dwellers the opportunity to sell off a few family heirlooms or ancestral *objets* in an effort to raise a bit of cash to cover the repair of a tumbling turret or a leaky roof. Sales are normally held during the month of May.

• For information contact: Flore de Brantes, Le Fresne, 41310 Authon
  or Stéphane Renault, 9 cloître St-Aignan, 45000 Orléans; fax:
  02.38.62.94.08

Chilleurs-aux-Bois (Loiret)

Château de Chamerolles

Entirely dedicated to the world of perfume, this museum is an unexpected presence in this part of France, but it all makes sense once you learn that the area within 150 kilometers of Paris is referred to as Cosmetic Valley due to the large number of *parfumeurs* with facilities here. Although many natural essences are still concocted in the southern city of Grasse, most of the synthetic scents and actual compositions of fragrances are cooked up in laboratories surrounding the capital.

The spacious Château de Chamerolles houses both extensive temporary exhibitions and permanent ones relating to the innumerable aspects of this ever-changing world. What I enjoyed most about this museum, however, were the permanent displays that traced the history of perfume over centuries past. Truly the material of comedy skits, lifelike scenes have been recreated in a series of rooms to show the varying attitudes toward personal hygiene throughout modern history. During the sixteenth century, for example, as many as a half dozen people would sit around soaking in baths as if they were hanging out in armchairs in a salon; in the seventeenth century they wouldn't let water touch their skin, so the *toilette* (meaning washing) came into practice in the form of a toile, saturated with perfume, that they would rub over their skin several times a day. Thank goodness the use of the bathtub was rediscovered during the eighteenth century, and this time, the approach was considerably more private. Up until the mid-nineteenth century, people made their own perfumes at home, and thereafter began to buy them premixed from *parfumeurs*. There is much to learn within this château and on its neatly groomed grounds. The boutique sells a sampling of some of the oldest toilet waters known to France as well as a few more trendy products from L'Occitane.

- 45170 Chilleurs-aux-Bois; tel.: 02.38.39.84.66; fax: 02.38.32.90.91
  Museum/Boutique
  Open April 1–September 30 10 A.M.–6 P.M.; October 1–March 31
     10 A.M.–5 P.M.

Chouzé-sur-Loire (Indre-et-Loire)

Château des Réaux

Ideally located approximately 40 kilometers from Tours and 20 from Saumur, the Château des Réaux serves as an excellent base for exploring the many sights of the Loire Valley and Western Loire regions. Even more enticing is the fact that Réaux promises the quintessential French castle experience, making you feel as though you have become one of the noble players in this fairytale land. The jaunty Florence Goupil de Bouillé, the proprietor of this stately dwelling, immediately sets the tone for the highly convivial ambiance and distinction that reigns here. Don't expect the sort of comfort that you enjoy at a chain hotel; there are no telephones, minibars, or TVs, and as my most proper *châtelaine* mentioned in the jaw-clenched speak of *la noblesse*, "It is truly a show of poor taste to put an elevator in a château." The well-worn look of the rooms only adds to the overall charm, but if sleeping in tired beds poses a problem for you, check in to the local Mercure, the French equivalent of a Holiday Inn.

- Chouzé-sur-Loire, 37140 Bourgueil; tel.: 02.47.95.14.40.; fax:
     02.47.95.18.34
  Château-Hôtel/Dinner by reservation for guests: Moderate-
     Expensive
  Open year-round

Orléans (Loiret)

Main shopping streets: rue Royale, rue Jeanne d'Arc, rue de la République
Market: Marché de la Source Thursday and Saturday 7 A.M.–noon
Flea Market: bd Alexandre Martin Saturday 7 A.M.– 7 P.M.

Classic in appearance, proportion, and spirit, Orléans is a town where Parisians feel comfortable—so much so, in fact, that many have actually moved here and commute to the capital for work. This helps to guarantee a standard of shopping a cut above that of your average *ville de province*. Locals and out-of-towners rejoice at **La Chocolaterie Royale** (51 rue Royale; tel.: 02.38.53.93.43; fax: 02.38.52.15.10), the city's best source for superior-quality chocolates, founded in 1765. One of the oldest chocolate shops in France, it sells sweets fit for royalty in fleur-de-lis–emblazoned royal blue and gold packages.

It may be hard to resist sampling the box of chocolates you've earmarked as a gift, and a good bottle of wine can be just as problematic—it's always a welcomed souvenir, but the gift giver is often tempted to uncork it in the end-of-the-day tranquility of his or her hotel room.

If you're planning to buy a take-home bottle, an *eau-de-vie Poire Williams d'Orléans* for just under 200F fits the bill quite nicely. A pear-shaped bottle of these spirits is not only beautiful but is also typical of the region. **La Vinithèque** (tel.: 02.38.54.13.51) on the rue de la Main qui File sells this delicious firewater along with a large selection of regional wines including St-Nicolas de Bourgueil, Vouvray, Quincy, Sancerre, Pouilly Fumé, and many more.

Mailfert-Amos

If I didn't tip you off ahead of time you'd most likely think every single piece of superbly crafted furniture showcased within the elegant *salons* of this venerable old establishment is indeed an antique. *Mais non.* Only the magnificent Renaissance town house may be classified as *de l'époque*—all the rest have been painstaking carved, sculpted, assembled, upholstered, gilted, lacquered, varnished, patined, and inlaid with marquetry by the forty or so craftspeople who work in the Mailfert-Amos atelier.

After learning about the exquisite furniture that this house has been making since 1907 for countless discriminating clients including King Fahd of Saudia Arabia (Mailfert furnished his whole yacht), I asked why someone would want to buy a reproduction when they can afford the real thing. I was told that finding a real antique in the Louis XV or Louis XVI style is as rare as finding a dinosaur egg—most of those pieces were destroyed during the Revolution, and the few that remain command out-of-the-stratosphere prices. Also, when you order pieces crafted especially for you, you can design them to your exact specifications. Each of the Mailfert rooms has been decorated in the style of a particular era, so a visit here is like touring through a museum of decorative arts–a real (or should I say faux?) treat for anyone who appreciates fine French furnishings.

- 26 rue Notre-Dame-de-Recouvrance, 45000 Orléans; tel.: 02.38.62.70.61; fax: 02.38.53.71.15
  Open Monday 2–6:30 P.M.; Tuesday–Saturday 10 A.M.–12:30 P.M. and 2–6:30 P.M.

Outside Orléans (Loiret)

Le Château de la Ferté-St-Aubin

I've noticed that whenever I visit an historic residence, the kitchen fascinates me the most. Maybe that is where I capture the greatest sense of hearth and home, or maybe I can more easily imagine myself working among old copper pots and wooden bowls than sleeping in a stubby bed or taking tea in a parlor, parked on a most uncomfortable chair. In any event, I was in historic kitchen heaven at this château, whose main attraction is a seventeenth-century *cuisine* accompanied by a boutique of the same theme. With a vaulted ceiling and a blazing wood fire as background, a folklorishly dressed *cuisinière* affectionately whips up a batch of fresh *madeleines* for everyone to taste warm from the oven. The boutique sells packets of those same spongy little tea cakes along with a delectable selection of jams, jellies, honeys, and other treats, as well as French baguette baskets, metal coffeepots, giant-sized breakfast bowls (used for hot drinks), and a large selection of beautiful books, including one entitled *L'Art de la Pique Nique.*

- 45240 Ferté-St-Aubin; tel.: 02.38.76.52.72; fax: 02.38.64.67.43
  Open daily March 15–November 15 10 A.M.–7 P.M.; November 16– March 14 Wednesday, Saturday, and Sunday, and school vacations 2– 6 P.M.

Tours (Indre-et-Loire)

TGV: 1 hour from Paris
Main shopping streets: rue Nationale, rue de la Scellerie, rue des Halles
Market: Les Halles daily 7 A.M.–8 P.M.
(vendors in the surrounding streets Wednesday and Saturday 7 A.M.–1 P.M.)
Flower market: boulevard Béranger Wednesday and Saturday 7 A.M.–7 P.M.

An hour from Orléans and Paris, this lively city is easy to reach by train. You owe it to yourself to stop in at **Briocherie S. Lelong** (13 place du

Général-Leclerc; tel.: 02.47.05.57.77), a bakery just across from the train station that has been making their own version of *brioche* since 1870. They sell nothing but these slightly sweet, eggy breads in a variety of shapes and flavors, including chocolate chip!

If you love breads, don't miss **Au Vieux Four** (7 place des Petites-Boucheries; tel.: 02.47.66.62.33), a bakery committed to making *pain à l'ancienne*. Walk down toward the *quartier de la cathédrale*, then on to this little square where you'll encounter a number of magnificent sixteenth-century Renaissance town houses, one of which houses this tradition-driven *boulangerie* best known for its old wood-burning oven. You can choose from about thirty-five different kinds of bread (of the seventy in their repertoire) for sale here on any given day.

A haven for antique seekers, the rue de la Scellerie in Tours may leave you furiously searching for ways to transport your newly acquired stash back home. The entire area, encompassing the street and **L'Espace de la Scellerie** (a sort of mini-mall of nine dealers at 45 rue de la Scellerie), boasts an ecclectic selection of antique offerings both from *la touraine* and elsewhere. For more regional pieces, try **Antiquités 28** (28 rue de la Scellerie; tel/fax: 02.47.61.12.22), keeping in mind that the Loire Valley style is far less rustic than those of the other provinces. Marie Tagger's boutique, **L'Esprit Maison** (55 rue de la Scellerie; tel.: 02.47.64.18.38) has a tasteful collection of home décor items from England and France; French accents include fanciful frames, tole pieces, and Limoges boxes. Whether you're just browsing or scouting about with the intention to buy, doll lovers and teddy bear fans will revel in the adorable collection of goods at **Boucle d'Or** (75 rue de la Scellerie, 37000; tel.: 02.47.66.40.47). I'll leave the rest of the antique prospecting on this street up to you!

As you tour around Tours (sorry, I couldn't resist), you're bound to work up a bit of an appetite. The cream-colored tea salon of the *pâtissier/chocolatier* **Poirault** (6 rue Nationale) can provide you with a pick-me-up: the lunchtime buffet upstairs is a hit with the locals, but save room for at least one of the four bonbons that have earned this nearly 200-year-old establishment its reputation for excellence. Each of the four candymakers who reigned *chez* Poirault since 1807 left their mark by creating their own toothache-provoking sweet: sugary prunes filled with an apricot/apple mixture, *flambé au rhum*; Grand Marnier–enhanced milk chocolate truffles called *muscadines*; coffee and orange-flavored dark chocolate coins referred to as *La Livre Tournois*; and the less decadent alternative: red and yellow hard candies, presented in an old-fashioned looking tin. Go for it!

L'Atelier de la Martinerie

Just before you enter the thick of the antique shops, it's hard to miss the brightly colored tapestries hanging in this gallery. The fruits of the energy and creative spirit pooled by three local women, these woven wonders appear to glorify the powers of the universe in figurative designs featuring the sun, stars, and angels. A mixture of old and new, Asian influences and organic inspiration, the results convey serenity, spirituality, and poeticism. Each piece radiates a distinct luminosity, as much from the blend of silk with wool as from the intensity of the motifs and the colors. Prices begin at 2,000F for a small picture-sized work and loom to about 130,000F for a majestic wall mural of great definition and size.

- 20 rue de la Scellerie, 37000 Tours; tel.: 02.47.05.41.13
  Open Tuesday–Friday 3–7 P.M.; Saturday 10:30 A.M.–12:30 P.M. and 2:30–7 P.M.
  Also in Amboise during the spring and summer at 7 bis rampe du Château; tel.: 02.47.57.37.51
  Open at varying hours

Manufacture des Trois Tours

As you visit the magnificent châteaux of the region, you will undoubtedly marvel at the volumes of sumptuous fabrics required to dress such expansive interiors and to upholster many an elegant armchair. The most beautiful, of course, have been woven out of silk, and although their provenance may be mostly French, not all of them come from Lyons, the city of France most associated with *la soie*. First introduced in Tours by the Italians during the fifteenth century, the silk industry prospered greatly here during the next couple of centuries, largely from orders placed by wealthy nobles. During the seventeenth century, half the population of Tours lived from the silk business; now the only remaining *soierie* is the Manufacture des Trois Tours.

Within the confines of this centuries-old showroom and atelier (ask to take a peek if you're not shy), the restoration of old silks and the weaving of new ones keeps nimble fingers almost as busy as the rickety old looms. And even though they mainly respond to the needs of neighboring châteaux, museums the likes of the Getty, distinguished textile houses such as Clarence House and Braunschweig & Fils, and the often persnickety demands of European royalty, it is not at all unusual for them to sell a bit of brocade to individuals determined to refurbish their favorite settee with a top-drawer *étoffe*.

- 35 quai Paul-Bert, 37100 Tours; tel.: 02.47.54.45.78; 02.47.54.14.89
  Call for appointment

Jean Bardet

You can relish in the gastronomic delights of chef Jean Bardet in a parklike setting, considered *une des plus grandes tables de*

Tours, only about five minutes from the center of town. With her husband in the kitchen all the time, Sophie Bardet had to find some way to express her creative talents, so she decided to open up a small shop within this restaurant/hotel establishment that would reflect her fanciful taste. Classic items include the pink, green, and gold Limoges breakfast service used at the hotel; her own homey-looking breakfast cups in periwinkle blue, monogramed with a large "B"; and a selection of wines from the region. Other, more unexpected accessories such as evening bags, stockings, toilet waters, and dog dishes are also for sale—just in case guests forget to bring their own.

- 57 rue Groison, 37100 Tours; tel.: 02.47.41.41.11; fax: 02.47.51.68.72
  Boutique and Four-Star Relais & Châteaux Hôtel/Restaurant: Very Expensive
  Open year-round; restaurant closed Sunday evenings and Mondays from November to March and Mondays at lunch from April to October

Villaines-les-Rochers (Indre-et-Loire)

Vannerie Villaines-les-Rochers

Although most of the world's basketmaking takes place in the Far East, Eastern Europe, and certain parts of Spain where the cost of labor permits such manually intensive handcrafting, the little town of Villaines-les-Rochers could hardly cease its wicker-work activity, from the growing of the osier to the ultimate crafting of the basket, that has taken place here since the sixteenth century. Depending on what time of year you pass through Villaines, you might witness the cutting and sorting of this type of willow in January, the drying and bundling of the reeds during the months of May and June, or the weaving of the baskets throughout the year in workshops dispersed around town, most of which have been installed in little caves to conserve humidity and render the wicker more malleable.

Founded in 1849, the cooperative centralizes the osier "harvest" and distributes it to its craftspeople. It also serves as an excellent starting-off point for learning more about this unique craft and for viewing its many final products, including bird cages, baguette baskets, French shopping carts, and cheese platters, to name a few. They will ship to the U.S. and they do special orders for such customers as Hermès and one of France's most celebrated bread makers, Poîlane. Check their wicker-worker map for an itinerary to many of the artisans' workplaces.

• 37190 Azay-le-Rideau; tel.: 02.47.45.43.03; fax: 02.47.45.27.48
Open Monday–Saturday 9 A.M.–noon and 2–7 P.M.; Sunday 2–7 P.M.
   (Easter–September Sunday 10 A.M.–noon and 2–7 P.M.);
Wicker workshop open July and August Monday–Friday 10 A.M.–7 P.M.

Charcuterie Hardouin

Heading out of Tours toward Blois on the N152, you can take in many of
the *maisons troglodytes*, or grotto-like houses, carved out of the hillsides, so
typical of this region. There's not much to indicate in Vouvray except for
this *charcuterie* (a sort of French delicatessen), known throughout the region
for delicious pork products called *rillettes* and *rillons*. People normally associate the fat-fortified pork spread, called *rillettes*, with Le Mans, a town in the
Western Loire, but it actually originated in Tours; and to further complicate
things, when I asked in Tours where I could find the best *rillettes*, everyone
mentioned Charcuterie Hardouin in Vouvray. As awful as they may sound
(and look), the fresh or preserved *rillettes* and *rillons* (whole pork pieces) taste
succulent served on a crusty piece of French bread accompanied with a cool
glass of Vouvray. You can buy bottles of this local white wine here as well
in varieties ranging from dry to sparklingly sweet.

• 8 rue de la République, 37210 Vouvray; tel.: 02.47.52.65.33;
   fax: 02.47.52.66.54
Open Monday–Thursday 8:30 A.M.–1 P.M. and 3:30–7:30 P.M.; Friday
   8:30 A.M.–1 P.M.; Sunday 8:30 A.M.– 1 P.M.

CENTRAL LOIRE

La Borne (Cher)

Just about midway between Sancerre and Henrichemont, the little village of
La Borne has been known for its pottery since the sixteenth century. Toward
the early 1900s about eighty potters worked here, and now La Borne counts
nearly fifty *en permanence*. The shift from industrial pottery to artistic creations occurred during the first half of this century, and since then the village
has taken on a more outgoing approach, adapting to the fickle and often
peculiar needs of artists—so different from the more consistent demands of
laborers. Today's scene has become quite international; the village's artist
colony frequently engages in exchanges with potters from all over the world,
most of whom work with clay, while others' proficiencies lie in mediums
such as painting or engraving. I sensed a real camaraderie among this colorful
mix of bohemians.

Spread throughout the village and its environs, some artists occasionally open their workshops for visitors, but most remain fairly reclusive. **La Borne Centre de Céramique** (tel.: 02.48.26.96.21), housed in an old school in the heart of town, however, presents a cross section of the artists' works on permanent display along with a mini-bookstore devoted to the ceramic arts. Everything is for sale at fairly reasonable prices. Make sure you visit the **Musée de la Poterie** next door in the old church; the exhibition changes yearly, although they always feature old pottery from La Borne, the most endearing of which are the figurative pieces that transform basic utilitarian works such as jugs, tobacco pots, or roof ornaments into whimsical icons of humor.

Just a short distance away from La Borne in Morogues, the **Château de Maupas** (tel.: 02.48.64.41.71) offers an eyeful of ceramics of a whole different genre. Sometimes referred to as the sanctuary of faience, the stairway of this eighteenth-century dwelling showcases some 900 antique plates, handmade by *faïenceries* from all over France, Delft, and even as far away as the Far East!

L'Epicerie de la Borne

The card of this little tea salon/boutique states, "From the ordinary to the extraordinary," and that is exactly what you can expect to encounter in this popular gathering place of locals and out-of-towners-in-the-know. A tasteful and authentic mix of elements of French country décor, savory dishes, people from all over the world, and trinkets for sale from near and far, engage in a multicultural *java* evocative of the exuberant spirit of the artists of La Borne.

• 18250 Henrichemont; tel.: 02.48.26.90.80
Boutique and Bistrot: Inexpensive
Open Tuesday–Saturday 9 A.M.–12:30 P.M. and 6–7:30 P.M.;
Sunday 9 A.M.–12:30 P.M.

Cathédrale Jean Linard

My travel companion and I scoured the countryside surrounding Henrichemont in search of the atelier of artist Jean Linard and his near-famous work *Cathédrale*. After a bit of confusion at the hamlet called Les Poteries, a farmer told us to look for the colorful house above this tiny community and insisted that "you can't miss it." As we finally approached this rather bizarre abode, bedecked with shiny and vibrant mosaics and flailing metal sculptures, we concurred with the farmer. Unlike any other cathedral that you may visit in the world, this one embodies the artistic expression and personal convictions of Jean Linard, a passionate *visionnaire*, who, if it weren't for his old Gauloise stogie, might be mistaken for Jesus Christ himself. *Cathédrale* is best visited on a fair day.

Inside this old farmhouse, Jean presents smaller and considerably less abstract versions of his creative genius in two different mediums: ceramics and paintings. Dramatically displayed against black walls, a mixture of materials and textures renders the artist's works even more dynamic in spirit and movement, as in the case of the flying bird (2,000F), a terra-cotta piece partially covered in a glossy bronze glaze to suggest flight. Jean's almost Impressionistic paintings of classic regional scenes provide a startling contrast to his more madcap abstractions in the garden. His energy rings loud and clear in his choice of vivid colors and dashing brush strokes so indicative of his ardent personality. Prices run about 5,000F.

• Les Poteries, Neuvy Deux Clochers, 18250 Henrichemont;
    tel.: 02.48.26.73.87
  Exhibition/Gallery
  Open daily 9 A.M.–6 P.M.

Dordives (Loiret)

Carenton Porcelaine

Just as you exit *l'autoroute du sud* on your way to Gien from Paris, you will pass through a short, unattractive stretch of factory warehouses and workshops, of which one complex belongs to Carenton Porcelaine, specialists in Limoges boxes. Although made in Limoges, these porcelain miniatures await their hand-painted decorations here where a team of skilled craftspeople take to their brushes under the watchful eye of Monsieur Carenton. All are for sale at very reasonable prices.

• Z.A. des Ailes, 45680 Dordives; tel.: 02.38.92.75.04; fax: 02.38.92.86.54
  Open Monday-Friday 8:30 A.M.–12:30 P.M. and 2–5:30 P.M.

Gien (Loiret)

Market: place de la Victoire
Saturday 8 A.M.–1 P.M.

Unlike Limoges, Gien is both the name of the town and the brand name of all of the handsome faience that has put this small French city on the map. Since much of the town was destroyed during the war, a number of its buildings are modern and unattractive; its faience factory, however, more than warrants a visit. You can easily spend a whole day in Gien. The *faïencerie* will indeed take up a good deal of your time, and if any remains, you can spend it at the **Musée de la Chasse** (tel.: 02.38.67.69.69; fax: 02.38.38.07.32), a hunting museum whose richly illustrated exhibits could fascinate even the most fervent animal rights activists in the crowd.

People tend to scoop up old pieces of Gien faience as fast as they can, and although some of the most treasured pieces are showcased in antique stores throughout the world, you can find magnificent works at the *vente annuelle*, or annual sale, that takes place in the city's auction house, usually during the month of December. Contact the Salle des Ventes, Commissaire Priseur Maître Renard, quai de Nice, 45500 Gien; tel.: 02.38.67.01.83 for information.

Gien

In terms of French faience, Gien's appeal rivals that of Quimper in the eyes of many impassioned shoppers. Both started to pop up in every other speciality shop and mail-order catalogue throughout the U.S. around the same boom-time period of the late 1980s. With Baccarat as its U.S. distributor, how could Gien not become a near household name among home décor aficionados, lovers of French country or not?

Founded in 1821 by Englishman Thomas Hall, Gien has mastered the art of *la tradition* by conserving many of its classical patterns and a good number of its nineteenth-century techniques while constantly expanding its extensive tally of motifs in order to keep in step with today's tastes. One can easily flounder when describing a typical Gien design because there are so many of them, sweeping from traditional themes of Renaissance inspiration to more modern versions of French country, such as the popular blue and white basketweave pattern highlighted by brightly colored fruit. These décors are handmade rather than hand-painted, most of them are actually carried out by an old English technique which involves a sort of stenciling of colors on the plates as opposed to actual painting.

A tour of the manufactory can explain this process and many others far better than I, and certainly that is one of the reasons for traveling to this provincial town. The Gien museum may prove to be another, particularly if you are interested in purchasing one of the museum-quality reproductions of old patterns referred to as *Gien tradition/faïence d'art*. I suspect, though, that the real thrill of your visit will occur upon entering the large factory store, where shoppers push around grocery carts to stock up on favorite Gien patterns at savings of about 25 to 30 percent less than regular French retail prices. Many of the items are seconds, some may be discontinued, but no matter—every time I have come here I have zeroed in on at least half a cartful of items to buy!

- place de la Victoire, 45500 Gien; tel.: 02.38.67.00.05; fax: 02.38.67.44.92
Discount Store/Museum/Factory Visits
Boutique open Monday–Saturday 9 A.M.–noon and 2–6 P.M.
Museum open May–September Monday–Saturday 9 A.M.–6:30 P.M.;
    Sunday and holidays 10 A.M.–6 P.M.; October–April Monday–
    Saturday 9 A.M.–noon and 2–6 P.M.; Sunday and holidays 10 A.M.–
    noon and 2–6 P.M.
Factory visits by appointment for groups only; tel.: 02.38.67.89.92.; fax:
    02.38.67.44.92

Sancerre (Cher)

Very much like the neighboring region of Burgundy, Sancerre consists of many small domaines that sell simply and directly to their clients without the formalities characteristic of other wine-producing provinces such as Bordeaux. My quest for one key wine shop specializing in a selection of fine Sancerre wines in this personable little town was squelched by the fact that you rarely find wines from more than one winegrower under one roof (except in a restaurant, of course). The good news is that the *dégustations* are often carried out in a convivial manner; and whether it be white, rosé, or red, a glass of Sancerre tastes even better accompanied by a bit of *crottin de Chavignol*, or goat cheese, from the nearby village of Chavignol.

I did, however, discover that the town bookstore, located on the main *place* and appropriately named **Le Verre et la Plume** (tel.: 02.48.54.11.02). The name means the glass and the feather, as in fountain pen, and the store sells excellent guidebooks and attractive coffee-table books on the wines of the Loire and the region itself. If it's sugar you're after, you must stop at **Le Lichou** (7 pl de l'Église; tel.: 02.48.54.00.32) to pick up a little sachet of their *specialités sancerroises*; a panoply of sweets consisting of several decadent varieties of chocolate and almond-flavored treats.

Le Grenier à Sel/Domaine Vacheron

Out of all of the domaines represented in town, I found the Vacheron wine bar to be the most charming, and better yet, to be the one with the most delicious wines. Locals crowd around little wooden tables ideal for intimate tastings in this wood-beamed fifteenth-century interior. Expect young floral aromas from these and other Sancerre wines. You can also buy bottles to go for about 50F each.

• Nouvelle Place, 18300 Sancerre; tel.: 02.48.54.35.37; fax:
  02.48.54.01.74
  Wine Bar/Boutique: Inexpensive
  Open daily 3–7:30 P.M.; July and August 10 A.M.–12:30 P.M.
  and 3–7:30 P.M.

Château de Beaujeu

If you feel comfortable enough with your French to carry on a decent conversation, and if you want to sample true château life without the slightest bit of pretention, reserve a room here (there are only two) well in advance, along with a place or two at the *table d'hôtes* of Monsieur and Madame de Pommereau, your humble hosts at Beaujeu. In a setting nothing less than grand are all the essential elements of a château: family portraits galore; a resplendent staircase, big enough for an opera house; a few Aubusson tapestries; and picture-perfect bucolic views of cows grazing in pastures just outside your bedroom window. The rooms are just as lovely, and although I woke up a little snarly from a restless sleep in a saggy bed, the otherworldly honey cream that I discovered on my breakfast tray more than made up for my discomfort.

• Sens-Beaujeu, 18300 Sancerre; tel.: 02.48.79.07.95; fax:
  02.48.79.05.07
  Château-Hôtel/Dinner may be reserved for guests: Moderate–
  Expensive
  Call ahead

LORRAINE
Lorraine

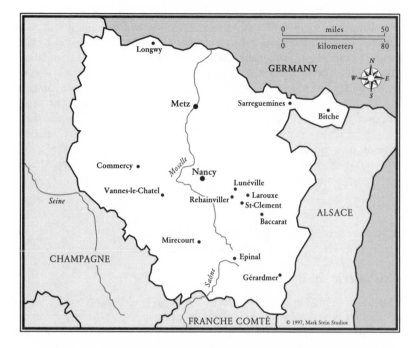

Longwy

GERMANY

N
W · E
S

0 miles 50
0 kilometers 80

Metz

Sarreguemines

Bitche

Commercy

Moselle

Nancy

Lunéville

Larouxe
St-Clement

Vannes-le-Chatel

Rehainviller

Baccarat

Seine

ALSACE

Mirecourt

CHAMPAGNE

Epinal

Saône

Gérardmer

FRANCHE COMTÉ | © 1997, Mark Stein Studios

madeleines • faience • crystal • *confiture de Bar-le-Duc* • reduced-priced house linens • hand-colored prints and cards • wines • blueberry jam • enameled faience • rustic furnishings • chocolates • lace • mountain honeys • handcrafted string instruments • Art Nouveau–inspired stained glass • *bergamotes de Nancy* • creative glassworks • *macarons* • *pâte de verre*–accented crystal • *eaux-de-vie* • *mirabelle* liqueur • antiques • jewelry and home décor accessories of a botanical theme

SHOPAHOLICS, BEWARE–LORRAINE could lead to your dreaded, over-extended credit card demise. It's pretty hard to sit quietly in a bistrot, nibbling on a healthy piece of *quiche lorraine*, without thinking about all of the wonderful crystal, faience, linens, and unusual home décor items that await you–always within a short distance away, and often at factory-reduced prices that only encourage you to buy more. If you happen to preface one of these potential shopping sprees with a visit to a museum directly connected to the history, tradition, and *savoir faire* of these many wonderful products, then you've hit your credit limit before you even make it to second base: you'll find that the more that you know about these exquisite goods, the more you'll want to acquire them. And if you find yourself hankering for a $10,000 violin, you may want to take the next flight home—unless, of course, you happen to be a dedicated musician wishing to fulfill the dream of a lifetime by buying a handcrafted instrument in one of the world's most reputed outposts for artisanally made string instruments, the city of Mirecourt in the Lorraine region of France.

It's misleading to treat Alsace and Lorraine as one place with one identity. As much as both of them have stood cheek-to-jowl confronting the perils imposed upon them during different periods of history, and despite their geographically intertwined location, I still perceive them as two very different regions. Now it's up to you to test the waters, to give your credit card a dry run, and then to assimilate the nuances of Lorraine—and maybe even Alsace.

Baccarat (Moselle)

Market: place du Général
Leclerc Friday 8 A.M.–1 P.M.

Cristallerie du Baccarat

Out of a population of 5,000, 900 of this town's inhabitants work for the prestigious crystalmaker of the same name. Founded in 1764, the Baccarat company chose this site for its close proximity to the forest to assure an ample and readily attainable supply of wood for the firing of the furnaces, the central component of the glassmaking process. Although these gigantic ovens are no longer wood-stoked, you can still hear their incessant hum today as you stand quietly on the Baccarat premises. Having first produced only ordinary glass, Baccarat switched to crystal in 1816, and now all of its products contain approximately 30 percent lead, a high percentage indeed (only 24 percent is required by law in France to be classified as lead crystal). All of the Baccarat crystal sold throughout the world has been crafted by hand in this town by highly skilled craftspeople, many of whom figure among the most recognized artisans of France.

Although factory visits remain off limits to tourists, you can view a ten-minute video in the Baccarat museum which traces the company's history and takes you through the eleven steps required in the making of a crystal glass. Housed in the former home of the first owner of Baccarat, the museum also displays prized pieces from its collection, some of which illustrate the different techniques applied in the ornamentation of crystal, including engraving and gilting.

By now you're probably begging for the seconds shop, but stop looking, because this highly scrupulous house does not let one single goblet eke by in anything less than superior quality; all of the questionables are smashed and melted down. The store adjacent to the museum, however, proves irresitible. The whole collection glistens here at prices that run about 30 percent less than those abroad. The store willingly ships anywhere, and be sure to ask for the *détaxe*. A word to the wise: Be careful shopping around town in the stores that sell crystal of inferior quality. Look for the Baccarat trademark, which has been engraved on the bottom of authentic pieces since 1936.

- BP 31, 54120 Baccarat; tel.: 03.83.76.60.06; fax: 03.83.76.60.10
  Museum/Boutique
  Open daily April 1–November 1 9:30 A.M.–12:30 P.M. and 2–6 P.M; from November 2–March 31 10 A.M.–noon and 2–6 P.M.; Closed December 25 and January 1

Bitche (Moselle)

Cristallerie de St-Louis

I almost felt goosebumps as I descended upon this old factory, firmly grounded in the still of the valley, encircled by an early morning mist. The thought of more than 400 years of history taking place here at this same secluded spot where sand and a few other essential ingredients have been transformed into sparkling finery moved me more than anything else that I had visited. As I conjured up images of this leading crystalmaker's sybaritic showcase in Paris, it occurred to me that certainly one of the greatest strengths of this sort of cultural and artistic stronghold lies in a neverending ability to adapt to current tastes and times. St-Louis has positioned itself well with its near *objet d'art* collection of brilliantly colored crystal, already a signature trademark of this renowned house.

Visits to the glassworks reveal the fascinating beehive of activity surrounding the two huge ovens (one for color, one for clear). Burly men in shorts and sneakers work around the clock blowing, molding, and cutting the taffylike molten glass into graceful forms. Explanations are mostly conveyed in *franglais*, somewhere between French and English—but that really doesn't matter, because you learn much by pure observation.

The factory showroom/boutique is not nearly as lavish as the company's boutique in Paris, but it does feature a large selection of discontinued items and seconds at 30 to 40 percent off regular French prices. One more reason to make the hike out to this far-eastern corner of Lorraine!

- St-Louis-les-Bitche, 57620 St-Louis-les-Bitche; tel.: 03.87.06.40.04; fax: 03.87.06.81.37
  Factory Visit/Boutique

Open Monday–Saturday 9 A.M.–noon and 1–5 P.M.; Sunday 2–5 P.M.;
   closed holidays
Visits are conducted hourly.

Commercy (Meuse)

A la Cloche Lorraine

After making several inquiries, I learned that this lovely little sweet shop is
regarded as one of the best places to buy *madeleines*, the scalloped-shaped
sponge cakes that are gobbled up throughout all of France. Although they
are sold in supermarkets and bakeries all over the country, there is something
special about buying them here in the town where they originated. Legend
has it that a young servant by the name of Madeleine from the town of
Commercy whipped them up for King Stanislas in 1755 when the royal
pastry chef steamed out of the kitchen during a particularly festive event
without leaving a dessert behind; forever indebted, the king dubbed these
scrumptious treats *madeleines de Commercy*.

Here they sell in three different varieties, but be sure to buy the *royale*,
the most buttery. You can pick up just a few or purchase them packaged in
pretty containers: I selected a cornflower blue oval-shaped box, painted with
a vibrant sunflower design, that I now use for keepsakes. The assortment of
chocolates, marzipan, *dragées* (candy-covered almonds) from Verdun, and
fruit-tinged *eaux-de-vie* (spirits) adds more strength to the shop's regional
product hit list, although the *confiture de Bar-le-Duc* outdoes them all.
Deemed a luxury product since the sixteenth century, the origins of these
exclusive red and white currant jams from the nearby town of Bar-le-Duc
date back to the fourteenth century. One silver spoonful tells you that the
recipe has not changed since then; sweet and delicate floral aromas fill your
mouth with every tiny burst of these caviar-like berries. It is said that small-
handed young girls gingerly deseed each individual currant with a goose-
feather so that these minuscule fruits can be tossed into the burning syrup
intact—a centuries-old method that conserves the flavor and translucency of
the currants. One tiny jar costs about 75F, but many would argue that this
is a small price to pay for such a divine treat and more than 600 years of
tradition!

• 8 place du Charles-de-Gaulle, 55200 Commercy; tel.: 03.29.91.25.19; fax:
   03.29.91.20.20
   Open daily 8:45 A.M.–noon and 2–7 P.M.

Epinal (Vosges)

Market: place des Vosges and in streets surrounding the covered market
Wednesday and Saturday 8 A.M.–1 P.M.

Imagerie d'Epinal

Situated on the quai de Dogneville a bit of a distance from the center of town, it took some doing to find this more than 200-year-old print workshop, but once here, there was much to see and buy. I started off with a short guided tour of the printshop; although the tour is conducted in French, you can learn about some of the different printmaking processes without speaking the language. Made entirely by hand on nineteenth-century presses using woodblock or lithography techniques, the true particularity of Epinal prints lies in their coloring. Vibrant colors incrementally enliven the basic black-and-white prints with each separate application of gouache; the traditional method of handcoloring called *pochoir*, or stenciling, is still used on the majority of the workshop's production.

The vast collection of images occupies most of the cellar, revealing in print after print the sheer diversity of subject matter: real and storybook characters such as St-Nicolas and Little Red Riding Hood vie for attention with more militaristic themes the likes of Waterloo or naval scenes of *la flotille nationale*. There's often a story to be told or a lesson to be learned, particularly in the classic albums such as *Les Fables de La Fontaine*, or The Taking of Constantine. Prices begin at 4F for postcards and reach about 400F for more contemporary-looking collages of varying themes. This is a great place for kids!

- 42 *bis* quai de Dogneville, 88000 Epinal; tel.: 03.29.31.28.88;
  fax: 03.29.31.12.24
  Open Monday 2–6:30 P.M.; Tuesday–Saturday 8:30 A.M.–noon and 2–6:30 P.M.; Sunday 2–6:30 P.M.; closed holidays

Gérardmer (Vosges)

Market: around the church
Tuesday, Thursday, Friday, and Saturday 8 A.M.–1 P.M.

There are two different routes to take from Epinal to Gérardmer, one rather precarious, the other quite navigable. The D11 had my driver clench-fisted on the steering wheel and seething to the point that we were going to have to hire someone to drive us back from Gérardmer (thankfully we learned about the easier route, the N57, the next day). Many of you might not find it so bad, but when night has fallen and you're twisting and turning through the Vosges mountains, frazzled by a couple of leadfoots nipping at your heels, it can be pretty frightening. Much to our delight, we ended up saying that it was well worth the unexpected adventure–otherwise we might never have discovered this mountain resort town nor all of the other untrammeled attributes, to this unique part of Lorraine.

Jacquard Français Factory Store

If this name does not sound familiar to you, then you are well overdue for acquainting yourself with some of the most best-loved house linens that exist within the hexagon. Long associated with Primrose Bordier/Descamps, Jacquard Français produces fine-quality table linens that always reflect the harmonious marriage of country French with town elegance in their innumerable patterns. Densely colored all-cotton damask dishtowels must be some of the biggest sellers on earth, and they are made so well you're apt to lose them before they ever wear out. The *nid d'abeille*, or waffleweave hand towels, give a very European accent to *la toilette*. This seconds store has discounts of 30 to 40 percent.

- 35 rue Charles-de-Gaulle, 88400 Gérardmer; tel.: 03.29.60.09.04; fax: 03.29.60.05.92
  Open Tuesday–Saturday 10 A.M.–12:30 P.M. and 2–7 P.M.

Maison de la Montagne

It's hard to miss this mountain house in the center of town, stocked solely with products from the Vosges. Every imaginable type of locally made foodstuff takes front and center: pâtés, cheeses, honeys, jams, and *eaux-de-vie*, to name a few. More obscure products include candies made from blueberry liqueur and *bluet des Vosges*, a delicious jam, also made from blueberries, that the locals often eat with meat (apparently it's a big hit with the Japanese,

---

Les Bas Rupts

Obviously a popular weekend getaway for visitors from Lorraine and Alsace, this hotel/restaurant stridently exhibits all of the right criteria for ensuring a pleasurable stay: scenic mountain views; warmly decorated, chaletlike guestrooms; friendly and efficient service; and most of all, a *cuisine* that leaves you satiated with regional *saveurs!*

- 88400 Gérardmer; tel.: 03.29.63.09.25; fax: 03.29.63.00.40
  Hotel/Restaurant: Moderate–Expensive
  Open daily year-round

too). Images from Epinal and handcrafted wooden toys highlight the shop's selection of nonfood gift items.

• place du Vieux-Gérardmer, 88400 Gérardmer; tel.: 03.29.63.21.93
Open at varying hours

Outside Gérardmer (Vosges)

Anne de Solène Factory Store

Just before Remiremont about 15 kilometers outside of Gérardmer is a small sign for this factory store. Another reputable brand of fine-quality French house linens sold in large department stores throughout France, the Anne de Solène look varies considerably according to current fashions and demands. The savings here run about 40 percent off regular French retail prices.

• 29 route Usine Julienrupt; 88120 Julienrupt; tel.: 03.29.61.10.11; fax: 03.29.61.11.07
Open Monday–Saturday 8:30 A.M.–noon and 1:30–6 P.M.

Longwy (Moselle)

If you've read about the enamels of Limoges in the Limousin chapter, you should already be somewhat familiar with this rich art form. Far to the north of Lorraine, the town of Longwy is also highly acclaimed for its enamels; here they are applied to ceramics, while the enamels of Limoges, the porcelain capital of the world, oddly enough are done on a metal surface. The Longwy tradition began toward the latter part of the nineteenth century at a time when major artists including Gauguin, Rodin, and later Cocteau dabbled in this colorfast medium, knowing full well that their chosen hues would never fade. The entirely handmade enamels of Longwy turned out to be a big invention of the nineteenth century, and not surprisingly, this freshly acquired direction in the arts gained momentum along with the peoples' heightened interest in modernity—sweet revenge after the rigid classicism of the Louis XVI and Empire styles.

Greatly influenced by the artistic techniques and *exotisme* of Istanbul, China, and the Far East, Longwy enamels emerged as a new and exciting art form and suddenly started to show up on everything from umbrella holders to champagne buckets. Inspired from an Egyptian blue, the turquoiselike *bleue Longwy* became all the rage, a shade that continues to typify Longwy enamels today. As you look around in some of the shops, you might feel a bit overwhelmed by the prices; keep in mind, however, that with these works, the color is achieved through the labor-intensive process of building up the enamel drop by drop to a raised thickness.

Emaux d'Art de Longwy

In their no-nonsense boutique just next to the bus station in the lower part of town, Monsieur and Madame Leclerq feature stunning pieces of traditionally decorated enamels. Honored with the country's prestigious *meilleur ouvrier de France* (Best Worker of France) award, Christian Leclercq's finely detailed creations enchant you with a flourish of flowers and birds, unmistakably inspired by Oriental art. In keeping with the true Longwy spirit, many of these same exotic motifs embellish the collection of antique pieces that make up the other half of the shop; the older vases, plates, figurines, and other assorted knickknacks cost about 20 to 40 percent more than the recently-made enamels.

- 2 bis place Giraud Gare Routière; 54400 Longwy; tel.: 03.82.25.71.46; fax: 03.82.23.19.61
  Open Monday 2–7 P.M. and Tuesday–Saturday 9 A.M.–noon and 2–7 P.M.

Faïenceries et Emaux de Longwy

Boldly colored enamels of an entirely different, contemporary style run riot in this more design-oriented store. Circus and celestial themes, and different animals and creatures such as polar bears and starfish, have replaced the more typical subjects of classic Longwy. The huge ginger-jar lamps in crackle-glazed melon, almond, and cream, priced at 3,500F each, further emphasize the shop's deliberate slant toward home décor.

- 3 rue des Emaux, 54400 Longwy; tel.: 03.82.24.30.94; fax: 03.82.23.53.52
  Open Monday–Friday 9 A.M.–12:30 P.M. and 1–6 P.M.; Saturday
  10:30 A.M.–12:30 P.M. and 1–6 P.M.

Faïencerie St-Jean l'Aigle

I hope that they've put up a sign for this château since the time I visited; situated a bit outside of town, it isn't easy to find, but is worth a visit if you're interested in Longwy enamels. If you're lucky you might have a chance to meet Jacques Peiffer, a true expert in ceramics who has authored some twenty books on the subject; he now curates the museum tucked away within this old structure. About fifteen people work in the adjoining atelier, hand-throwing and hand-painting the enameled faience for the château's collection and special orders. The selection in the showroom is rather small but highly selective; an Asian-inspired teapot in traditional Longwy blue, for example, fetches about 2,000F—certainly better suited for a curio cabinet than for pouring tea!

• Château de la Chiers, 54440 Herserange; tel.: 03.82.24.58.20; fax:
  03.82.24.43.76
  Open Monday–Friday 9 A.M.–noon and 2–5 P.M.

Lunéville (Meurthe-et-Moselle)

Mention Lunéville to well-informed lovers of country French and they will
immediately conjure up images of scallop-edged plates decorated with fresh
springtime bouquets of pink tulips and tiny yellow-faced flowers. This, along
with a similar décor referred to as Strasbourg, has come to exemplify the
faïence de l'est, or the faience from the east, a country-kitchen earthenware
that can stand up to the best-dressed tables. Visit the museum of the **Château de Lunéville** in the center of town to discover an incomparable collection of old faience from the region.

Faïenceries de Lunéville/St-Clément

Once in Lunéville, follow signs for the train station, then look for the *zone
des faïenceries* toward the outskirts of town to find this huge, warehouse-like
space that sells faience manufactured in the nearby town of St-Clément.
Most of the store has been allocated to seconds, discontinued majolica, and
contemporary pieces from the St-Clément production, all of which have
been marked down by 30 to 40 percent. Don't expect a price break on the
classic Lunéville patterns, however, unless you happen to stumble upon a
special promotion like an end-of-the-season sale. Although rather out of
place in this hangarlike setting, the upstairs museum offers an honest over-
view of the history of faience, particularly that of Lunéville.

• 1 rue Trouillet, ZAE des Faïenceries, 54300 Lunéville; tel.: 03.83.74.07.58
  Open Tuesday–Saturday 10 A.M.– noon and 2–6:30 P.M.

Outside Lunéville (Meurthe-et-Moselle)

Guestin J.

I discovered this little shop on my way to Baccarat and quickly concluded
that this is a far better place to buy Lunéville faience than in the cold,
impersonable showplace in town (especially since the prices remain the
same). Besides the classic pink tulip Lunéville motif, I was able to admire a
good showing of the not-too-dissimilar Strasbourg pattern along with another
design, quite similar in color and spirit, known as the rooster of St-Clément.
The store also recently added a blue and white rooster to their collection as
an alternative to the already longstanding bird of Moustiers, a rather scanty-
looking creature in an olive green color scheme.

After a bit of prying, I learned that the designs are in fact serigraphed on to these pieces and that only the fine line that traces the rim has been hand-painted. *Peu importe*—they were charming enough for me to start calculating the cost of bearing in mind the 75F price of a single plate. I also spotted a separate glass case featuring Lunéville of a noticeably superior quality. It took more insistent questioning until I learned that those pieces were entirely hand-painted, and although they were not dishwasher-safe and cost nearly seven times more than the others, it was nice to know that the top-drawer quality was out there if you wanted it!

• 5 rue de la Division-Leclerc, 54950 St-Clément; tel.: 03.83.72.60.16
Open Monday-Saturday 9 A.M.–7 P.M.

Charles Ledermann Antiquités

Coming from Lunéville just before St-Clément on the right side of the road, keep an eye out for this château, which has been partially converted into a fine antique showroom. You'll encounter several antique dealers along the route to Baccarat, but this one struck me as one of the most reputable. Monsieur Ledermann's collection of *faïence de l'est* consists of eighteenth- and

---

Château d'Adomenil

Whenever I hear mention of Relais & Châteaux, a little flashing light systematically goes off in my head. I had heard that there was one near Lunéville, so I decided to take the back road that would lead me there via rambling fields and then farther on, through an impeccably manicured *parc*. It was late morning, the most quiet time of day at such establishments, a perfectly peaceful moment sandwiched in between the rush of the morning checkout and the midday lunch, when I peeked in to take a look around. And what to my wandering eyes did appear . . . but a roomful of tables dressed in traditional Lunéville table gear! The Château d'Adomenil table settings pay an impressive homage to the arts and traditions of the region.

• Rehainviller, 54300 Lunéville; tel.: 03.83.74.04.81; fax: 03.83.74.21.78
Relais & Châteaux Hôtel/Restaurant: Very Expensive
Open year-round; restaurant closed for lunch Monday and Tuesday. Restaurant also closed Sunday evening November 1–April 15.

nineteenth-century pieces from Lunéville and St-Clément, as well as from *faïenciers* no longer in existence, such as those of Epinal and Rambervillers (prices range from 200F to 4,000F a plate). A few old pieces of Baccarat top off the table arts collection, and certainly the biggest attractions here happen to be the most voluminous: the sturdy oak furnishings from Lorraine.

Totally different from the painted pine and walnut furniture of Alsace, the beauty of these regional pieces lies almost exclusively in their design. Look for armoires with a drawer, a feature highly characteristic of the region; those built toward the beginning of the nineteenth century tend to be the most beautiful, largely because superbly crafted accents of inlaid work often became the focal point of the piece during this decorative period. Count on spending 30,000F to 40,000F for such a handsome furnishing.

• Château des Landes, 31 route Nationale, 54950 Laronxe; tel.: 03.83.72.60.17; fax: 03.83.72.66.62
Open daily except Wednesday 10 A.M.–noon and 2–7 P.M.

Metz (Moselle)

Main shopping streets: rue Serpenoise, rue des Clercs,
place St-Louis, En Nouvelle rue, En La Chaple rue
Market: place de la Cathédrale and place St-Jacques
Tuesday, Thursday, and Saturday 7 A.M.–1 P.M.
Flea market: parc des Expositions 6 A.M.–1 P.M. the first
and third Saturday of almost every month

Arriving at Metz once night has fallen is totally awe-inspiring. I will never forget the overpowering image that struck me so hard and fast—that of the hundreds of illuminated spires and flying buttresses of the town's great cathedral, a gem of flamboyant Gothic architecture. It is a city to be seen in the dark—but also by the light of day so that you may better forage for antiques, of which there are many to be unearthed. This is a town devoted to the fine-tuned art of antiquing, and even better, the fun of rummaging through a heap of bric-à-brac with the hope of coming up with a piece of gold. The big event of the year takes place mid-September, attracting people from all over Europe in search of something old and interesting at an alluring price at the **Grande Foire à la Brocante**. Contact the tourism office at the place d'Armes ahead of time for the particulars (tel.: 03.87.55.53.76; fax: 03.87.36.59.43).

The bimonthly Metz flea markets or **Marché aux Puces** also prove to be a good draw, and like the September fair, distinguish themselves particularly by their abundance of merchandise from the eastern part of France. This is an excellent place to pick up *faïence de l'est*, jewelry and decorative arts pieces influenced by *l'Ecole de Nancy* (the Art Nouveau Movement started in the town of Nancy), and even a hefty piece of regional furniture or two if you can arrange shipping.

As you're touring around town, do as the *messins* (the people from Metz) do and stop into one of the country's most reputed chocolatemakers, **Pierre Koenig** (20 En Nouvelle rue, tel. 03.87.36.72.72), for a little treat in the form of a *palet au café* or *palet au thé*. As suppliers to France's top gourmet food shops, Hédiard and Fauchon, and with three shops in Metz and one in Nancy, Koenig could easily be called the king of chocolate of eastern France—even if Koenig wasn't his name (*Koenig* means "king" in German)!

You will notice that beer is consumed heavily in this part of France, although the people here also imbibe in wine and spirits produced in Lorraine. If you can chart your way to **Les Caves Saint-Clément** at 6 rue Gambetta (tel.: 03.87.63.92.92), check out their selection of popular regional products that include wines from Toul and a lip-smacking line of *eaux de vie*, the most traditional made from *mirabelle*, a thumbnail-sized golden plum native to Lorraine.

Only about two bridges away from the cathedral, the restaurant **Du Pont St-Marcel** (1 rue du Pont St-Marcel; tel.: 03.87.30.12.29) promises more breathtaking views of the city at lunch and dinner seven days a week. During the warm months you can sit on the terrace facing the Moselle river, and when there's a nip in the air, you'll be warmed by the rustic, colorful interior of this 350-year-old establishment. The centuries-old wood beams have to blend perfectly with the vibrant hues of the dining room's frescoes, merry scenes that depict the city of Metz during the seventeenth century. *Côté cuisine*, you'll revel in the regional specialities, which include frogs' legs and *potée lorraine* (a sort of pork stew with cabbage)—all politely served by a staff in folkloric dress.

Mirecourt (Vosges)

This town might not impress you from the outside, but within its walls it perpetuates two unrelated traditional crafts: string instruments and lace. Developed during the sixteenth century, the tedious and time-consuming tradition of lacemaking would probably have faded by now if it were not for an enthusiastic organization of women determined to keep it alive. A ladies' club of sorts, this gregarious group of women comes together several times a week in their own special meeting hall to fastidiously maneuver their dozens of spindly spools. The ambiance alternates between convivial and serious, as the women work to advance another fraction of an inch by the end of the day. For about 1,400F you can spend a week at a lacemaker's house attending a lacemaking workshop, guaranteed to leave you with your own tiny doily along with many memories of such a shared cultural experience as a souvenir. For more information about this or other aspects of this dedicated group, contact **Association Promotion et Renouveau de la Dentelle,** Centre d'Initiation à la Dentelle aux Fuseaux, avenue de Lattre-de-Tassigny, 88500 Mirecourt; tel.: 03.29.37.03.62.

If you are not quite ready to immerse yourself into such an esoteric domain but want to know more about the history of lacemaking in Mirecourt, a visit to the *Hôtel-de-Ville* (city hall) in the center of town could bridge the gap. Two rooms have been set aside to pay tribute to the town's most glorious crafts: the lace exhibition includes one large piece representing at least 250 hours of work as well as another bit of *dentelles* that dates back to the sixteenth century. The other room honors *la lutherie,* or string instrument making.

A few of the dozen or so instrument workshops spread around town are open to visitors by appointment; call the ateliers mentioned below ahead of time or contact **Mirecourt-Information** (03.29.37.05.22) Monday through Friday 3 to 5 P.M., to set up a special tour. Why does this small town claim so many *luthiers?* Introduced to Mirecourt toward the end of the sixteenth century, the craft has been kept alive largely by the presence of the *Ecole de Lutherie,* or the string instrument–making school, the only one of its kind in France. Potential *luthiers* come from all over the world to participate in this highly specialized program. People also travel great distances to shop in Mirecourt for the instrument of their choice; this steady stream of business further encourages the craftsmen to work directly with musicians or orchestras instead of passing through the intermediary of stores. The rapport between the *luthier* and the musician plays a vital role indeed, an important concept to bear in mind if you are able to arrange any workshop visits.

I started off in the highly polished atelier of **Jean-Jacques Pagès** (tel.: 03.29.37.11.33; fax: 03.29.37.01.92), a craftsman who specializes in violins and cellos. This elegant man explained to me that he has made about 160 instruments within the past twenty years in addition to repairing and maintaining a good number of others. Count on spending 35,000F to 60,000F for an entirely handmade violin, which requires about a month of attention (two weeks to craft it, then another two to apply the ten to fifteen coats of varnish).

The scrappy workroom of senior *luthier* **Lucien Gerome** (tel.: 03.29.37.11.85) offers up a completely different experience. As I waded through a sea of old wood fragments and shavings, I learned about the 100-year-old history of this atelier, dating three generations back to when Monsieur Gerome's father was in charge. It was nice to learn that the cutting and bending of the wood takes place in much the same manner today, giving way to the guitars' and mandolins' classic voluptuous shapes at prices (1,500F to 10,000F) that still seem fair, with or without their fancy inlaid work.

If all of this is still just a bit too much for you, pick up a chocolaty, praline-filled violin at **Daniel Crux**, the town *chocolatier* next to city hall!

Nancy (Meurthe-et-Moselle)

Main shopping streets: rue Gambetta, rue des Dominicains,
rue des Carmes, rue St-Dizier
Market: Les Halles, rue St-Dizier, and place Henri Mangein
Tuesday–Saturday 6 A.M.–6 P.M.
Flea market: in the Old Town every
second Saturday of the month 8 A.M.–6 P.M.

You must allow yourself at least a couple of days to explore this splendorous city—not only because it is the capital of Lorraine but also for the simple reason that there is so much to do and see here. As Nancy unfurls before you, you will surely detect a Parisian air about the city, particularly in its architecture; Nancy, like Paris, may be considered a relatively new town in France, mostly because few vestiges of the Middle Ages have remained. Instead, you are greeted by a hugely expansive place Stanislas, surrounded by magnificent eighteenth-century buildings, gilted gates, and elaborate fountains—all Versailles-esque in grandeur and distinction.

This, however, is not where Nancy has left its real mark; you only have to walk a short distance toward the more residential neighborhoods of the city to discover some of the eloquent Art Nouveau buildings characteristic of this lovely city. A testimony to the late nineteenth-century riches of the province, this return-to-nature style descended upon Nancy like locusts on a cornfield between 1880 and 1910. The leader of this movement was the renowned Emile Gallé, followed quickly by the Daum brothers, ancestors to the celebrated crystal house of today. To see just how widespread this new artistic style became, duck into the Crédit Lyonnais bank on the rue St-Georges to admire the recently restored stained-glass ceiling by Jacques Gruber, another front runner of the Art Nouveau style; imbued with pale yellow and soft lavender shades, the light, airy feeling of this *verrerie* transports you to a country garden on a fresh spring day.

Before you wander much farther, you really should visit the **Musée de l'Ecole de Nancy**, an exquisite museum that has integrated countless decorative arts pieces in the Art Nouveau style into the décor of this once private town house. The **Musée des Beaux Arts**, or Fine Arts Museum, makes for an excellent next stop, and although you can admire many beautiful paintings inside, the real highlight of this art-honoring fortress is its superb collection of Art Nouveau and Art Deco glassware, most of which was created by Daum. At this time, Daum worked mainly with frosted glass and *pâte de verre*, or glass paste. It wasn't until after World War II that Daum started working with crystal; today most of their pieces embrace a handsome harmony between *pâte de verre* and crystal.

If these richly hued creations seduce you enough to want to buy, go to the **rue Stanislas**, the street that promises the most successful antiquing in Nancy. **J. C. Jantzen** at number 13 (tel.: 03.83.35.20.79) outdoes them all in Art Nouveau: ceramics and glassware by Gallé, glass and crystal by Daum and Lalique, faience from Lunéville and Longwy, and other exquisite pieces from Muller, Walter, and many more reign here in artistic splendor. As long as you're in the art mode, stop in at the **Galerie Art International** (17 rue d'Amerval; tel.: 03.83.35.06.83), one of the city's best showcases for contemporary works, including glass and paintings by local artists as well as some of the more cutting-edge Longwy enamels.

Those more interested in the old and the traditional should visit the **Musée des Arts et Traditions Populaires** (Folk Arts Museum; 66 Grand'Rue; tel.: 03.83.32.18.74), where you can marvel at the stupendous collection of pharmacy jars in faience along with a heartwarming display of country furnishings.

Atelier Bassinot

Now that your appetite for florid home décor accents has been whetted, you might be thinking about how to introduce some of these same sensual themes into your own home. A luminous glass panel, blooming with insouciant botanical motifs, would start you off with an earnest statement. Some people might wonder where to put this sort of piece, but it's easy to place once you start thinking about all of the clear glass panes in a house that you could happily replace with such a decorative work. In the stained-glass business since 1930, this atelier works in many styles other than Art Nouveau; I feel, however, that if you're going to purchase such a piece in this city, let it be one of inspiration from *l'Ecole de Nancy*.

• 16 rue Cristalleries, 54000 Nancy; tel.: 03.83.35.50.03; fax: 03.83.32.74.17
   Open Monday–Friday 8 A.M.–noon and 2–6 P.M.; Saturday 8 A.M.–noon

Baccarat

See page 184 for description.

• 2 rue des Dominicains, 54000 Nancy; tel.: 03.83.30.55.11; fax: 03.83.36.49.62
   Open Monday 2–7 P.M. and Tuesday–Saturday 9:30 A.M.–noon and 2–7 P.M.

Daum

It's likely that from now on whenever you look at a piece of Daum's *pâte de verre*–enhanced crystal, it will be hard not to think of the whole Art Nouveau movement that took hold here. Even the more recent, highly publicized line of cactus-topped carafes, designed by Hilton McConnico, harken back to this rapturous study of nature and form. Like the Baccarat boutique, Daum occupies a prestigious selling space within the center of Nancy, two shimmering reminders that these big names preside over the region.

Baccarat does not sell seconds, but Daum is generous with its less-than-perfect castoffs. Nearly hidden away in a huge storeroom setting close to the center of town, the sizable selection of Daum and Cristal de Sèvres items sold here at dangerously reduced prices could well send shoppers into a frenzy. Daum's discontinued pieces, (signed Daum) are marked down 20 percent; the slightly defective creations (signed Nancy), have been marked down by at least 40 percent. This may be your opportunity to pick up a good bargain or two; I found a *pâte de verre* and crystal fruit bowl, originally priced at 4,900F, reduced here to 800F!

- Daum Boutique: 22 rue Héré, 54000 Nancy; tel/fax.: 03.83.32.21.65
  Open Monday 2–7 P.M.; Tuesday–Saturday 9:30 A.M.–12:30 P.M. and
  2–7 P.M.
- Daum Factory Store: 17 rue des Cristalleries, 54000 Nancy; tel.:
  03.83.32.14.55
  Open Monday–Friday 9:30 A.M.–12:30 P.M.

Lalonde

You don't have to be a hard-candy connoisseur to appreciate the delicately perfumed ambrosial flavor of *les bergamotes de Nancy*, the amber-colored sweets created here in 1850. The rinds of the bergamot fruit, which resembles a pear-shaped orange, yields essential oils frequently used in perfumery; you rarely encounter this aroma in anything except Earl Grey tea. I was so delighted with the taste that I bought a whole quantity of them to share with others. You'll probably do the same, and I would guess that your only hesitation will be over what type of tin to select–Art Nouveau, or a classic view of the place Stanislas.

Other traditional Lorraine treats include marzipan, mirabelle-flavored bonbons, and *chardons*, whose pink-and green-coated, liqueur-filled candies resemble thistles.

- 59 rue St-Dizier, 54000 Nancy; tel.: 03.83.35.31.57; fax: 03.83.32.51.83
  Open Monday 1:45–7 P.M.; Tuesday–Friday 9 A.M.–noon and 1:45–7
  P.M.; Saturday 9 A.M.–12:15 P.M. and 1:45–7 P.M.

Maison des Soeurs Macarons

The distinguished façade of this more than 200-year-old establishment speaks of Old World charm, graciously announcing the quality of goods that you can expect to find inside. Many of them resemble the kinds of sweets sold at Lalonde, but, as the name indicates, the real specialty of this venerable old house happens to be the *macaron*, the faintly almond-flavored meringue-like treat that seems to pop up, in one form or another, throughout all of France. Here they are fresher than fresh, and if your French proves passable, the salesperson will probably ask you *"Pour manger quand?"* meaning "To eat when?" As with a good Camembert, a difference of a day or even an hour can mean an awful lot. If you're looking to pick up something that will keep for travel, consider the sugary fruit jellies (*pâtes de fruit*) instead.

- 21 rue Gambetta, 54000 Nancy; tel.: 03.83.32.24.25; fax: 03.83.32.07.36
  Open Monday–Saturday 9 A.M.–noon and 2–7 P.M.

Brasserie Excelsior

My first introduction to Nancy took place in this bustling brasserie, and during the whole meal I could hardly keep my eyes on my plate or my lunch partners—I was too enraptured with the décor. I noticed that I was not the only one with eyes roving from one element of this spectacular Art Nouveau interior to another, and I knew we would not be the last. There's no way you can be blasé about all of the superb workmanship on view here: a profusion of elaborate trimmings in the form of ferns, pine branches, and ginkgo leaves, ethereal glass panels signed Gruber, and leafy wrought-iron chandeliers weeping with *pâte de verre* light fixtures created by Daum. I can't remember what I had to eat but I'm sure it was delicious.

- 50 rue Henri-Poincaré, 54000 Nancy; tel.: 03.83.35.03.01; fax: 03.83.35.18.48
  Brasserie: Moderate–Expensive
  Open daily 7:30 A.M.–midnight except Christmas Eve

Grand Hôtel de la Reine

If you reserve a room here, be sure to specify that you want one facing the place Stanislas. This hotel is part of the well-reputed Concorde Hotel chain, so you are sure to enjoy the same comfort in their rooms as you would in any international hotel of grand standing. The bonus asserts itself in the omnipresent European pomp, regal features that render this luxurious establishment truly worthy of its prestigious location. Expect lots of high ceilings, giltwork, and heavy draperies.

- 2 place Stanislas, 54000 Nancy; tel.: 03.83.35.03.01; fax: 03.83.32.86.04
  Four-Star Hotel/Restaurant: Expensive
  Open year-round

Sarreguemines (Moselle)

Known as an extremely important center of faience from the end of the eighteenth century up until the early part of the 1900s, this town has only one factory today, and even that one doesn't hold much interest since it mainly manufactures tiles. The history of Sarreguemines cannot be erased, however, and in many respects has proved to be as indelible as all of the striking colors locked within its magnificent ceramics. If your enthusiasm for faience is not on the wane, plan a visit to the **Musée de Sarreguemines** in the center of town; if you're short on time, go directly to the first floor to admire the deliciously color-splashed winter garden, created in 1880, as well as a few other rooms—all of which have been plastered with vibrant ceramic tiles to create majestic allegorical scenes of enormous proportion. Neo-Renaissance and Baroque influences lended themselves marvelously to the grandiose majolicas that also emerged around that time, and thank goodness for us that many fine examples can still be viewed here today. As an extension of the museum visit, take a look around **Jadis Antiquités** (6 rue de Verdun; tel.: 03.87.98.62.04), an antique shop in the center of town that prides itself on its large collection of Sarreguemines faience.

Sarreguimines Factory Store

You'll discover a real hodgepodge of faience styles here. Two of the most traditional patterns of eastern France sell here at 30 to 40 percent off on the seconds and 10 to 15 percent off on the discontinued pieces; the *bouquet champêtre*, or country bouquet, signed Agreste takes the prize for one of the best-loved French classics, whereas the Obernai motif, which depicts the town of Obernai in Alsace, trails in noticeably further behind in popularity. A few Lunéville patterns also sell here, although not at greatly reduced prices, as do some majolica and contemporary pieces of a far more neutral order.

- rue du Colonel-Cazal, 57200 Sarreguemines; tel.: 03.87.98.68.51
  Open Monday–Saturday 10 A.M.–noon and 2–6 P.M.

Vannes-le-Chatel (Meurthe-et-Moselle)

On the very fringes of the crystal route lies this little hamlet, a popular destination for a Sunday afternoon drive. I first stopped at **Cristal de Sèvres** factory discount store (tel.: 03.83.25.41.01), where I had to elbow my way through a series of rooms in this old house to glimpse at the discounted goods that seemed to be attracting everyone's attention. You might not be familiar with this brand, but it features some lovely crystal, and sells here for 30 to 70 percent off. As at Daum in Nancy, this store also features a scant showing of seconds and discontinued items from Daum's collection.

The **Cristal Innovation Développement** (rue de la Liberté; tel.: 03.83.25.47.38; open daily 2–5 P.M.) represents another busy hub of activity where people divide their time between visiting the glass blowers' ateliers and touring through the showroom across the street that exhibits their creations. Their works vary considerably in creativity and price, beginning at 35F for a miniature glass-blown fruit and reaching well up into the four-digit range for more otherworldly expressions of artistry. Be sure to visit the vaulted cellar, where you're apt to discover some of the most exciting pieces.

Lyons and Romans
Lyon et Romans

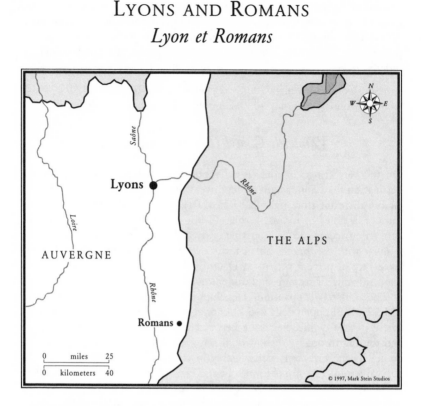

designer shoes at discount • hand puppets • silks • antiques • chocolates • silk wedding and evening dresses • marionettes • fanciful ribbons • books about the silk industry • *saucisson de Lyons* • plush towels and bathrobes • luxurious home décor items • chic luggage • silk ties, scarves, and fashions

LYONS AND ROMANS are two very different cities with one thing in common: they are both situated just off of *l'autoroute du soleil*, the busy highway that leads travelers to sunny destinations in the south. The A6 just clips the city of Lyons, making it possible to spend a half day here, although there is so much to see that you'll probably want to stay longer. Farther south toward Valence, Romans is only a twenty-minute drive from the Tain Hermitage exit—the sort of side trip that can furnish welcome relief from long stretches of driving.

By train, Lyons is a breeze—particularly if you take the TGV. (Trains don't run as speedily or as regularly to Romans, but, as always, if there's a will there's a way.) Keep in mind that the surrounding area has much to offer, especially toward l'Ardèche, the wonderfully wild province of France where people go to hike, kayak, and to run the river's rapids. If you're near St-Pierreville, be sure to visit the **Ardelaine Wool Museum** (04.75.66.61.97) and store (04.75.66.61.97)—the one place that I was sorry to have missed during my travels. Don't forget to send me a postcard!

Lyons (Rhône)

TGV: 2 hours
Main Shopping Streets: rue Edouard-Herriot, rue de Brest,
rue Victor-Hugo, rue Emile-Zola, rue des Archers
Market: Les Halles de Lyon
Tuesday–Saturday 7:30 A.M.–10:30 P.M.; Sunday 7:30 A.M.–2 P.M.
Flea market: Villeurbanne, 1 rue du Canal
Thursday and Saturday 8 A.M.–1 P.M.; Sunday 6 A.M.–1 P.M.

Strategically situated at the crossways of the Rhône and the Saône rivers, Lyons's importance as a major commercial center throughout history was nothing less than inevitable. As the second-largest city in France, Lyons continuously builds upon the cultural and economic stature that it has accumulated over the centuries. Although lovely Lyons cannot compete with powerhouse Paris in shopping opportunities as brazenly as it does in gastronomy, the overall scene is nonetheless quite spectacular.

Before you delve into the buying of the goods, start off with a visit to the **Musée des Tissus** (34 rue de la Charité), or Textile Museum, to learn about Lyons's most famous product: its silk (soie). Various exhibits trace the history of silk throughout the ages from its earliest beginnings in ancient China right up through Lyons's most celebrated silk houses of today—*soieries* the likes of **Tassinari et Chatel** who continue to create luxurious interiors of great refinement and others who work for the world of *la haute couture*. You will learn that the Italians introduced silk to the region during the sixteenth century when they came to this important European trading place to sell spices and fabrics. By the end of the seventeenth century, Lyons had surpassed Italy in both creation of designs and actual production of the silk; the raising of silkworms had in fact become so prevalent that there were even mulberry trees, the worms' food source, planted in the Tuileries gardens (production ceased between the two world wars, and since World War II, the French have bought their silk supply from Japan and Korea). Many of the most sumptuous silks were created during the seventeenth and eighteenth centuries, a period that also produced a significant volume of fabrics to accommodate the custom of changing draperies and slipcovers twice a year, for summer and for winter, while women of the upper classes never wore the same dress twice!

Although scantily stocked, the museum boutique sells some lovely silk scarves (450F to 750F) printed with motifs from their collection in addition to several books, in both French and English, about the museum and the silk industry in general.

The logical next stop on the silk history tour is **La Maison des Canuts** (10–12 rue d'Ivry; tel.: 04.78.28.62.04), an old silk workers' house that acts as a living museum for the demonstration of the silk-weaving process. Two massive looms greet you as you enter this workshoplike space, one used for the weaving of traditional silks, the other reserved for velvets. These manually operated looms tackle rich intricate patterns that modern machines cannot, requiring the majority of tedious tasks to be carried out by hand (and by foot—each tap on the pedal provokes a clack-bam-boom, heralding another passage of threads). To further illustrate the laborious steps involved to operate these cantankerous dinosaurs, it takes about one month of fastidious maneuvers just to set up a loom and put the nearly 1,000 bobbins in place for the creation of such elaborate works.

Behind the boutique across the street, you may be able to see (and certainly will hear) the mechanical loom in action, a noisy monster that epitomizes both the progress and decline brought on by the Industrial Revolution. I was not impressed by the quality of the silk products sold in the highly touristy boutique, however, when I asked about buying pieces of their hand-loomed silk, the less-than-helpful saleswomen did acknowledge that pillow-sized remnants sell for about 3,000F.

As you walk around this Croix-Rousse section of Lyons, ask someone to point you in the direction of the *traboules*, the covered passageways that were built around this hill so that the silk workers could transport their goods from place to place without having to worry about being rained upon. If you head back down toward the chic part of town, stop in at **La Droguerie** (12 rue de la Monnaie; tel.: 04.78.42.37.71; fax: 04.78.38.00.76) to admire, and perhaps even to buy, some of their spectacular ribbons and trims, most of which were made in the passementerie capital of France, the nearby town of St-Etienne.

In the nineteenth century, the Italians also inspired the *lyonnais* to embrace another tradition when characters from the commedia dell'arte suddenly became the fashion. The hand puppet Guignol was born along with a lively entourage of *personnages* bubbling with diverse personality types, a motley cast of characters that served as a clever vehicle of expression of opinions among the people of Lyons. This unique form of theater lives on today at **Le Guignol de Lyon** (2 rue Louis-Carrand; tel.: 04.78.28.92.57; fax: 04.78.30.00.52), a company under the direction of Christian Capezzone, a passionate man who talks about his more than 300 puppets the way a proud father would boast about his brood. Throughout most of the year, 30-to-45-

minute shows are presented in this adorably diminutive theater on Wednesday, Saturday, and Sunday afternoons and almost daily during school vacations excepting summer, when the troupe often hits the road to perform elsewhere. It's important to understand French if you want to have a total grasp of the story line, otherwise adults and children can just take it in much like the Kabuki theater in Japan. Call ahead to reserve.

Once you've been exposed to these endearing characters, you might feel the urge to buy one. Le Guignol de Lyon sells small (190F) and large (380F) puppets along with a few T-shirts and pins in the entrance hall of the theater. Just a few steps from here in the thick of *Vieux Lyon*, the old section of the city, l'**Atelier de Guignol** (4 place du Change; tel.: 04.78.29.33.37) showcases a large selection of handpuppets and marionettes of varying themes in a colorful boutique; not all are made in France, however, so take a close look before you buy. In any event, these two addresses give you good reason to cross the Saône to visit the old part of Lyons, a historic and picturesque portion of the city.

Lyons antiquing offers two very different experiences: one in traditional little shops within the heart of the city, the other in a shopping-mall setting way at the other side of town. Just off of the expansive place Bellecour, the neighborhood traversed by the rue Auguste-Comte is home to a good number of Lyons's most reputable *antiquaires*. Situated in the far reaches of the city in an area called Villeurbanne, **La Cité des Antiquaires** (117 boulevard de Stalingrad; tel.: 04.72.44.91.98) is not easily accessed by public transportation, and by taxi, it'll cost you a hefty fare. Opened Thursday through Sunday, this modern showplace of *le vieux* does, however, house some 150 dealers, so if your main focus is antiques, you should probably plot your way here.

If you have visited just a fraction of the silk, hand puppet, or antique businesses that the city has to offer, you might feel hungry by now in a *lyonnais* sort of way. The people of this great gastronomic capital also love to eat and drink simply in bistrots that they refer to as *bouchons*. With tables typically dressed in red-and-white-checked tablecloths and red wine served by the carafe to accompany hearty fare, the ambiance of these often family-run establishments is one of unfettered neighborliness, rather uncharacteristic of the French indeed. **Le Garet** (7 rue Garet, tel.: 04.78.28.16.94; fax: 04.72.00.06.84) is one *bouchon* among hundreds—but whatever you do, don't leave Lyons without having sampled at least one.

KHA

If you begin your silk shopping here, you're starting at the top. I discovered this ravishing boutique late one evening just before its closing. I was actually in search of another luxury store located on the same *place* **Epsilon Décoration**, a stunning home-interiors showcase that had already battened down its hatches for the day. As I encircled the palatial place des Célestins, I stumbled upon the brightly colored shopwind ows of this fairly new boutique and felt drawn to the opulent goods presented inside.

The shop primarily features creations by André Claude Canova along with other upscale women's fashions by Nina Ricci and Hervé Leger. Canova creates fabrics for Ferragamo, Chloë, and Cartier collections with exuberant color schemes and fantastical designs that embrace the same concern for detail, quality, and refinement found in the shop's own line of goods. You can go for broke and plunk down about 4,000F on a vividly patterned *chemise* or spend a more conservative 850F for a silk twill scarf or 390F for a classic tie—all items that you will most likely treasure for a lifetime. Other lofty temptations include elegant silk and cashmere shawls, deep-pile bathrobes and towels, and handsomely constructed luggage bearing a dapper golfer print.

- 8 rue Gaspard-André, 69002 Lyon; tel.: 04.78.38.02.02; fax: 04.78.37.97.32
  Open Tuesday–Saturday 10 A.M.–7 P.M.

L'Atelier de Soierie

You may already have gathered by now that two different types of silk-making typify the silk industry: weaving and printing (*impression*). Situated at the end of a courtyard in a little street within the garment district with a rather dubious-looking entrance, this silk-printing workshop is one of about ten companies still operating in Lyons. Although created with tourists in mind, the workshop is not just here for show because as the pervasive smell of intoxicating paint indicates, the silkscreening and stenciling of silks is carried out here on a regular basis. The fruits of this atelier's production sell in the mini-boutique upstairs in the form of scarves, shawls, and neckties. Some of the items are so classic that they look boring while other pieces cry out in a jubilant expression of creation. Most of these works were confectioned in the adjoining atelier, where the hand-painting of silk chiffon in soft, fluid designs is the primary occupation. For a real signature piece of this order, don't miss the billowy shawls highlighted by *panne de velours*, or panne velvet (850F to 950F), a look originally brought into fashion in the 1930s and then relaunched during the nineties.

- 33 rue Romarin (near the place des Terreaux), 69001 Lyon; tel.: 04.72.07.97.83; fax: 04.78.28.61.84
  Open Monday–Saturday 9 A.M.–noon and 2–7 P.M.

Bernachon

As long as you are taking in Lyons's *produits de luxe*, find your way over to Bernachon, undoubtedly one of the world's best makers of luxury chocolates. Chocolate lovers can choose from more than fifty different kinds of chocolate, all sold only in this boutique. If you're wondering which is the most celebrated, try the *palet d'or*, a divine melange of chocolate and Normandy double cream enrobed in a dark, glossy *couverture*. *Couverture* does not just mean covering; in fact, the word refers to the essential ingredient of the chocolate-making process, bars that are melted down to make everything from a chocolate cake to a *ganache* center. The key to Monsieur Bernachon's success probably lies in the fifteen different kinds of *couverture* that he creates from the finest cocoa beans harvested in South America and Asia. The master *chocolatier* refers to these different varieties of *couverture* as *crus*, a word usually employed in the classification of wines, the same attention goes into the selection and blending of these beans as that devoted to the grapes in the making of a fine wine. Make your choice with the knowledge that Monsieur Bernachon has been artfully creating these chocolates in his backstage *laboratoire* for more than forty years.

- 42 cours Franklin-Roosevelt, 69006 Lyon; tel.: 04.78.24.37.98; fax: 04.78.52.67.77
  Open Tuesday–Sunday 8:30 A.M.–7 P.M.

Bianchini Férier

Also in the silk quarter, not far from the Croix Rousse métro station, the Bianchini Férier factory continues to puff away as one of the most prestigious silkmakers of Lyons. Bargain seekers will be thrilled to learn that this longtime supplier to the big-name designers had the largesse to open up a factory discount store featuring high-quality silks at affordable prices. I quickly zeroed in on three richly patterned ties (220F apiece) for three elegant men in my life. I resisted the desire to pick up another scarf or shawl (500F to 1,500F) to add to my collection, and as I turned to admire their huge and widely colorful selection of fabrics, I only wished that I sewed or at least knew of a good seamstress who could turn them into a few flowing numbers for my wardrobe. Look for the signs that lead you to this store, which is hidden amid the offices upstairs.

- 4 rue Vaucanson, 69001 Lyon; tel.: 04.72.07.31.00; fax: 04.78.27.90.30
  Open Monday–Wednesday 1:30–5 P.M.; Thursday 12:30–5 P.M.; Friday 1:30–4 P.M.

Bocuse & Bernachon

Back at "the Bernachon block," the street with three different Bernachon establishments in a row, the Bocuse & Bernachon alliance has been successful in more ways than one (the daughter of world-famous chef Paul Bocuse married Monsieur Bernachon's son). Bocuse & Bernachon sells an array of delights fit for a king's banquet. Try some of the farm-fresh products, such as creamy cows' milk cheeses from St-Marcellin and savory sausages from Lyon called *saucissons de Lyons* or *rosette*, along with a bottle of fine wine to accompany this regional snack. Other less perishable items include a variety of jarred homemade pâtés and prepared dishes, ready for long-term storage in your gourmet pantry. If you want to be a real show-off, ask about the special Bocuse & Bernachon gift packages filled with exquisite treats sure to impress your favorite gastronome back home.

- 46 cours Franklin-Roosevelt, 69006 Lyon; tel.: 04.72.74.46.19;
  fax: 04.72.74.46.24
  Open Tuesday–Saturday 9 A.M.–noon and 2–7 P.M.

Lise Tarraud Creations

As I was antiquing along the rue Auguste-Comte I fell upon this dreamy space which I soon realized was a boutique for princesslike brides-to-be. I was immediately greeted by the warm and smiling Madame Tarraud, the *créatrice* behind the gorgeous gowns and sartorial suits presented here–all superbly made-to-measure from the finest Lyons silks. How marvelous it would be for a future bride to buy her wedding dress here–not only in France, but better yet, in Lyons, one of the silk capitals of the world!

Madame Tarraud assured me that she has mailed off expertly packaged dresses all over the world. The clients make their choice by looking at the selection of prototypes on view in the boutique as well as by glancing through her collection of photos of other specially designed creations. Once the choice has been made, Madame can produce the muslin pattern within a few hours for a quick fitting, and by the end of that same day, the actual dress in the desired fabric is ready for a second fitting. All that remains are the finishing touches before this precious cargo is shipped to destinations within or beyond the borders of France. The collection of styles impressed me almost as much as this expedient manner of handling out-of-towners; if you want to go all out, you can splurge with an eighteenth-century-inspired re-embroidered silk organza gown, or if you're a modern bride, you might opt for a more understated cream-colored silk taffeta suit. Prices begin around 8,500F and quickly climb toward the 15,000F to 20,000F mark. Those who do not fall into the "bride-to-be" category need not stay away either, because many of these fancy frocks can double as evening dresses; men open to the purchase of an elegant silk brocade vest can have lots of fun here, too!

- 40 rue Auguste-Comte, 69002 Lyon; tel.: 04.78.37.62.65
  Open Monday–Saturday 10 A.M.–noon and 2–7 P.M.

Richart

Immaculately packaged chocolates are the trademark of this high-quality chocolate maker. The Richart chocolates, as well as their boxes, have a purity of line and form that is best appreciated by sophisticated chocolate lovers. Each of the geometrically shaped chocolates is arranged in a white glossy box, complete with pull-out drawers for easier and more aesthetically pleasing consumption.

- 1 rue du Plat, 69002 Lyon; tel.: 04.78.37.38.55; fax: 04.72.41.73.57
  Open Monday 2–7 P.M.; Tuesday–Saturday 10 A.M.–1 P.M. and 2–7 P.M.

Bernachon Passion

The third member of the Bernachon trilogy can be a lifesaver when you find that you need an energy-inducing treat after wearing yourself out around town. Although this restaurant/tea salon is open for breakfast straight through dinner, I recommend stopping here around teatime to indulge in a chocolaty treat. Bernachon's best-known chocolate cake is a good bet in all seasons except summer, when the house takes a break from making this fragile creation for fear that its trademark mountain of chocolate shavings would melt into a gooey brown blob. This is not your ordinary *gâteau au chocolat*; Monsieur Bernachon created this candied fruit and chocolate cream-filled spongecake for Valéry Giscard d'Estaing when his buddy, Paul Bocuse, received the prestigious *legion d'honneur* award. The cake has, of course, been called *le président* ever since!

- 42 cours Franklin-Roosevelt, 69006 Lyon; tel.: 04.78.52.23.65
  Restaurant/Tea Salon: Moderate
  Open Monday–Saturday 9 A.M.–6:30 P.M.

Hôtel Plaza

The name sounds ritzy, but this is in fact a modestly priced establishment that offers comfortable, clean, and pleasantly decorated accommodations in a convenient central location. The interior was recently renovated in a contemporary style, yet not so contemporary that you feel the chill of a minimalist décor. A double room costs about 600F per night.

- 5 rue Stella, 69002 Lyon; tel.: 04.78.37.50.50; fax:
  04.78.42.33.34

Three-Star Hotel: Moderate
Open year-round

Le Nord

Yet another member of the Bocuse family, the ninety-year-old *brasserie* Le Nord has thankfully retained its Old World charm of yesteryear. Its red and green interior provides an idyllic, cozy refuge on a blustery night, and the restaurant's jovial squadron of waiters scurry about in traditional dress with long white aprons just about skirting the tops of their shiny shoes. I dined here alone on the classic roast chicken served with a copious helping of *pommes frites* (French fries) and not once did I feel lonely or out of place—just another indicator of the festive ambiance that reigns in this enclave of French bonhomie and good food.

- 18 rue Neuve, 69002 Lyon; tel.: 04.78.28.24.25; fax: 04.78.28.76.58
Brasserie: Moderate
Open daily for lunch and dinner

Romans (La Drôme)

Even though the leather-crafting industry of Romans dates back to the fifteenth century, it wasn't until the beginning of this century that the shoe-making business started to emerge here. It really took off during the 1960s, and today this small town serves as home to a handful of France's most upmarket shoe manufacturers, including Charles Jourdan, Robert Clergerie, and Stéphane Kélian. In view of the town's status as an important historical and industrial stronghold for the making of shoes, it only seemed natural to create a museum directly linked to this preeminence. In founding the **Musée de la Chaussure**, or Shoe Museum, the people of Romans outdid themselves: never before have I seen such an extensive and attractively presented collection of footwear (shoe fetishists take note!).

Housed in an old convent that was built during the seventeenth and nineteenth centuries, the visit starts out rather routinely with a look at some of the machinery and tools used in the crafting of shoes. Once you go upstairs, however, you learn about the entrancing history of shoes, the people who wore them, and their motives behind covering their feet with a certain type of protection and ornamentation. The space lends itself extremely well to the exhibits, which are presented in separate quadrants that were originally the nuns' tiny cells.

You begin by learning that the first sandals were made out of papyrus in Egypt, and that leather didn't appear until much later. Then you discover that emperors wore shoes for ceremonial purposes, and that during the Middle Ages, when shoes were still quite rare and expensive, a man's wealth was measured by the length of his shoe. Heels emerged during the Renaissance. The exhibition takes you through *les grands classiques français* when red heels symbolized aristocracy; in accordance with the shift in politics, heels were eliminated entirely during Napoleon's reign. The next time that you hear yourself complaining about sore feet, just think about the pain and suffering that our ancestors had to endure; up until 1870, there was absolutely no distinction between a shoe for the left and the right foot. If you start to study the wealth of shoes from other continents, you may very well find yourself lost here until the end of the day. A few Turkish slippers, American Indian moccasins, and Japanese platforms later, you're apt to leave with a yen to add at least a couple of exotic pairs to your collection.

You're in the right town, because Romans's factory outlet shoe shops feature fashion-conscious footwear from the most in-step labels of the industry. In most cases, these self-serve shops sell the previous year's collection at about 50 percent off the retail price:

Charles Jourdan. Men's and women's shoes and accessories; also sells Dior and Chanel footwear for women.

• Galerie Fan 'Halles, 26100 Romans; tel.: 04.75.02.32.36
  Open Monday 10 A.M.–noon and 2–6:45 P.M.; Tuesday–Friday 9 A.M.–noon and 2–6:45 P.M.; Saturday 9 A.M.–6 P.M.

Robert Clergerie. Women's shoes; Fenestrier and Unic shoes for men.

• rue Pierre Curie, 26100 Romans; tel.: 04.75.05.59.65
  Open Monday 2–7 P.M.; Tuesday–Saturday 9:30 A.M.–12:30 P.M. and 2–7 P.M.

Robert Clergerie Espace. Women's shoes and accessories.

• Galerie Fan 'Halles, 26100 Romans; tel.: 04.75.02.87.97
  Open Monday 2–7 P.M.; Tuesday–Friday 10 A.M.–noon and 2–7 P.M.; Saturday 10 A.M.–12:30 P.M. and 2–7 P.M.

Stéphanie Kélian. Women's shoes; some Maud Frizon.

- 11 place de Charles-de-Gaulle, 26100 Romans; tel.: 04.75.05.23.26
  Open Monday–Friday 9 A.M.–12:30 P.M. and 1:30–7 P.M.; Saturday
  9 A.M.–7.30 P.M.

Tchilin. Maker of men's and women's shoes for well-known brands.

- 52 quai Chopin, 26100 Romans; tel.: 04.75.72.51.41
  Open Monday 2–7 P.M.; Tuesday–Saturday 10 A.M.–noon and 2–7 P.M.

You will encounter even more shops around town.

NORMANDY
Normandie

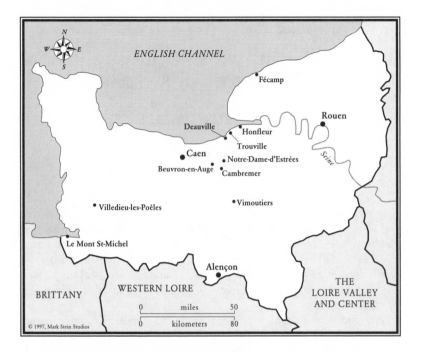

copperware • faience • chic clothing and accessories • cider • Bénédictine • rustic furnishings • cheeses • pewter • antiques • prints • Calvados • bells • nautical knitwear • lace • Camembert labels and posters • World War II memorabilia, books, and tapes • pommeau • apple jelly • Impressionistic and Postimpressionistic paintings • *confiture de lait* • seafaring casualware • butter cookies

WHEN MANY FOREIGNERS hear mention of Normandy, they often first think of the World War II landing beaches or the highly gentrified string of resort towns (which I call the Northern Riviera) just east of the region. Le Mont St-Michel draws people from every corner of the earth to marvel at its very existence. And although this precious gumdrop of land is listed in many guidebooks as part of Brittany, it is officially Norman. The Breton influence does, however, nudge "Le Mont" much the way *un certain air de Paris* hovers over the Northern Riviera and other trampled haunts, including Monet's rapturous Giverny in Vernon.

As fascinating as all of these destinations are, if you want to see, feel, and experience the uniqueness of this part of France, you must go to the apple-and-cheese region, the delightfully rural part of Normandy where there is not much to see other than cows, half-timbered farmhouses, apple trees, fields, and more cows. This endearing countryside will undoubtedly steal a piece of your heart, and leave you aching to give away just a tad more.

THE NORTHERN RIVIERA

Deauville (Calvados)

Main shopping streets: rue Eugène-Colas, rue Desiré-Le-Hoc
Market: place du Marché Tuesday, Friday, and Saturday 8 A.M.–1 P.M.;
fish market in Trouville daily (closed for lunch)

A speedy two-and-a-half-hour drive from the capital, Deauville rates high on the list of favorite Parisian weekend destinations. Aside from socializing, gambling, and playing golf, the favorite thing to do in this pristine seaside resort is to walk along *les planches*, one of the most famous boardwalks on earth. Even on blustery days you can spot pleasure-seekers strolling along as the wind snaps at the myriad brightly colored parasols and their thick sashes of contrasting hues.

Another activity that scores major points as a popular Deauville pastime is shopping. One look around this perfectly manicured storybook town and you can see why: **Dior, Nina Ricci, Yves Saint Laurent, Hermès, Cartier,** and **Polo/Ralph Lauren** are just some of the big-name boutiques that typify this luxury-driven bastion of the elite. Set up mostly on the streets surrounding the casino, these chic showplaces look like satellite boutiques of their larger mother houses back in Paris. If you walk inland toward the heart of the commercial district, you'll see further evidence that Deauville is *the* Norman town *à la parisienne*; the impeccable half-timbered houses, the irreproachable flowerbeds, and their Haussmann-like alignment of streets create a look far more refined than what you would expect in a quaint Norman town. There are so many *traiteurs* (a more upscale version of our delis) here that you'd think that you were in the 16th arrondissement in Paris. Between these pricey takeouts and the plenitude of restaurants, it's clear that second-residence dwellers don't cook at home much.

I set out to discover the best, and particularly the most authentic, addresses in Deauville for regional comestibles, and sure enough, I found it at the opposite end of town from the casino. A visit to **La Ferme Normande** at 13 rue Breney makes the distance worthwhile because once inside, you feel as though you've just entered an old Norman creamery; oak cabinetry and little white lacquered tables display their abundance of farm-fresh cheeses and locally made goods such as cider, Calvados, and Bénédictine liqueur in a downhome style so different from the rest of the food shops in town. If you can't find just the right *calva* here, try looking around the corner at **La Cave de Deauville**, 48 rue Mirabeau, a wine shop/liquor store known as the best-stocked and most serviceable in the region.

If you're in search of antiques you're in the wrong town, but what Deauville lacks in that domain, it more than makes up for with its dining. **Chez Miocque** (81 rue Eugène-Colas; tel.: 02.31.88.09.52) is one of the most chichi addresses in the area, a popular meeting place better known for its crowd than for its food or setting. In a far different category, the plush, theatrical interior of the handsome half-timbered **Hôtel Normandy** (38 rue Jean-Mermoz; tel.: 02.31.98.66.22; fax: 02.31.98.66.23) beckons at teatime. You may also want to contemplate a stay in this grand establishment—perfect for a cozy weekend *à deux*. Ask for a room with a Channel view. If you're into pampering, see what program of treatments might suit you at the **Thalasso Deauville** (10 avenue Marie-Louise; tel.: 02.31.87.72.00).

Next to Deauville (Calvados)

Les Vapeurs Brasserie

Obtaining a table here for Saturday lunch is like finding a quiet spot on the beach during the month of August. Here you can at least reserve in advance—just like *les habitués* who ritually race up the highway from Paris in time for the midday meal *aux Vapeurs*, THE unofficial start of the weekend. Once here, you will be greeted by effusive salutations of *bonjour madame, bonjour monsieur* in typical *politesse française*, but the hurly-burly of this popular seafood restaurant keeps the waitstaff busy enough that they won't fawn over you—in fact, you may be left to debone your exquisitely prepared *sole meunière* all on your own. Their *moules meunières* taste just as delectable, and if you want to order like the locals, you'll have the mussels, then the sole, followed up by *fraises melba* (strawberries and whipped cream)! As you languish on their lobster-red banquettes, you'll have a fine view of the marvelous photos, advertising posters, and neon signs that plaster the yellowed walls like mementos in an old scrapbook.

- 160 quai Férnand-Moureux, Trouville; tel.: 02.31.88.15.24
  Brasserie: Moderate–Expensive
  Open year-round

Honfleur (Calvados)

Market: place de l'Eglise Ste-Catherine Saturday 8:30 A.M.–1 P.M.

The drive from Deauville/Trouville to Honfleur is one of my favorites in all of France. Be sure to take the road that borders the sea, and plan to leave yourself adequate time to cruise this scenic stretch in a leisurely fashion. In the summer you don't have much choice, because the heavy traffic automatically reduces you to a snail's pace. The views of rolling pastures, knobby fields, and big brown-eyed cows are actually far more plentiful and beguiling than those of the coast. Antique dealers and cider and Calvados producers dot the landscape to capitalize on the near-constant flow of well-to-do travelers; I was not overly impressed with the few that I visited, but I'll leave the final judgment up to you!

Once in Honfleur, you will probably feel overwhelmed by this picturesque old fishing village and by the hordes of tourists that flood it as regularly as the daily tides. When I see such historic places so overrun by swarms of visitors and the multitude of eateries and tacky tourist shops that go along with them, I automatically feel my stomach sink. In Honfleur I set out to comb the maze of old streets in search of just a few establishments that didn't have "tourist" written all over them. The task seemed insurmountable, but by the end of the day I felt confident that I had unearthed a few good finds.

Exploring the back streets is a must, and the first few times I visited Honfleur, I foolishly overlooked them; instead I stayed glued to the old port in awe of the jumble of stone houses and grey-blue slate-faced dwellings that surround the harbor. I hadn't even made it to the handsome fifteenth century Ste-Catherine Church and its adjacent weather-worn shingled bell tower, two unique structures built out of wood—real exceptions in France. The tiny half-timbered house just next to the bell tower shelters **Marin Normand** (24 place Ste-Catherine; tel.: 02.31.89.14.79), a shop open 10 A.M. to 8 P.M. 365 days a year for mariners and even pseudo-mariners in need of clothing worthy of a ship's mate!

La Brocanterie

I found this shop on my way to putting another coin in the parking meter. Don't let the name mislead you, because there's much more for sale here than simple *brocante* (secondhand goods). It could, in fact, be called Art & Antiques since the merchandise is of top-drawer quality, most of it procured from estate sales within the region. Many of the treasures circulate from one estate to another via La Brocanterie, because some of the shop's best clients are Parisians looking to add a few interesting pieces to their nearby vacation homes. The selection is quite ecclectic: at any given time you can expect to find many delicate little bibelots carved out of mother of pearl or ivory in addition to the shop's diversified collection of silver, crystal, glassware, china, faience, and copperware from varying provenances. Some splendid pieces of Norman furniture captured my attention the day I visited, including an exquisite eighteenth-century clock and a milkmaid's pantry in solid oak.

Interspersed among all of these old things are new creations made by a local woman who expresses her artistic talents primarily through basic lamps; the décor is achieved by applying pieces of paper or fabric inside transparent lamp bases and afixing them with coordinating sprays of color. Themes vary as much as the hues in the innumerable collages that spring from this artist's imagination: roses and butterflies swim in a turquoise blue sea, angels float in stardust, and a still life of richly colored fruits blanket an ochre background. Refreshingly opalescent in effect and topped off with pastel-colored shades, their 2,000F price tag seems fair for such original work.

Painters flocked to Honfleur toward the latter part of the nineteenth century, initiating a perpetual ebb and flow that continued right up through the early 1900s. Prominent artists from this period included Henri and René de Saint-Delis, two brothers who were contemporaries of Raoul Dufy, a native of Honfleur who was also influencial in leaving his mark in this *colonie de peintres*. Probably the most famous of the two, Henri de Saint-Delis is recognizable for his heavy-handed stroke and strong colors. Paintings, engravings, and pastels by the Saint-Delis brothers, as well as works by another prominent figure, André Le Maître, hang upstairs in seeming anticipation of interested art enthusiasts. The subject matter primarily consists of historic Norman scenes, so visitors can cherish the unspoiled views of Honfleur that are so few and far between today.

The owner of this lovely shop also presides over **Les Arts de l'Enclos** (tel.: 02.31.89.19.13), a gallery on the quai St-Etienne that highlights works from Norman painters of varying styles. With a clientele predominantly composed of art amateurs from Paris, the exhibitions meet cosmopolitan standards.

- 11 cours des Fossés, 14600 Honfleur; tel.: 02.31.89.05.36;
  fax: 02.31.98.72.25
  Open daily 10 A.M.–12:30 P.M. and 2:30–7 P.M.

Galerie Arthur Boudin

The owner of this gallery is not related to Eugène Boudin, the frontrunner of the Honfleur school of painting, as one might think, although you might encounter a few of this famous artist's works on exhibit here. Oils, pastels, and a few drawings from a good number of *les peintres de l'estuaire* (estuary painters), along with works from many twentieth-century artists such as Bernard Loriot, an artist known for his Impressionistic touch, make up this gallery's permanent exhibition. You have undoubtedly heard the nineteenth-century painters talked about more in connection with la Ferme St-Siméon than with the estuary. According to the owner of this gallery, only some of the estuary painters would congregate at St-Siméon (then a family farm, today a four-star hotel) along with artists from Paris and other parts of the world.

- 6 place de l'Hôtel-de-Ville, 14600 Honfleur; tel.: 02.31.89.06.66
  Open Monday, Tuesday, Friday, and Saturday 10 A.M.–1 P.M. and 3–7 P.M.; Wednesday, Thursday, and Sunday 3–7 P.M.

Gribouille

Boutiques specializing in regional products have overtaken Honfleur with as much zeal as the day-trippers, making the decision of which one to sample a real conundrum. I triumphantly found the one that pleased me with its fine selection of products and from-the-heart décor. The meaning of the word *gribouille* as a noun refers to a shortsighted idiot, and as a verb means to scribble. I'm not sure which one applies to this tasteful hodgepodge of secondhand items and top-quality foodstuffs—but in any event, virtually everything in this quaint little shop is for sale. More than 100 different egg beaters hang from the old wood-beamed ceiling and a scramble of baskets, crates, old farm furniture, and metal display racks like the ones used in French bakeries serve as authentic props for the variety of goods so pleasingly presented in this shop. You can start off with the apple jelly or *confiture de lait* (a milk jam made in a variety of flavors), then work up to more vociferous products the likes of onion and shallot compotes, which are delicious with grilled meats, only to arrive at the perfect crescendo of at least 70 different kinds of Calvados!

- rue de l'Homme-de-Bois, 14600 Honfleur; tel.: 02.31.89.29.54
  Open daily except Wednesday 9:30 A.M.–noon and 2–6 P.M.

THE APPLE-AND-CHEESE REGION

Beuvron-en-Auge (Calvados)

One of a handful of villages that punctuates *la route du cidre*, Beuvron-en-Auge is indisputably the prettiest of them all. Officially classified as one of the most beautiful villages of France, this haven of peace and quiet could lead you to fantasize about shopping in Beuvron for provisions from your Normandy dreamhouse. All of these perfectly preserved half-timbered houses, abloom with colorful flowers, appear fresh out of the pages of a children's book, and after you've taken one look at the surrounding countryside, it's only normal that you'd contemplate coming back regularly. **Epicerie P. Langlois**, the village grocery located in the heart of town, sells many enticing goods which include a fine selection of homemade regional products such as cider, cider vinegar, apple jelly, apple juice, Calvados, and fresh butter, cream, and cheese from the neighboring towns. If you're looking for a good country meal such as a classic *escalope normande* (veal scallop with cream), **l'Auberge de la Boule d'Or** (tel.: 02.31.79.78.78), just across the street, fits the bill nicely. In true Beuvron spirit, remember to order cider as your beverage of choice instead of wine.

Caen (Calvados)

Memorial Boutique

With more than 400,000 visitors per year, this museum/monument/multimedia showplace devoted to worldwide peace through the recounting of the traumas and triumphs of World War II is not to be missed. I include it in this book not only for these reasons but also because it touts one of the very best museum shops in all of France, and you even can stop here without entering the exhibition spaces. The boutique focuses on an extensive selection of books pertaining to war-related subjects that range from general topics to highly specific ones including the Resistance, the Third Reich, peace and human rights, the life of de Gaulle, and the Liberation of the Calvados Department, to name a few. You can find works that you might never find elsewhere in German, Italian, and Dutch, in addition to the far more prevalent English and French editions. Documentary and entertainment videos also figure among popular items, along with an aficionado's collection of World War II model planes, boats, and tanks. I fell right into the swing of things by purchasing Claude Bolling's *Big Band Victory Concert* tape, a compilation of peppy tunes from '44 and '45 that kept me hopping and humming on my drive through the hilly Norman countryside. A bit pricey at 85F for the cassette, but I'd say that I got my money's worth.

- No address: just follow the Memorial signs in and around Caen;
     tel.: 02.31.06.06.44; fax: 02.31.06.06.70
  Mail order available
  Boutique/Museum
  Open daily 9 A.M.–6 P.M.; closed January 1–15

Cambremer (Calvados)

Old-fashioned market: village center 9:30 A.M.–12:30 P.M. Easter, Pentecost, and July–August

Calvados Pierre Huet

If you continue on the *route du cidre* just outside of the village of Cambremer, you should spot a sign or two for the Pierre Huet distillery, one of the most prestigious names in Calvados. After a drive through the undulating terrain of the apple orchard–festooned cider region, you'll be ready to sample a few of the delicious products of this sector. There are enough distilleries to visit along the way to keep you on this meandering route for days, but if you want to avoid running into an errant cow, play it safe and only stop at one or two.

The amber-colored spirit called Calvados has been made in this region since the Middle Ages, and it all begins with cider. French *cidre* resembles what we call hard cider; it has a fizz and a bit of a kick to it that can easily creep up on you after a couple of glasses. Once this cider has been distilled by the same method used for cognac, it is left to age in barrels to take on the full flavor and color of apples. Calvados from *les Pays d'Auge*, the area that encompasses the cider route and beyond, often undergoes the distillation process twice, which partly explains why these *calvas* rate among the best. Many of the apply *eaux-de-vie* from Pierre Huet's production have won awards and as a result are served at some of the finest restaurants in France. The selection in the woodshedlike boutique includes cider; eight different kinds of Calvados, ranging in age from two to thirty years old (100F to 425F); and pommeau, a mixture of apple juice and Calvados that is delicious served chilled as an apéritif.

- Les Fontaines, 14340 Cambremer; tel.: 02.31.63.01.09; fax: 02.31.63.14.02
  Distillery Visits/Boutique
  The boutique is open year-round; Monday–Friday 9 A.M.–12:30 P.M. and 1:30–6 P.M.; Saturday 9 A.M.–12:30 P.M.; half-hour visits of the distillery and the cellar are conducted Easter–November 1 in French and English

Musée du Camembert

One of the best parts of a visit to the Camembert Museum is the ride there! The scenery from Caen to St-Pierre-sur-Dives then to Livarot on the D4 truly takes your breath away. The fairy-tale views of contented cows grazing on the rolling hills and soft sloping valleys, interrupted only by an occasional Norman farmhouse or lordly castle, indicate that you are in the heart of France's greatest cheese region, where the cows are treated as well as (or even better than) the inhabitants. You can stop in Livarot to visit its cheese museum, or go directly to Vimoutiers, where the tiny Camembert Museum occupies most of the tourism office.

An audio-guided tour available in several different languages walks you through the various exhibits that illustrate the making of this popular cheese. I was particularly fascinated by the more than 1,400 Camembert labels displayed to show that so-called Camembert cheeses have been made as far away as Tasmania. The really good Camembert, of course, is made only in this part of France from raw cows' milk; look for a label marked *au lait cru* (unpasteurized cheese) and *moulé à la louche*, which you rarely will see outside of France since unpasteurized cheeses are prohibited in most other countries. Most visits end with cheese tastings accompanied by a glass of cider on the museum's backyard terrace. As far as souvenir shopping goes, I was intrigued by the packets of colorful Camembert labels to purchase for any number of fun craft projects. In case you're wondering . . . there is a village called Camembert just down the road with a population of 170 people and who knows how many cows!

- 10 avenue du Général-de-Gaulle, BP 32, 61120 Vimoutiers;
    tel.: 02.33.39.30.29
  Museum/Boutique
  Open March, April, November, and December Monday 2–6 P.M.,
    Tuesday–Friday 9 A.M.–noon and 2–6 P.M. and Saturday 9 A.M.–noon;
    May 1–end of October Monday 2–6 P.M., Tuesday–Friday 9 A.M.–
    noon and 2–6 P.M., Saturday 9 A.M.–noon, and Sundays and holidays
    10 A.M.–noon and 2:30–6 P.M.

Notre-Dame-d'Estrées (Calvados)

Hotel au Repos des Chineurs

Just a notch away from the cider route, a world of elegance, charm, and refinement awaits you at this centuries-old postal inn that has been transformed into a hotel, tea salon, and antique shop—all in one delightful package! Madame Steffen, the owner of this homey establishment, in fact promotes a whole *style de vie* (way of life)—one that many visitors would like to take home. You can't take the pastoral views home with you, but you can purchase much of what you enjoy inside. It doesn't take long to realize that the old creaky country armoire in which you store your belongings, the delicately carved bedside table for your water glass, the retro lamp that you read by, the fine English porcelain cup that you raise to your lips, the pressed glass pitcher that you use to pour a second goblet of fresh apple juice, the silver toast holder, and countless other collectibles that you encounter here are all for sale! In fact, every object bears a price tag; those on the more regularly washed items, however, have worn a bit thin.

If you don't plan to spend the night, you can stop in for a delicious Norman breakfast of fresh eggs, bacon, herb sausages, baked apples, and Camembert, or just have tea and cakes in the afternoon. The art of *la chine* (a nearly untranslatable word that more or less means to ferret out old objects) can be done at any time, since a good portion of Madame Steffen's treasures are on permanent display in the salon. One last tip: If you do stay overnight, try to reserve the yellow rose room where you can gaze upon the glorious view of the illuminated church of Notre-Dame-d'Estrées until you fall quietly asleep on your soft milky-white sheets. *Quel bonheur.*

- Chemin de l'Eglise, 14340 Notre-Dame-d'Estrées; tel.: 02.31.63.72.51; fax: 02.31.63.62.38
  Boutique/Hotel/Tea Salon: Moderate
  Open year-round

OTHER PARTS OF NORMANDY

Alençon (Orne)

Market: place de la Madeleine and place de Plénitre
Thursday and Saturday 8 A.M.–1 P.M.

At the southernmost point of Normandy, teetering on the department of the Sarthe, a province in the Western Loire, Alençon is a city that conjures up images of lace of great workmanship and finesse. Much to my disappointment (and I'm sure yours as well), Alençon has no workshops that churn out yard after yard of this exquisite lace. In fact, this lace was never turned out in huge quantities since the crafting of such fragile finery is carried out at a snail's pace. So don't be fooled if you hear the term Alençon lace tossed around: chances are the lace was only inspired by *la dentelle d'Alençon* and machine-made.

After a visit to the **Musée de la Dentelle**–Lace Museum–(31–33 rue du Pont-Neuf; tel.: 02.33.26.27.26), you'll know the difference between lace that is truly handmade and so-called handmade lace that is assembled by hand but made with a machine. You'll also understand why a simple postage-stamp piece of handmade lace costs as much as 1,000F. A fifteen-minute video followed by a brief tour of this tiny museum shows you exactly how fastidious and time-consuming it is to work with the *point d'Alençon* or Alençon stitch, a needle-and-thread technique that involves meticulous hand sewing without the help of bobbins. The only craftspeople to work this way today are the twelve members of the Lacemaking School, an organization created in 1903 to perpetuate the tradition of this nearly lost art. Most of the school's creations are offered as gifts to visiting heads of state; others sell here in the museum for a great deal more than souvenirlike prices!

Near Alençon (Sarthe)

Château de St-Paterne

Experience the grandeur of sleeping in a fifteenth-century château (certain parts were also built during the seventeenth century) run by the dashing Charles Henry de Valmay. You'll receive a warm and charming welcome and learn how Charles Henry's ancestors lived many moons ago. Each room has its own distinct personality: the room that was once his grandmother's, for example, features an auspicious canopy bed and romantic trompe l'oeil murals draped with garlands. In the *chambre* Henri IV, the main attraction is the bathroom where a regal Renaissance ceiling, exquisitely painted with the arms of the aforementioned king, might entrance you to such a degree that you'll find it difficult to leave the tub!

- 72610 St-Paterne; tel.: 02.33.27.54.71; fax: 02.33.29.16.71
  Château-Hôtel/Dinner by reservation for guests: Moderate–Expensive
  Best to call ahead.

Fécamp (Seine-Maritime)

Market: Town center Saturday 8 A.M.–7 P.M.

Palais Bénédictine

Even if you are not a fan of this aromatic, golden-honeyed liqueur, plan a visit to the Bénédictine Palace, a tourist destination in and of itself. Little known to most foreigners, the coastal views within the vicinity of Fécamp and its neighboring Etretat are nothing short of spectacular: chiseled cliffs drop off into the sea as sharply as the waters crash on to the shore. Perhaps this dramatic scenery inspired Alexandre Le Grand, the founder of the Bénédictine distillery, to erect his extravagant palace-factory; a behemoth of

Neo-Gothic/Renaissance architecture, typified by its pinnacled, flamboyant, and highly ornate edifice, this unique structure could serve as a metaphor for the many mysteries surrounding this ancestral cocktail. Some 120,000 visitors per year spend hours touring the actual distillery and visiting the various art collections and exhibitions prominently presented inside. You will learn just enough about Bénédictine's unique recipe of twenty-seven herbs and spices, which undergo a complex two-year distillation and aging process, to pique your interest—but no secrets are given away here. Originally developed as an elixir by a Bénédictine monk, this intriguing liqueur is served straight up, on the rocks, or mixed with other beverages as a long drink. The Palace's boutique supplies many ideas for innovating this age-old liqueur as well as a few that feature B&B (Brandy & Bénédictine), the company's other bestseller.

• 110 rue Alexandre-Le Grand, BP 192, 76400 Fécamp; tel.: 02.35.10.26.00; fax: 02.35.28.50.81
Museum/Distillery Visits/Boutique
Open mid-May–September 1 daily 9:30 A.M.–6 P.M.; mid-November–December 31 and January 2–mid-March, visit at 10:30 A.M.; mid-March–mid-May 10 A.M.–noon; early September–mid-November 2–5:30 P.M.

Le Mont St-Michel (La Manche)

Under "The Shops" section of the Mont St-Michel tourist brochure, the shopkeeping tradition carried out here for the past 1,000 years sounds quite charming and quaint, but be prepared to find a mountain of schlock. Although this kind of commercialization for the masses probably is necessary for economic reasons, I hate to see such a glorious place become so exploited for the sake of tourism.

I have visited the Mont several times at three different seasons, and if you have the opportunity, here is one way to proceed: arrive during the off-season late in the day to walk around the village and its outskirts; have dinner and spend the night at the historic establishment, La Mère Poulard; then rise early the next morning to join in a guided visit to the abbey so that you leave the premises by noon before the afternoon crowds arrive. The tour ends at the **gift shop situated within the abbey**, where you can pick up lots of tasteful souvenirs in a saintly setting. Expect to find books in many different languages about Mont St-Michel and the region, as well as religious music, videos, T-shirts, models of the Mont, and much more.

La Mère Poulard

I had heard quite a bit about this restaurant, known for its world-famous omelettes, before having the opportunity to try it. After hearing that the eggs are vigorously beaten in huge copper bowls before your very eyes, I had imagined a folksy setting and was thus surprised to discover such a formal Victorian décor. Founded in 1888, the restaurant has a red velvet, heavily furnished interior reminiscent of that era and poses an interesting contrast with the ancient architecture that typifies the Mont. Several years ago the owners (*la mère poulard* died in 1931) decided to share the rich history of this venerable institution with the rest of the world by framing their collection of more than 3,000 photographs, autographs, and various other mementos of the celebrated people who dined here. These images now hang throughout the dining rooms, hallways, bar, and bedrooms for everyone to enjoy.

Before you settle in to an elegant dinner of regional specialties (one does not order just a simple omelette), take a look at the boutique, which occupies a small, intimate space next to the bar. Highlights of this signature shop include china, tins of butter cookies, and various bottles of fine Calvados—all marked with the rooster red Mère Poulard label. The many pieces of copper have been stamped with the name of the house as well as that of Villedieu-les-Poêles, the nearby town where they are made—two stamps of excellence which might help to explain why these prices run considerably higher than those simply marked Villedieu. The shop also sells a few well-executed prints and watercolors of the mystical Mont St-Michel!

- BP 18–Grande-Rue, 50116 Le Mont St-Michel; tel.: 02.33.60.14.01; fax: 02.33.48.52.31
  Restaurant: Expensive Three-Star Hotel: Moderate Boutique also
  Open year-round: restaurant open 11:30 A.M.–10 P.M.; boutique open 7:30 A.M.–11 P.M.

Outside of Le Mont St-Michel (La Manche)

Boutique Saint-James

Created in 1889 to outfit sailors with basic knitwear of durable quality, the Saint-James label today is as much associated with *le chic* as with *le pratique*. An all-time favorite among the BCBGs preppy types of France, this is the brand of choice among properly dressed French people for classic navy blue cardigans and blue-and-white striped tunics. Although all items originally were made of 100 percent wool, slightly more fashion-oriented outfits (about 1,500F for a skirt and sweater) have been added for women in acrylic/cotton blends in less traditional colors such as jonquil, sky blue, and powder pink. Other marine-inspired sportswear includes weathered cotton casuals from Mât de Misaine, heavy raingear by Michel Beaudoin, and Guy Cotten's forever-popular white slickers, priced at about 500F.

- 15 rue du Mont St-Michel, 50170 Beuvoir; tel.: 02.33.60.59.45
  Mail order available
  Open daily 10 A.M.–12:30 P.M. and 2–7 P.M.

Rouen (Seine-Maritime)

Main shopping streets: rue du Grosse-Horloge, rue des Carmes
Markets: place du Vieux-Marché Tuesday–Sunday 7 A.M.–1 P.M.
place St-Marc Saturday 7 A.M.–7 P.M.; Sunday 7 A.M.–1 P.M.

As you drive through this busy urban center you probably won't notice its most noteworthy shopping attribute: tremendously rich antique shops, most of which are clustered on the streets surrounding the cathedral. Before you unleash yourself onto this antique maven's terrain, visit the **Musée de la Céramique** (tel.: 02.35.07.31.74) in town and the **Musée des Traditions et Arts Normands** (tel.: 02.35.23.44.70), one of the best crafts and folklore museums of Normandy at the Château Martainville, a stout castle 9 kilometers outside of Rouen on the N31. Many of the traditional crafts, costumes, faience, and furnishings sold in Rouen are displayed here in heart-warming settings that resemble the way Norman countryfolk once lived. *Note*: Among the reputed *antiquaires* of Rouen, a good number also showcase highly refined pieces representative of the way the wealthy *rouennais* merchants adorned their interiors centuries ago.

Atelier Saint-Romain

If you're looking for a Norman antique that you won't have to worry about shipping home, the amiable Francis Lefèbvre should be able to dig up a print or two to your liking. He has been collecting engravings, lithographs, pen-and-inks, and watercolors of the region for more than twenty years, and I would guess that all of the business he has conducted with overseas dealers in search of French treasures partly explains his mastery of the English language. One could easily call him "the source" for nearly every imaginable view of the Rouen cathedral ever put to paper as well as other images of Rouen landmarks, many of which were destroyed during the war. Views of surrounding Norman sites such as Le Havre, Fécamp, Dieppe, and the Mont St-Michel are nearly as plentiful as Monsieur's decorative pieces, which include countless images of fruit, flowers, horses, and birds. Prices range from 30F to 3,000F.

- 28 rue St-Romain, 76000 Rouen; tel.: 02.35.88.76.17
  Open daily 10 A.M.–noon and 2–7 P.M.

Carpentier

Just next door to the print shop, the workshop/boutique of Carpentier perpetuates the faience-making tradition that was once a major activity in Rouen. In fact, the pattern *vieux Rouen* is one of the oldest designs in the history of French faience, a décor whose monochromatic blue, or blue and red-brown, motifs on white backgrounds are mainly composed of tendrils and lambrequins originally inspired by Chinese ceramics. Eons away from the light and airy feel of Quimper faience, the Rouen look is richer and infinitely more ornate, making it quite suitable for country French interiors of a more polished order. Everything is made on the premises, and the prices are a bit steep: count on spending about 500F for a teapot.

- 26 rue St-Rouen, 76000 Rouen; tel.: 02.35.88.77.47
  Open Tuesday–Saturday 9 A.M.–7 P.M.

Villedieu-les-Poêles (Manche)

Market: Town center Tuesday 8 A.M.–1 P.M.

The literal translation of this town's name is "God's town the frying pans," and that alone should give you an inkling of what you'll find here. Frying pans, saucepans, stockpots, and decorative items such as planters and fanciful molds are just a few examples of the copperware that fills this small town. It all began during the eleventh century when a group of religious knights from Asia settled here and began to practice their skill as metalworkers; today you can still hear the rat-a-tat-tat coming from workshops located within inner courtyards as craftspeople work much the same way their ancestors did.

Don't be misled, however, in thinking that all of these rosy-gold creations have been hammered out by hand by coppersmiths bent over their workbenches for hours on end. While it's true that a certain amount of the Villedieu copper production is handmade or at least hand-finished, the greatest quantities roll out of more industrial settings. This does not necessarily mean that the mass-produced pieces are of inferior quality; the majority of the copperware that bears the Villedieu-les-Poêles stamp is among the most handsome in the world. You should also be aware that buying directly from the manufacturers can represent price savings of 50 percent or more. The selection is rather daunting, and since the overall ambiance of the town is less than charming, your main focus should be to look, learn, and eventually buy.

The streets are lined with such an array of shops, all shimmering with seemingly similar copperware, that you can't help but feel a bit wary. Make sure that whatever you buy is stamped Villedieu-les-Poêles. If you plan to make a major purchase, such as a five-piece set of pans, do your research and think about what you want, details include the thickness of the copper, the type of lining you desire, the choice between bronze or iron handles, riveted or not, and so on.

Generally speaking, stainless-steel–lined, rivetless copperware of about a 2.5mm thickness works best for the average home cook. If you consider yourself more of a gourmet cook, you might prefer the tinned, 3mm weight, but remember that these heavier pieces can be unwieldy and that you will have to find an appropriately trained craftsman to retin them every few years. Prices on copperware of equal quality run about the same throughout town; count on paying about 2,300F for a five-piece set of nonriveted, stainless-steel–lined copper pans of a hefty weight plus a bar on which to hang them. To ship all of this to the U.S., add on about 600F more.

L'Atelier du Cuivre (54 rue du Général-Huard; tel.: 02.33.51.31.85; fax: 02.33.51.04.96) is one of the best places to shop and to learn about copperware, because in addition to viewing a video, you can actually visit the workshop out back to see the coppersmiths cutting, plying, hammering, and burnishing various works to spangling perfection. Cuivres Pitel-Couetil (2 rue Carnot; tel.: 02.33.51.88.22; fax: 02.33.61.25.22), a shop on the main thoroughfare, features pieces from Mauviel, another reputable copperware maker that supplies many of the major restaurants in France. Just across the street, you may want to visit the Maison de l'Etain (15 rue du Général-Huard; tel.: 02.33.51.05.08; fax: 02.33.51.04.96), to admire a few of the handsome pewter pieces handcrafted here as well as many others that come from other parts of France. You'll see signs and leaflets for the bell foundry, La Fonderie de Cloches (tel.: 02.33.61.00.56; fax: 02.33.90.02.99), in the center of town, yet another craft that has gripped Villedieu for centuries.

You can't escape the town without visiting the Musée du Meuble Normand, the Norman Furniture Museum (9 rue du Reculé; tel.: 02.33.61.11.78), which, although stark, features countless examples of country furnishings of extraordinary quality. If you are looking to buy such superb pieces, go directly to Erick Hervy (28 rue Pontchignon; tel.: 02.33.51.18.51), a bona fide specialist in this domain. For centuries-old pieces of copper and assorted bibelots, try poking around at the second Erick Hervy establishment (48 rue Carnot; tel.: 02.33.51.18.51), an inconspicuous-looking shop in the center of town amid all of the gleam and sheen.

PICARDY AND THE NORTH
Picardie et le Nord

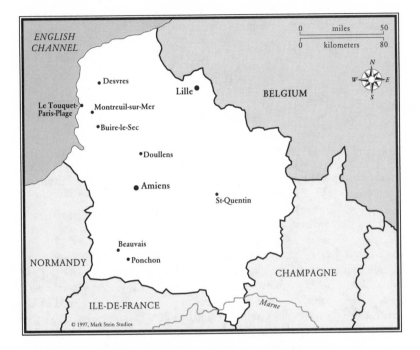

reduced-priced textiles • stained glass • *macarons* • antiques • chocolates • faience • marionettes • cast iron cookware • *gauffres* • chic, casual, and classic children's clothing • fish soup • discount shopping • top-quality house linens • country French ceramics • smart casualwear • puppets

THE FRENCH OFTEN unjustly pooh-pooh the idea of visiting their northernmost provinces. Despite the stigma of lack of sun and too much rain, the weather is not much worse here than in Paris, and there are so many wonderful places to visit in Picardy and beyond that the *météo* should not be a primary consideration. The northern cities of Amiens, Lille, and Arras possess an architectural heritage that resembles the fairy-tale aspects of the most famous Flemish cities farther north; the cultural and artistic riches of these provinces is equally outstanding, particularly when you consider that so much of what was destroyed during the wars had to be built back up again. This certainly was the case for the Beauvais Tapestries Manufactory, and even Jean Trogneux, owner of the oldest and most renowned sweetshop in the region, stressed that after every war his family would just start over and forge on. This sums up the spirit of the northern people quite accurately: they are hardworking and determined, and this fortitude probably helped the North become one of the most heavily industrialized regions of France—a major reason why the shopping is none too shabby!

PICARDY

Amiens (Somme)

Main shopping streets: rue Delambre, rue des Trois-Cailloux,
rue de Noyon
Market: place Parmentier and off of the boats in the nearby canals
Thursday and Saturday 8 A.M.–1 P.M.
Flea market: place Parmentier and place du Don
second Sunday of every month 8 A.M.–6 P.M.

Among travelers, Amiens is one of the most overlooked cities in France, and I admit that its multitude of colorful and charming facets came as a surprise to me. I first heard mention of Amiens many years ago during a visit with friends in Antwerp; they had made plans to visit the city's renowned cathedral on their way to the south of France. When I set my eyes upon this notable wonder, I could understand their short detour and was also thrilled to discover that the entire city is worth a visit.

The quartier St-Leu is a picturesque and animated section of the city whose villagelike qualities contrast greatly with the cityscapes that make up most of the rest of the town. Often referred to as the "Little Venice of the North," this part of Amiens is divided by the Somme River into a jumble of quadrants and canals, each lined with colorful little structures that house a variety of quaint boutiques and bistrots brimming with fun-loving folk. Two life-sized sculptures mark the entrance to the atelier/boutique of **Jean-Pierre Facquier** (67 rue Don; tel.: 03.22.92.49.52), a sculptor who works with his wife to create marionettes representative of the life in Picardy during the eighteenth and nineteenth centuries; most of the works are entirely hand-sculpted, and prices range from 650F to 1,500F. At one time Amiens had about ten marionette theaters; today there is only one, and some shows are performed in *picard*, the old language of the region.

On the other side of the Somme, the sumptuous antique shop **André Coll-Rotger** (1 rue de la Dodane; tel.: 03.22.92.40.22) can't help but capture your attention. Uncontestably one of the most reputed antique dealers of Amiens, Monsieur Coll-Rotger's forte lies largely in traditional pieces of

Picardy such as a *traite*, a long buffet prevalent during the nineteenth century, which was typically constructed of sculpted oak. These pieces often incorporated clocks and shelves, making them so massive that they usually were built right in peoples' homes. Many of them are so beautiful that you might just go to the trouble to ship them home!

If you find yourself in Amiens on a Thursday or Saturday morning, be sure to visit the *marché sur l'eau*, the market where all of the *hortillons* (farmers who cultivate their crops near the outlying marshlands) sell their produce directly from their boats, which congregate in the canals.

Galerie du Vitrail

Plan a visit to this gallery, just a few steps away from the cathedral, around 3pm for the opportunity to enter a reverential world of stained glass. Some of the most spectacular examples of *vitraux* have lovingly been assembled within one space by Claude Barre, a man who has worked for more than fifty years with this brilliant art form. As you step into the depths of the building's thirteenth-century vaulted cellar, you are sure to marvel at many of the rare treasures from the owner's private collection, which includes jewel-like pieces that date back as far as the eleventh century. Upstairs the kaleidoscope continues, this time in a flourish of delicate flowers, birds, and foliage awash in subtle hues—all characteristic of the nineteenth-century style. If any of these ravishing creations leave you wanting one of your own, stop at the middle floor atelier to see if your favorite piece can be duplicated.

• 40 rue Victor-Hugo, 80000 Amiens; tel.: 03.22.91.81.18;
   fax: 03.22.92.14.27
   Museum/Gallery
   Open Monday–Saturday at 3 P.M. for visits

Jean Trogneux

Since 1872 the Trogneux family has been the chief supplier of top quality sweets for the *amiénois*, and with six different addresses spread throughout the region, it looks as though they are satisfying most of the sugar cravings in the north today. They excel in a variety of mouth-watering chocolates, and their prize-winning *macarons* are to die for! Out of all of the *macarons* that I sampled throughout my travels in France, I savored these most. Wrapped in gold paper, these chewy treats stay fresh for about two weeks. According to the bright-eyed Jean Trogneux (the 5th), the secret of their scrumptiousness is in the quality of the almonds. Almonds, sugar, and honey must always be present in a true *macaron*, yet the variations on this one theme are near infinitesimal. Egg whites are frequently added, and as in the case of certain macaroons, coconut often replaces the almonds, a substitution far too inferior for most of the French.

- 1 rue Delambre, 80000 Amiens; tel.: 03.22.91.58.27; fax: 03.22.71.17.11
  Open Monday 1:45–7 P.M.; Tuesday–Saturday 9 A.M.–12:15 P.M. and
  1:45–7 P.M.

Beauvais (Oise)

The town of Beauvais suffered some of the worst damage in WWII, so today only a smattering of this city's historic buildings remain. **La Manufacture Nationale de la Tapisserie**, the national tapestry factory, was nearly destroyed and did not reopen until 1989. Fifteen people work there, weaving mostly contemporary creations to be used by the state, much the way the Gobelins Tapestry Works function in Paris. Visits are conducted at the Beauvais factory in the center of town Tuesday, Wednesday, and Thursday from 2 to 4 P.M. Next door, **La Galerie Nationale de la Tapisserie** pays the Beauvais tapestries the homage they are due in an immense space that features changing exhibitions of works from the factory's archives. Depending on when you visit, you might view an installation of eighteenth-century Beauvais tapestries or perhaps a show of Beauvais and Gobelins creations mounted according to theme. The life-sized paintings, or *maquettes*, that were used as models for many of the tapestries are also often exhibited, a real treat since many of these oils were painted by the most skilled artists of the time. Unfortunately, there is no museum shop. As you head out, notice the imposing edifice on your right, a centuries-old palace that houses **Le Musée Départemental de l'Oise**. This museum contains many magnificent works, particularly in the ceramics section—a true reflection of the importance that the industry once held in this province. A look around here serves as a good introduction for the following entry, a visit to a *faïencerie* in Ponchon.

Beyond Beauvais (Oise)

Sylvie Thémereau

About fifteen minutes from Beauvais heading in the direction of Paris on the N1, keep a sharp lookout for signs indicating Ponchon. The town once housed eight *faïenceries* that turned out tiles, mostly for kitchens, but all activity ceased in 1916. In 1991 Sylvie Thémereau decided to relaunch the tradition by opening up her atelier/showroom in an old *faïencerie* situated across the courtyard from her little brick house. She employs the same techniques and motifs as the original *faïence de Ponchon*, executing every step of the process by hand including the actual cutting of the stencils used to decorate each piece, recognizable by their repetitive geometric motifs in blue-on-white backgrounds. If you've ever seen Monet's kitchen in Giverny, you've had the opportunity to admire one of the finest and most famous existing assemblages of these tiles.

Most of these *carreaux* must be special-ordered, although Sylvie has applied the simple and fresh designs to hand-turned pitchers, bowls, vases, and a variety of other country kitchen accessories. Blue and white predominate, although touches of sun yellow, violet brown, red brown, and green creep into the traditional color scheme. Prices range from 75F for a mug to 250F for a pitcher. A friend of Sylvie's has stenciled coordinating motifs onto quintessentially French blue-and-white-checked cotton tablecloths, placemats, and dishtowels. If you have time to visit more ceramicists in the region, ask Sylvie for information about the *potiers du Pays de Bray*.

- 645 rue des Faïenceries, Hameau de Pierrepont, 60430 Ponchon; tel.: 03.44.03.40.55; fax: 03.44.03.28.76

No credit cards

Best to call ahead.

Doullens (Somme)

Château de Remaisnil

The northern Picard town of Doullens lies within a short country drive to many of the highlights of Picardy and the North. Once you enter the alluring world of grandeur at the superbly-appointed Château de Remaisnil, it is doubtful that you will want to leave. The debonair Adrian Doull and his soothing wife, Susan, welcome you to their eighteenth-century rococo castle in such an unpretentious manner that you feel as though you've arrived to spend a weekend with friends. If you hit it off with their Manhattan-transferred cat, coyly referred to as Fish, then your initiation into the world of ex-pats is near complete. I knew that Susan was American, but I was surprised to learn that Adrian is not French (he is in fact South African); I had thought that Monsieur Doull must certainly be one of the great descendants of Doullens. *Mais non!* It was just a coincidence, fate, or a little of both that brought the Doulls to Doullens in 1987 after they saw a newspaper ad announcing the sale of Laura Ashley's country estate in France. Remaisnil may be in the heart of the French countryside, but the style is far from country French, so be sure to pack elegant attire for a formal dinner or two. If you're looking to purchase a few antiques of your own, ask *madame* about the auctions that regularly take place in town.

• 80600 Doullens; tel.: 03.22.77.07.47; fax: 03.22.77.41.23
Château-Hôtel/Dinner by reservation for guests: Expensive–
Very Expensive
Open year-round except for the last three weeks of February

St-Quentin (Aisne)

Textiles Bochard

Located on the fringes of town toward the top of a garden called Les
Champs-Elysées, this is the last remaining textile factory in St-Quentin, a
city long associated with *le textile*. As it turns out, Bochard manufactures
house linens for some of the biggest names in France, including Descamps
and Porthault, so most of what you can expect to find in their factory store
is of the finest quality. Only some of the merchandise can be classified as
seconds, and the majority of the table and bath linens consist of fine 100
percent cotton weaves or cotton/linen blends. A kimono-style bathrobe of
the factory's well-known waffleweave material sells here for about 250F. You
can pick up a damask tablecloth for even less, and handsome French dishtowels are practically a giveaway at 25F to 40F! Before you leave, you might
want to throw a respectful glance at the old loom set up incongruously in
the center of the showroom, a veritable historic monument that once produced many of Coco Chanel's own luxurious fabrics.

• 2 rue du Général-Legrand-Girarde, 02100 St-Quentin; tel.: 03.23.08.17.84;
   fax: 03.23.08.28.91
No credit cards
Generally open only Friday 9 A.M.–noon and 2–6 P.M.–however, if you
   ring for them at these same times Monday–Thursday, they will open
   for you; open also weekends before Christmas and Mother's Day;
   closed in August

Beyond St-Quentin (Aisne)

Le Creuset

The factory and factory discount store of this world-famous French cast-iron
cookware specialist are located just a short distance from St-Quentin, although bargains on these reduced-priced kitchen helpers are often rivaled at
discount stores outside of France. Much of the colorful cookware is attractively presented here along with Weber barbecues and Screwpull corkscrews

(definitely no big savings there) Le Creuset pieces cost about 30 to 40 percent less here than in regular French retail stores.

- 880 rue Olivier-Deguise, 02230 Fresnoy-le-Grand; tel.: 03.23.06.22.22; fax: 03.23.09.06.82
  Open Tuesday–Saturday 10 A.M.–12:30 P.M. and 2–6:15 P.M.

THE NORTH

Buire-le-Sec (Pas-de-Calais)

Espace Marionnettes

If you love puppets, stop here to discover Philippe Malin's collection of marionettes from all over the world, including Indonesia, Greece, Czechoslovakia, nineteenth-century China, and many more exotic lands. Theater presentations occasionally take place here for groups and individuals. The selection of puppets sold in the boutique flaunts almost as much international flavor, although if you're looking for a made-in-France model, choose among the clown and hobo marionettes–great gifts for kids and reasonably priced at 70F.

- 62870 Buire-le-Sec; tel.: 03.21.81.80.34
  Open weekends and holidays 2:30–7 P.M. and daily except Tuesday during school vacations.

Desvres (Pas-de-Calais)

The name of this tiny town itself is synonomous with faience, a local tradition that supplied many other regions of France with earthenware for centuries. The oddly shaped and tiled, modern structure of the **Maison de la Faïence** (tel.: 03.21.83.23.23) in the town center is a good place to learn about the history of the craft that was once such a vital part of this city's existence. Today the industry has been greatly reduced, but the boutique **Desvres Tradition** (1 rue du Louvre; tel.: 03.21.92.39.43; fax: 03.21.92.39.63) is the best place to find faience made in a relatively artisanal manner. The pieces are hand-decorated with a technique similar to the one used in Gien. Most of the designs produced in this town resemble those of Rouen in Normandy or Moustiers-Sainte-Marie in Provence. Probably the most traditional items here are the handsome *plaques de maison* or house plaques (250F), which you can have personalized and shipped to you.

Lille (Pas-de-Calais)

TGV: 1 hour from Paris; 3½ hours from Lyons
Main shopping streets: rue de la Grande Chaussée,
rue de la Monnaie, rue Esquermoise
Market and flea market: place de la Nouvelle-Aventure
Sunday 8 A.M.–1 P.M.

Lille has received much attention in the past few years as a gateway city to the new Europe, mostly because of its strategic location along the TGV/ Chunnel path. Remnants of the city's rich history as the capital of Flanders and the home of wealthy textile merchants for centuries create an architectural symphony here that speaks glowingly of the North.

Small and quaint shop-filled streets snake around the *vieux ville* in a villagelike formation, unique to a city of such importance. Two reputable establishments described in the Amiens entry skirt the parameters of this old section of town, making them good places to begin or to end your tour through this network of winding streets: the *chocolatier* **Jean Trogneux** at 19 place du Théâtre (tel.: 03.20.06.91.91); and **La Galerie du Vitrail** at 80 rue Royale (tel.: 03.20.42.10.37), open Tuesday through Saturday, which sells a number of stained-glass home accessories such as lamps, mirrors, and assorted *objets*.

Chic boutiques clamor for your attention back in the heart of the old section of town; however, if you are more interested in discovering the lesser known haunts of the *lillois*, seek out the tiny rue au Pétérinck, just off of the place aux Oignons. Here two very different shops cater to the little darlings in your life, giving you the choice of dressing them with all the pomp and circumstance that a French *couturière* can muster up at **Tambours and Trompettes** (tel.: 03.20.51.35.66), or by clothing them in comfy togs fashioned out of fabrics from exotic lands at **Kayata** (tel.: 03.20.31.68.45).

The elegant rue Basse has enough richly stocked antique shops to keep you whirling and contemplating purchases for hours, particularly since prices here run a good 30 percent less than those in Paris. If you're looking to go all out on a bargain-hunting bonanza, plan to attend the **Braderie de Lille**, a colossal event that takes place annually the first weekend of September, where you can unearth everything from discarded old chotchkes to fine quality antiques!

Olivier Desforges

The name might not mean much to you, but once you see all of the fine-quality house linens displayed within this centrally located boutique, you will understand why Olivier Desforges is one of the leading textilemakers of the region. If you want to buy from the current collection, stay on the main level; if bargain hunting beckons, take the small staircase that leads you down to the large, medieval vaulted cellar, which houses linens from previous collections. Discount shopping doesn't get any better than this; prices have been slashed in half on lovely bed, table, and bath linens, sleepwear and personal accessories for adults and children, and play clothing for properly dressed kiddies. Nearly everything is 100 percent cotton in an array of classic prints that will never go out of style.

- 15 place du Lion d'Or, 59800 Lille; tel.: 03.20.78.04.17
  Open Monday 2–7 P.M.; Tuesday–Saturday 10 A.M.–noon and 2–7 P.M.

Meert

To experience part of the Saturday afternoon tradition in Lille, you can have a beer in one of the many pubs or elbow your way in for tea *chez* Meert. If you choose the latter, arrive before 4 P.M. to snag one of the Louis XVI styled tables in the front room. With walls the color of *crème pâtissière* and huge mirrors clouded by the passing of time, you can't help but feel like one of the *bourgeoisie de Lille* sitting in this distinguished space. The shop section of this *pâtissier/salon de thé* also conveys great prestige with its elaborate Napoleon III décor, and if all of this historic finery has distracted you to the point that you don't know what to buy, just pick up a package of their *gauffres*, sweet waffle cookies that were once the favorites of the late General de Gaulle.

- 25–27 rue Esquermoise, 59000 Lille; tel.: 03.20.57.07.44
  Boutique/Tea Salon: Moderate
  Open Monday 2–7 P.M.; Tuesday–Saturday 10 A.M.–noon
  and 2–7 P.M.

Next to Lille (Pas-de-Calais)

L'Usine

This whole part of northern France is splotched with textile factories, many of which have opened discount stores either on the premises or in nearby towns. The one complex, however, that regroups about eighty stores under one roof is L'Usine in Roubaix, an old factory that has been converted into a discount mall. Unfortunately most of the brands sold here remain little known to those outside of the French mainstream shopping loop, although that is not to say that you can't pick up some smart finds at affordable prices. As usual, most of the merchandise is from last year and sells for nearly half-price.

- 228 avenue Alfred-Motte, 59100 Roubaix; tel.: 03.20.83.16.20; fax: 03.21.86.36.36
  Open Monday–Saturday 10 A.M.–7 P.M.

Montreuil-sur-Mer (Pas-de-Calais)

Auberge de la Grenouillère

The epitome of a French country auberge, this cozy establishment's old farm interior will leave you with a feeling as radiant as the wood fire that burns in the immense hearth. The low wood-beam ceilings, the rustic furnishings, and tasteful array of folksy accents makes for the perfect setting for a convivial meal; throw an eclectic collection of frogs into the picture and you've added a whimsical note of humor that automatically ups the ambiance! The most amusing froggie touches are the yellowed frescoes from the 1920s that depict *les grenouilles* as people, all dressed up and indulging in fine food and Champagne! Things haven't changed much since then—only now, you only see people feasting and feting at La Grenouillère, and I would guess that the frogs have all gone back to the neighboring ponds.

- La Madelaine-sous-Montreuil, 62170 Montreuil-Sur-Mer; tel.: 03.21.06.07.22; fax: 03.21.86.36.36
  Restaurant: Expensive
  Four Guest-rooms: Inexpensive–Moderate
  Closed Tuesday and Wednesday except during the tourist season

Le Touquet-Paris-Plage (Pas-de-Calais)

Market: Place du Marché Thursday and Saturday 8:30 A.M.–1 P.M. (Monday, too, in summer)

Certainly the most stylish *station* of the region, le Touquet became known as Le Touquet-Paris-Plage largely because so many Parisians flocked here toward the beginning of the century. Parisians and visitors from other parts of France and the world still marvel at le Touquet's long and large beaches, expansive swathes of sand that make this resort town an ideal spot for the International Kite-Flying Championship that takes place here annually.

The shopping scene is *à la hauteur*, and you have only to see all of the chic sportswear boutiques that have thrown anchor along the rue St-Jean to see why. High-end antique shops and art galleries fill in the gaps on this busy thoroughfare and along some of the side streets, but don't expect to find too many real bargains.

You can't come here without visiting two of the town's classics of two entirely different orders: stop first at **Pérard** (67 rue de Metz; tel.: 03.21.05.13.33; fax: 03.21.05.62.32) for a healthy serving of Serge Pérard's fish soup, made from seven different types of *poisson* from the Channel and the North Sea; if you don't have time to sit down, you can always buy a few jars of this delicious blend to go. If you haven't overindulged in *soupe de poisson* and other seafood delicacies from the sea *chez* Pérard, you should be in just the right state to sample some of the chocolaty sweets at the old-fashioned candy store by the name of **Au Chat Bleu** (47 bis rue Saint-Jean; tel.: 03.21.05.03.86; fax: 03.21.05.42.47); an institution of sorts, you can't miss spotting its shopfront filled with blue cat-covered candy boxes.

POITOU CHARENTES
Poitou Charentes

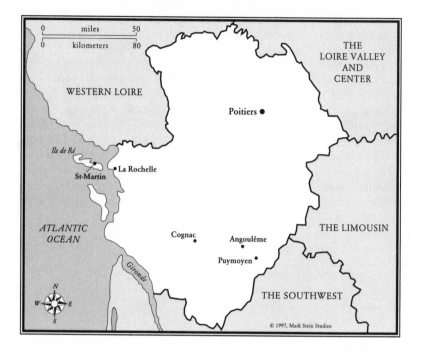

cognac • artisanally made paper • marine books, prints, and navigational maps • perfumes and bath accessories • faience • *pineau des charentes* • chocolates • comic books • old books, postcards, and publicity posters • artful ceramics • sea salt and sea salt products • *chocolats au cognac* • avant-garde crystal • nautically inspired jewelry • antiques • *charentaises* • cognac accessories

FOR MOST PEOPLE the name Poitou Charentes means next to noting. If you tell them about the highlights of this region, however, which include the cognac country and destinations along the Atlantic coast such as La Rochelle, visitors begin to develop a clearer vision of this land, said to be one of the sunniest regions of the country! The startling contrasts of this region amazed me as I went from the rambling ramparts of Angoulême, through the lyrical countryside of Cognac, to the windswept seascapes of La Rochelle and Ile de Ré. The scenery changed three times over the course of three hours, and as usual, I left with a list of more places to discover on a return visit.

Angoulême (Charente)

Main shopping streets: rue de Périgueux, rue St-Martial, rue des Postes
Market: Les Halles, place des Halles daily 6 A.M.–1 P.M.; additional
vendors in surrounding streets Wednesday and Saturday
Flea market: place Mulac the third Sunday of the month from October
through May 8 A.M.–6 P.M.

I had circled Angoulême on my map because I knew that this name was long associated with the paper industry, but little did I know that the city itself possessed such a rich cultural heritage. The unexpected beauty of this little known town draws from important examples of Romanesque and medieval architecture: the sedate and solidly proportioned Cathédrale St-Pierre crowns the mount on which Angoulême was constructed, eleventh-century houses cling to its rocky hillsides, and nearly the whole town is encircled by ramparts that were progressively added and rearranged throughout the centuries. The city's many terra-cotta tile roofs cast a rosy light on the sand-colored buildings as if to signal that the south lies just a short distance away—and in fact, it does.

Somehow the connection with the paper industry determined that Angoulême would house the only museum in France entirely devoted to comics. **Le Musée de la Bande Dessinée** (tel.: 05.45.38.65.65) traces the 150-year history of French comics in addition to highlighting many of the best-known strips from throughout the world. True fanatics might want to attend the **Festivale de la B.D.** (Comics Festival), which takes place annually toward the end of January. More good news for "funnies" fans: all kinds of comic books sell in the museum gift store.

Shopping for fine-quality sweets is a cinch in Angoulême as well. If an alluring setting stimulates your spendthrift tendencies, beware of the exquisitely-decorated **Duceau** (tel.: 05.45.95.06.42), just across from the Hôtel-de-Ville. The angelic eighteenth-century décor of this more than 120-year-old establishment might romance you into buying one of the regal red and gold-trimmed boxes filled with almost a pound of chocolates—a splurge that will set you back about 240F. The *chocolaterie* **Letuffe** (10 place F-Louvel; tel.: 05.45.95.00.54) is apt to overwhelm you more with its assortment of chocolates than with its peach-colored display cases; specialties consist largely of confections made from cognac. After sampling the candied chestnuts *au cognac* and the almond-encrusted truffles *au cognac*, I felt so completely satiated that I had to save their famous *marguerites d'Angoulême* for later (I can attest that these dainty daisy-shaped chocolates will woo you, too)!

If you're not too sugared out by now, you need to drive toward the outskirts of town on the route de Libourne to discover the next shopping highlight: **Majoliques d'Angoulême** (198 rue de Montmoreau; tel.: 05.45.61.06.35). This small, corner boutique and workshop arose from a husband-and-wife team's undying love for faience; Claude and Simone Roux met and also fell in love with each other at Renolleau, a *faïencerie* founded in the nineteenth century, where they both worked until the company went bankrupt in 1960. They summoned up all of the savoir faire and courage they could muster to open a small atelier of their own, then later moved to this location in 1980, where they both work with the help of only one assistant. Monsieur handles the special orders while the ladies design and paint works from the regular collection; typical motifs include those traditional of Charentes such as roses, roosters, pears, and grapes in a fête champêtre palette of dusty pink, cornflower blue, and wheat.

Around Angoulême (Charente)

Moulin du Verger

You may want to ask for specific directions in town to find your way to this secluded mill, located almost in the hinterlands just a bit southeast of Angoulême in Puymoyen. One of two paper mills in Charentes that makes *papier à l'ancienne*, this *vieux moulin* allows visitors to step three or four centuries back in time. Paper was first made on this site in 1539, and the structures that you see here today date back to 1636. Informal tours conducted in a mixture of French and English year-round show how paper was fabricated during these times. I don't suggest you come here on an empty stomach, because a dank and musty smell similar to that of wet woolen socks permeates the wet room, making it rather difficult to breathe. Here, water is churned up with fiber in huge vats, then spread out onto screens, pressed free of water, and hung to dry in the adjoining building.

Many of the paper products sold in the upstairs shop are far less rustic than the mill itself. The sheets of paper that have been crafted here, however, are quite lovely; look for those textured with bits of ferns or scraps of *Le Monde* newspaper.

- 16400 Puymoyen; tel.: 05.45.61.10.38; fax: 05.45.61.68.08
  Open Monday–Friday 9 A.M.–12:30 P.M. and 1:30–6 P.M.; Saturday and Sunday 3–6 P.M.

Cognac (Charente)

The first thing you notice when you arrive in Cognac are the blackened buildings, which somehow become more attractive when you learn that this sooty-looking patina is a byproduct of the various cognac-making processes of distillation, blending, and aging that take place inside virtually every other building of this town. Twenty million bottles of this deep caramel-colored spirit are produced within the region annually and that's not counting the 3 percent of the production lost through evaporation, much of which ends up on the city's façades.

Necessity is the mother of invention, a dictum that explains how the wine merchants of Cognac began to distill their cargo toward the end of the sixteenth century so that it would not sour during the long voyages to the British Isles, Holland, and Scandinavia. A land already known for its grape-growing and winemaking capabilities, Cognac later became renowned throughout the world for its twice-distilled spirits of varying ages. Many of the big-name "merchants" who began to distribute this revered drink around the world more than 200 years ago form the Cognac biggies of today; and as in Champagne, most of them readily welcome visitors for tours of their cellars, and in some instances, parts of their distilleries. You can visit Rémy Martin in a little train or travel to the Hennessy warehouses in a ferry boat, followed by tastings (or the gift of a sample) and a tour through the showcase boutiques. You can create a library of Camus's famous cognac-filled Limoges porcelain books or impress your friends with a set of Hennessy's divine crystal tulips—supposedly the best glasses for cognac (they're small enough for you to warm this tawny-colored liquid in your hands). Check at the tourism office (16 rue du 14 juillet) to find out which visits appeal to you the most or go directly to the various houses to join a tour.

La Cognathèque

A veritable cognac-arama, this one-of-a-kind boutique overflows with at least 200 different bottles of cognac and a variety of cognac-y gift items including *chocolats au cognac* from Letuffe. Before you feel overwhelmed in front of such an extensive selection of spirits, you may want to consult with Monsieur Arron, the owner of this fine shop who, of course, knows his cognacs. Monsieur stresses that there are two important factors to consider when selecting a cognac: age and geography, information that should be on the bottle's label. The classification system for cognac begins with three stars for spirits that have been aged a minimum of thirty months and progresses incrementally through V.S.O.P., Napoléon, and Réserve, which are all a blend of spirits that have been aged at least four and a half years, until you reach XO and Paradis—bottles that range from fifteen to eighty years of age! The geographic consideration requires a certain knowledge of the *crus* of Cognac and also a sense of what proportion of grapes from different parts of the region are likely to produce the best blends. If you're feeling stumped you can always check the price tags, which tend to be indicative of quality: when I asked about the best cognacs I was directed to Hennessy No. 1. Priced at

3,800F, it's understandable why Monsieur only sells about four bottles a year.

If you find cognacs too strong for your palette, try the *pineau des charentes*, a sweet nectar made from cognac and grape juice, normally served as an apéritif. You can sample them here in white, rosé, and red.

• 8 place Jean-Monnet, 16100 Cognac; tel.: 05.45.82.43.31; fax: 05.45.82.53.97

 Open in season Monday–Saturday 9:30 A.M.–7 P.M.; Sunday 9:30 A.M.–12:30 P.M. Hours vary during off-season

Outside of Cognac (Charente)

Maison Brillet

Halfway between Angoulême and Cognac on the *route de Cognac* (RN141), turn onto the D63 toward Vibrac, then take the D155 to St-Amand-de-Graves to find your way to this almost 150-year-old maker of cognac. Although it's a bit out of the way, the drive presents many scenic views of the vineyards and the Charente River, the two principal reasons for the emergence of the cognac industry in this part of France in the first place. Take a good look at the vines within the vicinity of J. R. Brillet, because they grow in two of the most valued land areas of the Cognac region, those referred to as *grande champagne* and *petite champagne*. The other geographic locations consist of sectors called *borderies, fins bois, bons bois*, and *bois ordinaires*. Most cognacs are made from grapes selected from several different areas; however, blends rarely represent the mixture of the top two *crus*, collectively referred to as *fine champagne*. (The origin of the word champagne is believed to stem from two different sources: a derivative of the word *campagne*, meaning country, and also in reference to these areas' chalky soil which is similar to that of the Champagne region.)

Such is the case *chez* Brillet, a highly reputable house that believes these origins should be respected, a selective approach shared by a half dozen cognac makers of the region. Just as unusual, Brillet is among the few who carry out each stage of the process itself, from grape-growing, to distillation and aging, to the final stages of commercialization. This semi-artisanal approach yields products of such superior quality that they are sold by some of the finest boutiques and restaurants around the world. You can buy here at prices that serve as the reward for having come so far off the beaten path; if you call ahead, the staff will make time for a guided tour of their down-home operations.

• "Les Aireaux," Graves, 16120 Cognac; tel.: 05.45.97.06.74; fax: 05.45.97.34.74

 Open Monday–Friday 9 A.M.–1 P.M. and 2–6 P.M.

Ile de Ré (Charente-Maritime)

One of France's best-kept secrets, Ile de Ré (pronounced ray), is a favorite summertime place for many of Paris's cognoscenti and middle- to upper-class funseekers who prefer to avoid the crowds at more widely known destinations. The island doubles as a year-round refuge for artists and craftspeople attracted to the incomparable luminosity of this primarily flat landmass and the pleasant, carefree life it fosters. A bridge was built a number of years ago to link this seventeen-mile-long island to the mainland, yet aside from an influx of day-trippers who cluster primarily around the island's more touristy sections, Ile de Ré has preserved its natural beauty. It's a great place for riding bikes, exploring long stretches of beaches, and taking in the authentic charm of picturesque fishing villages—although I still recommend avoiding a visit in August.

The island has a hint of Nantucket ambiance, although the little white, pink, and yellow houses, accented by shutters of varying shades of green, brown, and blue, create a picture that is distinctively French. The *rétais* cleverly established their most stylish enclave at Les Portes, the farthermost point of the island, which was once an old fishing village. A multitude of trendy shops and quaint boutiques dot the rue Jules David and the other tiny side streets that make up this village's postcard-perfect configuration of stone and whitewashed houses.

The island's shopping highlights focus mostly on arts and crafts, although a stop at the **Maison du Marais Salant** (tel.: 05.46.29.03.83) in Loix enables you to pick up organic bounty the likes of sea salt, bath salts, seaweed-flavored mustards, and delicious saltwater caramels. Salt has been collected in the surrounding marshes for centuries, and today fifty people still farm *le sel* throughout the island. Tours of the saltmarshes, some of which are conducted in English, begin here at various times.

In terms of ceramics, the island touches upon everything from the fantastical to the functional. Longtime resident **Albert Pesché** stands out as one of the community's most creative forces; his figurative wall sculptures and murals, composed of mosaic-like terra-cotta and glazed pieces, draw inspiration from sources as varied as the Aztec Indians to the sky over the Ile de Ré. Prices range from 3,000F to 15,000F. Call ahead to visit his atelier at 2 bis rue de St-Martin at Le Bois-Plage-en-Ré (tel.: 05.46.09.18.69). Monsieur Pesché takes as much pleasure in working with the island clay as Francine Durand, from **Atelier Terre**, derives from mixing and mashing local vines, seaweed, and other sediments from the ocean into her own unique glazes—blends that veer predictably toward a palette of faded blue-grey hues. Francine works with porcelain and stoneware, materials that lend themselves to her sculptural bird, fish, and modern madonna designs—poetic pieces that play on the contrasts between soft and shiny. Prices range from 140F to

1,800F in her atelier/showroom located at Terre des Grenettes, Le Bois-Plage-en-Ré (tel.: 05.46.30.11.87).

The gorgeous tiles of Salernes (in Provence) have hit Ile de Ré bigtime at **Alain Vagh**, a brightly colored showroom located at Le Moulin d'Angibeau, Quartier Bel Air in La Flotte-en-Ré (tel./fax: 05.46.09.54.59). I would guess that most of the beautiful homes on the island have been decorated with these exquisitely glazed works; even if you're not looking to pass an order for a kitchen-scaled supply of tiles, you can pick up some trivet-sized pieces, each priced at 250F, that have been handmade on the island and painted with blue and white sailboats, fishermen, sand dunes, and other ocean-inspired motifs.

Chances are you'll visit St-Martin-de-Ré, the most important village of the island. Outside of town you can take in the **Cristallerie de l'Ile de Ré**, a small crystal-making complex located on the route de la Flotte (tel.: 05.46.09.42.73; fax: 05.46.09.04.66). Most of the works aim to please the masses with their classic designs and shapes; however, Fabrice Steiner really shows off his crystal-making prowess (he started in the family tradition at the age of thirteen) in his avant-garde sculptures: colorful cartoonlike works that demand art gallery prices the likes of 12,000F.

Feasting on fresh seafood makes up much of the dining experience on the island, and one of the most fashionable places to begin is **La Baleine Bleue** on St-Martin-de-Ré-sur-l'Ilot (tel.: 05.46.09.03.30), which features the freshest catches of the day. If you want to truly "get with the swing of things," don't refuse the suggested cognac-based apéritif!

La Rochelle (Charente-Maritime)

TGV: 3 hours from Paris
Main shopping streets: rue Chaudrier, rue du Palais,
rue du Temple, rue des Merciers
Markets: Place du Marché daily 8 A.M.–6 P.M.
Flea market: la rue St-Nicolas Saturday year-round 10 A.M.–6 P.M.;
also open Thursdays June–September

One cannot help but fall under the Old World charm of La Rochelle. History is everywhere you turn, and the town's rich and diverse architecture often makes it difficult to tell that you are indeed in a port city, one that balances tourism, seafaring activity, and urban culture in an amazingly harmonious manner. It is in fact this mix of old ocean town and centuries-old buildings (primarily from the Renaissance) that makes La Rochelle unique. The city has four ports, two for pleasure boats and two devoted to commerce—a juxtaposition that only adds to the city's sprinkling of cosmopolitan flair. If you're not sitting along the port sipping a glass of pineau des charentes, strolling under the city's more than 9 kilometers of arcades can transfix you from numerous historic and shopping perspectives.

If you're a lover of *le luxe,* fine jewelry of both classic and nautical inspiration may prompt you to sail in to **Chauvin et Fils** (16 rue du Temple; tel.: 05.46.41.00.28). Luxury in the form of truffles flavored with cognac-soaked raspberries (*La Reine Jeanne*) or bonbons filled with cognac or coffee praline (*Les Rochelines*) reign supreme at **Jeanne d'Albret,** one of the city's most renowned sweet shops (tel.: 05.46.41.17.40) at 10 rue Chaudrier. La Rochelle was once an important exporter of this heavenly brandy, and an abundance of cognacs and pineaus are for sale around town. You may also visit two cellars here that sell their own blends of spirits: **Paul Bossuet** at 21 rue Gargoulleau (tel.: 05.46.41.31.92) and the centuries-old establishment of **Godet** at 1 rue du Duc (tel.: 05.46.41.10.66; fax: 05.46.50.59.90).

La Rochelle, like so many other cities of France, once had a couple of faienceries that turned out utilitarian and decorative pieces for the region during the eighteenth and nineteenth centuries. Both of these have long disappeared, but across the street from Godet, the shop **Poteries La Rochelle** (29 quai Maubec; tel.: 05.46.41.38.14) features locally made pieces that embrace the spirit of La Rochelle faience from the eighteenth century. Blue roosters, blue roses, and blue and pink country bouquets dominate the design schemes, many of which have been hand-painted on predominantly white backgrounds and enhanced by yellow and green accents. Prices are among the best that I've encountered in France. To see older pieces of this country French faience, go to the **Musée d'Orbigny-Bernon** (tel.: 05.46.41.18.83 at 2 rue St-Côme).

Most of the really fine pieces of antique faience from La Rochelle sell at high-end *antiquaires* in Paris, but you never know when you might unearth a rare find in the antique shops that populate the rue St-Nicolas and the nearby streets. The overall shopping scene is in fact quite quaint, speckled with gifty home accessory boutiques such as **Au Fur & A Mesure** at 11 and 15 rue St-Nicolas (tel.: 05.46.41.12.90). The shop's selection of country French fabrics particularly warmed me, and in addition to classic *toiles de Jouy* and Alsatian prints, I found a prettier and far more complete selection of Cholet textiles than those that I saw in Cholet in the Western Loire region!

Although perfumes are not typically associated with Poitou Charentes, Monsieur and Madame Séris have made it their passion to collect bottles from all over the world. Their **Musée du Flacon à Parfum** (Perfume Bottle Museum) upstairs at 33 rue du Temple (tel.: 05.46.41.32.40; fax: 05.46.41.92.34) displays some real rareties that have earned this little showcase collection a noteworthy reputation among devotees. The ground floor of this temple of scents lures you in with its fragrant, beautifully packaged products and bath accessories.

Pampering for other people comes more in the form of *pantoufles,* or slippers, which in this region usually means *charentaise*, a sort of house shoe that figures among *les grands classiques français*. Stop in to **Chaussures Denis** (36 bis rue des Merciers; tel.: 05.46.41.13.93), a shoe store that appears locked in time, to survey the collection of *charentaises* for men, women, and children. The store's appearance may seem dated, but you will never be considered out-of-date (at least not in France) by wearing these shoes. As a matter of fact, their recent resurgence onto the fashion scene led to the creation of more fantasy-type models, such as a blue-violet plaid in addition to their more classic browns. You may choose wool, synthetic, or cashmere linings, but their felt bottoms, badgelike insignias, and dowdy shapes remain their most distinctive traits; prices range from 70F to 200F. The store also has the best selection of entirely French made (mostly from Brittany or Normandy) galoshes and clogs I've ever seen, and in summer you'll find a good choice of classic and trendy espadrilles from the most authentic Basque brand, Bayona.

If you are a fan of marine navigational maps and other printed materials concerning the sea, stop at **Librairie Maritime** (33 place des Coureauleurs; tel.: 05.46.41.81.95; fax: 05.46.41.81.62)—or go directly to **André**, a bar/restaurant at 7 rue St-Jean (tel.: 05.46.41.28.24), which sings the praises of the Atlantic in its cuisine and its décor. What started as a bar for fishermen has become one of the favorite haunts for the *rochelais*, (townspeople). Choose from several different settings for drinks or dining either at the bar, the terrace, or in the dining rooms: one has a warm and rustic, nautically inspired décor, while the other has a more elegant, art-oriented sophistication. Note the cognac stills and barrels displayed throughout—a simple reminder of the integral part spirits and the sea have played in the history, culture, and economy of this section of France.

PROVENCE
Provence

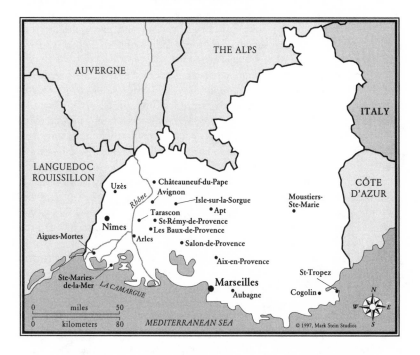

lavender sachets, bouquets, and pillows • *le croquant Villaret* • rugs • olive oil • wine • *anchoïade* • pottery • *tapénade* • embroidered house linens • dried-flower topiaries • French cowboy wear • *piqués de Marseille* • Provençal prints • *calissons d'Aix* • homemade jams and honeys • *navettes* • handmade tiles • hand-painted faience • antique jewelry • trendy womenswear • antiques • *santons* • old garden furniture • paper sculpture • *savon de Marseille* • trompe l'oeil plates • cicada-inspired creations • sandals • boating attire • table arts • candy-colored candles • pastis • truffles • fashion trimmings • images of Cèzanne • *herbes de Provence*

I WAS TWENTY the very first time that I arrived in this intoxicating land. I was staying with friends in a wonderful old *mas* (a large, one-level farmhouse in Provence) not far from Apt in the Lubéron mountains. The days were paced and planned according to the sun, and if I remember correctly, during the entire ten days I was there, we didn't see one single cloud. The funny thing is that I scarcely remember having gone shopping at all. We did take a day trip to Avignon, but only wandered through the streets.

Little did I know that there was a whole other world out there. Of course, I had already fallen under the spell of the region, but I had become so entranced with the laissez-faire atmosphere of Provence that I didn't feel the need for more than life's simple pleasures: the warmth of the intense sun; the aromatic scents of rosemary, lavender, and thyme in the air; and the constant creek-creek of the crickets at night.

When I returned about four years later, I realized that in addition to the heavenly countryside, there is quite a lot to see. My true discovery of Provence began with the enchantingly beautiful hilltop village of Gordes; then with the mystical Abbaye de Senanque; then on to the curious mountainous landscape of Les Baux; and then finally to the astonishingly unique scenery of La Camargue. I became hooked, and each little village and charming Provençal town had yet another market, shop, or product to discover.

I quickly learned that when in Provence, one must dress *à la provençale*. Souleiado became a given and *les indiennes* (the Provençal prints) of Les Olivades, Les Indiennes de Nîmes, and Valdrôme soon followed. Now even when I'm not in Provence and I wear those clothes, I feel transported back to the land where life is easy.

A few lavender sachets later, I learned to appreciate the skilled craftsmanship that each *santon* (clay figurine) requires. No longer could I look at them as touristy trinkets that are sold along the souvenir-saturated rue de Rivoli in Paris. I now hope to acquire a complete nativity set from one of the finest *santon* makers in Provence.

Just as I began to grasp the essence of Provence, it seemed as though everybody else started to glorify its attributes as well. First there was all of that talk about the *triangle d'or*, the golden triangle that one could imagine between the fast folk of Arles, St-Rémy-de-Provence, and Tarascon. Then came Peter Mayle and all that he had to say about "his own backyard." Suddenly it seemed as though "my Provence" was under siege. It wasn't until I went back recently that I could rest assured. Provence is still there— just as it was before. It simply sells more lavender-scented pillows and pieces of pottery than it ever did before.

Aix-en-Provence (Bouches-du-Rhône)

Main shopping streets: rue Espariat, rue des Cordeliers, and side streets in between
Provençal market and flea market: place des Prêcheurs, place de la Madeleine, and place de Verdun
Tuesday, Thursday, and Saturday 6 A.M.–1 P.M.

It was named the capital of Provence during ancient times and has maintained its place and prominence as a major converging point over the centuries. Aix (pronounced like X) is a big university town, which partly explains its exuberance and free-wheeling spirit. (Whenever you mention Aix to the French, eyes brighten and mouths draw contented sighs.)

The town hops the highest on Friday night, and to seize the effervecense, start out by driving down the cours Mirabeau, the comely tree-lined avenue that is home to most of the city's landmark banks and cafés. Not even the shroudlike branches of the massive plane trees can temper the energy; in fact, the wind rustling through the leaves only adds background music to the din of the crowds. The more than forty fountains dispersed within the city appear to be set out like dancing props on a stage.

The overall shopping is abundant, although the selection of charming and unique boutiques is less prolific. The large **Souleiado** store at 8 place des Chapeliers is one of the most recent additions to this Provençal powerhouse, but I found it far too citylike for my taste (the welcome was rather stiff as well). **Terre du Soleil**, a shop that features brightly colored Provençal pottery at 6 bis rue Aude provided a much sunnier experience. Antiquing in Aix is not what it once was, but you will find a smattering of interesting shops around the place des Ormeaux. And if you haven't yet found the *santon* of your dreams, try visiting **Santons Fouque** just outside of Aix at 65 cours Gambetta. Although touristy, this is one of the best known makers of *santons* in Provence.

One thing you will see much of is images of Cézanne. The painter is the city's most famous son, and although he wasn't appreciated here during his life, he is now immortalized through the usual pictures, postcards, and prints. You'll notice that much has been named after him, including streets, cafés, and even a health clinic—but if you wish to see any of his major works, you'd be better served in Paris, London, or New York.

Calissons d'Aix du Roy-Rene

It may seem unfair for me to mention only one *calisson* maker here because there are quite a few good ones in Aix, but I don't have the space to list them all. These little candies are sold in nearly every bakery, grocery store, and sweet shop in Provence and in many other parts of France as well. This pale, lozenge-shaped treat is directly entwined with the history of the city; legend says that it first appeared during the marriage celebration of King René in 1473. You are apt to find the subtle flavor and dense, pasty consistency unusual, but consider it a test of the finesse of your palate. Although each recipe varies somewhat, the basic ingredients include almonds that have been ground and blended with a syrup made from *fruits confits* (candied fruits, in this case melons and oranges). The mixture is glazed with a glossy icing and the entire candy rests upon a wafery-thin host most likely introduced many centuries ago as a reminder that God is forever present in this world. The *calissons* keep for a fair amount of time although it is best to consume them quickly once the package is opened.

• 7 rue Papassaudi, 13100 Aix-en-Provence; tel.: 04.42.26.67.86;
     fax: 04.42.24.41.94
  Open Tuesday–Saturday 9 A.M.–noon and 2–7 P.M.

Jacquèmes

Provence has so many wonderful food products that you surely will want to bring a sampling home–or on a picnic. Jacquèmes is a family-owned business (three generations since 1930) that takes great pride in promoting the best of the region. It offers seven different types of French olive oil and some of the Italian, too. The selection of olives, *tapénade, anchoïade,* and herbs is equally impressive, and if you choose a bottle of wine and a few locally made goat cheeses, the only thing missing is a crusty baguette!

The regional wines are indeed noteworthy, and if you are not familiar with the juices of Bandol, Cassis, Gigondas, and Tavel, they definitely merit some consideration. If you are shopping for something to bring home, I suggest you buy a bottle of Muscat de Beaumes de Venise (98F), a succulent white wine from a small town in Provence that is usually served chilled as an apéritif. Nonalcoholic delights, such as a jar of pink apricot or watermelon jam from Octave, an exalted jam-maker in Apt, may be deserving of your attention as well.

• 9 rue Méjanes, 13100 Aix-en-Provence; tel.: 04.42.23.48.64
  Open Monday 2:30–7:15 P.M.; Tuesday–Saturday 8:30 A.M.–12:15 P.M.
     and 2:30–7:15 P.M.

Les Deux Garçons

Very much an institution for the people of Aix, this is a great place to have a bite to eat or just to while away a couple of hours on the shaded terrace accompanied by a good book and a cool glass of *pastis*. Chances are, though, that you will be too distracted by people-watching to become engrossed in your book. If you're alone, why not consider a newspaper?

• 53 cours Mirabeau, 13100 Aix-en-Provence; tel.:
     04.42.26.00.51
  Café/Restaurant: Moderate
  Open daily 6–3 A.M.

Villa Gallici

Sheer comfort, elegance, and luxury—this must be how the gentry lived in Provence 200 years ago—albeit without all of today's modern conveniences. This hotel is not in the heart of town so you won't be able to do much touring on foot. Not to worry—you won't have much desire to leave here anyway.

- avenue de la Violette (Impasse des Grands-Pins), 13100 Aix-en-Provence; tel.: 04.42.23.29.23; fax: 04.42.96.30.45
  Four-Star Hotel: Very Expensive
  Open year-round

Apt (Vaucluse)

Market: Town center Tuesday and Saturday 7 A.M.–1 P.M.

It's worth a trip to Apt just to see the rough and rugged scenery of the Lubéron mountains. The town itself is a little dreary, so you may want to visit on a market day when the atmosphere becomes far more animated. Apt is known for its rich, terra-cotta–colored soil, which has been used for centuries in the making of faience and tiles. **Vernin Carreaux d'Apt** (RN 100–Le pont Julien, 84480 Bonnieux; tel.: 04.90.04.63.04; fax: 04.90.74.00.47), is another well-known tile maker of Provence. Its artisanally made tiles look just like all of the wonderfully rustic reds and pinks that you see in most of the houses of this land.

Apt's reputation for *fruits confits* (candied fruits) is nearly as fierce (one look at the abundance of fruit trees in the region and you'll understand why). Stop in to **Richaud** at 48 quai Liberté in the center of town to sample these sweet, color-rich treats.

Faïence d'Apt/Atelier Bernard Jean Faucon

The highly artistic works of Jean Faucon merit a visit all by themselves, particularly if you are looking for a regional piece unique in its design and quality. Monsieur Faucon has carried on the tradition of mixing color-soaked clays that began in a little village of the Lubéron more than 200 years ago. Heir to six generations of savoir faire, he himself learned this unusual technique from his grandfather and has perpetuated most of the same marbleized color schemes while developing a few of his own. In addition to a range of natural earth tones, this master ceramicist has added bursts of more daring pigments such as midnight blue and vermilion to his repertoire.

The overall feeling of these pieces is actually quite Baroque, and different from most of the other ceramics normally associated with Provence. Their originality lies in the classicism of their forms (many of which are based on eighteenth-century pieces of faience and silver) and the ornateness of their ornamentation (mostly flowers, olives or grapes with realistic-looking leaves, branches, and vines). The prices are just as high as the quality of the works, but remember, this is art. Count on spending about 500F for a dinner plate.

- 12 avenue de la Libération, 84400 Apt; tel.: 04.90.74.15.31; fax: 04.90.74.30.51
  Best to call ahead

Arles (Bouches-du-Rhône)

Main shopping streets: rue de la République,
boulevard Georges Clémenceau, boulevard des Lices
Markets: boulevard des Lices Wednesday 7 A.M.–1 P.M. and
boulevard des Combes Saturday 7 A.M.–1 P.M.
Flea market: boulevard des Lices all day
the first Wednesday of every month

I had had the opportunity to briefly visit Arles numerous times over the past ten years, but my senses were not seized by its true essence until the day I arrived with the hungry eye of a reporter in quest of maximum information in minimum time. I can't believe that I didn't "get it" before. Sure the little snippets of Arles I had already experienced touched on the main attractions of the city–the ancient bullfighting arena, the antique theater, and other remnants from Roman times–but nothing filled me with as much of the veritable fervor of Arles as the day I started my search from the inside out: I began within the depths of the town and worked my way out toward the main thoroughfares.

Start at the place du Forum, a large centrally located square (more of a longish triangle) that serves as a popular gathering place for the different types of people you're apt to encounter in Arles. The café ambiance here is totally unpretentious. Christian Lacroix's *haute couture* may be largely *arlésienne* in inspiration, but there is nothing chichi about Arles or its inhabitants. In fact, this world-renowned *couturier* has based his whole concept of fashion on the *gaïeté* of Provence and the wonderful mix of colors, textures, and prints that have been present here over time in the peoples' often fanciful, yet basic, way of dressing.

Go to the **Museon Arlaten** (29 rue de la République) next to fill your heart and mind with visions of the Provençal history. This museum is a gem and certainly the best of its kind in all of Provence. Its strength lies in its vernacular depictions of the everyday life in Provence and the objects that filled it: furniture, religious relics, costumes, and a variety of other adornments that explained how these people lived and what mattered most to them. There is even a typical house (complete with thatched roof and whitewashed walls) from the nearby wetlands of the Camargue! To the modern eye it appears deliciously folkloric, but to the people then it was a way of life.

If you are lucky enough to be here for the *fête d'Arles*, a celebration that takes place yearly around the first of May, consider dressing up like so many of the town folk as a true *arlésienne*. After drawing inspiration from the magnificently clad mannequins at the Museon Arlaten, you can go directly over to the boutique, **L'Arlésienne** (12 rue du Président-Wilson), to be outfitted. If you are short on time, consider renting a ready-made costume for a mere 700F. And if you want to think ahead toward your next costume party, this is the place for all of the marvelous fabrics and trims you'll need to look like a well-turned-out Provençal lady back home.

Costumes are only one way to use the exquisite silk taffetas, velvet ribbons, and intricately made laces hidden within this tiny shop. Many of the accessories are equally alluring: the gloves, fans, and hand-embroidered kerchief like scarves, called *fichus* or *pèlerines*, in cotton organdy—which practically require a Ph.D. in folding and pinning in order to wear them properly!

And what is a costume without its jewels? Very plain, of course, so naturally the Provençal women traditionally are big on jewelry, particularly crosses, many of which are encrusted with garnets and ornate in their detail. Delicate antique chains, brooches, and earrings with a sizable amount of filigree work, also are very fashionable.

To buy authentic old jewelry go to **Li Beloïo** (11 rue Porte-de-Laure). For considerably less expensive reproductions, the best address is **Bijouterie Pinus** (6 rue Jean-Jaurès), which has been making classic Arlesian pieces for over four generations. Its panoply of *cigales* (cicadas), the symbol of happiness in Provence, is also vast and reasonably priced at 150F to 360F.

Thank goodness I didn't have time to spare in the **Christian Lacroix** boutique (52 rue de la République), because with its new, lower-priced Bazaar line and the super-friendly reception from the sales help (so un-Parisian), I could have gone on a rampage like a bull in a *corrida*!

Camille

The name of this store is quite feminine, but the top of their business card states *tout l'habillement masculin* (all clothing for men), and that is most of what is sold here. Camille is a sleepy old establishment founded in 1931 that doesn't seem to draw crowds, although it has become an institution in Arles.

If you shop here, chances are that if you run into anyone it will be a *gardian* (the name for the man who takes care of the horses on the ranches), because this is where they outfit themselves for both work and play. Don't be too astonished, though, if you run into Princess Caroline of Monaco or France's famous race-car driver, Alain Prost, who have been known to shop here, too. This is truly a great place to pick up reasonably priced Western wear with a Provençal twist.

- 5 boulevard Georges-Clémenceau, 13200 Arles; tel.: 04.90.96.04.94
  Open Tuesday–Saturday 9 A.M.–noon and 2–6:45 P.M.

F. Dervieux

The pickings are rather slim when it comes to shopping for "antiquities" in Arles, but fortunately the goods at F. Dervieux more than fill this void. The selection is not enormous, but what Monsieur Dervieux lacks in quantity he more than makes up for in quality. The Dervieux family has been in this business for more than four generations, and as you pull open the door to this centuries-old town house you are instantly enveloped by a feeling of Old World tradition and savoir faire.

The fact that you enter practically face-to-face with the *atelier de restauration*, where ardent workers are rubbing and polishing away with great skill, instantly reassures you that these are the kind of people who know and love antiques of the finest kind. Their specialty is in eighteenth- and nineteenth-century Provençal furniture, particularly armoires and commodes, most of which are made of walnut. You'll notice that the hardware on these pieces is decorative and this, combined with the sculptural ornamentation of flowers or curlicues, is indicative of the region's love for a bit of whimsy.

Spaced intermittently amid the furniture are old costumes and fabrics, much like those from the Museon Arlaten, that draw a fair amount of interest from devotees and serious collectors despite the sometimes astonishing prices.

Grand Hôtel Nord Pinus

This hotel makes you feel so much a part of the town. Maybe it's because it sits directly on the place du Forum, or maybe it's because the matadors who once stayed here have left behind a dash of excitement. In any case, bullfighting memorabilia accents an interior that marries the new with the old without compromising either sophistication or authenticity.

- place du Forum, 13200 Arles; tel.: 04.90.93.44.44; fax: 04.90.93.34.00
  Four-Star Hotel/Restaurant/Bar/Terrace/Boutique: Expensive
  Open year-round

• 5 rue Vernon, 13200 Arles; tel.: 04.90.96.02.39; fax: 04.90.96.44.42
Open Monday–Saturday 9:00 A.M.–noon and 2:30–7 P.M.

Aubagne (Bouches-du-Rhône)

When it comes to pottery, the three "biggies" in the south of France are Vallauris, Anduze, and Aubagne. Each city has been associated with ceramics for centuries, and potters in each town work on a range of scales (from artisanal to semi-industrial) to create pieces of varying qualities. In addition to its close link with ceramics, Aubagne differs from the other two in that it is also well known for its *santons,* the hand-painted clay figurines so typical of Provence.

Although a bit touristy, "Le Petit Monde de Marcel Pagnol," is a must for visitors to Aubagne. It is hard not to be charmed by this diorama, which consists of hundreds of *santons* gaily clad in meticulously designed Provençal frocks and set in scenery identical to that of Aubagne and its environs. This is the town's way of showing off some of its artistry in an homage to one of France's most famous writers, Marcel Pagnol, whose celebrated works were set primarily in the rough and arid countryside of this region.

There are approximately thirty different workshops and manufacturers within the city limits, all of which specialize in the creation of ceramics and/ or *santons*—and many even do both. Works come in a wide range of styles and sizes, meaning that there is something for almost everyone's taste. The following descriptions are a sampling of what you can expect to find in Aubagne. A complete list of the town's craftspeople is available at the tourism office (avenue A.-Boyer).

Barbotine/Estampille

The name of the street where this boutique/atelier is situated, rue Frédéric Mistral, is as melodious as the poetry that was written by this *grand monsieur.* Unfortunately, the street is not very attractive; if it weren't for the sizable grouping of ceramic and *santons* shops here, there wouldn't be much reason to amble over to this part of town. Just as I was beginning to feel a bit discouraged, I stumbled upon Barbotine/Estampille, where I was warmly welcomed by a handful of potters eager to show me their creations and the workshops from which they grew.

Talk about the proverbial needle in a haystack: I unearthed a few plates from within the depths of their basement that I wanted to purchase, but was gently turned down after having been told that they were made exclusively for a certain high-end department store in the U.S. Aha. This small yet exceedingly creative workshop has been churning out a number of handsome patterns for the past few years now, and their success is growing.

Nearly all of their ceramics (both pottery and faience) speak distinctively of *la provence*, and most of them appear as small studies of *l'art populaire* from days gone by. Each piece exudes a warm rusticity (most of them have been hand-turned), and nearly all are hand-painted in traditional hues of cobalt blue, olive green, creamy yellow, or ochre. My favorite pieces were those that combined several earthy colors in a marbleized swirl reminiscent of the jasper of Provence (I liked them even more once I saw similar dishes at Pierre Deux in the U.S. for about five times the price).

- 30 rue Frédéric-Mistral, 13400 Aubagne; tel.: 04.42.70.03.00;
     fax: 04.42.84.03.59
  No credit cards
  Open Monday–Saturday 9 A.M.–noon and 2–7 P.M.

Maison Louis Sicard

As I pulled into the courtyard of this old *faïencerie* I was greeted by a *vieux monsieur* who endeared me to him not only with the warmth of his singsongy Provençal accent, but also by his whole demeanor, which spoke of many long years of craftsmanship and hard work. He was sitting outside on an old stool, expertly sculpting a piece of wood into a little bird on a branch.

When he introduced me to the shop I was able to see the sweet-faced *santons* in their final phase—this time in hand-painted clay, some of which were dressed up in native attire and accompanied by all of the necessary accoutrements. As I admired statuettes of an old fisherman from Marseilles and a granny eating a piece of cake, I noticed that virtually all of the *santons* depicted older people. I learned that this is quite typical, and apparently the reason is that old faces are said to be far more interesting. *Touché!* Here they are sold in a variety of models and sizes, with prices beginning at about 100F.

Sicard is also known for its ceramics: it was the first to create the cicada in faience. I found these pieces to be a little too kitsch for my taste, but they reminded me of the sort of souvenirs that you see in backwoods areas like the Adirondacks. Another service in a bright yellow called *le jaune d'Aubagne* could work in the right nouveau French country décor.

- 2 boulevard Emile-Combes, 13400 Aubagne; tel.: 04.42.70.12.92;
     fax: 04.42.84.45.39
  Open Monday–Saturday 9 A.M.–12:30 P.M. and 2:30–7 P.M.

Poterie Ravel

This is the kind of place that you can enjoy visiting even if you don't buy a thing. In fact, if you do buy anything you will probably need to have it shipped, since most of what is sold here is huge garden planters, vases, and urns. It is all very Mediterranean in spirit and design, and this is a great place to come to when you need a few substantial accessories for your villa, terrace, or garden. Here since 1837, the site and showroom are attractively maintained.

• Z.I. des Paluds, avenue des Caniers, 13400 Aubagne; tel.: 04.42.84.47.73; fax: 04.42.82.00.87
Open Monday–Saturday 9 A.M.–12:30 P.M. and 2:30–7 P.M.

Avignon (Vaucluse)

Main shopping streets: rue Joseph-Vernet, rue St-Agricol
Markets: in front of train station
Saturday and Sunday 7 A.M.–1 P.M. and Les Halles
daily except Monday 7 A.M.–1 P.M.

Like much of Provence, Avignon truly comes alive during the summer months with a full schedule of cultural events. While Aix bursts into song, Avignon excels in the performing arts, and theater aficionados are said to come from all over the world for a taste of some of the city's high drama during the month of July. August can be a much quieter time and certainly more advantageous for those of you who want to leisurely take in the sights and shops without much hassle.

Avignon is easily explorable by foot, and the stores are all heavily concentrated within the center of town. The rue Joseph-Vernet, one of the main shopping streets, reminded me of a provincial version of the rue du Faubourg St-Honoré in Paris. There aren't nearly as many big-name boutiques here but the feeling of a long, narrow street snaking its way around to busier thoroughfares is quite familiar. The many eighteenth-century *hôtels particuliers* (town houses) also make me think of Paris, and a good place to start is right inside number 58 at Le Vernet. Lunch in their courtyard is particularly delightful in this casual-chic restaurant, and if you haven't drunk too much rosé in the sun, you will leave here feeling rejuvenated and ready to visit the city during the remainder of the afternoon.

Hervé Baume

Located in the heart of the *quartier des antiquaires* is this stunning boutique that reigns supreme over the world of interior design for all of Avignon. Monsieur Baume, himself an interior decorator, is the creative innovator behind the deliberate and intuitive jumble of furniture and objects, both old and new, that fills this store pellmell from top to bottom. Many of the pieces are one-of-a-kind, such as a twelve-foot eighteenth-century armoire from a château in Burgundy or a particularly old and well-preserved *vase d'Anduze* (urn from Anduze) marked at 60,000F—eek!

New pieces from Hervé Baum's well-reputed collection of clear-colored, handblown crystal hurricane lamps are more manageable in both size and price.

- 19, 19 *bis*, 19 *ter* rue de la Petite-Fusterie, 84000 Avignon; tel.: 04.90.86.37.66; fax: 04.90.27.05.97
  Open Monday–Saturday 9:30 A.M.–12:30 P.M. and 2:30–7 P.M.

Terre è Provence

The sister shop of Terre du Soleil in Aix, Terre è Provence also keeps Poterie Augier in St-Tropez well-stocked with a supply of richly made Provençal pottery. The quality of these pieces really is a cut above most of what you see around; so much so, in fact, that I quickly spotted the colorful window display of this store through a swarm of shoppers on a busy Saturday afternoon in Avignon. This pottery is sold (at considerably higher prices) in the U.S. and Japan at high-end stores such as Barney's.

- 26 rue de la République, 84000 Avignon, tel.: 04.90.85.56.45; fax: 04.90.14.03.02
  Open Monday 2–7 P.M.; Tuesday–Saturday 10 A.M.–12:30 P.M. and 2–7 P.M.

Hôtel de la Mirande

This is about as close as you can come to spending the night in the *palais des papes*, the main attraction of Avignon, which provided sumptuous quarters for popes during the fourteenth century. Your budget might not allow you to sleep here, but try to allocate a lump sum to experience Provençal cuisine at its finest. The dining room brims with Old World charm and comfort, due largely to the effusive use of flowery fabrics by the famed Parisian designer Manuel Canovas. If you are feeling less self-indulgent, at least slip into one of the rattan chairs in the winter garden for a refreshing glass of Perrier.

- 4 place de l'Amirande, 84000 Avignon; tel.: 04.90.85.93.93; fax: 04.90.86.26.85
  Four-Star Hotel/Restaurant/Bar/Terrace: Very Expensive
  Open year-round

Les Baux-de-Provence (Bouches-du-Rhône)

This little village is perched on top of a conglomeration of oddly shaped, cavernouslike mountains referred to as Les Baux-de-Provence. It was interesting to take a look around at this historical site, the best vantage point for appreciating the full magnitude of this wondrous area is from down below, poised on the elegant terrace of the hotel **L'Oustaù Baumanière** (tel: 04.90.54.33.07; fax: 04.90.54.40.46).

I'll never forget the time I brought my mother here: she was completely awestruck, and felt even more privileged to have experienced such an incredible view particularly after having seen Les Baux and Baumanière featured on the television program *Lifestyles of the Rich and Famous.* The setting in fact looks as though it was created for a Hollywood production; and it appears that the glorious terrace and pool as well as every cypress tree, olive branch, and odd rock formation was left behind for the guests' full aesthetic enjoyment. (Jean Cocteau did some filming in the ominous-looking hills, but the result was not at all like Hollywood glam.)

Boutique Baumanière

A night or even a meal at the prestigious L'Oustaù Baumanière is sure to set you back a bit, but the boutique features a wide range of gift ideas at varying prices. It started out as a small shop that primarily sold the luxurious linens and china exclusively designed for them in the hotel's signature floral print by Porthault and Bernardaud. Their success was so great that they expanded and more than doubled their size by adding on an entire section for kitchen items and a wine cellar as well. Here you can pick up a pure white honeycomb-weave cotton dishtowel marked Baumanière in blue lettering on the side or a fine bottle of their special reserve from the Côteaux des Baux—each for about 60F a piece.

- 13520 Les Baux-de-Provence; tel.: 04.90.54.33.07; fax: 04.90.54.57.28
  Open daily except Wednesday and Thursday 9 A.M.–12:30 P.M. and 1:30–6 P.M.

La Camargue (Bouches-du-Rhône)

A special man in my life first introduced me to this part of France in 1987 and we both became so enchanted by this unusual place in the sun that we returned at every opportunity. Often referred to as France's wild, wild west, the Camargue is much more than a region—it's a whole way of life, unique not only to France but to the entire world.

Geographically speaking, the Camargue is defined by two rivers, Le Rhône and Le Petit Rhône, and one sea, the Mediterranean to the south.

This unique triangular section of earth is made up of a highly varied terrain consisting of long stretches of dry, bush-tufted lands broken up by an occasional swamp. The fauna and flora are just as surprising: this may be the only place in France where you're likely to see big black bulls grazing within charging distance of delicate-looking pink flamingoes. Hundreds of acres of wetlands serve as a stopping point for northern European birds en route to or from Africa—or to the patchwork of muddy waters allocated for the cultivation of rice!

Le cheval Camarguais is probably even more typical of the Camargue, and you will see these strong white horses either in semiliberty or tucked away on a ranch. There is so much to experience and so many visits to make to not-so-distant places like Arles or St-Rémy that you can easily get through a stay without one single go-round on a horse. Most of the hotels are ranches, though, which means that you will be lulled to sleep at night by the sound of neighing horses, croaking frogs, and the ever-present crickets (or are they cicadas?) of Provence. The **Boumian** (tel.: 04.90.97.81.15; fax: 04.90.97.89.94), a moderately priced three-star establishment, in Stes-Maries-de-la-Mer is a favorite for its warmth and friendliness, not to mention its delicious meals served poolside.

The town of Stes-Maries-de-la-Mer is best known for its bullfights and gypsies (the musical group Gipsy Kings are from the Camargue). If you're looking to outfit yourselves for the arena, the men should go to **Tout Pour le Gardian** (rue Victor-Hugo, tel.: 04.90.97.82.33), the counterpart of Camille in Arles—you'll be all set for the action!

If you're not on Provençal print overload by now, take a look around at **Souleiado** at 16 rue Jean Jaurès (tel.: 04.66.53.74.28). Most of the rest of the shopping in this town is pretty iffy.

Aigues-Mortes is really the most interesting town in Camargue particularly if you come here at the end of the day as the sun casts a warm, bronzy glow on the old, weathered stones of the castle and its adjacent ramparts. Plan time to look around a bit: once again many of the stores are very touristy with the exception of **Maria-Maria** (rue Sadi-Carnot; tel.: 04.66.53.72.97) and **Soulieado** (16 rue Jean-Jaurès; tel.: 04.66.53.74.28).

For a casual dining experience that will leave you clapping to the gypsy beat, try **La Camargue** (19 rue de la République; tel.: 04.66.53.86.86).

Maria-Maria

Named after Marie Sara—who is blond, beautiful, and very brave—because she is France's only female matador! You probably won't encounter Marie Sara here in her quaint little fashion boutique, but you can try on a blazing red bolero and imagine how you would look in front of an angry bull.

The clothing really is fun—casual and colorful in a sensuous senorita-takes-to-the-ring kind of way. Expect to see a lot of little embroidered jackets and vests with coordinating skirts and pants. Many of the jeans have been embellished with her monogram, signature roses, or the cross of Camargue (part cross, anchor, and heart). The prices won't knock you out of the arena, either.

- 7 place des Remparts, 13460 Stes.-Marie de la Mer; tel.: 04.90.97.71.60
  Open Tuesday–Sunday 10 A.M.–12:30 P.M. and 2:30–9 P.M.

Châteauneuf-du-Pape (Vaucluse)

As my travel companion and I discussed our day's itinerary, we realized that the ancient village of Châteauneuf-du-Pape was just a short distance beyond Avignon. Being the wine lovers that we are, we decided that if we didn't linger too long over breakfast we could squeeze in a visit there toward the end of the day.

Once beyond the outskirts of Avignon, the drive turned out to be delightful. Our search for some of the finest wine of the world took us over hill and dale and in and out of a series of quaint little towns until we arrived at our ultimate destination. We knew that we were there when we spotted a particularly large truck ambling down the road with a huge load of plump, ripe grapes as its cargo. We had arrived right in the middle of the *vendange*—the grape harvest—which only heightened our anticipation about the wine-tasting adventure that we were about to embark upon.

Château Mont-Redon

I chose to visit the vineyards of Château Mont-Redon because I wanted to go to one of the best. The choice was a good one because the wine from this château generally ranks within the top three for Châteauneuf. The fact that you can't buy their wine in the U.S. (they only sell to top restaurants) made the trip seem all the more worthwhile. I had thought that Châteauneuf-du-Pape was only reputed for their reds; but the white wine I tasted won first prize for the world's best white in a recent competition.

The reason the wines of Châteauneuf-du-Pape are so incredibly delicious begins with their soil, which is barely soil at all but rather small, smooth stones called *galets* that may have made up the Rhône riverbed hundreds of thousands of years ago.

- 84230 Châteauneuf-du-Pape; tel.: 04.90.83.72.75; fax: 04.90.83.77.20
  Open daily except Wednesday 8 A.M.–noon and 2–6 P.M.

Cogolin (Var)

Manufacture des Tapis de Cogolin

Just outside of St-Tropez sits Cogolin, a town I was tempted to classify as just another one of the pretty little villages of Provence until I discovered the Manufacture des Tapis de Cogolin—one of *the* best places in France to buy a rug. If you know the shopping scene in Paris well enough, you may find some of the pieces here similar to those at the exclusive Art Curial gallery. The most typical rugs of this manufacturer are stunning ecru models in cotton and wool that are made on the old looms that reside behind the glass windows of this contemporary-looking showroom.

The nearly twenty looms that labor tirelessly over these near masterpieces began their lives in Aubusson where they were used for the weaving of fine silks. This explains why the starting width of these Cogolin carpets is only 70 cm wide, they either remain this way to be used as runners, or are sewn together to create much larger salon pieces (plan to spend about 10,000F for your average living room). This company has done work for numerous Arab princes, the King of Morocco, and the embassies of France—and when I heard that Lauren Bacall was one of their clients, I was totally won over!

- boulevard Louis-Blanc, 83311 Cogolin; tel.: 04.94.54.66.17;
  fax: 04.94.54.47.93
Open Saturday and Sunday 8:30 A.M.–noon and 2–6 P.M.

L'Isle-sur-la-Sorgue (Vaucluse)

Market: town center Thursday and Sunday 7 A.M.–1 P.M.
Flea market: avenue des Quatre-Otages 9 A.M.–7 P.M. Saturday and Sunday

The crowds are overwhelming at first, but once you get the knack of navigating them you'll have a wonderful time here ferreting out vintage items, assorted bric-à-brac, and antiques of remarkable quality. This is probably the one place in France that can rival the famed Paris flea markets at St-Ouen, and some of the shops are as appealing as those you would expect to find in the capital.

The bonus is that the backdrop is totally Provençal and that most of the goods are as typical of this region as the tall plane trees standing stoically alongside the river Sorgue. Your best bet is to come early to get a parking space and see the freshly arrived goods that the dealers have just unwrapped. There is of course a great agglomeration of goods here and the showplaces are equally as varied: sprawled out along the river, the flea market will perhaps grab your attention first, but be sure to take in many of the other dealers who are grouped together in mini-villages such as the **Isle aux Brocantes**, the **Village des Antiquaires**, and the **Près de la Gare**. Do note, though, that the flea markets and most of the antique shops are open only on Saturday and Sunday. Some antique shops are open on Monday as well.

If you're looking to quadruple your fun, plan to visit at Easter or during the week surrounding the August 15th holiday when there is an even bigger gathering of dealers.

Michel Biehn

As I pushed open the door to this nineteenth-century town house and shop, I felt as though I was about to enter someone's private home. Michel Biehn (pronounced bean) does in fact live here and the strong but sweet smell of sautéed garlic that wafted from the kitchen doors aroused one of my worst fears—that I had interrupted his lunch, a sacred time of day in all of France, but even more so in Provence.

After a brief exchange of greetings Monsieur Biehn confirmed that although he and his wife live here, he was more than happy to let me have a look around the shop. I quickly discovered that his handsome selection of goods reflects the Provence of today without playing on exaggerated sentiments of nostalgia. Monsieur Biehn is a decorator and a specialist in many Provençal products—particularly old fabrics and clothing (I'm sure that certain fellow dealers have looked upon his collection of eighteenth-and nineteenth-century prints with an envious eye).

The Biehn emporium is divided into three principal areas that feature both old and new items of varying themes. As you walk in you'll encounter a whimsical little old-fashioned grocery store stocked with jars of gourmet jams and jellies, cookbooks, and more exotic items such as blown-glass ratatouille and terra-cotta pumpkins. Monsieur Biehn also sells dishes, many of which were made exclusively for him in traditional tones of vanilla, sun yellow, and jade green.

The couture corner, however, is what truly distinguishes Monsieur Biehn from all the rest. In addition to the antique items, this man of great taste and sensibility has created a small but highly select collection of pieces inspired from traditional garments of years past. The result is very up-to-date, and if you slip on one of the fully gathered plaid skirts with a T-shirt, you'll look as though you're ready to greet the casually clad jetsetters at St-Rémy!

• 7 avenue des Quatre-Otages, 84800 L'Isle-sur-la-Sorgue;
    tel.: 04.90.20.89.04; fax: 04.90.38.45.09
 Open Saturday, Sunday, and Monday 10 A.M.–1 P.M. and 2–7 P.M.;
    Tuesday–Friday by appointment

Nicod

Gérard Nicod and his wife, Mick, who is originally from L'Isle-sur-la-Sorgue, make up the team that has transformed this eighteenth-century *relais de poste* (postal inn) into an eye-catching showcase for discriminating, late twentieth-century shoppers. The look is contemporary, perfect for people who enjoy giving old things a new life without worrying about chipped paint or lackluster finishes. Rust is big here, and it seems as though the more a piece is worn, the richer the patina promises to be.

Wrought iron is especially popular, whether it's from an old piece of garden furniture or forged into an intricately worked sign, like the one marked *République Français* that once towered over the entrance to a local city hall. Everything here comes from the south of France except Nicod's clients, who tend to be largely Parisian, American, or British.

Eclecticism seems to run in the family, because the Nicods' son Xavier has helped to perpetuate his parents' passion for the old and the unusual with his newer and slightly more sophisticated selection of trendsetting goods next door.

- 9 avenue des Quatre-Otages, 84800 L'Isle-sur-la-Sorgue; tel.:
  04.90.38.35.50 or 04.90.38.07.20; fax: 04.90.20.73.09
  Open Saturday, Sunday, and Monday 10 A.M.–1 P.M. and 2:30–7 P.M.

Le Carré d'Herbes

Stop here as soon as you arrive to reserve a table for lunch at this popular, garden-style bistrot with many furnishings from Nicod. Elizabeth Bourgeois, still presides over the eloquent Provençal restaurant Le Mas Tourteron in Gordes, but here heads up a brigade of women who zealously turn out meals that embrace the savors of the region. Favorites include *petits farcis provençaux* (baby vegetables stuffed with seasoned meat) or thick, open-faced sandwiches topped with such winning combinations as goat cheese mixed with tomatoes, fennel, and basil.

- 13 avenue des Quatre-Otages, 84800 L'Isle-sur-la-Sorgue; tel.:
  04.90.38.62.95
  Bistrot: Inexpensive–Moderate
  Open daily except Wednesday for lunch and dinner

Karine Mesureur

Although this reputable antique shop was closed the day I stopped by, I couldn't help spending time peering into the distinguished-looking interior, which is sandwiched between Nicod and Biehn on the avenue des Quatre-Otages. Karine Mesureur is known for her crisp, classical approach to Provençal decorating *avec de l'ancienne*.

• 7 bis avenue des Quatre-Otages, 84800 L'Isle-sur-la-Sorgue;
  tel.: 04.90.38.45.47
  Open Saturday, Sunday, and Monday 10 A.M.–1 P.M. and 2:30–7 P.M. or
  by appointment

Beyond Sorgue

Edith Mézard

You're apt to miss this lovely place if you happen to blink when driving through this little village. The embroidery of Edith Mézard is as heavenly as the name of her château and village, Château d'Ange in Lumières—the angel's castle in light. Discreetly set back in the courtyard, Madame Mézard's showplace (which was in fact an old stable) is as elegant as a Madison Avenue boutique, without all of the fuss.

All entirely handmade, these exquisite house linens are a reflection of this noble-looking woman's persona—undisputably refined, yet entirely down-to-earth. She has revived the dying art of embroidery, and her crew of half a dozen seamstresses stitch and sew under her careful direction every morning, in performing the long, tedious hours of work that these splendid

---

Le Mas des Grès

When the famous French film actor Pierre Arditi tipped me off about this place, I instantly knew that I was being let in on one of the best kept secrets of L'Isle-sur-la-Sorgue. Jacques and Doune Hermitte are the hosts in this modest, yet totally endearing hotel that is sure to win you over as much as the region itself. The owners, Jacques (a former actor himself) and Doune, form an incredibly charming and sincere team whose main concern is that their guests feel at home. Don't leave without giving Marion Lamy's sculptural paper silhouettes a shopper's once-over (all are discretely displayed throughout the hotel).

• Route d'Apt, 84800 Lagnes; tel.: 04.90.20.32.85; fax:
  04.90.20.21.45
  Two-Star Hotel
  Dinner by reservation for guests: Inexpensive
  Open March–mid-November and the week of January 1

creations require. Each piece begs to be treasured and used countless times on the finest tables accompanied by the most brilliant crystal and china, then to be stored as family heirlooms for generations to come.

Prices vary considerably depending on the piece and can range from 980F for a very simple square linen tablecloth to 6,800F for a king-sized cashmere bedspread. Creamy hues of off-white, champagne, and taupe comprise most of the color scheme, although the day I was there Madame had a beautiful *ABCDaire* (a sort of sampler that represents the alphabet) bed throw in a soft, pale lavender color. Delectable pieces of Provençal pottery in milky-whites and beiges, which were made exclusively for Edith Mézard by Pichon (see Uzès, page 282), round out the subtle palette of colors that hints of "angels in lights."

• Château de l'Ange, 84220 Lumières; tel.: 04.90.72.36.41
  Open daily 3–6:30 P.M. and by appointment

Marseilles (Bouches-du-Rhône)

Main shopping streets: rue St-Ferréol, rue de Rome,
and the beginning of the rue Paradis
Markets: avenue du Prado Monday–Saturday 7 A.M.–1 P.M.;
La Plaine Tuesday, Thursday, and Saturday 7 A.M.–1 P.M.
Flea market: avenue de Cap Pinède Sunday 8 A.M.–1 P.M. and
Cours Julien the second Sunday of every month 8 A.M.–6 P.M.

Mighty Marseilles is the city with a pulse that is like no other in all of France. You will either fall in love with it or decide to leave after getting lost in its gridlocked pattern of one-way streets one too many times. My own attraction to Marseilles was magnetic. The city lives and breathes with the diversity of its inhabitants. There is a lot to see and do here, and even more to experience.

Culture is not lacking in Marseilles, and Italian influences dominate—particularly in the theater and the opera where the standard is set almost inordinately high (if a piece makes it in Marseilles, it generally means smooth sailing for the rest of France). Like Paris, Marseilles is divided up into *arrondissements*, and almost each one holds claim to a particular historical monument, museum, or characteristic that distinguishes it from the others. The antiquing is also in the image of Marseilles: a bit offbeat, weatherworn, and not incredibly upscale *du tout*. Most of these fun and funky sort of *brocantes* are situated on the crest of the city around the place Félix-Baret and the cours Julien.

The area surrounding the old port is certainly the most typical and undeniably the most picturesque. Sit in one of the cafés here in the morning in front of the sea and a *grand crème* to watch the fishmongers selling their catch. From here you might decide to walk over to **Les Docks,** the old docks of this maritime moneymaker, that have recently been restored and converted into a very "in" place to go for a bite to eat or for a bit of shopping.

The **tourism office** (4 la Canebière; tel.: 04.91.13.89.00; fax: 04.91.13.89.20) also faces *le vieux port,* and as I popped in here to pick up a map, I discovered that the headquarters are very sleek—complete with halogen lighting, modern accents, and a boutique corner that is one of the best places to buy the big rustic blocks of *savon de Marseille* (the soap that has earned Marseilles worldwide recognition) and T-shirts that are neither too tacky nor too expensive (about 150F).

By now you may be ready for another break, and **Les Arcenaulx,** another newly renovated complex not far from the port at 25 cours d'Estienne-d'Orves, could be just the thing for you. Their restaurant/tearoom appeared to be *the* meeting place for the women of Marseilles, and much to my delight, I heard only French being spoken here. It put me in the mood to read some Pagnol, so I poked around in the adjacent bookstore until I found a couple of choice volumes among a whole realm of books (in several different languages) on Marseilles, Provence, and the innumerable specialties of the region in every imaginable format. More regional products (of varying qualities) are sold in two other shops on the same premises.

If your promenade takes you even farther east toward the St-Victor Abbey, plan to stop at the **Four des Navettes** (136 rue Sainte), the oldest bakery in Marseilles that is famous for its cookielike snacks called *navettes.* Like the *calissons d'Aix,* the taste of these local specialties is quite foreign to the uneducated palate. The *marseillais,* however, have had plenty of time to become accustomed to the unusual taste and hard consistency of this Stella Doro–like cookie because the treats have been made here since 1782. The recipe is guarded like a state secret, although it is not difficult to detect a hint of orange-flower water and a touch of lemon. The perfect accompaniment to a cup of tea or coffee or even *un pastis* (the local anise-flavored apéritif), these shallow little boats, called *navettes,* last up to one year neatly packaged in their chartreuse yellow tin boxes.

Les Ateliers Marcel Carbonel

A longtime presence in the religious history of Italian culture, artisanally made figurines have been used extensively to depict the nativity scene in all of its sweet splendor. Marseilles was one of the first ports of call for these miniatures, and their use became particularly widespread toward the end of the eighteenth century during the uprisings of the French Revolution. Developing more secular ways of expressing one's faith became imperative and it didn't take long for the *santon* (Provençal for "little saint") to catch on throughout the region.

Soon the faces of the characters of the nativity became those of the people of Provence. When looking at these caricatural figurines it is easy to forget their original purpose and the religious significance that they once primarily represented. They have, however, become symbolic of *la Provence*, and each one offers up a different vision of this enchanting land. Whether it be a woman gathering up a bunch of lavender or an old ripply faced man stooped over his workbench, every piece is handmade from start to finish out of terra-cotta clay and then handpainted in gouache with great agility. Prices start at about 49F for *les puces* (the mini-flea–like versions) and increase progressively to about 460F for the largest size (about six inches tall). Although the store sells the fully dressed ten-inch kind, the clothing and adornment of the traditional *santon de provence* is always painted on—not crafted out of cloth.

Fully respectful of the proper and most traditional way to craft the *santons*, Les Ateliers de Marcel Carbonel create miniature wonders of superior quality. A visit to their establishment is a must to see how *santons* are made. A look at the video and a tour around their private collection, which consists largely of figurines from distant countries, will complete your education of this anecdotal character of Provence.

- 47 rue Neuve-Ste-Catherine, 13007 Marseille; tel.: 04.91.54.26.58; fax: 04.91.54.89.42
  Boutique/Museum
  Open Monday–Saturday 8:30 A.M.–1 P.M. and 2–7 P.M.

Faïences Figueres

A trip here is an excellent excuse to tour some of the outlying areas of Marseilles. The drive takes about twenty minutes from the center of town, and technically speaking you are still within city limits. It's hard to believe, however, from looking at the wild and sparcely populated terrain that lies on the fringes of the city center. Cruising along the coastal road that borders the Mediterranean is a thrill; the water here is clean as a result of the strong currents that run through this part of the sea. If you continue along this road a bit farther you will discover some of the famous *calanques* of Marseilles, the sharp, chalky-looking cliffs that enhance the already breathtaking views of the coast.

After a bit of searching, I finally arrived at the Faïences Figueres shop and atelier where I was greeted by Monsieur Figueres, a charming man whose almost curious resemblance to Pinocchio's woodcarver warmed me. There was no wood here, however, only handmade faience of two very different orders. The first collection features beautifully executed reproductions of eighteenth-century Provençal pieces based on the floral motifs of the well-known craftswoman la Veuve Perrin. The second and most recently created collection is far less traditional and certainly more original in spirit. You won't be able to eat off any of these pieces, however, because their trompe l'oeil ornamentation restricts them to a decorative function.

This ingenious idea of affixing ceramic versions of nearly lifesize fruits and nuts of the region to boldly colored, scalloped-edged plates of classical Provençal design has been a huge success for the workshop. Each one is a work of art and incredibly lifelike. The hardest decision you will have will be in choosing between olives, apricots, figs, green almonds, or the soon-to-arrive mussels, crabs, and bouillabaisse! Prices begin at 150F.

If you have more time to spare in the area and if old faience strikes your fancy, take a look around at the **Musée de la Faïence**, which is housed nearby in the lovely **Château Pastré** at 157 avenue de Montredon.

- 10–12 rue Lauzier, 13008 Marseille; tel.: 04.91.73.06.79;
  fax: 04.91.25.34.95
  Open Monday–Friday 8:30 A.M.–noon and 1–6 P.M.; Saturday 8:30 A.M.–noon

Galerie Wulfram Puget

If you have visited the Museon Arlaten in Arles or the Musée Souleiado in Tarascon, you have already been introduced to the beauty and uniqueness of traditional Provençal fabrics.

Museums can be frustrating, though, especially for people who want to buy, so I was only too happy to hear about this gallery that is highly reputed for its collection of eighteenth- and early nineteenth-century quilts and fabrics. Madame Beaumelle is the expert here and she proudly oversees her handsome collection with the knowledge, confidence, and expertise of the most respected museum curators.

Under Madame's most sincere tutelage I learned about *les piqués de Marseille*, the highly worked textiles for which the town and this gallery is most renowned. You could best describe them as quilts without patchwork—only an abundance of top-stitching that creates a quilted effect. The decorative work is incredible, and I can only imagine the hours of labor required for the exquisite rendering of flowers, petals, and other swirly motifs that distinguish these fabrics. (A woman's marriage skirt was usually made in *piqué* during the course of her engagement, a period which back then lasted several years.)

The historical background of the *piqués* is nearly as intricate. Marseilles has always been an important port, and it was here that the paisley and other flower-inspired fabrics (called *indiennes*, as in from the Indies) arrived from the Far East. The *piqué* was introduced as a means of dressing up these rather primitively designed cotton fabrics into more elegant and desirable fashion statements. Many of the works here are still in their original form of either a bedspread or an article of clothing, but they have become such prized pieces that most people put them on display, framed and under glass.

- 7 rue Wulfram-Puget, 13008 Marseille tel.: 04.91.76.42.85;
  fax: 04.91.76.42.85

Open Tuesday–Saturday 2–6 P.M.
Best to call ahead

Madame Zaza of Marseille

The name should clue you in to the sort of clothing and accessories you can
expect to find in this funky women's fashion boutique. The look is cosmopolitan in a trendy kind of way, but what speaks of Marseilles the most is its
exoticism. Much of the clothing resembles the brightly colored and multi-
patterned garb that is worn by the more exotic people of the city—only here
it has been reinvented with stretchy fabrics and more provocative cuts. Prices
run from about 500F for a clingy top to 1,650F for a fanciful jacket.

• 73 cours Julien, 13006 Marseille; tel.: 04.91.48.05.57
  Open Monday–Saturday 10 A.M.–1 P.M. and 2–7 P.M.

Le Miramar

Serendipity played a major role in the delightful evening I spent
at this elegant restaurant. My one reason for coming here was
to taste their famous bouillabaisse, but I was not destined to
revel in this fabulous dining experience entirely all alone. Instead
I found myself seated next to a familiar-looking man who happened to be talking "film" with his dining partners. It did not
take me long to figure out that this person happened to be a
famous French film actor by the name of Pierre Arditi. Soon we
were chatting up a storm, and not only did I not have to finish
the evening alone, but I also left with a slew of addresses that
could have been entitled "personal favorites of a movie star in
Provence."

• 12 quai du Port, 13002 Marseille; tel.: 04.91.91.10.40; fax:
  04.91.91.56.31
  Restaurant: Expensive
  Open Monday–Saturday for lunch and dinner; closed three
      weeks in August and Christmas week

Moustiers-Ste-Marie (Alpes-de-Haute-Provence)

Market: in front of the Hôtel-de-Ville Friday 8 A.M.–1 P.M.

In estimating how long it might take you to drive here, you must consider
that depending on what direction you come from, chances are that you will

find yourself on at least a couple of twisting and turning roadways. The views along the Grand Canyon du Verdon rival some of the majestic sites of the western United States, but your sightseeing could turn into an aggravating experience if you come here during the heat of the summer and get stuck behind an endless string of camping cars. Plan accordingly.

As long as you're mentally prepared, the journey is worth it. If you really want to do Moustiers the right way (without encountering masses of tourists), plan to spend at least a couple of days at the exclusive inn, **La Bastide de Moustiers** (quartier St-Michel; tel.: 04.92.70.47.47; fax: 04.92.70.47.48) which is run by star cuisinier Alain Ducasse of the famed Monte Carlo restaurant Le Louis XV and the recently opened Alain Ducasse in Paris. If you become tired of dining here, another fine restaurant **Les Santons** (place de l'Eglise, tel.: 04.92.74.66.48), is located in the center of town. Be sure to reserve a table on the terrace, where you can take in more spectacular views of the Alpes-de-Haute-Provence while dining on a handsome assortment of Villeroy & Boch china and faience from Moustiers-Ste-Marie.

It is once again the earth that has created this town's reputation, for Moustiers is most known for its faience (and now for its tourism, because the faience attracts so many visitors). You may want to begin with a brief tour around the town's tiny **Musée de la Faïence** (place du Presbytère), although by now you may have already seen more spectacular collections of old ceramics elsewhere in France.

The village of Moustiers-Ste-Marie is jam-packed with ceramic shops of every nature. It's up to you to hunt down the goods that best suit your tastes and pocket books. Most collections are inspired by traditional seventeenth- and eighteenth-century French faience, particularly those styles most typical of Moustiers. Highly refined and feminine in design, many of the patterns are characterized by wispy garlands, exotic birds, and delicate flowers (mostly from potatoes). The better pieces have been hand-painted with divine precision and prices tend to be rather high, although justifiable for the quality of workmanship.

Nîmes (Gard)

Main shopping areas: place de la Carré, place aux Herbes,
rue du Général-Perrier, rue de l'Espic
Market: Les Halles daily 6 A.M.–1 P.M.
Flea market: allées Jean-Jaurès Sunday 8 A.M.–1 P.M. and
Monday 8 A.M.–6 P.M.
Provençal market: l'Esplanade during *Féria* (Pentecost–end of September)

Nîmes could be easily referred to as the sister city of Arles. Both towns have two important attractions in common: bullfighting and Roman ruins. Much of the bullfighting in these cities takes place within their Roman ruins, and thus *les arènes* are a popular place of entertainment. I guarantee, however, that you will be bowled over by the stately beauty of La Maison Carrée, Nîmes's most significant Roman ruin. Set off by a huge plaza that enhances the beauty of this pure and simple wonder of nearly 2,000-year-old architecture, this monument should be viewed both during the day and at night. A few of the cities' nicest boutiques have set up shop here, including **Souleiado, Les Olivades**, and **Cacharel** (the president of this world-renowned company was for a long time the mayor of the city).

Like Marseilles, Nîmes also has a rich history associated with textiles. The word "denim" originated from *de Nîmes* (from Nîmes), and this is the sort of fabric on which the city built its reputation. Denim was exported through Gênes or Genoa: most people couldn't properly pronounce the name so it was transformed into jeans.

A quick look around the shops of Nîmes and you realize that the *nîmois* still favor the Provençal fabrics. The boutique **Les Indiennes de Nîmes** showcases Provençal prints much the way you would find them at Souleiado or Les Olivades. The difference here is that they are far less expensive, which means that the quality of the cottons and the vibrancy of the colors is not the same. Be a smart shopper, because they do have some great pieces. I spotted a near couturelike *bouffante* skirt, fashioned out of a chartreuse and royal blue–colored Provençal print and topped with black netting, which was designed by someone who had previously worked for Christian Lacroix.

When in Nîmes, you will in fact hear a lot about *La Féria* because this is when the city truly comes alive. The period lasts from Pentecost to the end of September and is filled with bullfights, folkloric festivals, and ceremonies.

If you're looking for haute Provençal cuisine in Nîmes, reserve a table at the garden restaurant of the **Hôtel Imperator Concorde** (quai de la Fontaine; tel.: 04.66.21.90.30; fax: 04.66.67.70.25). I also had the pleasure of spending the night here and found it difficult to leave, having been so charmed by the room's tasteful Provençal interior.

St-Rémy-de-Provence (Bouches-du-Rhône)

Market: place de la Mairie and its surrounding streets
Wednesday 6 A.M.–1 P.M.

Seductively chic, without all of the glitter–this is certainly part of the reason so many people find St-Rémy so attractive. It is indeed a charming Provençal town and its environs are equally desirable for both their beauty and their proximity to so many other great places of interest in Provence. Its sleepy confines and reputation for calm also make it attractive to celebrities.

Tranquility still pervades at St-Rémy and the T-shirt vendors have been kept at bay, although the town has most definitely swelled in its sophistication and subsequent flow of visitors. The shopping is not quite all that you would expect from a town that touts such celebrated second-residence dwellers as Caroline de Monaco, France's best-loved princess; Inès de la Fressange, the former model turned designer; or Jacques Grange, the famed Parisian decorator—to name just a few. I found the following boutiques to be the most Rémy-esque.

Le Grand Magasin

Far from provincial, Le Grand Magasin transcends the traditional ways of looking at the arts and crafts of Provence. The cosmopolitan-like displays of this store's diverse collection of bibelots would practically parachute you back into Paris or New York if it weren't for the nature of most of the wares. Francis Braun, the dynamic *provocateur* of Le Grand Magasin, is indeed a heteroclite who has knowingly carved out his niche among the fast-forward, fashion-conscious folk of St-Rémy.

Shimmering glass cases and shiny shelves provide the necessary support for the interesting mix of merchandise that includes lampshades, evening bags, sculpture, and pottery. The one thing all the items have in common is that they are first and foremost *objets d'art*. The majority of these goods have been made in the region or reflect the energy of this color-splashed land. Provence prevails with the presence of *la cigale* (the cicada), the consummate symbol of the region, which is ubiquitous here primarily in the form of costume jewelry. Creations from both today and yesterday tempt you in every imaginable sort of material including wood, Bakelite, lucite, resin, and ceramic in renditions that range from primitive to highly sophisticated.

- 24 rue de la Commune, 13210 St-Rémy-de-Provence; tel.: 04.90.92.18.79; fax: 04.90.92.35.76
  Open Tuesday–Saturday 10 A.M.–12:30 P.M. and 2:30–7:30 P.M.

Terra Nostra

France is slowly but surely going green, and this shop encourages everyone to do it with style. Terra Nostra's carefully honed selection of natural and recycled products promotes a whole concept that in the end should make you feel good about using them. The linens, table arts, beauty products, clothing, and home and personal accessories at this shop all are environmentally friendly. Not all of these goods come from Provence, although those that do are among the most fragrant.

In addition to the traditional *savon de Marseille*, the boutique features a whole other line of products, also from Marseilles, that capture the scents of the region in the form of luxurious bath gels and skin creams. Redolent scents of jasmine, rosemary, and orange have been sealed within blue-tinted medicinal-like bottles made of recycled glass, beautiful objects that elicit a cleaner way of life.

- 31 rue Carnot, 13210 St-Rémy-de-Provence; tel.: 04.90.92.58.23
  Open Monday–Saturday 10 A.M.–1 P.M. and 2:30–7:30 P.M.
  Also in Nice at 13 rue Massenet, 06000 Nice; tel.: 04.93.87.99.63; fax: 04.93.88.51.81

Le Château de Roussan

I stopped here on my way into St-Rémy from Tarascon in search of a cup of tea. The choice couldn't have been better, because as I basked in the golden sunshine of autumn, I drank in the untamed beauty of the château's immense grounds. Unlike regions to the north, châteaux are not common in the south of France—a fact that makes stopping at Le Château de Roussan, whether for a drink or to spend the night, all the more exceptional. The setting is devoid of any unnecessary formalities, which might explain why Americans make up the majority of their clientele.

- Route de Tarascon, 13210 St-Rémy-de-Provence; tel.:
  04.90.92.11.63; fax: 04.90.92.50.59
  Château-Hôtel/Restaurant: Moderate
  Open year-round

St-Tropez (Var)

Main shopping streets: rue Gambetta,
rue Georges-Clémenceau, rue Général Allard
Market/flea market: place des Lices
Tuesday and Saturday 7:30 A.M.–1 P.M.

The shopping scene in St-Tropez is explosive. In fact, this could describe the overall feeling of this world famous coastal resort. From the topless beaches to the trendy nightclubs, this place really swings. Underneath all of this French Riviera shimmer, however, lies a far more down-to-earth side that intimates the unaffected casualness of Provence. It is precisely this interesting juxtaposition of *la Provence* and *la Côte d'Azur* that makes St-Tropez unique.

There is no better place to capture this quality than at the Saturday morning market on the place des Lices. If you're coming by car, come early, because after 8 A.M. during the summer months you won't find a parking space. As you breathe in the sights and sounds of this typical Provençal market you may end up rubbing elbows with a frequent flyer of the jetset, a chic vacationer from Paris, a crew member from one of the visiting yachts—or just another tourist! This is also a great place to start your shopping because in addition to fresh food products, local vendors come down from the hills to sell their homemade honeys and jams, olive oil, pottery, and Provençal frocks.

From here you can either head off to some of the glitzy fashion boutiques or stay regional with shops like **Potier Augier** (rue Gambetta; tel.: 04.94.97.51.78) for boldly colored pottery or **L'Atelier de Provence** (24 rue Allard; tel.: 04.94.54.80.30) for cheery dried-flower arrangements and topiaries. If you are not in town on a market day, the regional offerings at **Artisanat Provençal** (13 boulevard Louis-Blanc; tel.: 04.94.97.77.43) just may fill the void. While you are here, stop in across the street at **Pierre Basset** (32 boulevard Louis-Blanc; tel.: 04.94.97.75.06), one of the most highly acclaimed pottery suppliers of the area who is best known for his exquisitely made collection of richly colored tiles from Salernes, a little town north of St-Tropez in the department of the Var.

If you really want to get into the thick of things, head down to the port. There is plenty more shopping here in trendy boutiques such as **Johnny Hallyday** (named after a local summertime resident who is France's equivalent to Elvis), which sells American casualwear souped up with a flashy, French rock 'n' roll twist. The two biggest attractions on the port are all of the incredible yachts and the nearly as exciting cafés that face them. **Sénèquier,** the sprawling café with its cramped arrangement of red directorlike chairs, is a veritable institution and possibly one of the best places in all of the south of France to people-watch.

One thing that you'll learn by observing the locals is that the real *tropeziens* wear boating attire by day and tantalizing glamour by night. Shops on the rue Gambetta sell scintillating fashions for the evening, although when it comes to elegant and particularly well-made togs for a serious day of sailing, the leader in all of St-Tropez is the boutique **Leader.** Situated right out on the port, Leader sells *la crème de la crème* of casual and durable boating attire.

If you just can't get enough of the boating scene, you absolutely must come here during the early part of October when the town becomes practically volatile with the Nioulargue, a sailing event that attracts many of the world's most beautiful and ostentatious yachts—and of course, a lot of B.P.s (Beautiful People) as well. Although I've never sailed on such a vessel in my whole life, I really felt like I was part of the event.

St-Tropez deserves strong mention all the way around. I was even surprised to learn that its antiques selection is fabulous and not overly priced as one might think: their prices need to be competitive since they work an international clientele of both individuals and dealers. Nearly all of the *antiquaires* and art galleries are concentrated in the little web of streets, referred to as **le Carré de l'Eglise,** that stretch out from the church of St-Tropez. This makes for the perfect place to seek solace from the hot afternoon sun *and* the crowds of tourists that sometimes plague this popular town. The streets, in fact, were constructed in this protected and rather hidden manner centuries ago in order to provide shelter from the *mistrals*, the relentless winds that often whip through Provence.

K. Jacques

The *sandale tropezienne* or the sandal of St-Tropez is probably the most typical product of this fashion-conscious enclave. It was in fact introduced to St-Tropez during the 1920s after one of the town's native sons happened to be in Rome and eyed a statue that was ceremoniously clad with these incredibly comfortable-looking sandals. *Voilà*, the *sandale de St-Tropez* was born. These classically designed sandals with their horizontal bands of plain beige leather still sell like hotcakes, but they now also come in a huge range of colors, including multicolored snakeskin.

K. Jacques is the best known sandal source, particularly since they have several boutiques in St-Tropez and even one in Paris. In addition to the classic, Roman-inspired model, they also show a whole realm of sandal styles (and even some enclosed shoes like moccasins) for men, women, and children. The snappy selection for women is certainly the most in sync with St-Tropez, although most of them are so sparsely designed they call for pretty feet!

• 25 rue du Général Allard; 83950 St. Tropez; tel.: 04.94.97.77.43
  Open in season daily 9:30 A.M.–1 P.M. and 3–8 P.M.; off-season Monday–Saturday 9:30 A.M.–12:30 P.M. and 3–7 P.M.

Muriel Grateau

This exquisite boutique features table arts and house linens of the finest quality. The *créatrice* of all of these luxurious products for the home is Muriel Gratineau, who formerly worked as a fashion designer in Italy. I could tell that she was accustomed to coaxing the best out of beautiful materials. This high priestess of style explained that she had recently set up shop here because her family has a home in St-Tropez. It all seemed to make sense; this brightly illuminated space is the perfect *vitrine* for all of her tasteful creations, and her goods correspond completely with the sophisticated tastes of the town's high-class visitors.

Upon admiring the sober yet eloquent place settings that Madame Gratineau had created in porcelain and faience, I learned that she has designed similar services for visiting yachtspeople to use on board their boats. Virtually everything here is a reflection of this distinguished woman's fine taste. There are scarcely any prints; instead, everything from china to glassware to linens (for both the table and the bedroom) plays on subtle nuances of color, and the palette is as extensive as the goods are expensive.

- 6 place de l'Hôtel-de-Ville; 83950 St-Tropez tel.: 04.94.97.12.70
  Open in season at varying hours

Rondini

Tucked away on this tiny yet highly commercial street is Rondini, makers of the classic St-Tropez sandal for even longer than K. Jacques (five years longer, to be exact: since 1927 instead of 1933!). They are the confirmed specialist of *spartiates*, (another name for the St-Tropez sandal) and here they sell in an even larger range of colors that include periwinkle blue and brick red. Prices on the classic models run about 500F; count on paying 600F for the snakeskin.

- 16 rue Georges-Clémenceau, 83950 St-Tropez; tel.: 04.94.97.19.55
  Open Monday–Saturday 8:30 A.M.–noon and 2:30–6:30 P.M.

Hotel Byblos

Did you say eccentric? Did you mention snobbery? Did you evoke vulgarity—or at least tasteful vulgarity, if there is such a thing? Yes, St-Tropez can be all of the above, and nowhere else will you find such a concentrated dose than at the Byblos. You would expect nothing less of St-Tropez nor of its premiere hotel—otherwise it would not be St-Tropez. The décor consists of a delicious mix of Greek, Lebanese, French, and Mauresque influences, and virtually every part of the establishment provides the opportunity to discover something (or even someone) new. If you can't swing a lengthy stay here, at least plan to make a night of it at Les Caves du Roy, the most happening nightclub on the coast.

- avenue P.-Signac, 83950 St-Tropez; tel.: 04.94.56.68.00; fax:
  04.94.56.68.01
  Closed mid-October–late March

Salon-de-Provence (Bouches-du-Rhône)

Market: place Morgan Wednesday 8 A.M.–1 P.M.

When I first conducted my preliminary research for this book, I sent out a mailing to the major tourism offices of France inquiring about the products most typical of their town or region. The responses did not always correspond with my expectations—especially in the case of Salon-de-Provence. A kind person took the time to send me a handwritten letter explaining that Salon was most known for its soaps and in particular its olive-oil *savons de Marseille*—which despite the name is fabricated here far more than in Marseilles. The landscapes of craggy olive trees that surround Salon lend credence to this: a pure olive oil soap must contain at least 72 percent virgin olive oil. The history of Salon's *savons* is rich, dating back to the nineteenth century when merchants became "fat" from their huge production of olive oil.

The **Musée de Salon et de la Crau** on the avenue Donnadieu commemorates part of this era, although if you want to buy any of these soaps you should go directly to the two *savonniers* who still make them in the traditional fashion: **Marius Fabre Jeune** (148 avenue des Grans, tel.: 04.90.53.24.77) or **Rampal-Patou** (71 rue Félix-Pyat, tel.: 04.90.56.07.28).

If all of these suds have you dreaming about taking a luxurious bath, try to reserve a *chambre* at the exclusive four-star Relais & Château hotel **L'Abbaye de Sainte-Croix** (tel.: 04.90.56.24.55; fax: 04.90.56.31.12), situated a short distance outside of town in an unparalleled Provençal setting.

Tarascon (Bouches-du-Rhône)

Market: rue des Halles and cours A. Briand
Tuesday 8 A.M.–1 P.M.

Souleiado

No other name signifies the spirit of Provence as completely as Souleiado. This old Provençal word actually refers to the indelible strength of the sun's rays after a storm: the company itself is considered the unofficial ambassador of this sun-drenched region throughout the world.

The wistful and vibrant fabrics of this classic old house affectionately communicate the vivacity of Provence in a way that is pure and simple, and most of all, void of any obstinacy. They speak of folklore and tradition and of a style of living that is better suited for the exterior than the interior. To embark upon the sentimental journey through the Souleiado fief in Tarascon, you must reserve a spot for one of their guided museum tours. The museum, which was recently established as a tribute to Charles Deméry, the most instrumental force behind Souleiado's success, is an ode to the culture and traditions of Provence.

Poetic visions of *la vie provençale* enliven the exquisitely decorated rooms of this seventeenth-century town house in an inviting manner that tempts you to move right in. As the tour leads you from kitchen to bedroom and from the ancient color laboratory to the rich display of regional costumes, you not only learn a great deal about the history of these boldly colored prints but also how to incorporate them into your own life.

The logical follow-up to this heartwarming visit is to take a look around the shop. Unfortunately, the boutique is as disappointing as the museum is captivating, which is all very deliberate so not to take business away from the other Souleiado establishments of the region. The shop sells mostly fabrics and only a fraction of the company's fashion and home-décor collections. You can pick up some good buys on sale items or discontinued merchandise, but if you really want to shop, you're better off hitting any one of the numerous Souleiado boutiques located throughout Provence.

- 39 rue Proudhon, 13150 Tarascon; tel.: 04.90.91.08.80; fax: 04.90.91.01.08
  Museum/Boutique
  Open Monday-Friday 8 A.M.–noon and 1:30–5:30 P.M.
  Museum by appointment only: 30F per person; visits usually conducted at 10 A.M. and 3 P.M.
  Boutique and museum closed weekends and during lunchtime

Beyond Tarascon (Bouches-du-Rhône)

Ciergerie des Premontres

Across the street from the Peugeot garage, this large but discreet atelier has made candlemaking a family affair for more than 100 years. Purveyors to many of the area churches and restaurants, this atelier is enrapturing as much for the slice of culture that it serves up as for its shopping: on any given day you are bound to see a half a dozen artisans judiciously hand dipping candles in a range of a dozen delicious colors, each of which has been specially blended for this purpose. The result is nearly edible, and the visual effect is one of a subtle moiré. It is no wonder that they are scooped up and sold at some of the finer establishments of the region for at least quadruple the price. Here the candles sell for 4F each, so the only thing that might hold you back is the room left in your suitcase.

- 13690 Graveson; tel.: 04.90.95.71.14
  No credit cards
  Open Monday–Friday 8 A.M.–noon and 1:30–5:30 P.M.

Uzès (Gard)

Market: Place aux Herbes Saturday 8 A.M.–1 P.M.
Flea market: at the Refuge (near the stadium) Sunday 8 A.M.–1 P.M.

A visit to this ancient village makes for the perfect day trip from Nîmes or Avignon, particularly since along the way you can make a stop at the Pont du Gard (an old Roman aqueduct), considered one of the most spectacular historical treasures of the whole world. The shopping scene at Uzès is quaint and refreshingly untouristy, with an emphasis on regional ceramics of noble quality.

The name **Pichon** dominates and it is apt to create a fair amount of confusion because it refers to two different ateliers, one of Véronique, the other of Jean-Paul—both Pichons and both ceramicists who seem caught up in a family rivalry. As I traveled through Provence, I would come across Pichon ceramics in many of the finer shops. I stopped asking which Pichon it was because the question seemed to stir some uneasy feelings. I suppose it doesn't really matter to us anyway because the pieces from both of these workshops are equally attractive and unquestionably similar in style and design.

As far as I could tell, the actual differences are most apparent in the choice of color: Véronique tends to use deeper, denser colors, such as lapis lazuli, squash, blood red, and ochre, while Jean Paul mostly sticks with the more muted tones of buttery yellow and sage green. Each collection, however, is comprised of many milky and cream-colored pieces that seem to be a Pichon trademark. These are all colors of the earth, and these dishes can be mixed and matched to create a gorgeous Provençal landscape.

The shapes have also drawn inspiration from traditional Provençal pottery, and two principal styles predominate: an octagonal shape trimmed with tiny pearl-like beads, and a more curvilinear form finished off with scalloped edges. Ceramic baskets that have been woven out of thick spaghettilike strips of clay are also typical of Provence and the beauty of these pieces is that they can really stand on their own without needing to be part of a set. The relationship between price and quality at both of the Pichon establishments is honest: **Véronique Pichon** (rue Jacques-d'Uzès; tel.: 04.66.03.06.46;) and **Jean-Paul Pichon** (6 rue St-Étienne; tel.: 04.66.22.36.31; fax: 04.66.22.71.59).

For more pottery, drive about 6 kilometers outside of town on the route de Bagnols to a little village called St-Quentin-la-Potérie. Known for its considerable output of ceramics through the centuries, this town recently experienced renewed interest in its craft, and now about a dozen different potters have formed a community here. In addition to periodic pottery festivals, many of these artisans' creations are on permanent display at the **Maison de la Terre in St-Quentin-la-Potérie** on a permanent basis. Special mention goes to the stoneware of **Jef Panthou** (31 avenue Maxime-Pascal; route de Bagnols; tel.: 04.66.22.70.56), whose greyish-blue and white bowls and vases incarnate reflective, Asian overtones.

Around Uzès

La Begude de Saint-Pierre

Less than a kilometer away from the Pont du Gard, this hotel is mesmerizing in its own quiet way. Like many Provençal homes, the harmony between the interior and the exterior enhances the natural beauty of this fragrant land to such an extent that if it weren't for the intensity of the Provençal sun, you might not be able to differentiate between inside and out.

Don't be surprised if you encounter a few baby swallows sailing through the house, their lilting presence will only add to the lure of this cajoling establishment. Luxury has not been spared, either; all of the rooms are air-conditioned and tastefully appointed with lively Provençal prints and furnishings. The cuisine is equally seductive, which comes as no surprise because the owner of this newly renovated establishment is a trained chef. If you can't spend the night, at least stop for a leisurely lunch on the terrace.

• D981, Les Coudoulières, 30210 Vers-Pont-du-Gard; tel.:
    04.66.22.10.10; fax: 04.66.22.73.73
  Hotel/Restaurant: Expensive
  Open year-round; restaurant closed Sunday night and
    Monday during off-season

THE SOUTHWEST
Le Sud Ouest

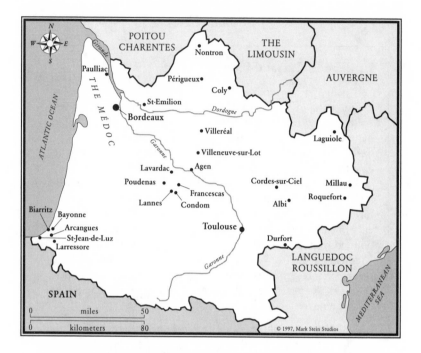

espadrilles • prunes • *makilas* • old books and engravings on wine • Basque linens • licorice-flavored chocolates • wines • surfing attire and equipment • *jambon de Bayonne* • handblown glass vases and lamps • Gothic and Renaissance antiques • handcrafted Nontron knives • armagnac • Toulouse-Lautrec mementos • floc de gascogne • handmade gloves • ewe's milk cheese • artisanal copperware • arts and crafts creations • Laguiole cutlery • model Airbus 340s • candied violets • Basque music and books • faience • vintage wines • *macarons* • hand-painted china • foie gras • eclectic antiques • *canelés* • Roquefort-emblazoned gift items • *beret basque* • fine chocolates

THIS CHAPTER COVERS the largest and most diverse region of all of those in this book, and it would take you well over two weeks to visit what I have chosen to include. Even at a marathon pace it would be difficult for you to take in all of the riches of this southwestern quadrant of France, and if you try, you might suffer certain inevitable consequences such as fatigue, or even worse, an acute case of gastritis. Although I'm not the gluttonous type, I confess that this is exactly what happened to me after so many samplings of *foie gras, confit de canard, cassoulet, roquefort, chocolat*, and much more—all of which had to be generously washed down with fine wines and fiery armagnacs. You'd have to have an ironclad system not to be affected by such glorious overindulgences. 'Tis a gastronomic land indeed, one that you'll want to savor little by little, so even if you do have a couple of weeks to spend here, don't make it your mission to taste all of the marvelous *spécialités* of each province.

Fortunately my damage was only temporary—particularly since my pocketbook had been spared from any superfluous expenses in the shopping department, a near-miraculous feat considering all the wonderful goods that the region has to offer. In this respect I felt perfectly content as a reporter, gathering information by seeing, touching, and when necessary, smelling a product to formulate my opinions. It also helped to ask a lot of questions, queries that sometimes left certain interlocutors dismayed by the challenge of summing up a couple centuries' worth of history in fifteen minutes or less! Thankfully I never felt that I had to buy a product to know it, but with food and wine, the problem presents itself differently. After all, one does have to eat—it's just a matter of how much and how rich.

The area that I refer to as the Southwest actually encompasses two administrative regions of France: Aquitaine and Midi-Pyrénées. Both of these regions share a number of similarities, and the most common one is their gastronomy. I have divided the region into five areas that should become apparent to you as you travel throughout the region. The blood-red half-timbered houses of the Basque country, for example, could not be more different in appearance and purpose than the fairy tale castles of the Dordogne. I hope that the uniqueness and distinct flavor of each province shines through with every city, shopping, and hotel and restaurant description that I have included. For the sake of space I had to sacrifice some of my favorite destinations, including the charming Basque villages of St-Jean-Pied-de-Port and Espelette, the enchanting town of Sarlat in Dordogne, the thick forest of Les Landes, and the oceanside resort of Arcachon. These you can include on your own itinerary with the assurance that you will never be too far away from a thick slice of foie gras or a glass of robust red wine.

THE BASQUE COUNTRY

Arcangues (Pyrénées-Atlantiques)

Arcangues, the adorable. This tiny Basque village awaits you only 7½ kilometers from Biarritz, perched on a hilltop surrounded by a lush green golf course. The typical features of Basque villages is instantly discernible: a church and cemetery; the city hall with an inscription usually written in Basque; and the *fronton*, the space where the tremendously popular sport of *pelote basque* (jai alai) is played. In Arcangues, you are sure to be touched by the unabashed candor of this happy threesome, a scene that appears to have been created for the photographic requirements of a travel brochure.

The best vantage point for admiring all of this is from a seat carefully positioned under the shade of the plane trees on the terrace of **Auberge d'Achtal**, a tiny restaurant that serves as another pole of attraction for this intimate community. After you've savored an *omelette aux cèpes*, the house specialty, be sure to peek in at the eclectic offerings of inveterate treasure hunter Jean-Marie Kocir at the neighboring **Loko** (tel.: 05.59.43.11.79). From Basque linens and crafts to antique finery, all that is so attractively presented in this inviting space has been hand-picked by Monsieur Kocir with a show of exceedingly good taste and style.

Bayonne (Pyrénées-Atlantiques)

Main shopping streets: rue Victor-Hugo, rue Thiers, rue de la Salie
Market: les Halles, Monday–Saturday 8 A.M.–1 P.M.; Friday 8 A.M.–6 P.M.

Knowledgeable francophiles will most likely associate the word *jambon* (ham) with Bayonne. It's true that the sale of *jambon de Bayonne* is widespread throughout France, but the better quality hams (aged 18 months) sell in Bayonne's specialty-food shops. **Pierre d'IbaïAlde**, a highly reputable *charcuterie* located at 41 rue des Cordeliers (tel.: 05.59.25.65.30; fax: 05.59.25.61.54), represents one such example, and although you might want to buy only a few slices of ham here for an impromptu picnic, more transportable Basque canned items include sweet red pepper–enhanced prepared dishes, like *pipérade*, an all-time favorite of the region.

You can't escape this old center of commerce without tasting some of Bayonne's best chocolate, either. The first French city to have been introduced to cocoa beans during the sixteenth century (via the Spanish conquistadors who surreptitiously brought them back from Mexico), Bayonne has upheld *la tradition du chocolat* ever since. Conveniently enough for us, the city's two best *chocolatiers*, **Daranatz** and **Cazenave**, are practically next door to each other at 15 and 19 Arceaux du Port-Neuf, respectively. Daranatz also prides itself on its fresh and tender *touron*, a sugary confection of Spanish origin. Cazenave truly wooed me with more than a dozen different sorts of chocolate bars, all of which have been temptingly wrapped in an array of brillantly-colored papers, and by its frothy hot chocolate—a delightfully soothing drink, especially when consumed in the tea salon with a serving of buttered toast!

Plans to open a Basque museum by the millennium in Bayonne are under way, but in the interim, Basque culture enthusiasts frequent the **Librairie Zabal** (52 Pannecau Karrika; tel.: 05.59.25.43.90; fax: 05.59.25.54.39). This small shop, filled with Basque music and books in the languages of Basque, French, and even some English, is a window onto the many dimensions of this fascinating culture. A sampling of their English titles includes *Basque Witchcraft & the Spanish Inquisition, Basque Violence,* and *Basque Sheep Herders of the American West.* For beautiful views of the Basque landscapes, ask to see the book *Argia,* which means "light" in Basque.

Biarritz (Pyrénées-Atlantiques)

TGV: 5 hours
Main shopping streets: rue Mazagran, rue du Port Vieux, place
Clémenceau, avenue Victor-Hugo
Market: Les Halles daily 8 A.M.–1 P.M.

Unequivocally the most glamorous resort town on the French Atlantic, Biarritz began as an old whaling station. Little remains from those days, but there's plenty of evidence to document the city's emergence as a spa town. Empress Eugénie's love for this seaside destination forever changed its destiny in the 1850s, and by the time the Belle Epoque rolled around, most of the European aristocracy followed. Over time, Biarritz became increasingly associated with *le sport,* a label that sticks just as firmly today.

You'll find that you have to do quite a lot of sports to burn off the calories that one can easily accumulate around town. Sweets seem to have besieged Biarritz in three popular forms: chocolates, caramels, and *touron.* The corner shop of *maître chocolatier* **Henriet** on the place Clémenceau supposedly is a favorite of designer Sonia Rykiel, one of France's best-known, self-confirmed chocoholics. I was assured that their *rochers de Biarritz,* a mouthwatering marriage of macerated orange peels and roasted almonds dipped in dark chocolate, can easily make the voyage across the Atlantic if you don't rip into their seashell wrapping paper first. Also on the place Clémenceau, **Miremont** and the neighboring **Dodin** can keep you prodigiously supplied in sweets, and their praline-and-almond-filled chocolate mussels, or *moules,* will remain indelibly imprinted on your mind. If it's lunch or teatime, settle yourself into the rather tattered *vieille France* décor at Miremont, where you can sit and stare transfixedly out to the sea.

Basque specialties of a less saccharine order make up part of the vast selection of gourmet products from around the world at **Maison Arostéguy**, the city's best answer to Fauchon at 5 avenue Victor-Hugo (tel.: 05.59.24.00.52; fax: 05.59.22.11.19). Since 1875, this bastion of Basque bounty has contented locals and visitors alike with regional foodstuffs including cheese, sausages, and *jambon de Bayonne*, as well as more exotic canned items such as *chiperons* (calamari in ink sauce) and the local delicacy, *hobrena-palombes* (large pigeons prepared in red wine). A small jar of ground *espelette* (the spicy red peppers from the town of Espelette) comes in handy when attempting to add a zesty note of Basque seasoning to your cooking at home.

On the sports scene, the town's top surf shop is a trendy spot by the name of **Quicksilver** at 2–4–6 place Bellevue (tel.: 05.59.24.34.05). I was shown their sizzling stuff by a sweet, blond-haired jock who explained to me that although Quicksilver was initially an Australian company that was bought out by Californians, much of what sells here is made nearby in St-Jean-de-Luz. Between this store and their beachfront outpost, you can pick up everything you need to tackle the famed surf of Biarritz. If it's winter and the idea of donning a wetsuit to unleash yourself onto the biggest waves of the year doesn't appeal to you, you can always buy a snowboard and head for another kind of surfing challenge in the Pyrénées mountains.

If you enter 27 place Clémenceau and walk upstairs to **La Fonda** (tel.: 05.59.22.35.21), you will find yourself in an expansive showroom that features mostly blue and white ceramics that have been handmade in the region. It's true that the space seems to overwhelm these airy pieces, yet I found it interesting to learn that the building was once an old English bank and that Queen Victoria had tea in this very room. The pieces displayed here have little to do with royalty except for an occasional fleur-de-lis popping up here and there; more local themes include stylized versions of the Basque cross, nautical knots, and a few Espelette peppers. Marie-Noëlle Mac-Donald (her husband is Scottish) designs most of the works, many of which have been inspired from traditional seventeenth- and eighteenth-century motifs. Prices range from 85F for a coffee cup to 125F for a plate.

There are enough high-end boutiques along the main drag to keep you shopping for hours, although if antiques are your interest you may want to try to take in a well-known **flea market** in the nearby community of **Anglet**. Only five minutes from Biarritz, this *marché aux puces* takes place at la place des Cinq Cantons year-round on the second Sunday of every month.

You could always squander any remaining spare cash at the **Casino de Biarritz**, the hard-to-miss play place that dominates the center of town. All recently renovated, the entire establishment is nothing less than spectacular, and even if you are not into *le jeu*, you can still relish a fine meal or simple moment inside or out on the oceanview terrace of the **Café de la Grande Plage** (tel.: 05.59.22.77.88). Tea, or–if you can afford it–a few nights' stay at the **Hôtel du Palais** (1 avenue Impératrice; tel.: 05.59.41.64.00; fax: 05.59.41.67.99), the palace in the center of town built for the Empress Eugénie by Napoleon III, may leave you reeling with delusions of grandeur, but such a splurge is nothing less than *obligatoire* when in Biarritz. Another form of expensive luxury awaits you nearby at the **Institut de Thalassothérapie Louison Bobet** (tel.: 05.59.24.20.80; fax: 05.59.24.87.24), where you can be sloughed, buffed, and pampered to your heart's content. Most of the center's spa goers reside at the adjoining four-star **Hôtel Miramar** (13 rue Louison-Bobet; tel.: 05.59.41.30.00; fax: 05.59.24.72.20), a sleek, modern facility that only adds to the pervasive sensation of living on a cloud without a care in the world.

Oceanfront lodgings of a more relaxed nature are difficult to pass up at the three-star **Villa l'Arche** (tel.: 05.59.51.65.95; fax: 05.59.51.65.99), only 4 kilometers outside of town on a magnificent site overlooking the Atlantic. Plan ahead to reserve one of their eight freshly decorated and reasonably priced rooms, a few of which offer near plummeting views of the ocean. More pedestrian types can walk just a few minutes along the beach to an excellent restaurant nearby, and with a low tide and a lot of energy, you can go the extra kilometers to arrive barefoot in Biarritz!

Between Biarritz and St-Jean-de-Luz (Pyrénées-Atlantiques)

Only a fifteen-minute drive separates these two oceanside towns, but it might take you longer than you think if you begin to stop at the many places of interest along the way. If you are an espadrille lover you must go to **Maison Garcia** (tel.: 05.59.26.51.27; fax: 05.59.54.75.65) in Bidart, one of the most renowned makers of this canvas-and-cord-confectioned footwear so characteristic of the region. If you're spending time in the area and you really want to get spiffy, bring in some of your favorite fabrics to have fashioned into your own personal models–creations meant to be matched with summery shifts and folksy frocks.

If more gastronomic inclinations have taken hold of you by now, plan to have lunch or dinner at **La Table des Frères Ibarboure** (tel.: 05.59.54.81.64; fax: 05.59.54.75.65), one of the most refined restaurants in the region, situated along the Chemin de Tallenia between Bidart and Guéthary. Anne Marie Ibarboure has installed a mini-boutique here, but if you pass through the area between Easter and mid-November, you must stop at **La Maison Dorrea** (tel.: 05.59.47.71.62), her half-hidden shop on the rue de l'Eglise in Guéthary. Passionate about Basque arts and crafts, Madame Ibarboure has stocked her homey space with goods made in the region, which include handmade linens and pottery, handcrafted gloves called *chis-*

teras used for *la pelote basque* (jai alai), walking sticks called *makilas*, and folkloric musical instruments unique to the Basque people. Less exotic gift items include books on the region and fine comestibles, some of which have been prepared by her husband's restaurant.

Larressore (Pyrénées-Atlantiques)

Ainciart Bergara

As I stood in this busy little five-man workshop, I struggled to converse with Monsieur Charles Bergara above the incessant rat-a-tat-tat of the other craftsmen who were tapping out *makilas*, the walking sticks that are the ultimate symbol of the Basque spirit. Each person was at a certain stage of workmanship of their makila, a so-called walking stick that serves as both a decoration and a weapon for its proud bearer. As Monsieur Bergara stooped slightly in front of his 300-year-old workbench, he talked about how he was born into the *makila* and how this has been part of his family's tradition for the past seven generations. When I asked about the actual origins of these handsome *objets*, I received only a slight shrug, accompanied with an off-handed remark to the effect that it has *always* been part of *la tradition basque*.

Every *makila* that leaves the Bergara workshop represents a sort of "labor of love," whether it is destined for a French minister, an African king, an emir, or the Pope. The craftsmanship of these pieces represents some of the finest work in all of France; virtually every piece is unique, although they all begin with a specially treated wooden support, finished by a woven braid of leather, and topped off with a hand-engraved ornamentation delicately carved out of 18K gold, sterling silver, or buffalo horn. A bayonet traditionally is incorporated into the overall design as if to serve as a reminder of the Basque peoples' inherent concern for defending themselves. The sky's the limit as far as fantastical designs and prices go, but even if you place an order for a modest 3,000F piece crowned in silver, you still may have to wait a year to receive it.

- 64480 Larressore; tel.: 05.59.93.03.05
  Open Monday–Saturday 9 A.M.–noon and 2–6 P.M.

St-Jean-de-Luz (Pyrénées-Atlantiques)

TGV: 4 1/2 hours
Main shopping street: rue Gambetta
Market: boulevard Victor-Hugo Tuesday and Friday 7 A.M.–1 P.M.;
also open Saturdays in summer
Flea market: across from St-Jean-de-Luz Mondays, summer only,
8 A.M.–7 P.M.

One of the most endearing resorts in the entire region, St-Jean-de-Luz truly lures in the vacationers from June to September. Calm, sandy beaches, a quaint fishing port, vacation villas from the 1930s and 1940s, medieval dwellings, and handsome town houses originally constructed by wealthy pirates (this port city was the pirate capital of Europe during the sixteenth century) form the backdrop of this nifty little Basque town. The royals also left their imprint when Louis XIV married L'Infante Marie-Thérèse in the Eglise St-Jean Baptiste on the rue Gambetta, a supreme example of a typical Basque church; note the wooden galleries whose upper levels are still reserved exclusively for men, while the women remain below. The attractive stone and brick house called **La Maison Infante**, where Louis's future Spanish bride awaited the ceremony, today houses temporary art exhibitions at different times of the year.

The royalist influence is also evident in many of the classic leather creations of **Laffargue**, situated on the rue Gambetta (tel.: 05.59.26.11.39). Easily recognizable by their hand-hammered stud and stylized fleur-de-lis accents, most of their bags and accessories have come to be known as typically Basque, although I did spot a studded leather belt, priced at only 400F, that looked amazingly like one from Hermès.

It's almost impossible to leave without succumbing to at least one of its celebrated sweet shops. If you haven't already tried **Dodin** in Biarritz, you can give it a go here at 80 rue Gambetta (tel.: 05.59.26.38.04). The *chocolatier/ confiseur* **Robert Pariès** also has a boutique on the place Clémenceau in Biarritz, but I tasted their specialties here at 9 rue Gambetta (tel.: 05.59.26.01.46); and like many of the locals, I think that I've become addicted to their famed *kanougas*, luscious caramels enrobed in rich chocolate. If you've had your fill of chocolates, caramels, and *tourons*, **Maison Adam** offers the perfect reprieve with their prized *macarons*; you can purchase them here at 49 rue Gambetta (tel.: 05.59.26.03.54) to accompany your midmorning espresso, which is, of course, best savored at one of the outdoor cafés along the port.

Bayona

If there is one region in France most associated with espadrilles it is the Basque country, and Bayona is indisputably the most authentic espadrille maker of them all. Since 1870, this Basque company has been making these cord-trimmed cloth sandals for men, women, and children, and today you can buy their traditional models along with an imaginative collection of more fanciful footwear, from slingbacks and platforms to open-toeds covered in lace. The signature Bayona trademark is visible hand-stitching along the exterior—quite unlike those made in China! Prices range from 49F for the classics, available in twenty-four different colors, and go up to about 300F for the funkier designs. Remember to buy tight because they always stretch.

- 60 rue Gambetta, 64500 St-Jean-de-Luz; tel.: 05.59.26.05.40
  No credit cards
  Open, Monday–Saturday 2:30–7:30 P.M.

Maison Charles Larre

One could argue for hours about which is more Basque: espadrilles or the *beret basque*. Real sticklers might say that the *beret basque* is not even made in Basque but rather in Bearn, a neighboring province. *Peu importe.* What is important is that the finest and most authentic version of this quintessential symbol of France sells here for about 180F. Some people might sneer that they can buy French berets for far less elsewhere, but these are the real thing: satin-lined, pure wool berets, trimmed with a thin band of leather along the interior to assure a snug fit. Black is the traditional color and they make excellent headgear for this often dewy climate. The store also features a sampling of folkloric costumes (perfect for children's dress-up) and traditional Basque table lines.

- place Louis XIV, 64500 St-Jean-de-Luz; tel.: 05.59.26.02.13
  Open Monday 2:30–7 P.M.; Tuesday 10 A.M.–12:15 P.M. and 2:30–7 P.M.;
    Wednesday–Saturday 9:30 A.M.–12:15 P.M. and 2:30–7 P.M.

Oyala

The origins of the Basque linens date back to the sixteenth century when peasants made their own toiles, which would reveal a certain amount of information about them through the color and width of the fabrics' stripes; their wealth and stature, for example, would be proudly displayed at village festivals when they would drape their oxen with these *mantes à boeufs*, decorative coverings that also protected the animals from the sun and flies.

The force at Oyala lies in their ability to have recreated these traditional linens by designing fabrics of far more colorful schemes and interesting patterns. Bright, bold stripes have replaced the more sober styling of traditional linens, and in some instances, decorative motifs of a floral or geometric nature have added a crisper, zippier look to fabrics that otherwise might be considered dull. Marigold, royal blue, and mint green work as terrific color accents for their more subdued beiges and whites that form the backgrounds of most cotton or cotton and linen blend fabrics. Count on spending 430F to 610F for a tablecloth.

- 17 boulevard Thiers, 64500 St-Jean-de-Luz; tel.: 05.59.26.96.96; fax:
    05.59.51.23.26

Open Monday 3–7:15 P.M.; Tuesday–Saturday 10:15 A.M.–12:30 P.M. and 3–7:15 P.M.

Outside St-Jean-de-Luz (Pyrénées-Atlantiques)

Jean-Vier

Jean-Vier has several outposts within the region, but I recommend that you stop in at this showcase emporium, situated at the entrance of St-Jean-de-Luz along the RN10 as you arrive from Biarritz. Some of the weaving for this leading Basque linen maker takes place here, and the minimuseum explains the importance of linens in the history of the region.

As the energetic Jean-Vier proceeded to show me the highlights contained within this reconstructed old farm, he voraciously discussed his more than two-decade-long passion with weaving and explained that most of the creations he designs himself. As you walk through the many alluring rooms of this rustic space, you discover not only a wealth of house linens inspired by Basque tradition, but also a collection of home and personal accessories from ham sacks for protecting your *jambons de Bayonne* to tote bags for carting your belongings to the beach. Many of the handsome table linens have matching china, and even the magnificent country antiques used to display this plethora of goods are for sale here at collectors' prices. A true ode to *l'art de vivre basque*, at Jean-Vier every item is beautiful, of the finest quality, and rather excessively priced—but it will all last a lifetime!

- RN 10, 64500 St-Jean-de-Luz; tel.: 05.59.51.06.06; fax: 05.59.51.18.19
  Mail-order catalogue
  Open daily 9 A.M.–12:30 P.M. and 2:30–7 P.M.; all day in July and
  August; afternoons on holidays

BORDEAUX AND ITS ENVIRONS

Bordeaux (Gironde)

TGV: 3 hours
Main shopping streets: cours Georges-Clémenceau,
place Gambetta,
cours de l'Intendance, allées de Tourny,
rue Ste-Catherine, rue Porte Dijeau
Market: place des Grands-Hommes, cours Victor-Hugo,
place du Marché des Chartrons,
Monday–Saturday 7 A.M.–1 P.M.

The fifth-largest city of France and certainly one of the most grand, Bordeaux might stun you with its opulent architecture and its resplendent style. One may think that most of this wealth comes from the wine trade, but as you delve into the history of the past 1,000 years of this fine city, you learn that much of Bordeaux's fortunes were bequeathed to its coffers long before *les affaires du vin*; the nectars of the region are the cherry on an already luscious cake. With such a history to live up to, the mentality of Bordeaux is often viewed as *bourgeois*, which can appear downright snobby to unsuspecting visitors. Don't let this impede your shopping adventures any more than such an attitude would affect you in Paris.

At the famed *chocolaterie* **Saunion** at 56 cours Georges-Clémenceau (tel.: 05.56.48.05.75; fax: 05.56.48.22.15) I found the welcome as austere as the décor. The nearby **Cadiot-Badie** (26 allée de Tourny; tel.: 05.56.44.24.22) pleased me considerably more with its alluring Versailles-esque interior and for the exquisite *truffes de Bordeaux*, truffles flavored with brandy made from Bordeaux wine. Their red and gold boxes of wafery-thin chocolates, or *palets*, seem to have been created for the sole purpose of accompanying a glass of wine or an eventual sip of coffee. You'll want to gobble up the *canelés*, the most reputed sweets of Bordeaux; usually served in miniature with coffee in the better restaurants of the area, these caramelized spongy flanlike treats also are sold in pastry shops around town. Some of the most delicious ones can be bought fresh from the oven at **Baillardan**, the city's *canelé* specialist, a tiny bakeshop with a few locations around town, one of which is hard to miss at the **Marché des Grands-Hommes** (place des Grands-Hommes).

Bordeaux's antiques market also reflect the city's riches—past and present—in a number of tastefully arranged shops along the rue des Remparts and the rue Bouffard. The warm interior of the boutique **Au Singe Bleu** at 41 rue Bouffard features a mix of the old and the new, a fashionable showcase reflective of the sophisticated tastes of the most up-to-date *bordelais*. If you are a believer in herbal medicines, step into **Le Tisanier d'Or** just across the street at 48 rue Bouffard for a look at an astonishing array of therapeutic herbs and elixirs, many of which may be difficult to unearth elsewhere. If you want to take in a number of antique shops in one fell swoop, go directly to **rue Notre Dame**, in the neighborhood referred to as Les Chartrons, where approximately ninety different *antiquaires* vie for your attention.

From here you can head over to the **Musée des Chartrons** at 41 rue Borie (tel.: 05.57.87.50.60), a small museum that illustrates the importance of the nineteenth-century wine merchants in the business of storing, bottling, and packaging wines. The proximity of this old building to the Garonne river is by no means accidental; by the seventeenth-century, similar long, narrow warehouses were already constructed here so that the first Dutch traders could stock their supply of Bordeaux wines and brandies. Prior to that, the English controlled most of the wine trade, which partly explains the acute British appreciation for claret!

Arts et Restauration Montaut

What better way to honor wine than through images? This dealer of old prints and books has obtained some of the best originals and reproductions of antique engravings that depict views as classic as a nineteenth-century representation of a wine harvest or as humorous as the seven stages of inebriation. Approximately 500 collectors within Europe anxiously wait Montaut's yearly catalogue announcing their most recent acquisitions of old, rare books on wine and gastronomy, some of which date as far back as the seventeenth century. Some of the centuries-old prints come from books, but I was assured that these works have been taken only from albums in a decrepit state and never from those fully intact. Historic views of the port city of Bordeaux also make up part of this rich collection, and lovers of other traditional prints should be happy to learn that more classical themes of flowers, fruits, birds, and architecture also have a special place reserved for them amid the rarities of this shop.

- 87 rue de la Course, 33000 Bordeaux; tel.: 05.56.81.96.38; fax: 05.56.44.81.03
  Open Monday–Friday 9:30 A.M.–noon and 2–7 P.M.

Les Chais Ryst Dupeyron

A visit to the Ryst Dupeyron cellars in the Chartrons quarter is a must if you want to find some of the best buys on Bordeaux wines. But before you start pushing your grocery cart through this self-service selling space (actually an old cellar), take a quick walk through their wax museum to learn about the history of wine and the wine-making process throughout the centuries. The visit ends with a few different videos on Bordeaux wine, the famous wine *châteaux* of the region, and the almost 100-year history of this venerable house. Their near warehouse-size selection of wines includes some real finds: a Château Beychevelle '85 (Saint-Julien), for example, sold here for 225F, roughly a third of the price it would fetch abroad. Shipping within or outside of France poses no problem for Ryst; to send five or six cases abroad, the cost would amount to approximately 700F for transportation and 10F per bottle for customs (depending on the country, of course). Don't pass up the special selection of whiskies, port wines, and armagnacs from their own delicious production in the Gers department—all of which can be purchased with your own personalized labels.

- 10–12 cours du Médoc, 33000 Bordeaux; tel.: 05.56.39.53.02; fax: 05.56.39.19.51
  Open Tuesday–Saturday 9 A.M.–12:30 P.M. and 2–7 P.M.

L'Intendant

I couldn't talk about Bordeaux without mentioning a wine shop, and certainly the most beautiful and one of the most reputable is L'Intendant, a four-story blond wood spiral that will seduce you as much by its high-pitched cylindrical shape as by its superb selection of wines. Over 15,000 bottles of Bordeaux are carefully housed within this climate controlled space, primarily arranged according to *cru* (growth). If you're looking to buy a truly exceptional wine that you don't have to wait to consume, climb to the fourth floor for a reverent display of old vintages, most of which date back to before 1970. Bad news is that the shop does not mail abroad.

• 2 allées de Tourny, 33000 Bordeaux; tel.: 05.56.48.01.29
  Open Monday–Saturday 10 A.M.–7:30 P.M.

The Médoc (Gironde)

The Bordeaux wine region encompasses such a vast area that if all of the vineyards were put together they would make up the world's largest landmass devoted to the production of quality wines. I have included the Médoc and St-Emilion in this chapter, although the other wine-producing sectors of Pomerol, Entre-Deux-Mers, Graves, and Sauternes should by no means be neglected. In any event, what is most important is to visit a handful of *châteaux* to experience part of the history and making of these world renowned wines from the source. The majority of the *châteaux* accept visitors (mostly by appointment), although tastings are unfortunately—and understandably—few and far between. You can purchase wine from some of the lesser-known *châteaux* or *domaines*, but as a general rule, the merchandising part of this highly controlled business is left more for the wine merchants than for the winegrowers.

It only takes a quick look at a map to realize that the Médoc is a peninsula; the micro-climate created by this geographic positioning between the Atlantic and the Estuary of the Gironde, is the reason this region came to yield such celebrated wines. By the mid-eighteenth century nearly all of the land areas were acquired by ennobled lawyers from Bordeaux, spurring a tradition often referred to as *noblesse de bouchon* (cork nobility). About twenty *grandes familles* preside over the Bordeaux wine world today, usually marrying among themselves so that this deeply embedded tradition remains as purebred as the horses the families ride during their weekend polo matches. Nowhere else in France does the word *château* stand up to its name as much as it does here (outside of the Médoc, *château* can be used to identify a wine, but that does not necessarily mean that an immense dwelling exists behind the name.). Here you can count on taking in many breathtaking views of elegant homes surrounded by neat rows of vines that seem to stretch as far as the horizon; this, of course, represents at least a fraction of the fun of touring around the Médoc in the first place, and there is no better place to begin than at **Château Mouton Rothschild** in Pauillac, *la grande dame* of them all.

Tours of this prestigious house are conducted regularly throughout the year, although it is best to call ahead for an appointment (tel.: 05.56.59.22.22 or 05.56.73.21.29). Once you enter this pristine and almost divinely immaculate establishment, you realize that this is not the sort of place you just barge into. After viewing a multiscreen slide show filled with many beautiful images of the vineyard, you enter into Mouton's near sacrosanct cellars where 250,000 to 300,000 bottles of their famed Mouton Rothschild repose in a seemingly blissful state. Learning about the making of the wine and studying their prized collection of artful labels (some designed by the Baron's artist friends during the early 1920s) is enrapturing, but your jaw will truly drop as you enter their **Musée du Vin**, a museum devoted to the representation of wine and the vine in art. Created in 1961, this exquisite space prominently displays wine-related artifacts from countless civilizations and varying ages collected throughout the world by the Baron and his wife, Pauline. From an ancient wine pitcher of Mycènes to a delicate pair of eighteenth-century Delft wine slippers, one cannot help but sense that this unique assemblage of *objets* was amassed with great love and refinement.

You may find yourself stopping in at the **Maison du Tourisme et du Vin in Pauillac** (tel.: 05.56.59.03.08; fax: 05.56.59.23.38) to inquire about other *châteaux* visits, and while you're here you can do a little shopping for wine. The selection is extensive, although the majority of the wines are indeed from Pauillac. The prices are the same as those at the *châteaux*, but don't expect any great bargains; I discovered that many of the same wines sell for only slightly more at large wine retailers such as Sherry-Lehmann in the U.S. It's always fun to pick up a bottle or two from the source, but it's even more exciting to stop for lunch or even a few nights' stay at one of the four-star luxury hotels and restaurants on the Médoc. If you revel in intimate surroundings, I suggest **Château Cordeillan-Bages** (tel.: 05.56.59.24.24; fax: 05.56.59.01.89), a Relais & Châteaux hotel in Pauillac; for a taste of grand living in a more spacious environment, try the **Relais de Margaux** (tel.: 05.56.88.38.30; fax: 05.56.88.31.73), located at the Bordeaux end of the Médoc in Margaux.

St-Emilion (Gironde)

The relaxed, down-to-earth approach that typifies the St-Emilion *châteaux* could not be any different from the imposing atmosphere and grand style that reigns on the Médoc. You are expected to call ahead at both locations to arrange a visit—but the difference stops there. The more physical characteristics of the St-Emilion *châteaux* might disappoint you (most of these *châteaux* look more like manors than castles), but the friendly, almost familylike environment more than makes up for it. I visited **Château Belair**, *1er grand cru classé* (tel.: 05.57.24.07.94 or 05.57.74.41.97), which produces only about 50,000 bottles a year of some of the world's finest wines, instantly realizing that this is the sort of place to come to if you truly love wine and are interested in sharing this passion with the people who work in this exclusive world. Here you can expect to be received by someone who works on the vineyard (not by a hostess as you'll find at the big houses), and although I can't guarantee any tastings, you may eventually be able to buy a bottle or two of a recent vintage.

The charming medieval village of St-Emilion only adds to the heartwarming sentiments that are sure to stir within you in this blessed land where wine has been made since the seventh century. You will most likely discover a few quaint shops as you explore the village's centuries-old streets, but be sure not to miss **La Tour des Vins** on rue de la Cadène (tel.: 05.57.74.47.62; fax: 05.57.74.94.02). The young and knowledgeable Ludovic Martin generally tends this wine shop, although if you are unlucky enough to find it closed, try looking for him down the street at the **Bar de la Poste**. Martin has the exclusive right to sell many St-Emilion wines that are not sold elsewhere in the village—gems that include wines like Château Tertre Roteboeuf '87 (360F), a rare vintage that is practically impossible to find elsewhere.

Ludovic is quick to show you commentaries from Robert Parker's *Comprehensive Guide to Wines* or the *Guide Hachette des Vins*, so virtually any purchase here should come with great assurance. The moment of ectasy comes when Ludovic presents his stockpile of big-name vintage Bordeaux wines the likes of a 1948 Château Montrose St-Estèphe, modestly priced at 1,800F.

Hardly a town, village or hamlet exists in France without a sweet shop, and in St-Emilion mouth-watering *macarons* are baked almost hourly with a recipe that dates back to 1620. It's hard to miss the busy little shop of **Madame Blanchez** at 9 rue Gaudet (tel.: 05.57.24.72.33), where clients are often piled up onto the street; so before you leave the village, be sure to pick up a box of these sugary almond treats, which melt even faster in your mouth when consumed with a velvety glass of Bordeaux. For a taste of regional specialties of far greater consequence, reserve a table at the **Hostellerie de Plaisance** (tel.: 05.57.42.72.32; fax: 05.57.74.41.11), an elegant establishment perched on the village mount (place Clocher) with extraordinary views of the countryside below.

THE DORDOGNE

Coly (Dordogne)

Manoir de Hautegente

A handsome fourteenth-century manor house awaits you just a short distance from the renowned prehistoric Lascaux Caves. If you are just passing through, you may want to stop at this beauteous dwelling to pick up a few gift packages that include select wines from the region and a variety of foies gras that have been expertly prepared by Madame Edith Hamelin, the lady of the house. You might be so charmed by Hautegente that you will want to taste some of the house specialities in the glow of the warmly decorated dining room or even spend the night in one of the well-appointed *chambres*. Plan ahead, though, because you will not be the only one to be enchanted by this elegant country establishment.

- 24120 Coly; tel.: 05.53.51.68.03; fax: 05.53.50.38.52
  Three-Star Hotel/Restaurant: Expensive
  Open year-round

Nontron (Dordogne)

La Coutellerie Nontronnaise

Nontron knives, the oldest cutlery in France, have been handmade in this small town since the fifteenth century. This fine form of Dordogne *artisanat* might already have died out by now had this little company not been bought out by La Forge, one of the most prestigious makers of knives, a few years ago. Thankfully the craft of carving each boxwood handle and affixing it to the finely forged blade has remained quite artisanal; today the atelier employs no more than ten cutlers who tend to every aspect of this knife-making process from start to finish, an attention to detail that is felt in each of these smooth-handled, polished blond wood knives. The characteristic Nontron signature lies in the burned engravings, rather primitive Indianlike designs that resemble a reversed letter V highlighted by a series of singed dots.

The tony oak interior of Nontron's showcase boutique further entices you to buy these handsome examples of refined rusticity, and once you take a look at their cost, you'll probably find it even harder to resist them; prices range from 100F to 200F for pocketknife models and 160F to 250F for classic pieces that can easily be used for elegant country fare.

- 33 rue Carnot, 24300 Nontron; tel.: 05.53.56.01.55; fax: 05.53.56.25.31
  Open Monday 2–6 P.M.; Tuesday–Saturday 9 A.M.–noon and 2–7 P.M.;
  open Sunday mornings in summer

Périgueux (Dordogne)

Main shopping streets: rue Limogeanne, rue St-Front
Markets: Les Halles and place du Coderc daily 8 A.M.–1 P.M.; place de la
Clautre and place de l'Hôtel-de-Ville
Wednesday and Saturday 8 A.M.–1 P.M.;
Marché au Gras: place St-Louis
Wednesday and Saturday 7 A.M.–noon
from mid-November to mid-March

I had the good fortune of visiting Périgueux one Saturday morning during the month of February. People were busy scurrying about this handsome town's maze of medieval streets, shopping for enough Dordogne bounty to carry them through much of the upcoming week. I had heard that one of the main regional attractions was to be experienced at the place St-Louis, the habitual marketplace for the *marché au gras*. Its literal translation, "fat market," can leave many a person wondering exactly what to expect here, but if it's any consolation, *gras* refers to the local geese and ducks that have been fattened with corn. The vendors proudly sell every imaginable part of these birds, from barbecued carcasses called *demoiselles* to plump livers awaiting the right preparations to be turned into succulent foies gras. I even spotted big tubs of fat as well as a few blackened nuggets of truffles which, of course, sold for considerably more! The ambiance alternates between folkloric and serious business, exuding a no-nonsense food-oriented animation unique to Dordogne.

For geese or duck products of the less perishable kind, you can choose from any number of prize-winning canned delicacies Tuesday through Saturday at the town's most reputable *ambassadeur*, **Loulou Bordas** at 8 rue de la Sagesse (tel.: 05.53.08.75.10; fax: 05.53.09.52.42).

La Galerie Medicis

Aside from its gastronomic delights, the Dordogne is also well-known for its antiques, a particularity that can be explained by the province's abundance of castles, most of which date back several centuries in time. As you walk along the narrow, almost pathwaylike rue Limogeanne, you'll have to duck (pardon the pun) into the courtyard of number 3 to fully appreciate the beauty of this town house's splendid sixteenth-century Renaissance architecture. The little antique shop occupying the corner space exhibits a collection of old and new goods that reflect the eclectic taste of owner, Yvan de Wilde. A unique *mélange* of neo-Baroque, Gothic, modern, and whatever else happens to strike Monsieur de Wilde's wildest fancy, his funky scramble of finds attracted the attention of Cher, the world-famous actress/singer, during one of her recent forays to the region. If you've ever seen her catalogue collection of medieval-inspired décor items, you'll understand why she practically bought out the store!

- 3 rue Limogeanne, 24000 Périgueux; tel.: 05.53.53.38.21 or 05.53.08.44.14; fax: 05.53.53.69.15
  Open Tuesday–Saturday 10 A.M.–noon and 2–7 P.M.

Serge Salleron

Monsieur Salleron's collection of impeccable furnishings from *le Périgord* (the other name for Dordogne) will make you feel as though you've just walked into the interior of a particularly well appointed *château*. Monsieur did indeed affirm that the surrounding area boasts a near obsessive number of *châteaux*, which explains why the immediate region is called *le pays de 1,000 châteaux* or the land of a thousand castles. Monsieur's forte is regional furniture from the Middle Ages through the seventeenth century, a span of nearly six centuries, during which time the pieces were massive and solidly built to accommodate the often rustic conditions of their stone fortresses. Most were crafted out of walnut, although some of the oldest were constructed of oak. Monsieur's cream-of-the-crop collection sells in perfect condition, and prices are far lower than what you might pay for the same pieces outside of France. A seventeenth-century regional armoire, for example, richly carved with deep diamond-shaped designs, sold for about 45,000F.

- 7 place de l'Hôtel-de-Ville, 24000 Périgueux; tel.: 05.53.08.21.56
  Open by appointment

AROUND AGEN

Condom (Gers)

Ryst-Dupeyron

No comment about the name of this town, but the Ryst-Dupeyron name— I know it well. I first tasted the delicious armagnacs of Ryst-Dupeyron in their Paris boutique, and the visit to their distillery helped me to appreciate even more the savoir faire that is poured into this family-owned operation.

The people of the region claim that the idea of distilling wine was introduced here by the Arabs, who intended it to be used as a medication; this occurred long before the process was tried in Cognac, and the *gascons* (the people from this part of France) would argue that their spirits are just as good—it's just that they never learned to sell them as well as the merchants of Cognac.

The variety of grapes is indeed the same for armagnac and cognac, although they *are* grown differently; in addition to this, armagnac undergoes a continuous distillation, producing spirits that are aged longer in oak barrels from the region. It's also important to remember that Armagnac country lies considerably more to the south than Cognac, a factor that influences how the grapes flourish and the type of soil. You'll be able to sample here, so it's up to you to discern which spirits you like the most.

- 32100 Condom; tel.: 05.62.28.08.08; fax: 05.62.28.16.42
  Open Monday–Friday 9 A.M.–noon and 2–6 P.M.; visits possible on the weekend by appointment

Lannes (Lot-et-Garonne)

Domaine de Cazeaux

The armagnacs produced by Michel and Eric Kauffer's family-run business sell only here and in a select number of restaurants in France. On a tour of the site, Eric explained that the distillation usually begins every year around December 31 and that he and his father alternately work the still for a week so that the process is not interrupted. The spirits are white when they emerge, and with time, they gradually take on the rich amber color that they absorb from the oak barrels. You can buy Kauffer's armagnacs here, aged from five to twenty-four years, ranging in price from 100F to 260F, along with other specialties such as sweet wines called flocs de Gascogne and jarred prunes copiously soaked in armagnac (delicious served over ice cream).

- 47170 Lannes; tel.: 05.53.65.73.03; fax: 05.53.65.88.95
  Open Monday–Saturday 9 A.M.–noon and 2–6 P.M.

Francescas (Lot-et-Garonne)

Le Relais de la Hire

Here in France's wild Southwest, like every other place in the provinces, business comes to a screeching halt at lunchtime, leaving you with little else to do than to enjoy a leisurely meal. Begin with a *pousse rapière*, the local apéritif concocted from

armagnac liqueur and white wine or Champagne, and settle
yourself into a meal of local epicurean delights in the comely
dining room of this veritable Gascon establishment. A serving
of foie gras is a must, particularly when savored with a glass of
Monbazillac, a regional wine similar to Sauternes.

• 47600 Francescas; tel.: 05.53.65.41.59; fax: 05.53.65.86.42
  Restaurant: Moderate–Expensive
  Open for lunch and dinner Tuesday–Saturday; Sunday lunch
  only

Lavardac (Lot-et-Garonne)

Market: *Marché Nocturne* in the town center
during the summer, 8:30–10:30 P.M.
Friday followed by a country banquet at 11 P.M.

Cristalleries et Verreries d'Art de Viannne

If you've shopped around France a bit you've probably already seen a good
number of the mushroom-shaped, semi-opaque, all-glass lamps that typify
this glassmaker's production. Primarily inspired from the florid works of Art
Nouveau, most of Vianne's mouth-blown and hand-engraved lamps, vases,
and ceiling and wall fixtures tout soft, natural motifs. My favorites include
the classic *pâte de verre* models, which come in a handful of blurry patterns
and colors; prices run about 1,025F for a largish lamp and around 365F for
a medium-sized vase. Allow yourself a good amount of time to tour through
the expansive museum before shopping in the factory store of this nearly
seventy-year-old French classic.

• 47230 Vianne; tel.: 05.53.97.55.05; fax: 05.53.97.50.28
  Open Monday–Friday 9 A.M.–noon and 2–6 P.M.; Saturday and Sunday
  3–7 P.M.

Poudenas (Lot-et-Garonne)

A la Belle Gasconne

If I could choose where to spend a relaxing sojourn in this region
so steeped in history and luxuriant cuisine, I would fall prey to
the graces of this elegant country auberge. Native of the picturesque little village of Poudenas, owner Marie-Claude Gracia

chose this rustic fourteenth-century mill to establish her temple of *la cuisine gasconne*. With five generations of skilled female cooks in her family, Madame Gracia exercises her own culinary expertise for the enjoyment of others in a setting that is truly the epitome of country charm and comfort.

- Poudenas, 47170 Mézin; tel.: 05.53.65.71.58; fax: 05.53.36.63.19
  Hotel/Restaurant: Expensive
  Open March 1–January 2

Villeréal (Lot-et-Garonne)

Château de Born

The only thing that disappointed me about this castle of prunes is that it is only open four months out of the year. The slide show that reveals how a plum becomes a prune is interesting enough, but the real highlights of Château de Born are stocked within their boutique, a unique shop of confections that sells nearly every form of prune imaginable. Reputed to figure among the *pruneaux d'Agen* of the finest quality, you have only to hear about the hand-harvesting of the property's plum trees to understand why. The transformation of the plums into prunes is handled with equal care so that the fruit retains its delicate flavor and moist texture. If you normally shudder at the idea of eating prunes, once you sample some of the château's homemade treats, I assure you that you will adopt an entirely different opinion of this often underappreciated fruit. Apprehensive neophytes should begin by tasting the prunes filled with creamy white or dark chocolate; it won't be long before you become enticed by their plain glossy fruits with just a hint of brandy to enhance their flavor and shine. Other delicious temptations include a jamlike mixture called cream of prunes, other prune confections filled with this smooth spread, and prune chutney, a spicy and fruity condiment that adds a bit of zest to savory dishes and a variety of meats.

- 47210 Villeréal; tel.: 05.53.36.03.03; fax: 05.53.36.63.19
  Open end June–end October daily 2:30–7 P.M.

Villeneuve-sur-Lot (Lot-et-Garonne)

Domaine de Clavié

This handsome guest house gives you another alluring lodging option in the region. The Domaine de Clavié consists of a noble seventeenth-century stonewalled dwelling, perfectly positioned upon its own stretch of glorious land. This is not a hotel, however, so plan well in advance to reserve one or more of its four charming rooms.

• Soubirous, 47300 Villeneuve-sur-Lot; tel.: 05.53.41.74.30; fax: 05.53.41.77.50
Bed-and-Breakfast: Moderate–Expensive; dinner by
   reservation for guests Wednesday and Sunday evenings
Open March 1–January 3

THE REST OF THE SOUTHWEST

Albi (Tarn)

Market and flea market: Cathédrale Ste-Cécile Saturday 8 A.M.–1 P.M.

Initially you may be drawn to this salmon-hued city by its famed Toulouse-Lautrec museum, but allow extra time to observe the many beguiling aspects of Albi, one of the prettiest towns in the Southwest. Touring through the astonishing collection of works at the **Musée Toulouse-Lautrec** (palais de la Berbie; tel.: 05.63.54.14.09) could take you a couple of hours; nowhere else in the world will you see such an extensive compilation of this celebrated artist's paintings, posters, lithographs, and drawings–a rightful homage that Albi pays to its native son. (This prolific collection was in fact donated to the city by the artist's mother after it was refused by the Palais du Luxembourg in Paris!) It's almost a given that you'll pick up a memento in the museum's gift shop, a modest boutique with an adequate selection of books, posters, slides, and postcards.

As you step outside of this medieval bishop's palace, take a look across the street at the Cathédrale Ste-Cécile. The strictly designed brick exterior of this massive structure gives you no clue that virtually every speck of the cathedral's plaster has been painted with brillant frescoes, a vibrant and most breathtaking display of fifteenth- and sixteenth-century artistry. Back out along Albi's sun-drenched streets, you'll encounter a few quaint shops, mostly along rue Mariès, rue de l'Oulmet, and rue de l'Hôtel-de-Ville. It's worth walking out, however, toward the town's fringes to discover the elegant offerings of *artisan chocolatier*, **Michel Belin**, at 4 rue Docteur-Camboulives (tel.: 05.63.54.18.46; fax: 05.63.54.07.12). If you allow yourself only one sinful indulgence, I suggest you choose one of his famed *Melissas*, a silky chocolate subtly flavored with *réglisse* (licorice).

Cordes-sur-Ciel (Tarn)

Market: place de la Bouteillerie Saturday 8 A.M.–1 P.M.

Just a short distance from Albi, the hilltop village of Cordes-sur-Ciel will impress you with its beauty, and if you're an art lover, by its significant population of artists. Classified as one of the most beautiful villages of France and also as one of the region's most fascinating fortified villages, or *bastides*, Cordes attracts visitors throughout the year, although most of its shops and galleries only open during the tourist season, from Easter to mid-October. As you trudge along the unforgiving cobblestones of its medieval streets, remember to occasionally stop and admire the deftly sculpted façades of so many of the village's exceptional Gothic town houses; this will also help you to spot an atelier or two, many of which remain discreetly hidden to all but sincerely interested art lovers. If you see a name plaque, don't hesitate to ring the bell, because any number of artists may be waiting behind their door to present works inspired by the uniqueness of this site.

From what I could see, the range of artistic expression leaps from hand-woven mohair jackets to mystical oil paintings. **Art'Cord**, (place de la Halle; tel.: 05.63.56.19.38) the artists' association of Cordes, is located in the center of the village, and in addition to showcasing a survey selection of most of their members' works, they also can contact the artists directly throughout the year to arrange for them to open especially for you. I found many of the creations fascinating, but was most intrigued by the colorful gouache paintings of **George Delcausse** (tel.: 05.63.56.04.71). In keeping with the medieval theme of the village, this humble man's intensely detailed works resemble illuminated manuscript pages from the Middle Ages; each labor-intensive piece requires three to four months of work, commanding prices between 50,000F to 100,000F. Fortunately, a good many posters and po-stcards reproduced from these works sell here at tourist-friendly prices. The atelier is open year-round.

Whether you decide to treat yourself to a repast or a stay of elegant proportion, or opt to move on to a more affordable option, at least sneak a look around at the village's grandest and most Gothic establishments: the three-star **Hostellerie du Vieux Cordes** (tel.: 05.63.53.79.20; fax: 05.63.56.02.47) or the four-star **Le Grand Ecuyer** (tel.: 05.63.53.79.50; fax: 05.63.53.79.51).

Durfort (Tarn)

Only forty-five minutes from the bustling hubbub of cosmopolitan Toulouse, Durfort is so small that you can barely call it a village. A rugged sight to behold, the view of Durfort's copper foundries nestled at the base of tawny-colored, rocky hills appears straight out of an old western film. The crafting of copperware first began here during the fifteenth century, and the same forceful waters that originally attracted the coppersmiths continues to provide the hydraulic force of today, a most necessary element for the propulsion of the essential tool of this trade: *le martinet*, or tilt hammer. The constant thump, thump, thump that resonates from within the **Pierre Vergnes** workshop is produced by one such hammer that hits the copper 150 times a minute to ultimately give it its desired shape. You can amble in to the Vergnes atelier for a look if your ears can tolerate the deafening noise.

As you can probably tell from the sweat of the brow of the forty or so workers who toil away within this one workshop, all of the Vergnes copperware is handmade, a distinction that must be taken into account when comparing these pieces with those of the better known Norman town of Villedieu-les-Poêles. Monsieur Vergnes claims that many a truck leaves here filled with copperware destined to be sold at Villedieu; I was not able to verify that, but if I were to choose where to make my rosy-colored purchase I would prefer to buy here, where both the setting and the products glow with authenticity. As I stepped outside of the workshop, I encountered a coppersmith crouched by a little stream of water rinsing his newly completed work—gestures, I supposed, that had been carried out like this for more than five centuries.

The Vergnes boutique (tel.: 05.63.74.10.52; fax: 05.63.74.19.90) showcases their copperware along with a small collection of pewter from elsewhere. Some of the pieces are reserved solely for decoration: those that can be used for culinary purposes bear a yellow ticket. You can buy a little decorative planter for 80F or a two-foot-long fish pan for about 1,000F; at 1,050F their five-piece copper casserole set sells for nearly half the price of those of Villedieu, but be sure to make the necessary comparisons (see Villedieu description, page 227). Most of you should be happy to learn that all of the Vergnes copperware has been specially patined (not varnished, as is often the case at Villedieu) so you never have to polish it!

Laguiole (Aveyron)

Unquestionably one of the most rural regions of France, the rugged terrain surrounding the small town of Laguiole in fair weather is typified by muddy-brown farmhouses accented by greyish-white shutters and near mountainlike meadows abloom with a medley of wildflowers. A perfect metaphor for the rustic yet fresh and eloquent knives that bear the name of this in-the-middle-of-nowhere town, a visit to the Aveyron department will leave you feeling as though you have just experienced some of the most untrodden land of France. Laguiole has been rediscovered in recent years thanks to the success of its knives, cutlery that was first crafted here in 1829 until all activity ceased around 1930.

Theirs, the other knife capital of France, took over the monopoly where about 80 percent of Laguiole knives are still manufactured to this day. As the Auvergne chapter explains, Laguiole actually refers to a particular form or style of knife, not a brand name. Much like china in Limoges, the curvilinear Laguiole knives come in varying qualities with the very best ones originating from the town of the same name. The first craftsmen to have relaunched the tradition of quality knife-making in Laguiole started the company **Le Couteau de Laguiole** (tel.: 05.65.48.45.47; fax: 05.65.48.48.50) in 1985; their boutique is located at place du Nouveau-Foirail, just across from the big bull statue in the center of town. All of their knives (and forks) are engraved with a bull, yet they are probably best known for their carbon blades. Although this cutlery is less expensive than other types, the maintenance requires more work since the blades rust easily (these blades are wiped rather than washed, an added effort that has its charm as well). Depending on the model, prices range from 126F to 5,000F.

In addition to the characteristic slender and stylized shape, all Laguiole knives are marked by a raised bee at the joint where the blade bends down into the handle. In the beginning, this served as a mark of quality initiated under the Napoleon regime; do not, however, automatically think that this is true today, because even the made-in-Taiwan Laguiole knives that often turn up in less scrupulous boutiques often bear this same imperial emblem. There's no doubting the quality of the goods at the fashion-forward **La Forge de Laguiole**, located at 8 allée de l'Amicale (tel.: 05.65.44.30.85; fax: 05.65.44.37.66). The striking apotheosis of a Philippe Starck creation, France's leading style dictator has once again wielded his illustrious sword in the designing of this sleek boutique. La Forge is the only company to claim that its pieces, including handles *and* blades, are entirely handcrafted by the ninety or so cutlers at work in their atelier. As you peer into the contemporary display cases at La Forge, you will most certainly marvel at their cutting edge pieces designed by Starck, Sonia Rykiel, and other prominent names that have been crafted out of exotic woods and synthetic materials such as Bakélite—but chances are you will settle on one of the true Laguiole classics, alluring pieces for even the most untraditional types. Their atelier on *route de l'Aubrac* is open Monday through Friday for visits, and you can also buy there at prices identical to those of their boutique.

Sophisticated types should not envision traveling to the near godforsaken town of Laguiole without considering a mega-splurge *chez* **Michel Bras** (tel.: 05.65.44.32.24; fax: 05.65.48.47.02). A lesson in refinement, simplicity, and harmony between minimalistic space and prosaic countryside awaits you here in this temple of *la haute gastronomie française.* You can expect nothing less than twenty-five different vegetables and herbs in your starter salad, an astonishing meadow mix selected from the neighboring hills by the innovative Michel Bras. The rest of what you find on your plates will only further elevate your palate, provoking an incomparable culinary sensitivity that will leave you looking at cuisine in an entirely different light. The utensils have been crafted into pure streamlined shapes by La Forge. Zenlike rooms in this luxury hotel may also be retained.

Millau (Aveyron)

If you begin to explore Millau, the glove capital of France, you may wonder why this town claims so many *gantiers*, or glove makers. The majority of the gloves made here have been fashioned out of lambskin, and Millau's activity is linked with that of nearby Roquefort, the town whose name is the same as the world's best-loved ewe's milk cheese. Cheese-making first began in Roquefort in the ninth century, and by the eleventh century locals caught on to the fact that the skins of these little lambs could also be put to use. Roquefort's activity engendered that of Millau, and by the nineteenth century, Millau prospered tremendously from the numerous tanning and glove-making businesses that capitalized upon the fashion of those times: the wearing of gloves for nearly every occasion, big or small.

Millau's handmade glove-making industry of today continues to flourish in more specialized areas, each of which caters to a number of different worlds: one maker satisfies the sporting arena with his gloves for boxing, golf, and motorcycling; another picks up the slack with his collection of ski, bicycle, and sports-car-driving gloves while someone else handles hunting and riding requirements, filling orders for celebrated houses such as Hermès. Others take care of special creations for the army and police, particular orthopedic needs, and, of course, *la haute couture.* Standard stylish gloves have not been forgotten, either, and you can discover *and* buy at the more than half a dozen ateliers dispersed around town.

The **Maison de la Peau et du Gant de Millau** at 1 rue St-Antoine (tel.: 05.65.61.25.93; fax: 05.65.61.35.87) can readily provide a list of these makers and more, but ask them to indicate which ones best correspond with your needs. I descended directly upon **Lavabre Cadet** at Impasse Charles-Gounod (tel.: 05.65.61.34.79), one of Millau's most exclusive glove makers whose atelier you can visit; they were working on flashy gloves for Claude Montana and Chanel the day I came by, but those weren't for sale. Their prices are as enticing as their gloves, all of which have been hand-stitched out of the most supple lambskin, kid, and even a few exotic leathers. Be advised that, as with the other ateliers, credit cards are not accepted.

Before you set out to achieve glove-buying nirvana, take a tour through the **Musée de Millau** at place du Maréchal-Foch (tel.: 05.65.59.01.08), a glorious glove museum, where in addition to permanent exhibitions about the history and trade of glove-making, exciting temporary exhibitions the likes of *Hermès à Millau* will captivate you by their information and presentation.

Roquefort (Aveyron)

Roquefort Société

Before you arrive at these famous cheese cellars, you will most likely spot a folkloric-looking gent in a simple countryman's cap and handlebar mustache on posters displayed around the area. By no means is this man, nor the hundreds of cheese wheels that surround him, a creation of an advertising whiz's imagination. This humble-looking *monsieur*, who epitomizes tradition and savoir faire at its country-French best, is in fact *le maître affineur* or master cheese maker at Roquefort, a company that produces 16,000 tons of cheese annually for over eighty countries throughout the world. This fact should tune you in to the authenticity and highly revered quality of this company's products, because as much as the actual cheese-making process has become more industrialized, the aging of every single wheel still takes place in the unique and naturally antiseptic environment of Roquefort's centuries-old cellars.

You will learn all about this and more during one of the regularly scheduled tours that takes place at Société's unpasteurized ewe's milk stronghold, and I assure you that you will never look at one of their cheeses the same way ever again. To further nourish this new found discovery, you may want to purchase some souvenir articles in their boutique, stocked with an abundance of cheeses, books, posters, Laguiole knives, and plates and knickknacks emblazoned with the green blue Société logo.

- 12250 Roquefort-sur-Soulzon; tel.: 05.65.58.58.58; fax: 05.65.59.97.14
  Open daily 9:30 A.M.–12:30 P.M. and 2–5 P.M.

Toulouse (Haute-Garonne)

TGV: 5 hours
Main shopping streets: rue du Taur, rue d'Alsace-Lorraine,
rue Croix-Baragnon
Markets: Les Halles, place Victor-Hugo Tuesday–Sunday; 7 A.M.– 1 P.M.
place du Capitole Wednesday 8 A.M.–1 P.M.
Flea market: St-Sernin Sunday 8 A.M.–1 P.M.

Toulouse is known as *la ville rose* (pink city) because most of it was built of rosy-colored bricks made from clay extracted from the Garonne river bed. No nickname could more appropriately describe the many attributes, both physical and otherwise, of this softly seductive urban center. With some 200,000 students making up almost half of the city's population, Toulouse can't help but buzz with animation; add to that a good dose of southwestern sunshine, and you have a town guaranteed to enliven the weariest traveler. The riches amassed by many a Toulousian family from the pastel dye trade of the sixteenth century left behind splendorous town houses that make walks through the city's streets today all the more interesting. (Don't hesitate to step into the courtyards to fully appreciate the architectural beauty of these Renaissance wonders.)

For a French cityscape of great proportion, go directly to the immense place du Capitole, the nexus of Toulouse, which becomes even more lively on Wednesdays when a large market occupies part of this seemingly endless square. Keep in mind also that a large underground parking lot lies underneath the *place*, which should prove useful if you are traveling by car. Situated just a short distance from Capitole is **Busquets** (10 rue de Rémusat, tel.: 05.61.21.22.16; fax: 05.61.23.88.37), a family-owned gourmet food and liquor store known to be one of the best in the city. All of the *spécialités du Sud-Ouest* are here in force: *foie gras, confit,* and *cassoulet* make up the Southwestern trinity, three cholesterol-rich foods that will leave you dreaming of this region long after you've enjoyed them at home. Myriad robust Southwestern wines are available to accompany these and many more savory dishes; you'll also find a good representation of armagnac, floc de Gascogne, and violet liqueur. Violets are in fact the flower of Toulouse, and if you are not able to experience the joy of buying a fresh bouquet on la place du Capitole during the short season that occurs in winter, you may want to buy a box or two of candied violets, precious blooms that have been forever locked in sugar. Perfect for decorating cakes or fresh fruit salads, these delicate confections will surely make a hit at your next gathering.

If you're looking for more goods made from *violettes*, try stopping in at the *pâtissier/chocolatier* **Régals** (25 rue du Taur, tel.: 05.61.21.64.86), a little pastry shop that sells a wide variety of violet-based products including this flower's delightfully scented *parfum de toilette*. Just a short distance away at 9 rue du Taur, you can give the prestigious chocolate maker **Michel Belin** (tel.: 05.61.23.40.31) a try, particularly if you missed his shop in Albi. If you're interested in hard-to-find books in *langue d'oc* (the regional tongue), go to **Librairie Occitania** at 46 rue du Taur (tel.: 05.61.21.49.00). For less esoteric literary or picture-book finds of the Southwest, visit the large bookstore **Castéla** at 20 place du Capitole (tel.: 05.61.23.24.24; fax: 05.61.29.03.24), where you'll find many beautiful books on the region's *châteaux*, *bastides*, Romanesque architecture, and much more.

Toulouse's history-laden grande rue Nazareth, rue Perchepinte, and rue Fermat offer antiquing at its finest. It's hard to get lost along this sweep of streets, each of which leads into the other, and you may want to seek out the side streets as well. There's enough to keep you going for hours—but whatever you do, be sure to plan a break at the nostalgia-imbued tearoom, **Rose Thé**, at 6 rue Fermat (tel.: 05.61.55.33.56). If you are a serious devotee of French antiques, plan to come here during November for the city's famed **Salon des Antiquaires**. Nearly every city of France claims an annual antiques show, although the offerings at this one remain among the most envious. Dealers and individuals alike clamor to lay their hands on prized goods from this great sale; and whether the merchandise is of investment-level range or of medium quality, it is known to be a bargain. This could very well be the sort of event to plan your trip around. For more information contact *le Salon* at tel.: 05.61.21.93.25; fax: 05.61.23.14.72.

In terms of accommodations, this leading city of French technology offers many options. The four-star **Le Grand Hôtel de l'Opéra** (tel.: 05.61.21.82.66; fax: 05.61.23.41.04), just off la place du Capitole, is the most obvious choice, but don't let its prominence deter you from discovering its more intimate charms. All of the rooms are decorated in a flood of cozy fabrics, and if you land one facing the courtyard, you may feel as if you are lodging at a Tuscan villa. Both of the hotel's restaurants will leave you reveling in the flavors of the Southwest; depending on your mood, level of fatigue, and budget, choose from the brasserie-style **Le Grand Café de l'Opéra** (tel.: 05.61.21.37.03) or the more high brow **Les Jardins de l'Opéra** (tel.: 05.61.23.07.76; fax: 05.61.23.41.04).

Outside Toulouse (Haute-Garonne)

Aerospatiale Taxiway

Despite my special contacts and assorted pleas, I was not allowed to visit Aerospatiale, the European headquarters for Airbus planes, without an appointment, especially when the staff heard that I was American. It didn't matter that the U.S. buys the greatest number of these Euro-designed and constructed airplanes; Americans and citizens of most European countries must phone at least forty-eight hours in advance to arrange a tour of these high-security facilities (the Japanese and visitors from other countries have to put in their request even earlier). Unlike the construction of planes at Boeing in Seattle, the assemblage and finishing touches of the various Airbus flying machines is more analagous to piecing together a giant puzzle, since most of the parts are flown in from around Europe in the bellies of Super Guppies.

If you miss the tour, pick up a few souvenir items in the Taxiway shop, most of which have been stamped with the Aerospatiale name and logo. Highlights include aerodynamically designed pens and lighters, sporty watches, model plane kits of their fleet, a variety of books and T-shirts, and more.

- avenue Jean-Monnet, 31770 Colomiers; tel.: 05.61.15.44.00 (to reserve); fax: 05.61.18.08.51
  Factory Visit/Boutique
  Open Monday–Saturday 9 A.M.–12:30 P.M. and 2–6 P.M.;
  Visits by appointment only

THE WESTERN LOIRE
Pays de Loire

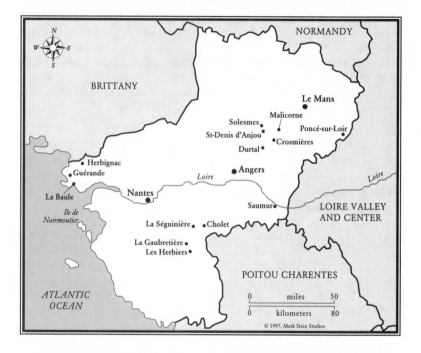

half hulls • *berlingots* • stoneware • fish soup • preppy clothes • artful ceramics • *sel de Guérande* • pottery • Petits Beurres • sablés • Cointreau • Gregorian chants • high-styled hats • marine attire and gear • antiques • art by local artists • equestrian boots • pewter • Saumur Brut • nautical décor items • faience • bluish chocolates • wines • classic house linens • bath salts • chic fashions • pipes made from morta • discount clothing and shoes

THE LOIRE VALLEY is one of the primary tourist destinations in France, known for the world's most spectacular castles. But what about the other part of the Loire Valley, which begins just east of Saumur and continues past Angers and Nantes until this broad and treacherous river finally empties out into the Atlantic? As a region, this part of the Loire is referred to as *les Pays de la Loire*, or the Western Loire.

People who promote tourism here always have to explain themselves—

humbly admitting that they are *the other Loire*. To make matters worse, the westernmost part of the Western Loire is often confused with Brittany.

Whatever way people refer to this part of the country, its geographic location provides it with tremendous advantages. Not only is it relatively close to Paris (Nantes is only two hours from the capital by TGV; Angers and Saumur are within a few hours' driving distance from Paris), but it also is situated at a major crossroads. Whether you're on your way to Brittany, the Atlantic coast, or the Southwest, traveling from Paris to the Western Loire represents only a minor detour. Not identifiable by one particular trait, *les Pays de Loire* offers a little bit of everything: fertile farmlands, green pastures, soothing seascapes, medieval fortresses, and even a château or two. And if you enjoy touring vineyards, there are many more of them here than in the "other Loire." Best of all, the shopping is great!

Angers (Maine-et-Loire)

TGV: 2 hours
Main shopping streets: rue St-Laud, rue Lenepveu, rue Toussaint, rue
St-Aubin
Markets: place Leclerc Saturday 9 A.M.–1 P.M.
Flea market: place Imbach Saturday 9 A.M.–1 P.M.

I had already visited Saumur, the vineyards of Anjou (the region surrounding Angers), and even Nantes a couple of times in the past, but for some reason I kept missing Angers. My preconceived notion of Angers was totally wrong. Somehow I had envisioned a more industrialized city, but in fact I discovered a pleasant town whose quiet yet stimulating spirit seems woven from the rich fiber of its past.

Visitors are first greeted by the most imposing landmark of the city, the Angers Castle, a mighty fortress constructed at the early part of the Middle Ages. I quickly found that its austere and forboding presence has little to do with the mood that permeates much of this fine city. College students hustle about in the nearby maze of medieval streets while shoppers browse around the store-lined pedestrian thoroughfares that distinguish the center of town.

Angers is an antique-lover's paradise and I was told that that is because the *patrimoine* (patrimony) is particularly rich in this part of France. Some of the best finds turn up at **EMMAUS**, a sort of French version of the Salvation Army, and dealers come from near and far in search of the best pickings at the lowest prices. EMMAUS is located in the village St-Jean-de-Linières along the RN 24 just outside of the city; open Wednesday through Saturday from 2 to 6 P.M.

Scanning the antique shops in the center of town is not as adventurous, but it will give you an opportunity to take in some of the more historic buildings and streets of Angers. Be sure to wear comfortable walking shoes as you navigate the cobblestoned ways of the medieval section. The array of half-timbered houses is particularly impressive, and although its touristy shopping may not be to your liking, **La Maison d'Adam** at the place Ste-Croix is a must. Most of the antique shops are situated along the rue Toussaint, but those on the rue Montault and the rue de l'Oisellerie should not be missed either.

Les Etains de France

Etain means "pewter," and this store presents three floors of it in an unparalleled setting that is worthy of the honorable *ducs d'Anjou*. This family enterprise has been crafting pewter since 1710, and it is all affectionately displayed in the warm and hearty interior of this resplendent fifteenth-century dwelling.

The top floor is a minimuseum that presents pewter pieces and tools from centuries past. Most of the towns of France had their own foundries during the eighteenth century; with the advent of faience and then porcelain, nearly all of them closed, making this one in Angers the most important.

Here the pewter has been crafted into a seemingly endless variety of traditional forms: candlesticks, platters, tea services, and lamps, to name a few. Three disparate finishes are used to give an entirely different feeling to each of the works: the polished finish makes the piece look like silver; the matte patina looks like the pewter, with which we are most familar; and the patina *à l'ancienne* creates the most rustic look of all. Prices start at 40F for a little trinket and go up as far as 4,000F for a soup terrine (with tray and ladle) *à l'ancienne*.

Unfortunately, the magnificent pieces of antique furniture used to display the pewter are not for sale.

- Logis de l'Estaignier (7 rue des Filles-Dieu), 49100 Angers; tel.:
  02.41.88.67.41
  Open year-round Monday–Saturday 9:30 A.M.–noon and 2:30–7 P.M.;
  closed Monday during July and August

Maison des Vins d'Anjou et de Saumur

If you don't have time to visit some of the outlying vineyards, or if you want the chance to taste the greatest number of local wines under one roof, don't miss this store. Located just across the street from the castle, this house prides itself on selling nearly fifty of the finest wines of the region, all AOC (*appellation d'origine contrôlée*).

The welcome is particularly heartwarming, and it's fun to taste and learn about the local wines with some of the people who know them the best. Unfortunately the store does not handle shipping so if you are looking to bring home more than a few bottles, you may want to taste-test here, then contact the wine growers directly.

- 5 bis place Kennedy, 49100 Angers; tel.: 02.41.87.43.01; fax: 02.41.86.71.84

  Open Tuesday–Sunday 9 A.M.–1 P.M. and 3–6:30 P.M. Closed January and February; closed Sunday in March and October–December.

La Petite Marquise

Blue slate roofs typify much of Anjou, so why not make a chocolate in honor of these legendary tiles? That was precisely why this *pâtissier/confiseur* created a candy called *Quernon d'Ardoise* in 1961. Instant success lead to near worldwide recognition, and now these little *Quernons* are sold in over 100 different locations in and outside of France (except the U.S., where the FDA said no to the bluish coloring of these treats). Buy them here, where they are made fresh every day.

As I bit in to this chocolate-covered toffee I instantly thought, Fanny Farmer, eat your heart out. The smooth, creamy texture of the outside (which is actually made from white chocolate), contrasted with the flaky interior, is equally as astonishing as the luminous blue-violet color of this sweet. The boxes are handsomely decorated with an old scene of tile workers toiling with Angers in the distance. Bright orange boxes contain other house specialties called *Rairies* (little chocolate "tiles" filled with a praline-and-Cointreau mixture) and *Plantagenets* (a mix of milk and dark chocolates).

- 22 rue des Lices; 49100 Angers; tel.: 02.41.87.43.01; fax: 02.41.87.70.13

  Open Monday 2–7:30 P.M.; Tuesday–Friday 9 A.M.–7:30 P.M.; Saturday 8 A.M.–7:30 P.M.; Sunday 8 A.M.–1 P.M.

Around Angers (Maine-et-Loire)

Cointreau

I always knew that Cointreau was French, but I didn't realize that it came from Angers. You can develop a far greater appreciation for this world-famous liqueur, found in every bar from Poughkeepsie to Johannesburg, by visiting the Cointreau distillery just outside of Angers.

The history of this venerated house is fascinating. Monsieur Cointreau started out in 1849 in the city of Angers as a *confiseur* (confectioner) and ended up becoming highly regarded for his assortments of *liqueur aux fruits*. The liqueur with the orange flavor was the most popular, and by 1875 Monsieur Cointreau was exporting his bottles of orange-flavored liqueur to the four corners of the world (hence the four-cornered bottle).

I almost swooned upon entering the distillery—not from the beauty of the stills, but from the heady aroma of orange peel that lingers in the air . . .

or was it the 96 percent alcohol that they achieve in the first part of the distillation process? I felt as though I was coming up for air as I entered the bar that concludes the visit.

Château de Noirieux

Who said that château life was not a part of the Western Loire? The Château de Noirieux is a perfect example of the sort of elegant, lordly living one can experience in this part of France. I suggest that you hole up here for a few days to enjoy the sweetness and tranquility of the Anjou countryside. There is much to see in the area, but the peacefulness of this site along the Loir river (yes, the Loir—not the Loire), the beauty of the immense park, and the comfort and exquisite décor of the seventeenth-century château and the fifteenth-century manor house just might keep you from going anywhere else.

If you have a penchant for flowery chintz and immense bedrooms and baths, you might never leave your luxurious *chambre*—if only for a contemplative visit to their sixteenth-century chapel or for a leisurely meal in their sunflower yellow dining room.

- 26 route du Moulin; 49125 Briollay; tel.: 02.41.42.50.05; fax: 02.41.37.91.00
  Four-Star Hotel: Expensive
  Open year-round; restaurant closed Sunday evening and Monday mid-October–mid-April

---

The drink of the day was the Caïpirinha, a margarita-like cocktail concocted with copious doses of fresh-crushed lime and ice. One of the members of the Cointreau family derived inspiration for this drink during a visit to Brazil, and it has become a favorite of the house ever since. The décor in the adjacent shop is quite ordinary, but it's fun to buy one of these red-ribboned bottles of Cointreau where it is produced.

- Z.I. St-Barthélemy; Croix Blanche; boulevard des Bretonnières; BP 79; 49181 St-Barthélemy-d'Anjou Cédex; tel.: 02.41.43.25.21; fax: 02.41.60.31.71
  Distillery Visits/Boutique
  Open June 15–September 15: tours Monday–Friday 10 and 11 A.M. and 2, 3, 4 and 5 P.M.; Saturdays, Sundays, and holidays 3 and 4:30 P.M.; September 16–June 14: tours Monday–Friday by appointment; Sundays and holidays 3 and 4:30 P.M.

La Baule (Loire-Atlantique)

Main shopping streets: avenue du Général-Charles-de-Gaulle,
avenue Pierre-Lotti, avenue Louis-Lajarrige
Markets: place du Marché Tuesday–Sunday 8 A.M.–1 P.M.
Flea market: jardin de la Victoire
Sunday 8 A.M.–1 P.M.

Most known for its 9 kilometers of beach, its glitzy casino, its reputed health spa, and its many golf courses, one of which is part of the Jack Nicklaus Academy of Golf, La Baule is one of the most overlooked resort destinations in France. Although it is not highly frequented by foreigners, the French love it—especially Parisians from the 16th arrondissement (or other points west) and the *haute bourgeoisie* of Nantes. These people, along with the abundance of sports and volumes of fresh, salty air, set a distinctively BCBG (*bon chic bon genre*) tone at La Baule. This version of French preppiness shows in everything from the classically styled boutiques to the well-heeled families actively participating in a range of open-air sports, from sailing to kite-flying on the seemingly endless sweep of sandy beach.

The main shopping street is the avenue du Général-Charles-de-Gaulle, which runs perpendicular to the waterfront. Like the people you encounter here, the shops along this street look distinctively *seizième*, or, in other words, very much like Eddie Bauer and L. L. Bean. The avenues Pierre-Lotti and Louis Lajarrige, along with the little mall (**L'Espace François André**) next to the Hôtel Royal, offer shops of a more cosmopolitan flavor.

Thalgo

France's thalassic spas or *centres de thalassothérapie* are mentioned in the Brittany and Biarritz chapters, but I can speak firsthand about the spa at La Baule because I had the luxury of spending a few days here, padding about in this mellifluous microcosm of the sea. If you spend only a short time browsing around the impeccably designed boutique, you, too, will realize why this center is inarguably one of the most sought-out in all of Europe. The luminous blond wood interior of this *thalasso* fosters a sense of serenity and relaxation. Once you shift into this mode, your body is ready to accept the many wondrous and often surprising treatments of the ever-so-discreet technicians of this seawater spa. Two of the most confounding include the *bain d'algues* (seaweed bath) and the *application d'algues*, in which I was slathered with a mixture of seaweed goo and then rolled and wrapped in a heated silvery blanketlike covering. Although I was being cooked, I felt a little like a human-sized sushi! These treatments (or in French spa-speak, *soins*), along with all of the other heavy-duty caretaking that goes on here, have been designed so that the rich elements and minerals of the saltwater and seaweed can best penetrate, massage, soothe, and consequently heal your body. Afterward, I was in such a jellyfish-like state that I was perfectly content to take a short snooze in the sublime solarium.

Thalgo offers several minitreatments that you can experience even if you are just passing through. They sell so many of their own fine-quality beauty products that you can easily continue their program of pampering long after you've arrived home.

- avenue Marie-Louise, BP 50, 44503 La Baule; tel.:
  02.40.11.99.99; fax: 02.40.60.55.17
  Spa/Boutique
  Open Tuesday–Sunday 9:45 A.M.–1 P.M. and 3–7 P.M.

Le Castel Marie-Louise

Originally the private home of François André, the man who developed La Baule as a fashionable seaside resort at the turn of the century and also founded the exclusive Lucien Barrière hotel chain, Le Castel Marie-Louise is certainly the most charming luxury hotel in the area. One could easily imagine Monsieur André's wife, Marie-Louise, for whom the hotel has been named, nodding approvingly at the choice of delicate floral prints and antique furnishings that adorn the hotel's thirty-one rooms and main dining room.

The ambiance is similar to what you might experience in a typical English manor, although instead of looking out upon a country landscape, you gaze out at the great expanse of the Atlantic. The main dining room becomes awash with such an intense amount of light that even on a grey day the luminous view can lift your spirits. With a menu composed of the freshest products that the region has to offer, you can experience both the beauty and the bounty of the Atlantic at this fine seaside establishment.

- 1 avenue Andrieu, 44504 La Baule; tel: 02.40.11.48.38; fax:
  02.40.11.48.35
  Four-Star Relais & Châteaux Hotel/Restaurant: Expensive
  Open year-round except from mid-January–mid-February

Hôtel Royal

If you decide to check yourself in to Thalgo for a few days or even a week of treatments (a two-week program is said to provide the maximum benefit), consider going the whole nine yards and reserve a room at this elegant establishment next door. The beauty of this is that you can stroll over to the spa in bathrobe and slippers without anyone batting an eye; you don't have to go outside, since a passageway was built for this very purpose. If your intention is to shed a few pounds, you can also benefit from the hotel restaurant's *menus diététiques*–although I preferred to indulge in their excellent cuisine. Even if you're not here for the spa, if you like big, beautiful seaside hotels, you'll enjoy staying here because le Royal is indisputably the grandest of them all.

- 6 avenue Pierre-Loti, 44504 La Baule; 02.40.11.48.48; fax: 02.40.11.48.45
  Hotel/Restaurant: Expensive
  Open year-round

Beyond La Baule (Loire-Atlantique)

Maison du Sel/Ets. Pradel

Someone once told me that a special salt called *sel de Guérande* was one of France's most extraordinary condiments. My visit to the salt marshes of Guérande later revealed the sheer uniqueness of this product. Although only 5 kilometers from the charming and historic medieval village of Guérande, the Pradel establishment takes some effort to find (I was later reassured that signs to more clearly guide visitors to this center would soon be posted). The first clue that I was going to experience the salt of the earth–or rather, the salt of the sea–came when I met Monsieur Charles Perraud, the head of this cooperative of more than 150 salt farmers who produce *sel de Guérande*.

Monsieur Perraud's weathered features, strong hands, and long, wavy hair made me think of him as a sort of *marin-fermier*–part sailor, part farmer. The process of harvesting the salt of the Atlantic has been carried out in this far-western corner of the Western Loire since the seventh century. The harvest takes place during the heat of the summer, mostly from June to September, when the wind and the sun cooperate to accelerate the evaporation of water from the intricate maze of canals that have been dug in the rich clay soil.

Once crystallization has occurred, the salt farmer delicately rakes off layer after layer of various types of salt.

The top crust, which is also the most refined despite its moist, milky appearance, is the *crème de la crème* of the Guérande salts. This is referred to as *fleur de sel*, and I was told that many a French chef both in France and abroad sprinkle a bit of this salt on their dishes just before they are served. The flavor is supposedly the richest in the world, and does wonders for dishes as simple as mashed potatoes or roasted chicken.

For those who consider salt to be an unhealthy component of your daily diet, it is important to note that *sel de Guérande* is so rich in calcium, magnesium, and potassium that it is sold in health-food stores as well as gourmet food shops throughout France.

In addition to several different types of salt, including bath salts, the coop's little shop (which looks more like a fish stand than a boutique) sells various types of vinegars and salt boxes as well as *salicornes*, an edible algae-like plant that grows along the marshes. Prices for this range of gift items start at 12F for a kilo of *gros sel* (typical sea salt) and go up to 150F for a gift package of products from Guérande.

On Sundays in the summer the cooperative runs an animated local market that offers a range of regional products, food, music, and dance for all.

• BP 44350 Guérande; tel.: 02.40.62.08.80; fax: 02.40.24.79.84
  Visits/Boutique
  Tours of the marshes are conducted daily from April to September

Patrice Sébilo

Traveling from Guérande to Herbignac provides a delicious sampling of some of France's wildest terrain. This region, which is referred to as the *Parc Naturel Regional de Brière*, furnishes views of relatively untouched marshlands and even an occasional glimpse at a rare bird that may have chosen this area as its stopping point en route to a warmer climate south of the border. Had I not been tipped off, I most certainly would not have found the unassuming shop of Monsieur Patrice Sébilo.

Nature seekers might enjoy the ride, but pipe smokers will rejoice at the small yet exclusive selection of pipes crafted by Monsieur Sébilo. Although the town of St-Claude in the Jura has long been known for its pipe making, Monsieur Sébilo is unique in his use of a certain wood, called morta, that has quietly soaked up minerals in the nearby marshland for over 5,000 years. This oak from the marshes is known for its deep ebony color and distinctive taste. Monsieur Sébilo proudly confided that he once received a letter from an Englishman saying his pipes were superior to those of Dunhill!

Prices on these entirely handmade pipes range from 200F to 3,000F. The supply, however, is limited; there were only twelve the day I stopped by, and only 350 are made per year. Monsieur explained that he has trouble finding this rare wood, and often there are too many cracks in a piece for it to be carved into a pipe. Monsieur also applies his carving skills to a collection of pens; prices run 550F to 900F for those made of rosewood, olivewood, and ebony, while those in morta cost as much as 1,500F.

- 16 avenue de la Monneraye, 44410 Herbignac; tel.: 02.40.88.98.08
  Open daily in season 9:30 A.M.–7:30 P.M.; closed Wednesday all day and Sunday afternoon during off-season

---

Crêperie Derwin

Just about five kilometers outside of La Baule, along *la côte sauvage*, this truly authentic crêperie serves crispy crêpes and steamy mussels in a handsome, rustic décor. You really have to be "in the know" to find this place. Even the calling card that I picked up in remembrance of a wonderful evening spent here with my mother many years ago was lacking a phone number, clearly implying that one can not reserve—so be prepared for a bit of a wait, especially in the height of the tourist season.

- Rue du Golf, 44740 Batz-sur-Mer
  Crêperie: Inexpensive–Moderate
  Open from Easter to end of September

Cholet (Maine-et-Loire)

Cholet (pronounced *show-lay*) and its surrounding region means shopping, mostly at factory outlet stores. Since the seventeenth and eighteenth centuries, textile production has been a major activity here, mostly because labor traditionally is less expensive in this part of rural France. Toward the end of the nineteenth century the shoe industry also took hold, and today it is the most important region in France for the manufacturing of *la chaussure*.

Unfortunately most of the brands that originate here are relatively unknown to foreigners, although many such as Naf Naf, Catimini, New Man, and Gaston Jaunet are favorites amongst the French and other Europeans. You will not find any big names, although *semi-luxe* articles abound. I have listed a few of my favorites among the twenty-five or so factory-outlet stores within the area. You can spot many of them in your travels, or ask for the complete listing at the tourism office in the center of town at the place Rougé.

La Bonne Toile de Cholet

This grandmotherly shop just a few steps from the tourism office is not a factory-outlet store but instead the showplace for a variety of fine-quality house and table linens that have been manufactured in Cholet for more than 150 years.

Although the setting does not complement them, most of the linens are of a very fine quality, particularly those from the house of Turpault, which has been in the textile industry since 1847. Look for the blue flower, which is the Cholet label of excellence, and try to envision the beauty of a 100 percent linen pillowcase (about 400F each) enveloping a fluffy pillow in your own home. Their red and white 100 percent cotton tablecloths (390F to 600F) lend themselves particularly well to a table for a country buffet.

The red and white pattern in these table linens, and particularly in the handkerchiefs, is the symbol of Cholet, and as the story goes the people from this region (*les Vendéens*) wore white hankerchiefs on their heads in 1793 during the war of the Vendée as a symbol of their loyalty to the crown. The handkerchief is more red than white, however, which represents the bloodiness of this ghastly war. You can buy three handkerchiefs for about 75F.

- 2 avenue Gambetta; 49300 Cholet; tel.: 02.41.62.29.70
  Open Monday 2–7:15 P.M.; Tuesday–Saturday 9 A.M.–12 P.M. and 2–7:15 P.M.

Club des Marques

The New Man label may not sound French, but their classically styled sportswear for men and women most definitely has a French flair. The clothing is manufactured here, so you are apt to find some of the best deals ever buying directly from this factory store. The same is true for Coup de Coeur, a wildly popular label in France that launched the trend of fantastical boxer shorts more than ten years ago. Their matching sleepwear and oversized slippers (for adults and children) can be just as addictive.

- Z.I. du Cormier, 49300 Cholet; tel.: 02.41.56.88.45
  Open Monday 2–7 P.M.; Tuesday–Friday 10 A.M.–noon and 2–7 P.M.; Saturday 10 A.M.–7 P.M.

Beyond Cholet (Vendée)

Albert

About 25 kilometers south of Cholet in Les Herbiers, this huge factory outlet sells trendy garb for babies, kids, and some adults. Fashions from French clothing manufacturers such as Naf Naf, Galipette, Kidokay, Chevignon, and would you believe, UCLA (pronounced *you-klah*) sell at 30 to 70 percent off. Some fashions are the previous year's; others are seconds or end of series.

During the summer season, you may want to combine a stop here with a visit to the Puy du Fou, (for information call 02.51.64.11.11), a château that features one of the best *son et lumière* (sound-and-light) shows in all of France.

• Zone La Buzenière, BO 104, 85503 Les Herbiers Cédex; tel.: 02.51.66.91.00; fax: 02.51.67.29.28
  Open Monday–Friday 9:30 A.M.–12:30 P.M. and 2–7 P.M., Saturday 9:30 A.M.–7 P.M.

Catimini

Wonderfully whimsical and colorful designs are the hallmark of Catimini's togs for babies and children. These well-made and highly creative fashions command steep retail prices, so plan to stock up at this outlet where the savings are great.

• 7 rue des Artisans, 49280 La Séguinière; tel.: 02.41.56.06.22
  Open Monday 2–7 P.M., Tuesday–Friday 10 A.M.–12:30 P.M. and 2–7 P.M., Saturday 10 A.M.–7 P.M.

L'Entrepôt

Shoes, shoes, shoes! If you have not heard of the brands Freelance or Pom d'Api, it is about time you get to know them. Some of the hottest French designs in shoe apparel are found under these labels, most of which promote an imaginative mixture of fun and funk. Pom d'Api takes care of the kids, but it's up to you to decide whether you're ready to plunge into a pair of clunkers from Freelance—all at factory discount prices.

• 38 rue du Commandant, 85130 La Gaubretière; tel.: 02.51.66.36.65
  Open Monday–Friday 10 A.M.–noon and 2–7 P.M.; Saturday 10 A.M.–6 P.M.

Nantes (Loire-Atlantique)

TGV: 2 ½ hours
Major shopping streets: rue Crébillon, rue Franklin, rue du Calvaire, quartier Decré
Markets: place Talensac and place Bouffay Tuesday–Sunday 7 A.M.–1 P.M.
Flower market: place du Commerce daily 8 A.M.–7 P.M.
Flea markets: place Viarme Sunday 8 A.M.–1 P.M.

Once the stronghold of the *ducs de Bretagne* and today the capital of the *Pays de la Loire*, the city of Nantes has a history and culture that represents a distinctive blend of the two westernmost regions of France: Brittany and Western Loire. At the crossings of the Loire and Erdre rivers and only 50 kilometers inland from the Atlantic, Nantes owes its prosperity to the sea, while the city's greenery is Loire-esque. This unique geographical position allows the *nantais* to embrace the riches of both the land and the water.

Commercial trade boomed here during the eighteenth century as Nantes became one of the most important ports of France, and the magnificent buildings are reminders that many a merchant became rich from the trade of everything from spices to slaves. Nantes is still considered one of the wealthier cities of the provinces, and this stroke of good fortune has endowed the city with an architectural affluence that only enhances a visit.

The shopping is not too shoddy either, and it seems to be the favorite pastime of the residents of this fine city. Most of the exclusive boutiques are lined up along the rue Crébillon, and from this name comes the verb *crébilloner*, which means "to browse or shop" along this lovely street. Start at the elegant place Royale and just *crébillon* your way up both sides of this street.

At the foot of the rue de Budapest along the rue Mercoeur and the rue Jean-Jaurès you will discover a number of antique shops that sell goods of collector's quality. Be sure to peek in at the **Librairie Guimard** at 23 *bis* rue Jean-Jaurès, where you will find a copious collection of posters, postcards, and old books.

Amarine

You are sure to find your way onto the rue Franklin, one of the most important shopping destinations of the city. At the lower end of this street, you will discover Amarine–La Mer en Boutique, a very attractive shop that sells a variety of *objets*, all with a nautical theme.

For your cruiser at home, you can pick up a few brass plaques (about 100F apiece) that indicate the various parts of your vessel, or a barometer or thermometer with French markings. What chic! If you don't have a boat of your own to outfit, you can content yourself with more ornamental works such as a model clipper ship (6,500F) or wooden eggs hand-painted with naïf seascapes (270F to 1,150F); you also can choose from a vast selection of wall decorations that represent the types of *noeuds marins* (marine knots) used in France, with such names as *jambes de chien* (dog's legs); *noeud de vache* (cow knot); and *noeud de chaise* (chair knot).

• 2 rue Franklin, 44000 Nantes; tel.: 02.40.69.60.18
  Open Monday 2:30–7 P.M.; Tuesday–Saturday 10 A.M.–12:30 P.M. and 1:30–7 P.M.

Les Caves du Belfroi

When in Nantes be sure to explore Le Bouffay, the medieval quarter of the city, which has a number of little bistrots within its labyrinth of streets. Nearby is this reputable wine shop, which in addition to offering a large selection of French wines stocks some of the best vintages from the Western Loire including Gros Plant, Muscadet, Saumur, Saumur Champigny, and wines from Anjou. Although lesser known to most foreigners, these wines are much appreciated by the French not only for their delicate aroma but also for their reasonable prices. You can pick up an excellent *appellation* (Sèvres-et-Maine) of Muscadet, for example, for as little as 40F a bottle.

You also can shop for a slew of products from Lu, the distinctively *nantais* company that has been making little tea cookies called Petit Beurre for more than 150 years. One could say that Petit Beurre is to France as Coca-Cola is to the United States. There was even a near uprising recently when the company opted to change the original scalloped pattern that borders each one of these delicate *biscuits* to one of a less distinctive nature. A package of these cookies may not create much of a stir at home (they are, in fact, rather dry), but you may want to pick up one of their cookie-filled tins or even a ceramic breakfast service, all which are decorated with the original Petit Beurre design.

Other gourmet gift ideas include salt and *salicornes* from Guérande, flavored vinegars, and canisters of *berlingots* (hard candies) prettily decorated with views from the famous restaurant La Cigale or the fountain at the place Royale.

• 12 rue de la Paix, 44000 Nantes; tel.: 02.40.47.04.12; fax: 02.51.82.36.70
Open Tuesday–Saturday 9 A.M.–noon and 2–7 P.M.

Gautier Debotté

This candy shop will dazzle you with its nineteenth-century interior. Built between 1850 and 1860 in a style characteristic of the Napoleon III epoch, this ornate shop is lavishly decorated with heavily carved mahogany presentation cases, elaborate gilting, and exquisite crystal chandeliers. Even the scales that accurately weigh the judicious quantities of treats are made of marble and embellished with bronze accoutrements.

The sweets themselves are equally seductive, and all are made entirely by hand on the premises. As in nearly all of the towns and regions of France, Nantes also has its special variance on sweets in addition to the more traditional offerings. The *berlingot* of Nantes is probably the best known, and the puffy triangular shape of these tiny hard candies is as endearing as their pastel-like colors. True decadence comes in the form of a flaky praline-filled sweet enrobed in chocolate and aptly called the *Mascaron Nantais (mascaron* is the name of the bas-reliefs that were used to decorate the edifices of wealthy peoples' houses during the 1700s). For those who relish liqueur-flavored chocolates, the *Muscadet Nantais* is a chocolate-covered grape oozing with a liqueur made from the local Muscadet wine.

The packaging is sublime as well, and whether you buy a tin of *berlingots*, a sepia-colored box of *Mascarons* depicting a classic bas-relief, or a package of *Muscadet Nantais* that illustrates a Muscadet vineyard and its surrounding village, these treats make for treasured gifts to take back home. Prices are a bit steep, but *ça c'est du luxe!*

- 9 rue de la Fosse; 44000 Nantes; tel: 02.40.48.23.19;
  Open Monday–Friday 9 A.M.–7 P.M.
  Boutique/Tea Salon: 3 rue de Budapest, 44000 Nantes; tel.:
    02.40.48.18.16
  Open Monday 10 A.M.–7 P.M.; Tuesday–Sunday 8:15 A.M.–7:30 P.M.

Passage Pommeraye

Just a few steps from Gautier Debotté between the rue de la Fosse and rue Crébillon is this elegant passageway, evidence of the opulence that Nantes has experienced over the past centuries. An architectural phenomenon that took hold throughout much of Europe during the nineteenth century, the Passage Pommeraye is quite different from the Paris passages in that it encompasses two levels.

Like today's shopping malls, these passages provided a protected environment for shoppers to browse through the various boutiques, free from the mud and dust of the cities' already congested streets. For the merchants these spaces ensured security, and even today, the main gates may be closed and locked at the end of each working day.

Characteristics of the passages include glass roofs, steel structures, elaborate woodwork, and mosaic floors. The Passage Pommeraye was built in 1843 (a bit later than those of Paris) in the classic *Restauration* style. One can hardly miss the heavenly statues of adolescents that portray the respected disciplines of the arts, commerce, science, agriculture, industry, and the sea. The four seasons haven't been left out, either.

In view of this stately setting, it is not surprising that two of the most reputable art galleries of the city call the Passage home. **La Galerie Moyon-Avenard** was established here in 1885, and for the past three generations the family has represented many of the finest artists of Nantes and the region. The octogenarian painter Jean Chabot is certainly one of the most distinguished and is best known for his realistic views of local seascapes in the form of watercolors (3,000F to 6,000F) and oils (10,000F to 20,000F). For more reasonably priced images of the area, ask to see the intricately designed engravings of de Lezardière or the watercolors of Maura. Although less regional in subject matter, I was particularly charmed by the highly decorative, *intimiste* watercolors and gouaches of local artist Chantal Delanoë.

La Cigale

No one should visit Nantes without going to La Cigale—it would be like visiting Nancy in Lorraine without seeing the Brasserie Excelsior. One must take in this marvelous Belle Epoque décor, so if you don't have time for lunch or dinner, you could always just stop here in between regular mealtimes for a drink or a brisk cup of tea.

Cigale means "cicada," of which you will see a few portrayed on the brightly colored tiles that adorn this brilliant interior, classified as a historical monument. Velvet floral motif wall coverings, painted wood-beam ceilings and trim, and vibrant ceramics give way to a sunburst of color that only accentuates the lively ambiance of this landmark brasserie. If you want to order like the locals, ask for a fresh seafood platter and a nicely chilled bottle of Muscadet.

- 4 place Graslin; 44000 Nantes; tel.: 02.40.89.34.84
  Brasserie: Moderate
  Open year-round

Hôtel la Pérouse

For such a provincial city, Nantes has revealed a more progressive side with the creation of La Pérouse, an ultra-avant-garde hotel. Although made of stone, the slightly skewed construction of this building distinguishes it from the more rigorous lines of its eighteenth-century neighbors. The real surprises await you inside, and I felt like a kid in a spaceship once up in my room as I tried to figure out the various workings of the light switches, the bathroom sink, and the window covers, which looked more like snap on sleeping bags than actual curtains. The result is a harmonious mix of contemporary design and warm elements such as parquet floors and wood furniture. The real bonus is that you can experience this architectural adventure for less than 600F a night.

- 3 allée Duquesne, 44000 Nantes; tel.: 02.40.89.75.00; fax:
  02.40.89.76.00
  Three-Star Hotel: Moderate
  Open year-round

La Galerie Art Comparaison on the ground level shows more contemporary works, including paintings and sculpture by artists of both national and international acclaim. I was deeply moved by the figurative paintings of Guillemard; the vibrant reds, dramatic blacks, and rich golds and browns provide an interesting contrast with the washed-out yet thick palette of ethereal seascapes by another highly acclaimed local painter Gilles Arzul.

If you are not yet feeling a cultural overdose, stop at **Beaufreton**, the bookstore where you will discover many attractive and informative books on the region, as well as many about Brittany.

- Entrances at rue de la Fosse and rue Crébillon
  Most stores are open Tuesday–Saturday 10 A.M.–7 P.M.

Ile de Noirmoutier (Vendée)

Markets: place de la République 7 A.M.–1 P.M.
Tuesday, Friday, and Sunday in summer; Tuesday and Friday
during off-season; Friday only in winter

After a glorious sun-drenched lunch at the Castel Marie-Louise, my most informative guide, Paul from the Western Loire tourism bureau, took me on a delightful ride to the island of Noirmoutier. I couldn't get over the fact that the skies were of such a deep blue while the rest of western France was hidden under a heavy mantle of grey. When Paul boasted that the skies are always blue here, at first I thought he was trying to convince me of the merits of his region, until he explained the scientific reason for this abundance of *beau temps*.

Much like Guérande, Noirmoutier is also known for its salt marshes. As the salt evaporates, the air above these two regions (as well as much of that in between) becomes so heavily salinated that the clouds are driven out, giving way to clear blue skies. No wonder so many artists and burned-out city dwellers have adopted Noirmoutier as their home. Even though the island is joined to the continent by a bridge, providing easy access for hordes of summertime visitors, it has somehow been spared the imprint of commercialism. Farming of salt and crops that draw upon the richness of the soil is particularly prevalent, and they say the finest potatoes in the world come from the depths of the Noirmoutier earth.

Fishing is also an important industry here, and the brightly colored boats that bob in the ports provide an amusing contrast with the low-lying white-washed houses that dot the rural landscape. The island offers nearly everything found at other quaint seaside destinations, including beautiful beaches and historic sites such as the St-Philbert Abbey or the Château of Noirmoutier.

The one thing, however, that remains unique to Noirmoutier is the Passage of the Gois, which is commonly called *Le Gois*. This is passable only at low tide, which occurs twice a day for barely three hours at a time. You will see signs indicating the Passage of the Gois right along the D758 quite a distance before you come to the bridge. *Mais attention!* You must be extremely respectful of the designated passing hours (which change daily according to the tides), because the water advances at such a rapid rate that once on the Gois, the only choice you have is to sink or swim!

Comptoir du Pêcheur

Just across from the fishing boats on the port of L'Herbaudière at Noirmoutier is the marine cooperative, where you will find everything you need to outfit yourself like a real *marin*. Fishermen, sailors, and pleasure seekers come here to buy clothing and gear necessary for life at sea.

Typically French fashion items include navy blue cable sweaters (580F) and the ultraclassic blue-and-white-stripe, three-button jersey (450F), both in machine washable 100 percent wool. If you want to look like you're a part of the French navy, pick up one of the navy blue berets topped with the traditional red pompom; if you're feeling less militaristic, you can choose a navy blue wool captain's hat. Both are priced around 75F.

• Port de l'Herbaudière, 85330 Noirmoutier-en-l'Ile; tel: 02.51.39.20.44; fax: 02.51.39.56.61
Open Monday–Saturday 9 A.M.–12:30 P.M. and 2–7 P.M.

Galerie P'tit Bleu

I met with Jean Michel Seiller on a chilly November evening in the clutter of his studio. Although here his creations were rather carelessly scattered about, I could easily imagine them making a magnificent ensemble in the gallery that he occupies at the place de la République during the tourist season.

Jean Michel captures the landscapes and seascapes of Noirmoutier and the surrounding area in masterly watercolors that evoke the quiet atmosphere of this region. His use of light and color creates images that are both tender in spirit and strong in composition. Prices start at 2,000F for the smaller works and go to 6,000F for those of a considerably larger size.

• place de la République, 85330 Noirmoutier; tel: 02.51.35.90.40
Open Easter through September at varying hours

Le Moulin de la Court

When I was first told about Marc Tourneux, an artisan who decided to make the island his home more than fifteen years ago, I didn't know anything about his special craft—that of *demi-coques*, or half hulls. After weaving through a series of back streets, my local guide finally landed me in a haven of peace marked by a centuries-old *moulin*, or windmill, just at the water's edge. As I stepped from the car grumbling that no one could ever find this place, I was greeted by a serene man who quietly explained to me that his lack of signs was deliberate—he didn't want to be disturbed by errant passersby, and people who really wanted to see his work would seek him out.

I don't know whether it was this man's quiet sense of confidence or the magic of his green eyes and sandy, salt-and-pepper hair that put me at ease and fueled my desire to see more. As I was led into the atelier, I quickly realized that I was not dealing with the average sort of craftsman. The rich smell of varnish hung thick in the air as I scuffed through layers of wood shavings that littered the floor.

I then discovered the *objects*, the famous half hulls (sculptural representations of half a boat's hull) that have become this man's passion. Marc's half hulls are poetic tributes to sailing vessels that are in and of themselves magnificent achievements. Each of these works is entirely crafted by hand, and the artist chooses from as many as forty different types of exotic woods for each model. Most of the designs are based on America's Cup originals, but from time to time Marc will execute a special order such as a clipper ship or a sloop. Each is finished with twelve coats of varnish applied by hand in typical eighteenth-century fashion, which explains why Marc may spend as much as forty hours on a major piece.

These creations, which range in price from 2,400F to 7,000F are mounted on wooden supports, and as the term half hull implies, no sails are involved. This may seem a bit strange to neophytes, but as you consider each piece, they evoke a supreme study of linear movement, architecture, and design.

After having worked with a couple of art galleries in the U.S. in the past, Marc's works are now found only in a few select places in France, but you also can buy directly from his workshop—if only you can find him.

• 85680 La Guérinière; tel: 02.51.39.67.08 or 02.51.39.00.91
  Call ahead for an appointment and directions

Poncé-sur-Loir (Sarthe)

Centre d'Artisanat et d'Art

It takes a bit of traveling on back country roads to arrive at this extensive arts and crafts center, but if you happen to find yourself within its proximity, it might be of interest to you. Most of the structure was an eighteenth-century paper mill; as you walk through this center's workshops, notice that the Loir river actually passes underneath in four different places. This constant flow of water creates a peaceful sensation that only adds to the bohemian atmosphere.

The center opened more than twenty years ago and since the beginning has emphasized educational demonstrations of various arts and crafts. You will always find at least two workshops functioning, whether for glassblowing, candlemaking, pottery, or carpentry. The end result is a little too touristy for my liking, although it is what the French would call *du bon tourisme*. The store is large and sells an array of folksy items, but the main draw is the creations of the two owners' children, who were brought up with arts and crafts and have taken what their parents started to a far higher level.

Venture upstairs to see Mathieu's innovative ceramics whose rich, earth-toned glazes typify his work. His pursuit of innovative enamels is constant, and at this point his prices do not reflect the time spent on each piece (figure about 500F for a medium-sized vase and approximately 2,000F for a larger piece).

Sister Céline sculpts in a different medium. She fashions unusual materials such as banana or pineapple fibers, resin, paper, or metal and more traditional fabrics such as silk organza, felt, or straw into hats that can be either classic or fantasylike in form and spirit. Céline studied at the Ecole des Beaux Arts in Paris, and her creations reflect her whole philosophy that there has to be a little humor and playfulness in each creation.

The biggest treat in stopping in at Céline's "boutique" is not only all of the fun you can have trying on her sculpted wonders but also the opportunity to meet this soft-spoken woman. The *créatrice* has a not-so-surprising knack for choosing just the right hat to fit the shape of each client's face and personality.

• Moulins de Paillard, 72340 Poncé-sur-Loir; tel: 02.43.44.65.12; fax: 02.43.44.08.27
   Open Monday–Saturday 9 A.M.–noon and 2–6:30 P.M.; Sunday 2:30–6:30 P.M.

The Sarthe

I first became acquainted with the department of *La Sarthe* through my friends Marie and François Benoît, who had the ambitious idea to convert their family château into a *château-hôtel* for paying guests. The Sarthe is what the French call *la France profonde*, or deep France, an expression that one could consider somewhat derogatory depending on whether you prefer flashy villas by the sea or massive, low-lying farmhouses that convey many years of toil and hard work.

This is most certainly farm country, and the rich soil of the Sarthe has provided fertile pastures for the grazing animals of the region as well as some of the richest clay for the making of sturdy ceramics. Ceramics have been made here since the sixteenth century. An entire village on the fringes of the Sarthe, just outside of Durtal, called **Les Rairies,** is made up of a series of manufacturers of terra-cotta tiles *à l'ancienne*. The most artisanal of them all is Yvon Cailleau, who still fires handmade tiles in his eighteenth-century brick oven on a regular basis.

The two neighboring towns of Solesmes and Sablé-sur-Sarthe vie for your attention on both a spiritual and epicurean level. **L'Abbaye St-Pierre de Solesmes** is one of the few monasteries in France where the monks still sing Gregorian chants. You can fill your heart and soul with these mystical hymns either by attending one of their masses or vespers or by purchasing one of their many recordings in their abbey boutique (tel.: 02.43.95.03.08; fax: 02.43.95.68.79).

Nearly every bakery in France sells shortbreadlike cookies called *sablés*. I always thought that their name referred to the granular, almost sandlike texture of these treats (*sablé* means "sand" in French), but in fact they refer to the town Sablé-sur-Sarthe. Each bakery claims to have their own special recipe, but you would have to organize an important *sablé* tasting to notice any significant difference. Those from the bakery **Drans** (38 boulevard Raphaël Elizé) in the center of town are known to be the most delicious.

The town of Durtal has gained international acclaim for its annual antique show that takes place the last Sunday of September from 6 A.M. to 7 P.M.—thirteen hours of craziness! Six hundred merchants show up to sell their goods, which range from old trinkets discovered in Granny's attic to near-museum-quality heirlooms.

Montgolfier

Just as I was beginning to feel a little itchy for a factory discount store, up popped Montgolfier, makers of quality stoneware and faience. All of the items sold here have been marked down about 30 percent from their regular retail prices; many of them are seconds but the flaws are minimal. Styles and patterns range from French country to rustic and their trademark piece is of course the *montgolfière* (hot air balloon).

• 49430 Durtal; tel.: 02.41.76.33.15; fax: 02.41.32.59.32
  Open Monday–Friday 10 A.M.–6 P.M.; Saturdays 10 A.M.–12:30 P.M. and 2:30–6 P.M.; Sundays and holidays 3–6:30 P.M.

Faïenceries d'Art de Malicorne

A craftsman from Nevers first brought the art of faience to the town of Malicorne during the eighteenth century. Although the overall production has diminished considerably, the town has perpetuated this tradition throughout the centuries. Today there are several small manufacturers, but if you only have time to visit one, let it be the *Faïenceries d'Art de Malicorne* (FAM). Their pieces, although costly, are simply superb, and this is their only retail outfit in France. You might occasionally come across their works in the U.S. in elegant shops, department stores, and even in a couple of mail-order catalogues, but buy here where the savings and the selection are the best.

All is beautifully presented, and a complete tour of their atelier allows you to develop a greater appreciation for the skill and craftsmanship that goes into each handmade and hand-painted piece. The visit begins with the making of the clay, which has been extracted from a nearby quarry, drained, and left to ferment for one to two years. This is only the beginning, and once you witness the precision it takes for each craftsperson to gingerly apply the colorful designs, you realize you are not dealing with ordinary pieces of faience.

The motifs have an unusual richness and cheeriness, and the pieces trimmed with the delicate cutwork designs are the most characteristic of the house. You may not feel ready to invest in an entire dinner service (plates average about 400F each), but a glorious fruit basket made of faience might be well worth the hefty price tag of 1,800F because you and your heirs will treasure it forever.

In addition to their more modern designs, owners Monsieur and Madame Deschang have respected the traditions of faience in its purest forms. A small

---

Auberge du Roi-René

The gastronomic offerings in this region are slim. Finding a good meal is one thing, but dining in a charming décor presents another problem. At this exceptional country auberge, you can relish what is on your plate as you revel in the warm and beautifully decorated surroundings as well. All the meals are prepared and served on an elegant service from Malicorne.

There are two main dining rooms, one adorned with bright floral motifs in typical eighteenth-century fashion, the other with a more somber, medieval mood perfect for candlelight dining. The auberge is in the heart of a picturesque medieval village, St-Denis d'Anjou, just a stone's throw from the border of the Sarthe department.

- 53290 St-Denis d'Anjou; tel: 02.43.70.52.30;
  fax: 02.43.70.58.75
  Restaurant: Moderate–Expensive
  Open year-round

museum behind the workshop houses a complete collection of faience from centuries past.

- 18 rue Bernard-Palissy; 72270 Malicorne; tel.: 02.43.94.81.18; fax: 02.43.94.73.03
  Boutique/Visit/Museum
  Open off-season Tuesday–Saturday 9 A.M.–6:30 P.M. Tuesday-Saturday 9 A.M.–noon and 2–6:30 P.M.; Sunday and Monday 2–6:30 P.M. from Easter to the end of September
  Visits: Tuesday–Saturday 9 A.M.–noon and 2–5 P.M. during the season; Sundays and holidays 2–5 P.M.

Haras de la Potardière

It took more than a little courage for two young Parisians to leave *la capitale*, their careers (*monsieur* an architect; *madame* a business-seminar trainer), and their friends to move with their children to the country and start a new life as fresh young up-starts in the hotel business. Success finally arrived after a lot of hard work, some luck, and the combination of their respective talents to transform the family château into a handsome and most welcoming country seat.

François employed his architectural savoir faire in the nu-merous renovations that were carried out both inside and out, while Marie wielded her skillful hand in the decorating of nearly two dozen *chambres*. Somehow they both manage to do all of this in a particularly laid-back fashion that makes guests feel perfectly at home. The spacious rooms and bathrooms match the grandeur of the grounds, and if you choose the room at the very eastern end of the château, you will most likely be awak-ened by either a bright beam of sunlight or the twittering of little birds.

- 72200 Crosmières; tel: 02.43.45.83.47; fax: 02.43.45.81.06
  Château-Hôtel: Moderate
  Open year-round

Saumur (Maine-et-Loire)

Market: place St-Pierre, place de la République, place de la Bilange
Saturday 8 A.M.–7 P.M.

If you approach Saumur from the N147 coming from the northern side of the Loire river, you will be awestruck by the sheer beauty of its château, an imposing structure high on a hill that towers majestically over this quiet little town. Part medieval fortress, part fairy-tale castle, the **Château de Saumur** deserves a visit. The Decorative Arts Museum housed inside has a splendid collection of Renaissance furniture, ancient tapestries, and countless superb examples of faience from all parts of the world.

Like most old houses and castles in the Loire, the château is made out of *tuffeau*, a chalky stone native to the region. Just outside of Saumur, you can visit some of the troglodyte dwellings that were carved out of the hillsides when the stone was quarried. The same is true for the kilometers of galleries that were dug underground and today serve as cellars for both the reputed wines and mushrooms of the region.

Saumur is also the French capital of horse-riding and home to both the *Ecole Nationale d'Equitation* (the National Academy of Riding) and the prestigious *Cadre Noir*, the most elite group of horsemen in France. Many champions come here to train, and if you visit Saumur during the spring and summer you will have the opportunity to view some of the finest horse competitions in the world.

Saumur Botterie

Heading out of Saumur along the *route touristique* toward Angers is Saumur Botterie, probably the most reputable of the several renowned bootmakers of the city. The shop is small and unimpressive, but this is *the* place to go for a fine pair of riding boots. The made-to-measures, which represent about thirty hours of work and a month's wait, are priced at about 12,000F. Even if you do not ride, these exquisite boots may tempt you because they can easily be adapted for city living. If you don't mind rubber instead of leather soles and do not insist on hand-stitching, you can buy a less costly version for 3,500F.

The shop also has a fine selection of classically styled ready-to-wear shoes for men and women. The smart little boots called *bottines* for women cost between 2,000F and 3,500F.

- place de la Sénatorerie, St-Hilaire-St-Florent, 49400 Saumur;
  tel.: 02.41.38.33.00; fax: 02.41.50.45.84
  Open Monday-Friday 8 A.M.–noon and 2–7 P.M.

Bouvet Ladubay

Most often referred to as Saumur Brut, *vin pétillant*, or even *vin à bulles*, this sparkling wine should never be called Champagne because we all know that Champagne with a capital C comes only from the Champagne region of France—right? After tasting this wine I had to stop myself from blurting out *ce champagne est délicieux* instead of *ce vin est délicieux*!

This wine is consumed mostly by true connoisseurs. In an actual taste-test you might find it difficult to distinguish a brut de Saumur from a Champagne, although the brut tends to be lighter with more fruity and floral overtones, while Champagne has a toastier aroma. You won't find it at your average liquor store—it is sold primarily to fine restaurants and specialty shops. Ladubay ships 300,000 bottles annually to the U.S., part of the nearly 20 million bottles produced in Saumur today. Bought out by Taittinger over twenty years ago, the quality and distribution of their selection of wines is increasingly on the rise.

A visit *chez* Bouvet-Ladubay is a must. The complex is exquisite and the forty-five-minute tour (followed by a tasting) leads you through most of the production process. Ask to take a peek at the *bibliothèque d'étiquettes* (not shown to everyone), a handsome chamber lined from top to bottom with hundreds of oak drawers that contain a library of over 6,000 different wine labels. Why so many? In the past most of the nobility had their own personalized labels, which now they serve to document the nearly 150 years of history of this venerable house.

Today the driving force behind Ladubay is Monsieur Patrice Montmousseau, an extremely vibrant man who is constantly developing ideas and projects to put the house a cut above the others. **Le Centre d'Art Bouvet-Ladubay** is a perfect example of this sort of progressiveness, and here in a voluminous space of over 900 square meters works are exhibited from today's frontrunners in contemporary art. Expect to find paintings and sculpture from many highly acclaimed French artists, such as César and Patrick Raynaud, in addition to works from other European and American artists as well. The exhibitions change every three months.

You might want to do some shopping at Ladubay, particularly since their wines sell at un-Champagne-like prices. My favorites included a sparkling red wine and a light fizzy white, appropriately named *Trésor* (treasure)!

- 11 rue J. Ackerman, 49400 Saumur; tel.: 02.41.83.83.83; fax: 02.41.50.24.32

  Museum boutique

  Open daily for visits October–May 8 A.M.–noon and 2–6 P.M.; June–September 8 A.M.–6:30 P.M.

THE PROVINCES IN PARIS

As I SAID in the introduction, Paris is the showcase for the best of France. One short stroll along the rue Royale, home to Paris's most celebrated table arts boutiques, reinforces that statement; there you will encounter many of the houses that I presented in previous chapters as well as a handful of other big names (Lalique, Christofle, and Ercuis, for example, do not readily receive visitors at their out-of-Paris operations). The following mini-index of boutiques is by no means a comprehensive shopping guide to Paris—that requires a whole book in itself! There is, however, enough information to keep you browsing and shopping around the capital for weeks. The accent, of course, is on the products of the regions—some of which are described in this book.

By now you may be wondering which products are the most *parisien*. A stroll down the pristine avenue Montaigne on the Right Bank will help to answer that query. The glorious shopfronts of France's famed couture houses feature displays that represent the apotheosis of the *le look parisien*. If you pass by these *grandes maisons* in the evening during the first few weeks of the months of January and July (the busy time before they present their collections), you will see workshops illuminated upstairs from their shimmering storefronts and realize even more rapidly that the ultimate Parisian product is of course *la haute couture*. Those extravagant creations are affordable to only a select few, so these listings focus on the more accessible establishments.

Note: Paris is divided up into twenty *arrondissements*, or districts; these are indicated after the name of the street (*8ᵉ*–8th arrondissement, e.g.).

REGIONAL SHOWCASES

Arranged according to type of product, these boutiques correspond with ones described in the previous chapters. This listing is by no means all-inclusive (the Paris store equivalents of the discount outlets in the regions, for example, have been deliberately left out). Refer to the designated chapter descriptions for details.

Atlantic-Based Beauty Products

• **Thalgo,** 218/220 rue du Faubourg St-Honoré, 8ᵉ 01.45.62.00.20; Métro: Ternes.
See Western Loire description, page 319.

Aubusson Tapestries

• **Atelier Robert Four,** 28 rue Bonaparte, 6ᵉ; tel.: 01.43.29.30.60; fax: 01.43.25.33.95; Métro: St-Germain des Prés.
See Limousin description, page 159.

Breton Faience

• **Quimper Faïence,** 84 rue St-Martin, 4ᵉ; tel.: 01.42.71.93.03; Métro: Châtelet.
See Brittany description, page 79.

Bordeaux Wines, Champagne, Armagnac, and Calvados

• **Ryst-Dupeyron,** 79 rue du Bac, 7ᵉ tel.: 01.45.48.80.93; Métro: rue du Bac.
See Southwest descriptions, pages 295 and 301, also Champagne and Normandy chapters.

Burgundy Mustards

• **Maille,** 6 place de la Madeleine, 75008; tel.: 01.40.15.06.00; Métro: Madeleine.
See Burgundy description page 90.

Burgundy Wines

• **Les Vins Georges Duboeuf,** 9 rue Marbeuf, 8ᵉ, tel.: 01.47.20.71.23; Métro: Franklin Roosevelt.
See Burgundy description, page 92.

Central Loire Faience

• **Gien,** 18 rue de l'Arcade, 8ᵉ; tel.: 01.49.24.07.77; Métro: Madeleine.
See Loire Valley and Center description, page 179.

Laguiole and Nontron Knives

• **Galerie Laguiole,** 1 place Ste-Opportune, 1ᵉʳ; tel.: 01.40.28.09.42; Métro: Châtelet.
See Southwest descriptions, pages 299 and 308.

Limoges China

• **Bernardaud,** 11 rue Royale, 8ᵉ; tel.: 01.47.42.82.66 (tea salon, too!)
• **Coquet,** 11 rue Royale, 8ᵉ; tel.: 01.47.53.78.65
• **Haviland,** Le Village Royal, 1 cité Berryer, entrances at 25 rue Royale and 24 rue Boissy d'Anglas; tel.: 01.42.66.36.36; The Métro for these boutiques is Concorde or Madeleine.

- **Laure Japy,** 34 rue du Bac, 7e; tel.: 01.42.86.96.97; Métro: rue du Bac.
See Limousin chapter.

Limoges China and Enamels

- **Madronet/Limoges-Unic,** 34 and 58 rue de Paradis, 10e; tel.: 01.47.70.54.49 and 01.47.70.61.49; fax: 01.45.23.18.56; Métro: Château d'Eau.
See Limousin chapter.

Other Limoges Items

- **Jean-Charles de Castelbajac,** 5 rue des Petits-Champs, 1er; tel.: 01.42.60.37.33; Métro: Pyramides.
6 place St-Sulpice, 6e; tel.: 01.46.33.87.32; Métro; St-Sulpice.
See Limousin description, page 160.

Lorraine Crystal

- **Baccarat,** 11 place de la Madeleine, 8e; tel.: 01.42.65.36.26; Métro: Madeleine. 30 bis rue de Paradis, 10e; tel.: 01.47.70.64.30; Métro: Château d'Eau.
- **Cristalleries de St-Louis,** 13 rue Royale, 8e; tel.: 01.40.17.07.74; Métro: Concorde or Madeleine.
- **Daum,** 4 rue de la Paix, 2e; tel.: 42.61.25.25; Métro: Opéra.
- **Madronet/Limoges-Unic,** 34 and 58 rue de Paradis, 10e; tel.: 01.47.70.54.49 and 01.47.70.61.49; fax: 01.45.23.18.56; Métro: Château d'Eau.
See Lorraine chapter.

Lyons Chocolates

- **Richart,** 258 boulevard St-Germain, 7e; tel.: 01.45.55.66.00; Métro: Solférino. 36 avenue Wagram. 17e; tel.: 01.45.74.94; Métro: Ternes.
See Lyons description, page 209.

Lyons Puppets

- **L'Atelier de Guignol,** 7 rue Bichat, 10e; tel.: 01.42.08.02.20; Métro: Goncourt.
See Lyons description, page 205.

Lyons Silks

- **Tassinari et Chatel,** 26 rue Danielle-Casanova, 2e; tel.: 01.42.61.74.08; Métro: Opéra.
- **Bianchini-Férier**, 51 rue Jean-Jacques Rousseau, by appointment only, 2e; tel.: 01.44.82.75.75; Métro: Halles.
See Lyons chapter.

Marseilles Fashions

- **Madame Zaza of Marseille,** 18 rue Ste-Croix-de-la-Bretonnerie, 4e; tel.: 01.48.04.76.03; Métro: Hôtel-de-Ville.
See Provence description, page 272.

Mediterranean Majolica

- **Fenouil,** 2 rue Amiral-Coligny, 1er; tel.: 01.42.36.78.93; Métro: Louvre.
See Côte d'Azur description, page 116.

Norman Copperware and Silver

- **Ateliers du Cuivre et de l'Argent,** Viaduc des Arts, 113 avenue Daumesnil, 12e; tel.: 01.43.40.20.20; fax: 01.43.40.60.60; Métro: Gare de Lyon.
See Normandy description, page 228.

Picard House Linens, and Home and Personal Accessories

- **Olivier Desforges,** 26 boulevard Raspail, 7e; tel.: 01.45.49.19.37; Métro: rue du Bac,
See Picardy description, page 236.

Provençal Prints and Home Accessories

- **Souleiado,** 78 rue de Seine, 6e; tel.: 01.43.54.62.25; Métro: Mabillon. 83 avenue Paul-Doumer, 16e; tel.: 01.42.24.99.34; Métro: La Muette.
See Provence description, page 280.

Riviéra-influenced Home Décor and Table Arts

- **Mise en Demeure,** 27 rue du Cherché-Midi, 6e; tel.: 01.45.48.83.35 Métro: Sèvres-Babylone.
See Côte d'Azur description, page 118.
- **Muriel Grateau,** 29 rue de Valois, 1er; tel.: 01.40.20.90.30; Métro: Palais Royal.
See Provence description, page 278.

Riviéra Footwear

- **K. Jacques,** 16 rue Pavée, 4e; tel.: 40.27.03.57; Métro: St-Paul.
See Provence description, page 278.

Sèvres China

- **La Manfacture de Sèvres,** 4 place André Malraux, 1er; tel.: 01.47.03.40.20; Métro: Palais Royal.
See Ile-de-France description, page 144.

BOUTIQUES WITH GREAT REGIONAL FLAVOR

You'll discover that the Paris boutiques best stocked with regional goods also happen to be among the most charming. Establishing a short list of these shops proved to be a rather daunting task, particularly since I had decided to limit it to my own personal top ten. Whether you're searching for products from the provinces or simply a few gift ideas that look distinctively French, the following addresses are some of the best places to begin in the capital.

Les Comptoirs de la Tour d'Argent

2 rue du Cardinal-Lemoine, 5ᵉ; tel.: 01.46.33.45.58; Métro: Cardinal-Lemoine or Maubert-Mutualité.

A carefully honed selection of gourmet food, wine, and spirits with a distinctive southwestern slant sell here along with this famous restaurant's collection of elegant signature gift items.

Coup de Torchon

15 rue de Turenne, 4e; tel.: 01.42.74.39.26; Metro: St. Paul.

The best place in Paris for taking in a survey view of the most traditional house linens of the provinces; country tablecloths from Alsace, Catalonia, Cholet, and the Basque country take center stage.

Dehillerin

18 rue Coquillière, 1ᵉʳ; tel.: 01.42.36.53.13; Métro: Les Halles.

One of the best-loved cookware shops of Paris, Dehillerin will make you delirious with their huge selection of kitchen necessities and frivolities consisting of wooden butter molds and copper pieces from Normandy, top-of-the-line culinary knives from Auvergne, cast-iron vessels from Picardy (such as Le Creuset), and much much more.

See Normandy description, page 213; Picardy description, page 229; and Auvergne description, page 62.

Dîners en Ville

89 rue du Bac, 7ᵉ; tel.: 01.42.22.78.33; Métro: rue du Bac.

Truly one of my all-time-favorite tabletop boutiques, Dîners en Ville showcases the provinces with their bountiful display of brilantly colored Beauvillé tablecloths from Alsace and decorative trompe l'oeil ceramics created by Christine Viennet in Béziers.

See Alsace description, page 53, and Languedoc Roussillon description, page 150.

L'Entrepôt

50 rue du Passy, 16ᵉ; tel.: 01.45.25.64.17; Métro: Muette.

Charm may not be the word for this warehouse-sized emporium of assorted goods, but it's fun to shop here for eclectic gift ideas from all over the world, including the provinces of France (their collection of *charentaises*, or slippers, is particularly impressive).
See Poitou Charentes description, page 248.

A l'Image du Grenier Sur l'Eau

45 rue des Francs-Bourgeois, 4e; tel.: 01.42.71.02.31; Metro: Rambuteau or St-Paul.

This gallerylike boutique in the heart of the Marais district is loaded with old publicity posters, prints, postcards, and photographs, many of which depict scenes from the provinces.

Pain d'Epice

29 passage Jouffroy, 9ᵉ; tel.: 01.47.70.82.65; Métro: Montmartre.

This delightful toy store gives you good reason to visit this animated passageway of Paris. Their finely crafted wooden toys from the Jura and artfully made marionettes will amuse both you and your kids.
See Franche Comté description, page 136.

Saponifère

59 rue Bonaparte, 6ᵉ; tel.: 01.46.33.98.43; Métro: St-Sulpice.

A bouquet of fragrances from the provinces sell here in this cheery bath shop in the form of attractive soaps from Provence, heady fragrances from the Côte d'Azur, and creamy beauty products from the environs of Paris.

La Tuile à Loup

35 rue Daubenton, 5ᵉ; tel.: 01.47.07.28.90; Métro: Censier-Daubenton.

It is worth going out of your way to discover the plethora of homey crafts featured in this folksy shop; pottery and assorted handwork from Savoy, Brittany, Burgundy, Provence, and sometimes other provinces reign here in rustic splendor.

Territoire

30 rue Boissy d'Anglas, 8ᵉ; tel.: 01.42.66.22.13; Métro: Madeleine.

A heartwarming jumble of goods awaits you in this French country store; regional highlights include hand-carved wooden fire starters from Auvergne, Laguiole and Nontron knives, wooden toys from the Jura, beautiful coffee-table books featuring the provinces, and table linens from Beauvillé in Alsace and Jacquard Français in the Vosges mountains.

See Southwest description, pages. 299 and 308; Franche Comté description, page 137; Alsace description, page 52; and Lorraine description, page 188.

Un Dimanche dans nos Campagnes

59 ter rue Bonaparte, 6e; tel.: 01.40.46.89.52; Métro: St-Sulpice.

Just next door to Saponifère on the boutique-packed rue Bonaparte, you'll be flooded with French country sentiments in this down-home store filled with clothing and home and table accessories by some of the most talented craftspeople of the provinces.

SURE BETS

Art and Antiques

The Paris antique and art scene is as wide and varied as that of the provinces; you can scavenge for discarded hardware at the flea markets or nobly inquire about a rare painting with one of the posh Right Bank dealers. Whatever your approach, and no matter what you're seeking, you can bet that the provenance of many of these goods is an old château, a family estate, or a farmhouse in the provinces. The following tips should help to point you in the right direction, but keep in mind that many interesting little shops pop up in some of the most unlikely places throughout the city.

High-End Right Bank Shops and Galleries

The rue du Faubourg-St-Honoré, avenue Matignon, and rue Boissy-d'Anglas near the Elysées Palace have a large concentration of showplaces. For an abundance of museum-quality pieces in a shopping-mall setting, go directly to **Louvre des Antiquaires,** 2 place de Palais Royal, 1ᵉʳ; tel.: 01.42.97.27.00; Métro: Palais Royal.

High-End Left Bank Shops and Galleries

The renowned *Carré Rive Gauche*, a squarelike formation of streets bordered to the north by the Seine and to the south by the rue de l'Université will keep you enthralled for hours with its art and antiques offerings of superior quality. Situated within this Left Bank quadrant on the rue Verneuil, between the rue du Bac and the rue de Poitiers, is a hamletlike assemblage of fourteen shops referred to as **Le Hameau de Verneuil**; Métro: rue du Bac. Farther south, you can continue the thrill of the chase at nearly 150 mini-art and antique showplaces installed at the **Village Suisse,** 54 avenue de la Motte-Piquet, 15ᵉ; tel.: 01.43.06.69.90; Métro: La Motte-Piquet (Note: Open only Thursday–Monday 10:30 A.M.–7 P.M.).

Marais Shops and Galleries

You can find medium ground, price-wise, at the quaint gathering of shops along the **rue St-Paul** and the **Village St-Paul** (the courtyard collection of dealers may be accessed by the rue St-Paul); Métro: St-Paul (Note: Shops are open every day except Tuesday and Wednesday noon–7 P.M.).

The Flea Markets

Although the words *flea market* often conjure up images of shabby goods, this is not the case in the provinces and even less typical of the Paris markets. While you might encounter a certain amount of junk and scrap metal *aux puces*, these showplaces of *le vieux* mostly feature goods that vary in quality from *brocante* to investment-level treasures—and the selection is astounding! The quantity of goods looms the largest at the flea markets of Porte de Clignancourt/St-Ouen, located on the periphery of Paris about a ten-minute walk from the Métro station at Porte de Clignancourt (Note: Open Saturday, Sunday, and Monday 7:30 A.M.–6:30 P.M.). For a considerably less overwhelming foray, go to the flea market of Porte de Vanves, also on the fringes of the capital, just a few minutes' walk from the Porte de Vanves Métro (Note: Open Saturday and Sunday 9 A.M.–6:30 P.M.).

Department Stores

If you can content yourself with one-stop shopping, then the Paris department stores, or *grands magasins*, may be just the place for you. Purchasing goods in rather impersonal surroundings almost guarantees a lackluster shopping experience for me, although the choice is highly individual. There's no doubt, however, that this is where you will find the largest quantity and greatest selection of products from the provinces under one roof. One last reminder: a couple of these giants have satellite stores in many of the cities in the provinces.

- **Galeries Lafayette,** 40 boulevard Haussmann, 9ᵉ; tel.: 01.42.82.34.56.
- **Printemps,** 64 boulevard Haussmann, 9ᵉ; tel.: 01.42.82.50.00.
- **The Métro stop** for both of these stores is Chaussée-d'Antin.
- **Le Bon Marché,** corner of rue de Sèvres and rue du Bac, 7ᵉ; tel.: 01.44.39.80.00 (their foodhalls and antiques department are terrific).
- **La Samaritaine,** 75 rue de Rivoli, 1ᵉʳ; tel.: 01.40.41.20.20; Métro: Pont-

Neuf (be sure to take in the views from their skytop restaurant, Le Tou-
pary).
• **BHV,** 52 rue de Rivoli, 4ᵉ; tel.: 01.42.74.90.00; Métro: Hôtel-de-Ville.

Gourmet Food Items, Wines, and Spirits

I'm sure that out of the multitude of delectable goodies described in previous
chapters, your salivary glands must have felt a bit overstimulated at least
once! If you refer back to those descriptions, you can easily plan a shopping
list of savory delights that you want to purchase in the capital. (To facilitate
your search even more, just glance through the "teasers" listed at the very
beginning of each chapter.) Keep in mind that in most cases, prices rise
exceedingly in these palatial Parisian emporiums. An assortment of regional
specialties sell in nearly every corner grocery store and neighborhood supermarket of the city, but the selection and packaging at these two stores are
among the finest.

• **Fauchon,** 26 place de la Madeleine, 8ᵉ; tel.: 01.47.42.60.11; Métro:
  Madeleine.
• **Hédiard,** 21 place de la Madeleine, 8ᵉ; tel.: 01.43.12.88.88; Métro:
  Madeleine. 126 rue du Bac, 7ᵉ; tel.: 01.45.44.01.98; Métro: Sèvres-
  Babylone. 76 avenue Paul-Doumer, 16e; tel.: 01.45.04.51.92; Métro:
  Muette.

And also . . .

Mostly Honeys:

• **La Maison du Miel,** 24 rue Vignon, 9ᵉ; tel.: 01.47.42.26.70; Métro:
  Madeleine (just behind Fauchon).

Mostly Wines and Spirits:

• **Lucien Legrand Filles & Fils,** 1 rue de la Banque, 2ᵉ; tel.: 01.42.60.07.12;
  Métro: Bourse.

Music and Books

Before you start your regional travels, stop here for tapes of some regional
music to put you in the mood. Upon return to the capital, you can pick up
more (perhaps CDs this time), and even a weighty picture book or two, to
remind you of your journey. The prices and selection in these hypermarkets
of entertainment are the best in the city.

- **FNAC,** 1 avenue des Ternes, 17ᵉ; tel.: 01.44.09.18.00; Métro: Ternes. 136 rue de Rennes, 6ᵉ; tel.: 01.49.54.30.00; Métro: Rennes.
- **Virgin Megastore,** 52 avenue des Champs-Élysées, 8ᵉ; tel.: 01.40.74.06.48; Métro: Franklin-Roosevelt. Also at the Carré du Louvre at 99 rue de Rivoli, 1ᵉ; tel.: 01.49.53.52.90; Métro; Louvre.

Miscellaneous

Alsatian armoires, painted in a variety of polychromatic scenes, are featured in the Marais at **Meubles Peints,** 32 rue de Sévigné, 4ᵉ; tel.: 01.42.77.54.60; Métro: St.-Paul; *See Alsace chapter, page 46.*

Basque linens from Jean Vier sell at **Etamine,** 63 rue du Bac, 7ᵉ: tel.: 01.42.22.03.16; Metro: rue du Bac. *See Southwest description, page 286.*

Cogolin rugs, made from the most art-oriented contemporary designs, are showcased on the Right Bank at **Artcurial,** 9 avenue Matignon, 8ᵉ; tel.: 01.42.99.16.16; Métro: Franklin-Roosevelt. *See Provence description, page 264.*

Provençal santons sell in the few religious shops located along the rue du Vieux-Colombier near the St-Sulpice church on the Left Bank; Métro: St-Sulpice. *See Provence chapter, page 250.*

Pottery from Provence, Corsica, Normandy, and Burgundy is brightly displayed at **La Maison Ivre,** 38 rue Jacob, 6ᵉ; tel.: 01.42.60.01.85.

Pipes from the Jura may be found along with many other fine smoking accessories at **La Civette,** 157 rue St-Honoré, 1er; tel.: 01.42.96.04.99; Métro: Palais Royal: *See Franche Comté description p. 133.*

Olives, olive oil, and related products from Provence are the specialty of **A l'Olivier** at 23 rue de Rivoli, 4ᵉ; tel.: 01.48.04.86.59; Métro: St-Paul.

Shopping Glossary

accessoires de cheveux–hair accessories

accessoires de cuisine–kitchen accessories

accessoires de maison–home accessories

accessoires de mode–fashion accessories

achats–purchases

acheter–to buy

antiquités–antiques

arts de la table–table arts

boutique–shop or store

boutique de luxe–luxury-goods store

boutique à réduction–reduced-price store

brocante–secondhand goods

cadeau–gift

carte de crédit–credit card

céramiques–ceramics

chaussures–shoes

cher, pas cher–expensive, not expensive

chèque, travelers–check, traveler's check

cosmétiques–cosmetics

couleur–color

couture–sewing (as in by hand)

couturier–couture designer

créateur/créatrice–male or female creator/designer

cristal–crystal

dégriffé–unlabeled designer clothing

délai–time limit

détaxe–tax refund

directeur/directrice de la boutique–shop manager

directeur/directrice du magasin–store manager

échange–exchange

espèce–cash

fäience–faience or refined earthenware

faire du shopping–go shopping

grand–big

grand magasin–department store

griffe–label

heures d'ouverture–store hours

linge de maison–house linens

linge de table–table linens

lingerie–lingerie, underwear

livraison–delivery

magasin–store

mannequin–fashion model

marché–market

meubles–furniture

la mode–fashion

modèle–model

paiement–payment

parfum–perfume

petit–small

porcelaine–porcelain or china

poterie–pottery

prix–price

prix à réduction–reduced prices, discount

produits–goods or products

produits de beauté–beauty products

produits de luxe–luxury goods

propriétaire de la boutique–boutique owner

propriétaire du magasin–store owner

les puces–the flea market

retouche, retouches–alteration, alterations

retoucheur/retoucheuse–men or women who do alterations

soldes–sales

style–style

styliste–designer

T.V.A.–VAT, or value-added-tax

taille–size

tissu–fabric

vendre–to sell

vendeur/vendeuse–salesman/ saleswoman

vente–sale

vente aux enchères–auction

verrerie–glassware

vêtements d'enfant–children's clothing

vêtements de femme–women's clothing

vêtements d'homme–men's clothing

vitrine–store window

For more shopping-oriented vocabulary, consult a phrase book.

INDEX

Discover The Enchantment of France

*as you cruise her tranquil waterways aboard
our luxurious hotel barges. Relax on the sundeck as
you glide past quaint villages and lush vineyards.
Walk and cycle through scenic countryside.
Join daily excursions to historic towns,
stately châteaux, and private wine cellars.
Dine on elegant provincial cuisine and fine wines.*

*Six-night cruises include air-conditioned
staterooms with private baths, all meals and wines,
bicycles, daily escorted sightseeing, and
transfers before and after the cruise.
Optional hot air ballooning.*

FRENCH COUNTRY WATERWAYS, LTD.

P.O. Box 2195   Duxbury MA 02331
800-222-1236   617-934-2454

ODDLY ENOUGH, THE IDEAL SPACE FOR WORKING IS THE IDEAL SPACE FOR FALLING ASLEEP.

Elsewhere, productivity and relaxation make for such strange bedfellows. But not in Air France's L'Espace 127 Business Class, where space is in generous supply. You sink into a richly-padded seat that reclines 127 degrees - the body's natural resting position in zero gravity. And when neither work nor sleep is of interest, you'll be tempted with gourmet food, fine French wine and a personal video entertainment system. For reservations, call your travel agent or 1-800-AF-PARIS. In a world where most airline seats are too cramped to allow you to work, ours tend to present the opposite problem.

AIR FRANCE ///

VACATION RENTALS
FRANCE, ITALY, SPAIN & PORTUGAL!

VACANCES PROVENÇALES VACATIONS

For portfolio catalogues, contact:
Vacances Provençales Vacations
1425 Bayview Ave., Suite 204,
Toronto, Ont., M4G 3A9
Tel: (416) 322-5565, 1-800-263-7152
Fax: (416) 322-0706
Web site: http://www.inforamp.net/~vpv

Ont. Reg. 2960556

We have a wonderful selection of Country Homes, Villas, and Apartments for rental in Europe. From the modest to the exquisite, from the cosmopolitan bustle to the country calm, we invite you to choose the surroundings that best suit your idea of a European Holiday. If France is on your agenda, choose the ideal Paris apartment, a country cottage or luxury villa with a pool in Provence or the Cote D'Azur, the charm of the Dordogne, Brittany and Normandy, or a comfortable chalet in the grandeur of the French Alps. In Italy choose a classic apartment in Florence or Venice, or a charming house in the Tuscan or Umbrian countryside, or a lovely Italian villa with pool.

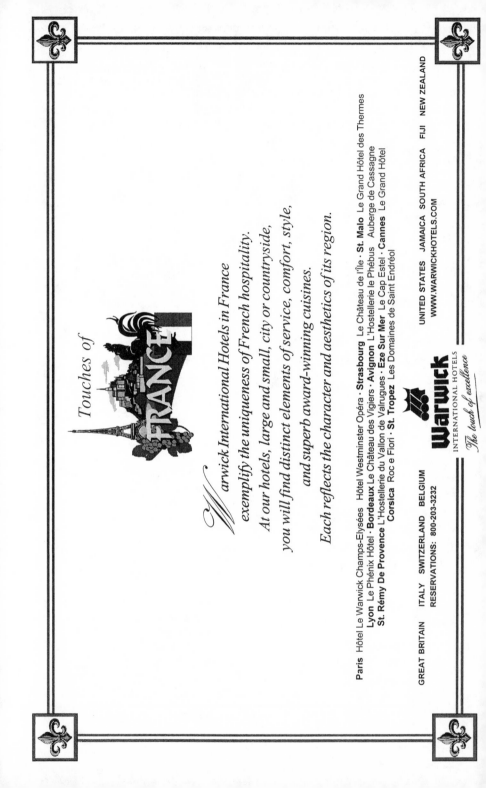

Touches of

FRANCE

𝒲arwick International Hotels in France
exemplify the uniqueness of French hospitality.
At our hotels, large and small, city or countryside,
you will find distinct elements of service, comfort, style,
and superb award-winning cuisines.

Each reflects the character and aesthetics of its region.

Paris Hôtel Le Warwick Champs-Elysées Hôtel Westminster Opéra · **Strasbourg** Le Château de l'île · **St. Malo** Le Grand Hôtel des Thermes
Lyon Le Phénix Hôtel · **Bordeaux** Le Château des Vigiers · **Avignon** L'Hostellerie le Phébus Auberge de Cassagne
St. Rémy De Provence L'Hostellerie du Vallon de Valrugues · **Eze Sur Mer** Le Cap Estel · **Cannes** Le Grand Hôtel
Corsica Roc e Fiori · **St. Tropez** Les Domaines de Saint Endréol

Warwick
INTERNATIONAL HOTELS
The touch of excellence

GREAT BRITAIN   ITALY   SWITZERLAND   BELGIUM
RESERVATIONS: 800-203-3232

UNITED STATES   JAMAICA   SOUTH AFRICA   FIJI   NEW ZEALAND
WWW.WARWICKHOTELS.COM

m/s Sea Cloud

Elegant's River Cruises
aboard the most *elegant* European Vessels

WEEKLY DEPARTURES, MAY THROUGH OCT. 1999

m/s River Cloud, m/s Blue Danube Cruise the Danube, Rhine and Main

m/s Cezanne Cruises the Rhone and Saone in France

A Millennial Event
Dec. 27, 1999 to Jan. 4, 2000
Cruise the Rhone River through the south of France aboard the luxurious CEZANNE

Sailing Cruises
aboard *Sea Cloud*

European Departures 1999:

April 16-22	Lisbon/Palma de Mallorca
May 7-12	Civitavecchia/Monte Carlo
July 17-24	Istanbul/Piraeus
August 20-28	Venice/Kusadasi (8 nights)
September 4-11	Piraeus/Kusadasi
October 21-29	Catania/Motril (8 nights)
Oct. 29-Nov. 5	Motril/Las Palmas

Transatlantic Sailing 1999:

November 5-20   Las Palmas/Barbados

Caribbean Departures 1999:
(All departures Antigua/Antigua except as noted)
March 27-April 3
Nov: 20-27   Barbados/Antigua
November 27-December 4

Upcoming For 2000:
March 25-April 4
Dec. 23-30 *(Christmas Cruise)*
Dec. 30-Jan. 6, 2001 *(Millennial New Year Cruise)*

m/s River Cloud

Elegant Cruises & Tours, Inc. 24 Vanderventer Avenue • Port Washington, NY 11050 • 800-683-6767 • Fax: 516-767-9303

I would like to hear from you.

As both an author and a travel enthusiast, I would enjoy hearing your impressions of various places of interest— both ones that I have clued you in on and ones that you've discovered on your own.

I also conduct tours to France from time to time, so I'd love to be able to keep you abreast of my activities and offerings. Please take a moment to sign on to my mailing list. Send your name and address to:

Maribeth Clemente
P.O. Box 5164
Saratoga Springs, NY 12866-8038